Exploring the
OLD TESTAMENT
BOOK BY BOOK

THE JOHN PHILLIPS COMMENTARY SERIES

Exploring the
OLD TESTAMENT
BOOK BY BOOK

An Expository Survey

JOHN PHILLIPS

Kregel
Academic & Professional

Exploring the Old Testament Book by Book: An Expository Survey

© 2009 by John Phillips

Published in 2009 by Kregel Publications, a division of Kregel, Inc., P.O. Box 2607, Grand Rapids, MI 49501.

All Scripture quotations, unless otherwise indicated, are from the King James Version. Italics added by the author.

All maps are reproduced with the permission of Moody Publishers, 820 N. LaSalle Blvd., Chicago, IL 60610.

ISBN 978-0-8254-3373-3

Printed in the United States of America
12 13 14 15 16 / 6 5 4 3 2

CONTENTS

The View from the Heights

Some two dozen rules govern Bible interpretation. Two of them, *structural analysis* and *Bible survey*, are of particular significance. *Structural analysis* involves breaking down any given passage of Scripture to its basic components. *Bible survey* involves examining larger portions of the Word of God. The one deals with the microscopic; the other deals with the telescopic.

I. The Microscopic Approach

Hans and Zachari Janssen of Middleburg, Holland, introduced us to the microscope at the end of the sixteenth or the beginning of the seventeenth century. We can well imagine the astonished unbelief of their critics when the Janssens announced the existence of living creatures so small that a single drop of water from a nearby ditch provided an ample ocean for these microscopic creatures.

As time went on, the specimens to be examined became increasingly small. A wag observed,

> Great fleas have little fleas upon their backs to bite them,
> And little fleas have smaller fleas, and so on *ad infinitum*, . . .
> And the big fleas themselves, in turn, have greater fleas to go on;
> While these, in turn have greater still, and greater still, and so on . . .
> —Agustus De Morgan,
> *A Budget of Paradoxes*

Nowadays we have electron microscopes, which enable us to see ever more clearly the innate structure of things. Objects as small as certain molecules can be seen and studied. Other wonders, too, have been revealed. Microbes have been discovered that can thrive in extreme environments, immune to conditions that spell instant death for ordinary forms of life. These creatures can thrive in temperatures far above and far below the freezing and boiling points of water.

What the microscope is to the scientist in his laboratory *structural analysis* is to the Bible explorer in his study.

II. THE TELESCOPIC APPROACH

The telescope was invented in 1609 by Hans Lippershey (c. 1570–1619), a Dutch optician. His marvelous invention literally opened up new and vast worlds for us to see. The Italian astronomer Galileo seized upon this marvelous instrument and announced to an unbelieving world that the planet Jupiter had moons. He had seen them! He had but touched the hem, though, of nature's stellar robes.

Now, of course, we have explored far, far beyond our solar system—itself a wonder in an endless infinity of wonders. It is 50 billion, billion times as voluminous as planet Earth, containing one star we call the sun, along with eight planets and 144 moons, millions of asteroids, and more than a trillion comets. It also hosts countless specks of dust, various gas molecules, and sundry atoms.

And so on, *ad infinitum!*

What the telescope is to the astronomer in his observatory, *Bible survey* is to the Bible student in his place of study.

This book is about Bible survey. It is an instrument that enables us to see the big picture, to see how the various parts of the Bible relate one to another. The higher we climb up the mountain, the more of the surrounding countryside can be surveyed.

Xerxes, the powerful Persian emperor, realized the value of a view from a high place. He had marched his vast army to the gates of Greece, had sailed his warships to the beckoning shore. He was ready to realize his dream—the conquest of Greece. Now he wanted to savor his victory to the full.

Should he display his banner on the pavilion where his generals and admirals within were deciding which moves to make? No! He had a better idea. He would get the big picture, the broad view. He would set his seat on high. He would see those great triremes of his make short work of the inferior warships of Greece.

High and lifted up, on his golden throne, he would see it all. And so he did. He saw his mighty fleet sail into the narrow straits between the mainland and the Salamas peninsula. But what did he see? His big battleships were all crowded together while the nimble Greek vessels rammed his, spreading havoc. Flaming arrows set his ships on fire, and Greek warriors swarmed aboard his stricken fleet. Now his army was imperiled. It was high time for him to go, lest he, himself, become a prisoner of war.

A survey view indeed!

It is this survey view of the Bible we will be studying here—the Old Testament book by book! It will help us sort things out; see how the Bible fits together. The prophets, for instance, judging by their close proximity, look like next-door neighbors. Some hundred years, though, separate them. Isaiah had to deal with the Assyrians, Jeremiah with the Babylonians.

Genesis begins with a creation and ends with a coffin. But what vast changes lie between.

The lists of names so characteristic of 1 Chronicles actually reflect the gospel of Matthew, which begins with a corresponding list of names. Yet four silent centuries lie between.

Still, Romans 9 is not to be divorced from Exodus 5–14.

Jonah should be set alongside Nahum.

Malachi and Matthew need to be compared with Daniel 11.

The "silent centuries" were not silent at all!

Years ago I saw a most extraordinary copy of the Constitution of the United States of America. It was a pen-and-ink rendering executed by a craftsman of unusual skill. Up close it was difficult to decipher because in places the words were crowded and cramped, almost falling over each other. In other places the words and letters were spaced far and wide. Looking at the manuscript up close, I could see little or no reason for such an arrangement. When I stood back, however, and took a general survey of the work, the writer's purpose became plain; he had not only written out the American Constitution, intact, but he had portrayed a portrait of George Washington—the cramped and crowded sections worked together with the spaced-out sections to form the lights and shadows of the face.

The Bible is like that. God's act of creating all the worlds of space is dismissed in five short words ("He made the stars also," Gen. 1:16). By contrast, the form and function of the tabernacle is spread over some fifty chapters of the Bible. Consider, too, the genealogies. We can scarcely pronounce them, let alone make much sense of them.

Why such choice and arrangement of material? The Holy Spirit has taken the Bible and, in all its pieces and parts, has given to us a perfect portrait of God's beloved Son.

Many centuries ago two sad and discouraged disciples of the Lord Jesus were making their way across the Judean hills. It had been a delightful dream while it lasted. They had known the Christ (as they believed Him to be) very well indeed. They had been awed by His miracles, thrilled by His parables. They had staked everything on Him. They had expected Him to cleanse Jerusalem of its corruption, rid the Promised Land of the Romans, and extend His empire to earth's remotest bounds.

But it was all over now. Their beloved Lord had been crucified and then buried in a Jerusalem tomb. True, certain women were circulating a story of a resurrection and an empty tomb, but there could be nothing to a tale like that! Only memories remained—dreams of what might have been.

Then somewhere on the hills they had been joined in their journey by Jesus, although they did not know it was Him. He joined their conversation. "Ought not Christ to have suffered?" He asked (Luke 24:26). Then beginning at Moses and all the prophets, He expounded to them things concerning Himself (Luke 24). In other words, He gave them a survey of the Scriptures. He put things in perspective. Christ was going to reign. Of course He was. But first He must redeem.

Their hearts burned within them. Suddenly Jesus was known to them. Just as suddenly He was gone. They could not wait until morning. Swiftly they locked up their house and made all speed to tell their tale to all in yonder upper room.

That was what a Bible did for them. That is what it will do for us.

John Dryden was poet laureate of Great Britain in the difficult days of Charles II. He lived in poverty but was buried with pomp in England's Westminster Abby. Dryden wrote these stirring lines about the Word:

> Whence but from heaven could men unskilled in arts,
> In different ages born, from different parts
> Write such agreeing truths?
> Or how, or why, should all conspire to cheat us with a lie?
> Fearful their pains,
> Unwanted their advice,
> Starving their gains
> And martyrdom their price.

Well, write it they did!

And nothing helps us more appreciate this Book of books than a Bible survey.

PART 1
OLD TESTAMENT HISTORY

CHAPTER 1

THE DIVINE LIBRARY: THE OLD TESTAMENT

The Old Testament's thirty-nine books deal with nine distinctive groups of persons, beginning with the patriarchs and ending with the poets and prophets.

I. THE PATRIARCHS: GENESIS

Genesis is a book of people, genealogies, biographies, and names. After a brief introduction describing the completion of creation and the commencement of the curse, the book gets down to its major theme, the story of the patriarchs. These were the fathers of the human race and the fathers of the Hebrew race. The names and aims of these people take up most of Genesis.

A. The Fathers of the Human Race

There are two sets of fathers. First are those who rose to prominence after the fall. The names highlighted during this period tell of two great developing civilizations. One, the Cainite civilization, centered around Cain and Lamech. It was a godless and lawless society that, while it produced a brilliant social and scientific culture, ruled out God and produced such violence and vice that God had to wipe it out.

The other collateral civilization were the Sethites, who produced men like Seth, Enoch, Methuselah, and Noah. Theirs was the world of the godly, of saints and seers who sought to walk with God amidst surrounding gloom.

The second set are the fathers who rose to prominence after the flood. The story is taken up with Shem, Ham, and Japheth. The Hamitic race produced

Nimrod, the great rebel, the founder of the tower of Babel and the leader of those lawless plans that brought a further judgment of God, the confounding of human language and the dispersal of ethnic groups. The Semitic race produced Terah and Haran and, finally, Abram, the man chosen by God to head a whole new race.

B. The Fathers of the Hebrew Race

The Hebrew race, which was to be God's instrument for giving the world the Word of God and the Son of God, had three titular heads—Abraham, Isaac, and Jacob. About half the book of Genesis is concerned with these three—father, son, and grandson—to whom God gave his great foundational promises, which form the basic constitution of the Hebrew people.

From Jacob sprang the twelve tribal heads. For the most part, the stories of these men , Jacob's sons, are woven into the story of their brother, Joseph. A quarter of the book of Genesis is concerned with this most remarkable man, who was detested by his brethren, sold as a slave into Egypt, and raised up by God to become prime minister of Egypt. He cared for the budding tribes in Egypt until such time as the purposes of God matured.

II. THE PROTECTORS: EXODUS

The Israelites remained in Egypt for about four hundred years, where they multiplied so rapidly that the pharaohs came to fear them. At length there came a pharaoh who transformed the Egyptian asylum into a ghetto and planned the gradual extermination of the entire Hebrew nation. Exodus is the story of how God used Moses and Aaron to foil Pharaoh's plots, humble Egypt, emancipate Israel, and bring the now populous nation out of Egypt to Mount Sinai in the Arabian peninsula.

The story is in three parts. We see God *saving* by sending Moses armed with a mandate and mighty power to break Pharaoh's hold on Israel. The climactic act of salvation was centered in the slaying of the Passover lamb. Next we see God *separating* by bringing the Israelites out of Egypt altogether and across the Red Sea into the wilderness. Finally we see God *sanctifying* by giving Israel the Law and teaching a code of conduct fitting for those gathered to Him. That code covered all that Israel needed to know, both for its walk and its worship in the wilderness.

III. THE PRIESTS: LEVITICUS

Leviticus is primarily the priestly book. It has four major themes, the first being the *way to God*, set forth in the five offerings and their laws. The next theme is the *walk with God*, given in a series of detailed laws dealing with various phases of life. The *worship of God* is treated next with special attention paid to the conditions under which Israel would be permitted entrance into the promised land of Canaan. Finally, Leviticus speaks of the *witness to God*, the great lesson of this book being that God insists on holiness even in the smallest details of life.

IV. THE PILGRIMS: NUMBERS

This book records two numberings of Israel. At the outset of their pilgrimage, the people who came out of Egypt were numbered; later, just prior to the entrance into Canaan, the new generation was numbered.

The book is largely concerned with *Israel in the wilderness*. Special attention is focused on the events that led up to the rebellion at Kadesh Barnea and to the wilderness wanderings that followed. The people who trusted God to bring them out of Egypt failed to trust Him to get them into Canaan. The later chapters show *Israel on the way* as the new generation is counted and conditioned for the coming conquest of Canaan.

V. THE PEOPLE: DEUTERONOMY

This book consists of ten addresses made by Moses prior to his death. It contains four perspectives—four looks, if you will.

First is the *backward look* as the people are reminded of past victories over the giants whose shadow lay dark over Canaan. This is followed by the *inward look* with a further reiteration of God's holy laws. Next is the *forward look* with special emphasis on the land laws of Israel. Finally, we see the *upward look* underlined in the death and supernatural burial of Moses.

The key phrase in Deuteronomy is the phrase "beware lest ye forget." Its kindred expression is "thou shalt remember."

VI. THE PATRIOTS: JOSHUA, JUDGES, RUTH

Joshua tells how the land was conquered. In a series of smashing victories, Joshua completely overthrew the foes in Canaan. First he drove a wedge into the center of the country by taking the key fortress of Jericho. Then, after a setback at Ai, he overwhelmed a coalition forming against him in the south. Next, he wheeled his army north and crushed a massive coalition formed against him there.

He made three political mistakes, however, leading to much of the disaster that followed: he failed to seize the coastline from the Philistines and Phoenicians; he made a fatal league with Gibea; he never completed mopping-up operations against the defeated foe. As a result, the Canaanite tribes were able to recover to a large extent and came to be a constant thorn in the flesh—both politically and religiously—to Israel.

Judges tells us how the land was contested. The resurgent Canaanite tribes repeatedly brought Israel into bondage. Again and again God raised up deliverers, or judges, to bring the oppressed people relief and a measure of revival. Othniel, Gideon, Barak, Deborah, Jephthah, Samson—these were the names of the more prominent judges.

The book shows a persistent cycle of sin, followed by servitude, sorrow, and salvation, followed again by sin, and so on, round and round. The Mesopotamians, the Moabites, the Amonites, the Amalekites, the Canaanites, the Philistines—these were Israel's oppressors and God's scourge for apostasy among his people. There were few days darker in Israel's history than the days of the judges.

The book of Ruth tells us how the land was conserved. It forms one of three appendices to the book of Judges, the other two being found at the end of Judges itself. Ruth demonstrates that God had a believing, godly remnant in the land even through those dark, apostate days.

The central character is Boaz, a lord of the house of Judah, who married the pagan Moabitess, Ruth, in accordance with the demands of the Mosaic Law. From this union, the line to the Messiah took a giant leap forward, for the great grandson of Boaz and Ruth was David.

The book of Ruth is the story of redemption, and it tells how God devised a means whereby His banished would not have to be expelled from Him. The goodness, the grace, and the outright godliness of Boaz is a delightful reminder that God always had in key places His people, through whom He can pursue His purposes.

VII. The Princes: Samuel, Kings, Chronicles

This long section tells of the march of the empire, the rise and fall of nations, the ebb and flow of dynasties. The story is in two parts.

A. March of History

The books of Samuel and Kings set before us the march of history. First Samuel relates the story of Israel's first king. The book is taken up with three great themes: the failure of the priestly office in Eli; the founding of the prophetic office in Samuel; the forming of the princely office in Saul.

Failure is everywhere in the book. Eli experiences failure as both a priest and as a parent. Samuel experiences his own sad failure with his sons. Saul experiences utter failure as Israel's first king.

Samuel, though, is the real hero of the book, a gentle, faithful servant of God, who began to draw the tribes together in true nationhood. The saddest character in the book is Saul, who despite early promise soon showed of what poor stuff he was made. Degenerating into a savage, vengeful, gloomy man, he became obsessed with getting rid of David, in whom he rightly discerned God's true heir-apparent to the throne.

Second Samuel relates the story of Israel's finest king. The Bible devotes more space to David than to any other person. When he became king, he found the nation torn by civil war, and a prey to its enemies. He left it united, respected, courted, and feared. It was he who put its archives in order, wrote half its hymnbook, organized its religious life, and left it a dynasty that would last until the coming of Christ.

For David, the book of 2 Samuel tells of the patient years, the time of waiting for the final dissolution of the house of Saul. Then comes the prosperous years when David could seemingly do no wrong. The book closes with the perilous years during which David paid in full for his murder of Uriah and his seduction of Bathsheba. The book is crowded with characters, all of whom need to be studied in the light of their relationship to David.

The two books of Kings deal with the history of Israel's subsequent kings. They deal first with the Davidic kingdom, focusing on the story of Solomon in all his glory and in all his tragic mistakes. For Solomon's serious backsliding, God foretold through His prophet that Solomon's kingdom would be rent in twain upon his death.

This rending apart is the further theme of the books of Kings, for they chronicle the story of the divided kingdoms. The history seesaws back and forth between Israel in the north and Judah in the south. Ten of the tribes, having rebelled, set up a rival kingdom in the north ruled from Samaria; the two other tribes, ruled from Jerusalem, remained loyal to the throne of David.

All the kings of Israel were bad; some were great; none paid heed to the true worship of God centered in the temple in Jerusalem. The three great kings of the North were Jeroboam, the first of them, who founded the calf-worship, which remained a constant religious snare to the tribes; Ahab, who married a pagan princess and who allowed her to debauch his people with Baal-worship; Jeroboam II, the last of the northern kings to reign with any semblance of divine authority.

The kingdom of Israel came to an end when the Assyrians invaded the land and captured Samaria. Judah continued for another 136 years until its fortunes came to an abrupt end at the time of the Babylonian invasion.

The same number of kings ruled over both the North and the South, but Judah's kings reigned longer on the average than Israel's kings, reflecting that a number of Judah's kings were good. Two of them were outstanding. Both Josiah and Hezekiah sought to bring the nation back to God—Hezekiah under the influence of Isaiah, and Josiah under the influence of Jeremiah.

If the books of Samuel and Kings set before us the march of history, the two books of Chronicles set before us the mirror of history. They cover much the same historical ground. They were written, however, after the Babylonian captivity rather than before. They concentrate mostly on Judah, and they give history from the viewpoint of the priests rather than the prophets. They were written to interpret to the returned remnant the significance of their history and to show that, while the throne of David was gone, the royal line still remained.

B. The Pioneers

Ezra, Nehemiah, and Esther close the historical section of the Old Testament. Ezra and Nehemiah are concerned with the conclusion of the captivity.

The seventy years of exile came and went. The Babylonian Empire gave place to the Persian Empire, and Cyrus, the Persian, magnanimously issued the decree that loosed the captives in his realm. The Jews were free to go home.

This gave rise to the pioneers. Led by three men, Zerubbabel, Nehemiah, and Ezra, a remnant of the Jews elected to return to the homeland and rebuild the wastes. As the captivity had taken place in three stages, so did the return. Only a small number of Jews responded; the majority had it too good in Babylon.

Ezra was a scribe, a priest of the family of Aaron. His book is concerned with (1) the rebuilding of the temple walls, a work entrusted to Zerubbabel, a prince of the royal family of David, and (2) the rebuilding of temple worship, a work pioneered by Ezra himself.

Nehemiah was a statesman. It took Zerubbabel twenty years to get the temple finished. Sixty years later, Ezra arrived to spur religious revival. Twelve years later, Nehemiah came to rebuild Jerusalem's walls. He finished this almost impossible task in just seven weeks.

As Ezra and Nehemiah are concerned with the conclusion of the captivity, the book of Esther is concerned with the character of the captivity. The Jews were well treated in Babylon, and many, in fact, rose to high office. Most became wealthy, or at least well-to-do. Thus, after the captivity ended the vast majority preferred their comfortable homes and solid positions in Babylonia to pioneering in Palestine. Yet they lived in danger. At the mere whim of a despotic king their position could change overnight from prosperity to peril.

Esther reminds us of this. God is not mentioned by name in the book, although His name is hidden there; He works behind the scenes. He is in the shadows, overruling in the affairs of men and working out His sovereign will. He will not allow Israel to be assimilated, allowing persecution, instead, to prevent it. Nor will He allow them to be exterminated. He acts providentially to hinder that.

VIII. THE POETS: JOB, PSALMS, SONG OF SOLOMON, PROVERBS, ECCLESIASTES

These five books give us the distilled wisdom of the Hebrew people, a wisdom gently collected drop by precious drop under the inspiration of the Holy Spirit. One book was written by a saint, one by a singer, and three by a sage.

Job was written by a saint. If ever this world entertained a suffering saint, that man was Job. It is a detailed study of the problem of pain. Job is seen in three positions. First, he is in the hands of Satan, then he is seen in the hands of men, and finally he is in the hands of God. Nothing ever written gives such insight as this book, the oldest in the world, into the causes and consequences of suffering.

Psalms was written by a singer, for thus David, who wrote half the collection, is called "the sweet singer of Israel" (see 2 Sam. 23:1). Other psalms were added by Moses, Solomon, Hezekiah, and others. A number are anonymous. All were written out of a deep emotional experience with God.

Joy and sorrow, despair and triumph, hope and fear, love and hate, horror and glory, peace and unrest—every possible emotion—are seen in the psalms. All contain a prophetic element, and some are clearly messianic.

Three of the books of poetry were written by a sage, Solomon. One of these deals with love, one with learning, and one with life.

The Song of Solomon was probably written when Solomon was young. It is a love song, written to commemorate Solomon's encounter with a Shulamite shepherdess who turned down cold his blandishments and offers of love.

Proverbs contains the pick of Solomon's epigrammatical sayings on nature, religion, psychology, human relations, and kindred themes. Ecclesiastes was probably written in Solomon's later years, toward the end of his misspent life. It gives the perspectives and prospects of a worldly minded man and, as such, is full of cynicism, despondency, and discontent. It shows that this world is simply not big enough to fill the eternal cravings of the human heart. Only God is big enough for that.

IX. The Prophets: Isaiah to Malachi

For the sake of convenience, the prophetic books are usually considered in two divisions: the major and the minor prophets. Since the distinction is based, for the most part, on the length of the respective books by these prophets, it is a somewhat arbitrary, although convenient, division.

A. The Major Prophets

Of the four major prophets, three focused on the Hebrew nations. The fourth, Daniel, had a much broader view.

We begin with Isaiah. His vision may be summed up in the word *Jesus*. Isaiah's very name can be freely translated, "Jesus saves!" He prophesied to Israel and Judah, living through the stormy era of the Assyrian invasions. Isaiah lived to see his prophesies against Israel fulfilled, in fact, by the Assyrian armies. He lived, too, to see the initial threat against Judah melt away to be replaced, in later years, by the rise of Babylon.

Always, though, his gaze comes back to the Messiah. No other prophet had such a clear vision of both Golgotha and the Golden Age.

Next comes the book of Jeremiah followed by the short book of Lamentations. The key word to Jeremiah's visions is *Judah*. He preached to the tiny kingdom, which was left shaken and stripped after the Assyrian incursions.

In Jeremiah's day the Babylonians were reaching for empire. His task was to preach the coming collapse of Judah and the inevitable Babylonian captivity. He wept out his heart to his people, was ignored by most, was denounced as a traitor, saw his writings torn up in contempt while becoming the object of persistent persecution.

The third in the trio of prophets was Ezekiel. The key word to his prophecies is *Jerusalem.* He himself was an exile, deported to Babylonia at the time of the second of Nebuchadnezzar's three invasions of Judea. Ezekiel's task was to tell the Jews still left in Jerusalem that their turn was coming. He also preached to his fellow exiles, acting out many of his prophecies in order to win their attention. After the final fall of Jerusalem he told his fellows that their city would rise again and would one day become the capital of the world.

While Isaiah, Jeremiah, and Ezekiel all mentioned other nations in their prophecies, they preached primarily to the two Hebrew nations. Daniel was the prophet who had the most to say concerning the heathen nations. Like Ezekiel, he lived in exile in Babylon. He rose to a position of great power, not only in the empire of the Babylonians but also in that of the Persians.

Daniel lived nearly all his long life in foreign lands, and his visions and prophecies largely concerned the great empires of Bible history—Babylon, Persia, Greece, and Rome. He foretold the exact date of Christ's triumphal entry into Jerusalem, detailed step-by-step the key events to transpire during the four silent centuries between the testaments, and depicted matters still awaiting fulfillment in the coming days of Antichrist.

B. The Minor Prophets

For convenience, we divide the twelve so-called minor prophets into the preexilic and postexilic prophets.

Of the nine minor prophets who delivered their message prior to the Babylonian captivity, six addressed themselves to national problems—problems confronting the Hebrew people.

Amos, Hosea, and Micah relate to the time of the first upheaval, the upheaval caused by the Assyrian invasions. Amos was a scornful farmer, a plain countryman sent to prophesy against the royal court of Israel's kings in Samaria. Popular at first because he denounced some of the petty neighboring states, including Judah, he was hated soon enough for thoroughly denouncing sinful Samaria.

Micah was a simple frontiersman who lashed out at both Jerusalem and Samaria, denouncing prophets, people, priests, and princes alike for their sins, which made judgment imperative. Hosea was a sorrowful father whose domestic woes were God-ordained so that they might illustrate the nation's woes to blinded Israel.

Two of the prophets, Zephaniah and Habakkuk, relate to the time of the further upheaval, caused by Babylon. Their words were directed against Judah.

Zephaniah was the princely prophet being the great, great grandson of godly King Hezekiah. He preached during the time of good King Josiah and helped promote the mini-religious revival that took place in that reign. He, together with his great contemporary prophet, Jeremiah, was unable, though, to stem the tide of national apostasy and decline.

Habakkuk was the puzzled prophet. He clearly saw the impending and inevitable Babylonian invasion and understood well that Judah's sins had to be punished. But how could God punish an unrighteous people, using as His instrument an even more unrighteous people? In wrestling with his problem, he made it quite clear to the Jews that their doom was not far off.

One of the preexilic, minor prophets focused on the final upheaval yet to take place at the time of the end. This was the prophet Joel. His great burden was "the day of the LORD," and while his visions might have had a partial, initial fulfillment at the time of the Assyrian invasion of Israel, his great vision went far beyond that event to happenings that have not transpired even yet.

Of the nine preexilic, minor prophets, then, six dealt with national problems. The other three, however, were concerned with neighboring powers. Two of them preached concerning a seemingly invincible city, the dread city of Nineveh. Of these two prophets, Jonah preached against Nineveh first, but the judgment he predicted was forestalled by the repentance of the Ninevites. Nahum preached against it some two hundred years later, and his predictions were literally fulfilled. With the fall of Nineveh the whole ancient world must have heaved a sigh of relief.

The remaining preexilic minor prophet is Obadiah. He, too, preached against a neighboring power, a supposedly invulnerable city. Seir was the impregnable stronghold of the Edomites, those people descended from Esau.

As there was little love lost between the twin brothers, Esau and Jacob, so there was a long history of enmity between the nations that sprang from them. When Nebuchadnezzar razed Jerusalem, the Edomites were delighted and even captured fleeing Jews, handing them over to their foe. Obadiah foretold Edom's inevitable doom.

Three of the minor prophets were postexilic, that is, they prophesied after the Babylonian captivity had ended. Of these, two are concerned with Israel's return to the land. They stood shoulder to shoulder with the pioneers who challenged the difficulties in the land in order to rebuild a nation for God.

Haggai was concerned with the temple of God. As a result of his passionate preaching, the long-neglected temple, started years before, was finally finished and dedicated.

Zechariah was more concerned about the truth of God. He was a prophet given to apocalyptic vision. Some of his visions dealt with things that will not be fulfilled until the time of Christ's return. He also foresaw the criminal folly of his people in their rejection and crucifixion of the Messiah.

The last of the prophets, Malachi, was concerned with Israel's relapse in the land. The Jews returned from Babylonia cured of idolatry but, as time went on, they substituted a host of different sins with which to provoke God. Sacrilege, profanity, witchcraft, adultery, fraud, and oppression came to flower. The formalism of Malachi's day was to come to fruition in the Pharisaism and Sadduceeism of Matthew's day.

Thus, as the Old Testament books are arranged in our Bible, Malachi closes the Old Testament canon. The book of Genesis begins with blessing; Malachi ends with a curse. But ahead lies the New Testament, unveiling God's great solution in salvation through Jesus Christ.

CHAPTER 2

GENESIS

The Book of Beginnings

Genesis begins with a rush and a roar. Countless stars and their satellites burst into being and head for the vastness of space. Prodigious orbits! Inconceivable velocities! Mathematical precision! Unimaginable destinations!

And all encompassed in one simple sentence: "In the beginning God created the heaven and the earth" (1:1). Ten short words! Isn't that just like God?

So then, Genesis begins with a creation—but it ends with a coffin. A coffin in Egypt. Something evidently has gone wrong. Why? What happened? Only the Bible can answer such questions.

Genesis is a book of facts, a book of firsts, a book of faith, a book of forecasts and—a book of funerals. In this book we have the beginning of everything except God. Genesis is an easy book to analyze. It can be done in eight words: creation, fall, flood, Babel, Abraham, Isaac, Jacob, Joseph.

With most of the books of the Bible in this survey, the reader will find included a summary structural analysis. These outlines enable the student to see how each book is put together. Here is the outline of Genesis.

I. Primeval History: Beginnings of the Human Race (1:1–11:32)
    A. The Creation (1:1–2:25)
        1. Introduction (1:1)
        2. Narration (1:2–31)
        3. Conclusion (2:1–7)
        4. Consummation (2:8–25)
    B. The Curse (3:1–4:15)

I. PRIMEVAL HISTORY: BEGINNINGS OF THE HUMAN RACE (1:1–11:32)

"In the beginning God . . ." Thus the Book begins. Genesis makes no attempt to prove that there is a God. The fact that God is, is taken for granted. It is a self-evident truth. God is mentioned by name thirty-two times in Genesis 1, and a further eleven times by use of personal pronouns, making a total of forty-three times. For that is the great work of the Holy Spirit—to bring us into the presence of God and to keep us there.

A. The Creation (1:1–2:25)

"And God said!" The expression occurs ten times, God's first set of commandments. They have all been kept to the letter. The words stand in contrast with God's second set of commandments (Exod. 20), none of which have been consistently kept—except by the incarnate Creator Himself.

 "After its kind!" The expression occurs ten times in Genesis 1. In biological circles it establishes the principle that, while there may be mutation within a given "kind," there is no transmutation between one "kind" and another "kind." *The order of creation* is interesting, too. It begins with the coming of light, the separation of the "waters below" from the "waters above," and the emergence of the land masses from beneath the ocean waves. It continues with the creation of herbs, grasses and trees, fish and fowl, cattle, creeping things, and beasts. It concludes with the creation of man. There is an ascending order, but that order is not the result of the working of chance or "natural selection." It is the result of continued divine involvement in the creation process.

The days of creation divide into two matching phases. On the *first* day, God separated light from darkness and established day and night; on the *fourth* day the sun, moon, and stars were appointed to function in relation to the earth. On the *second* day God separated the waters below from the waters above, the clouds from the seas, and established the firmament; on the *fifth* day fish were created to live in the sea, and fowls were created to soar through the sky. On the *third* day God separated the land from the sea, raised the continents, and covered the world with vegetation; on the *sixth* day animals and man were created to live upon the land. The *seventh* day was an appendix to the work of creation and was ordained by God to be a day of rest.

We can tabulate creation thus:

THE STAGES OF CREATION	
The First Phase	**The Second Phase**
1. Light established	4. The heavenly bodies ordained to function
2. The waters separated	5. Fish and fowl created
3. The continents raised from the sea and plant life established	6. Animals and man created

B. The Curse (3:1–4:15)

Man was made "in the image of God," a perfect being (1:27). Genesis 3 tells how man fell. All three kingdoms were involved in the fall. The animal kingdom was involved (the temptation came through the serpent), the vegetable kingdom was involved (the forbidden fruit was the object), and the human kingdom was involved (both Adam and Eve disobeyed God). The serpent tempted Eve first, and then Eve tempted Adam. The Bible distinguishes between the nature of Eve's sin and Adam's sin—Eve was deceived, Adam was disobedient.

Note that the Lord Jesus accepted the Genesis account of Adam and Eve as being true history (Matt. 19:4), and the Holy Spirit builds Romans 5 on the foundation of the historical accuracy of Genesis 3. Thus, the Bible is an organic whole. We cannot pick and choose what we will believe. To deny Genesis 1 and 3 is to attack the deity of Christ and the foundations of the gospel.

Sin, sorrow, suffering, and death all stemmed from the fall. Whereas Adam was created perfect, in God's image, Adam's children were born in his own fallen image (Gen. 5:3). The first sin separated man from God; the second sin, as told in the story of Cain and Abel, separated man from man. Christ came to restore both these lost relationships through the work of the cross.

We learn, too, from Genesis 3 that sin did not begin on earth, it began in heaven; it did not originate with a human being, it originated in the heart of Lucifer, the anointed cherub who stood at the very apex of creation. Sin was imported into this world as a foreign, exotic growth, and it has flourished here like a noxious weed ever since.

C. The Catastrophe (4:16–9:29)

Genesis 4 lists the descendants of Cain, and Genesis 5 the descendants of Seth. Cain's descendants were worldly minded, and their history climaxed in the wickedness of Lamech, the seventh from Adam. The Sethites were "otherworldly"; that is, they lived for the world to come, and their history of godliness climaxed in Enoch, likewise the seventh from Adam. In Genesis 6 the separation between the people of God and the children of the world disappears. Human apostasy reached to heaven, calling for judgment.

The story of Noah and his ark is quite literal. It was not only accepted as historically reliable by the infallible Son of God but was used by Him as the basis of one of His great prophetic utterances (Matt. 24:37–39). Many of the marks of antediluvian society are being reproduced in today's world, a sure indication that we are approaching the last days and that the Lord's end-time prophecies are about to be fulfilled.

D. The Coalition (10:1–11:32)

Noah's three sons, Shem, Ham, and Japheth, became the federal heralds of the human race after the flood. The first movement toward world empire was in the family of Ham, a son singularly unblessed by Noah because of his personal indecency and impropriety. Nimrod, a descendant of Ham, took the sword of the magistrate, which God had delivered to Noah after the flood, and converted it into the sword of the conqueror. Nimrod was the driving force behind

ADAM'S IMMEDIATE DESCENDANTS

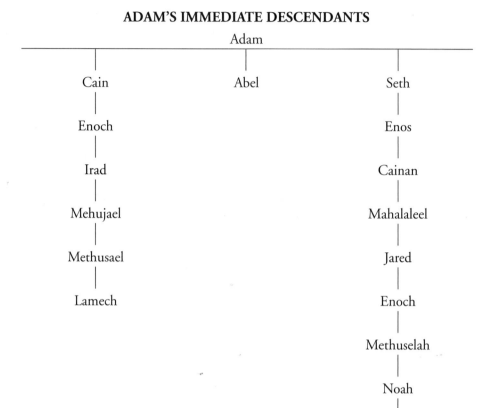

the building of the city and tower of Babel—monuments, indeed, to man's fresh defiance of God.

Nimrod had a world federation of nations in mind. All nations were to be under his rule. There was to be a one-world government with a common language, one world religious center, and one political commonwealth of nations. Mankind's first federation of nations was established in deliberate defiance of God's Word. It has all the hallmarks of the last one, the one that features prominently in the book of Revelation. It is beginning to cast its shadow upon our modern world. God came down from on high and judged that ancient, budding global empire. He did so by confounding human speech and scattering the human race far and wide around the world. In a coming day He will come down again and judge the world empire of the Beast.

II. Patriarchal History: Beginnings
of the Hebrew Race (12:1–50:26)

A. The Progenitor: Abraham (12:1–25:11)

By the time of Abraham, idolatry had spread over the entire earth. Possibly it was introduced to mankind by Nimrod himself. Ur of the Chaldees, where Abraham was born, was a center of moon worship. Abraham obeyed the call of God, left Ur, and became a pilgrim and stranger in the land of Canaan, the land of promise. God signed a covenant with Abraham and promised to give him and his designated seed this land forever.

The Holy Spirit lingers as long over the story of Abraham as He does over all the long ages of time that had preceded him. He calls Abraham "the father of all them that believe" (Rom. 4:11) and also "the Friend of God" (James 2:23 et al.). Many practical lessons concerning the life of faith can be learned from Abraham. We see him at times on the mountaintop, worshipping the gracious and living God, who had so changed and enriched his life. We see him at times falling flat on his face in failure, yet always soon restored to the path of faith.

Abraham had two principle sons—Ishmael and Isaac. The first of these was the fruit of unbelief, or at least, of half belief. Convinced that God had promised him a son and equally convinced that Sarah his wife was unable to give him that son, Abraham married Hagar, his wife's maid. The son born of this union was Ishmael, the progenitor of the Arab peoples. Later, God worked the miracle He had always intended to work and gave Abraham the true heir, Isaac, born to Sarah in her old age.

Many testing experiences were brought into Abraham's life. One of the greatest trials must have been the one recorded in Hebrews 11, where we are reminded that he "died in faith, not having received the promises" (v. 13). His only actual territorial possession in Canaan was a tomb. But God had not failed. In the early days of Abraham's pilgrimage, God told him that the promise would not be fulfilled until a far off future date (Gen. 15:13–21).

B. The Pilgrim: Isaac (25:19–27:46)

The covenant promises were confirmed to Isaac and later to Jacob. The word "overshadowed" gives the clue to Isaac's history. He is overshadowed even in the way his story is told in Genesis, only one chapter being devoted solely to him. He stands, for the most part, either in the shadow of Abraham, his illustrious father, or in the shadow of Jacob, his equally illustrious son.

Two great events in Isaac's life illustrate his being in the shadows. We see him going to Mount Moriah and yielding himself to be a burnt offering. Later we see him patiently waiting for the servant of Abraham to find him his bride. In both

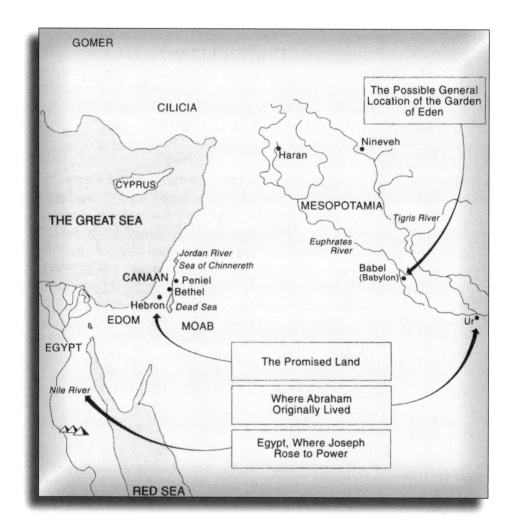

cases Isaac stood in the shadow of Abraham. We see him, too, in spite of himself, handing on the patriarchal blessing to Jacob—but it is Jacob who dominates the story. In that event, Isaac stood in the shadow of his son. The one chapter in which Isaac stands alone tells of his quiet persistence in digging wells despite the opposition of the Philistines among whom he dealt.

C. The Propagator: Jacob (28:1–35:29)

Jacob's history can be summarized in three words: Supplanter! Servant! Saint! His deceitful conduct toward his twin brother Esau, by which Jacob supplanted Esau as heir to the patriarchal birthright and blessing, laid the foundations for the national enmity that existed later between the nations of Israel and Edom. At

ADAM TO THE TWELVE TRIBES

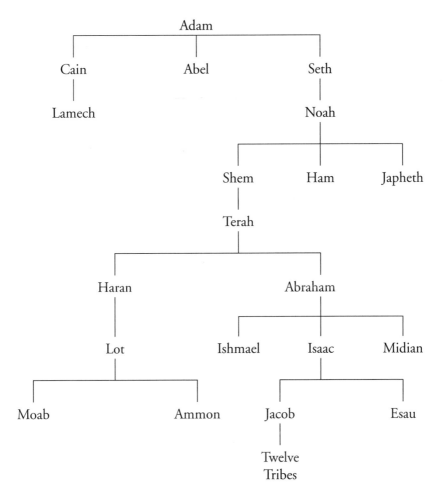

Peniel, where Jacob wrestled with the angel, both his name and his nature were changed. From Jacob (supplanter) he became Israel (he who strives with God, or prince with God). His sons became known as the "children of Israel." They were the founders of the twelve tribes, and their history occupies the greater part of the Old Testament. In the order of their birth, these sons were Reuben, Simeon, Levi, Judah, Dan, Naphtali, Gad, Asher, Issachar, Zebulun, Joseph, and Benjamin.

Jacob was the kind of person who filled every room he entered. Everyone around Jacob was cast in a supporting role. It was Jacob, for instance, who really founded the nation of Israel by giving the fledgling people its twelve tribal fathers.

Most of us can identify with Jacob because his faults and failings mirror our own. Yet, beneath it all, Jacob nursed a flaming faith. He never lost sight of his high calling in the purposes of God. We see him *lying* and *listening* and *learning* and *limping*, and, last of all, *leaning* on his staff preparing for the life beyond. Through it all we see a man with his eyes firmly fixed on heaven, even though his feet so often stumble on earth.

Doubtless that is why the *staff* is so prominent in Jacob's life. Abraham is identified with an altar, Isaac with a well, and Jacob with a staff. It marked him out as a shepherd and, supremely, as a pilgrim. His wanderings took him far and wide, but he never lost sight of the birthright and the blessing that became his, and which spoke of him as the chosen of God, destined to stand in a direct line to the coming Messiah.

D. The Provider: Joseph (36:1–47:26)

Joseph's life story is the stuff of which stories are made. The son of Rachel, Joseph ruled supreme in Jacob's heart as the father's well beloved son. More! He did always these things that pleased his father.

His brothers hated him, both for the life that he lived and for the truth that he told. His brothers, "the children of Israel," conspired against him and sold him for the price of a slave and handed him over to the Gentiles. He was triumphant over fierce temptation, was falsely accused and imprisoned for sins not his own. He lived long years in that dark place of death. It must have seemed that the years of his rejection would never end. And, while there in that prison, he triumphed and held the keys of that place.

Then came the butler and the baker, both of whom were under the displeasure of Pharaoh, and both of whom were disturbed by their prophetically significant dreams. Skilled in the interpretation of dreams, Joseph read to each man his future: for the butler, a new life beyond that dark place; for the baker, a second death far worse than mere imprisonment.

More time passed. The pharaoh himself had a pair of dreams that no one could unveil—until the butler recalled Joseph and mentioned him to the king. So Joseph interpreted the pharaoh's dreams, and the king, profoundly impressed, promoted Joseph to the rank of grand vizier. More, he gave him a name (Zaphnath-paaneah) above every name and decreed that at that name every knee should bow.

The years of plenty came and went as foretold in Pharaoh's dream. Then came the years of bitter famine.

In Canaan, Jacob sent his sons to Egypt to buy bread. Joseph recognized them, but they did not recognize him. And though they did not know it, they were about to be sorely tried. Joseph treated them as they had treated him. He knew them, they knew not him—they said of this time of trial, "We are verily guilty concerning our brother"—until at last he revealed himself to them, forgave them, brought them to himself, and brought fullness to the father's heart.

Touch the story of Joseph anywhere, and we instinctively think of Jesus!

E. Conclusion (47:27–50:26)

As the Genesis road turns its final bend, Joseph is on the throne, the days of his rejection are over, and the long day of his glory has come. The story could well end there. But the Spirit of God adds an appendix, telling of two notable deaths—the death of Jacob (47:27–50:21) and the death of Joseph (50:22–26).

The record of Jacob's death is lengthy but it can be briefly surveyed in two stages—his foreknowledge (47:27–49:27) and his funeral (49:28–50:21).

As Jacob lay on his deathbed, the Spirit of prophecy descended on him. He was able to see with remarkable detail the future of not just his sons, but of his people.

First, though, we are told where Jacob's *home* was and where his *heart* was. "And Jacob lived in the land of Egypt seventeen years" (47:28). For seventeen years Jacob had been surrounded by all the splendor the world has to offer. The world, though, has nothing to offer to the Israel of God. Israel was in Egypt, but Egypt was not in Israel. Jacob's heart was in Canaan, the land of promise, the place where God had put His name. Thus Jacob said, "Bury me where my fathers are buried" (see 47:30).

When the news at last came to Joseph, "Behold, thy father is sick" (48:1), Joseph, with his sons, Ephraim and Manasseh, in tow, hurried off to the patriarch. As soon as Jacob heard that Joseph was coming, "Israel strengthened himself" (48:2). The work before him was important, for it concerned the tribes of Israel for the rest of time.

But Jacob made a statement about *the present*: "And now thy two sons, Ephraim and Manasseh, which were born unto thee in the land of Egypt before I came unto thee into Egypt, are mine; as Reuben and Simeon, they shall be mine" (48:5). Jacob officially adopted Joseph's two sons into his family as *his* sons, to stand on equal footing with his own twelve boys.[1]

"When I came from Padan, Rachel died by me in the land of Canaan . . . and I buried her there in the way of Ephrath" (48:7). Thinking of Joseph's sons made Jacob think of their grandmother, Rachel, the only wife he had ever desired. All his sons would have been Rachel's sons if he had had his way. It was fitting, therefore, that Joseph, Rachel's firstborn, be given the inheritance rights of the firstborn. So Jacob gave the double portion to Joseph by bringing in Ephraim and Manasseh as full sons.

We now come to a prophetic utterance that can be compared for scope and detail only with Daniel 11. "And Jacob called unto his sons, and said, Gather yourselves together, that I may tell you that which shall befall you in the last days" (49:1). The expression, "the last days," is used here for the first time in the Old Testament. The expression has always been taken by the rabbis as referring, generally, to "the end time" of Daniel 12:4, 9, the terminal point in time to which all history leads.

Thus, the various dispensations of time in God's dealings with mankind were foreseen, as those dispensations affected Jacob's people.[2] The scene of Jacob's sons gathered about his bed prefigures, too, the judgment seat of Christ. Lives are brought up for review and rebukes, and rewards were meted out.

Reuben's sin had taken place forty years ago: "Thou wentest up to thy father's bed; then defiledst thou it." Since there had been no repentance and confession on Reuben's part, Jacob foretold, "Thou shalt not excel" (49:4). Here at the judgment seat, unconfessed sin was exposed and dealt with.

Neither had Simeon nor Levi confessed themselves wicked and wrong in their *criminal behavior* at Shechem (Gen. 34). "Simeon and Levi . . . instruments of cruelty are in their habitations . . . I will . . . scatter them" (49:5, 7).

Judah had apparently repented of his sins. Jacob said nothing of it; it was forgotten. Jacob's judgment seat was not convened to rake up confessed and forgiven sin. Rather, Jacob saw *the leader.* "Judah, thou art he whom thy brethren shall praise; thy hand shall be in the neck of thine enemies; thy father's children shall bow down before thee. . . . The sceptre shall not depart from Judah" (49:8, 10). We think at once of the Lord Jesus and the three classes who will one day acknowledge His supremacy—the Jews (His brethren according to the flesh); the Gentiles (in their end-time hostility toward Him); and the church (the Father's children). We recall that Judah had stood before the unknown Joseph in Egypt and pleaded Benjamin's cause. So at the judgment seat of Christ no stand taken for Christ will go unrewarded in the Kingdom.

Of Zebulun and Issachar, the Bible tell us little. Likely they were ordinary, unassuming persons. Yet Jacob's prophetic eye saw Zebulun's future *national and international interests*: "[Zebulun's] border shall be unto Zidon" (49:13). There is no proof that Zebulun's influence ever reached that far, but there is a *mystical* interpretation that needs to be considered. Zebulun's tribal inheritance included Nazareth and Cana of Galilee. Thus, Zebulun cradled that mighty movement that resulted, on the day of Pentecost, in the advent of the church, which soon thereafter set out to conquer the world.

Looking at Issachar, Jacob spoke of *his strength, his satisfaction,* and *his servitude*: "Issachar is a strong ass, . . . and he saw that rest was good, and the land that it was pleasant, . . . and [he] became a servant" (see 49:14–15). It was not a flattering likeness, yet is a picture of dependability and strength. In David's day the men of Issachar took the lead in welcoming David back to the throne (1 Chron. 12:32, 38–40).

Jacob saw in Dan *poison*: "Dan shall be a serpent by the way, an adder in the path, that biteth the horse heels, so that his rider shall fall backward" (49:17). It was Dan that first introduced idolatry into Israel as tribal religious policy (Judg. 18:30–31).

Jacob saw Gad as both *vanquished* and *victorious*: "A troop shall overcome him," but "he shall overcome at the last" (49:19). Gad was the first tribe to be carried away when Assyrian hordes came down on the fold, yet the prophet Elijah was from the tribe of Gad.

Looking at Asher, Jacob again saw two things. He saw *life's routine rewards* and *life's royal riches*: "Out of Asher his bread shall be fat, and he shall yield royal dainties" (49:20). Asher's inheritance in Canaan was the fertile strip running up the Mediterranean coast past Tyre. Much is made of the statement, too, that Asher also was to "dip his foot in oil" (Deut. 33:24). The modern port of Haifa is situated in Asher's territory today, and there pipelines from the Iranian oilfields terminate. Asher literally dips his foot in oil today.

Of Naphtali, Jacob put his finger on his son's *natural wildness*. "Naphtali is a hind let loose" (49:21). That disposition for freedom was capable of development for better or for worse. At the judgment seat, the Lord is going to look at what we have done with natural traits. Have we left them ungoverned, or have we brought them to the altar and allowed them in the Spirit's power to achieve new and nobler ends?

When Jacob's eye fell on Joseph, his delight, the word *blessing* came to his lips. And there it stayed—one blessing after another (49:25–26): the blessing of heaven, of sufficiency, of security, and of sovereignty. It was Christlikeness in Joseph that opened up that floodtide of blessing—that and that alone.

In Benjamin, Jacob saw his conquests. "In the morning he shall devour the prey, and at night he shall divide the spoil." Two illustrious Benjamites are found in Scripture—Saul of the Old Testament, Saul of the New. In the morning, Saul reigned as Israel's first king; in the evening Saul of Tarsus, the greatest of the apostles, seized the reins of the church, bearing a message that hammered at the very gates of Rome.

At the judgment seat, the experience had been painful for some, pleasant for others, but the verdict had been *perfect* in each case, delivered without bias. Each knew he had been fairly dealt with. And in Jacob's last words, "All these are the twelve tribes of Israel," is the first instance in Scripture of the sons of Jacob being referred to as such.

The Spirit of God now tells of Jacob's funeral (49:28–50:21). "I am to be gathered unto my people," he said. "Bury me with my fathers" (49:29). If Jacob suspected the Messiah was coming to Canaan, he may have wanted to be there when Christ came. Who could tell what wonders the Messiah would perform![3]

As regards the death and burial of Joseph, it is told in five short verses (50:22–26), and with that death the book of Genesis ends. It is significant, however, that when Joseph died, he said, "God will surely visit you, and bring you out of this land unto the land which he sware to Abraham, to Isaac, and to Jacob . . . and ye shall carry up my bones from hence" (vv. 24–25). It was the greatest and most illuminating act of faith in a life that was ablaze with faith.

He had something, though, to bequeath to his brethren, something priceless to them but worthless to the Eqyptians—his bones! In other words, he left them *a memorial body*. It was the last and final point in which Joseph typified Jesus. "This do in remembrance of me," Joseph might well have said as he spoke of his body.

"So Joseph died" (v. 26). That is the Holy Spirit's final comment in the book on the nature and tragedy of human sin, the final exposure of the Devil's lie: "Thou shalt not surely die." But Joseph, the most Christlike man in all the Bible, "died . . . and they embalmed him, and he was put in a coffin in Egypt" (v. 26).

CHAPTER 3

EXODUS

The Way Out

The great theme of Genesis is creation; the great theme of Exodus is redemption. Genesis begins with God and ends with man; Exodus begins with man and ends with God. In Genesis we witness the birth of the *Hebrew family* and in Exodus the birth of the *Hebrew nation*. In Genesis the priest who is introduced is the *royal priest*, Melchizedek; in Exodus the priest is the *ritual priest*, Aaron. In Genesis the *covenants* are prominent; in Exodus the *commandments* are prominent. In Genesis the lamb is *promised*; in Exodus the lamb is *provided*. In Genesis the emphasis is on *the land*; in Exodus the emphasis is on *the law*. In Genesis we hear the *promises* of God; in Exodus, the *precepts* of God: *grace* is the basis of the one, *government* of the other.

Exodus is the book of redemption. Its first word, *now*, links it onto Genesis. Leviticus, Numbers, and Deuteronomy also begin with conjunctions, making the Pentateuch one single book. Exodus begins with the expression, "Now these are the names," for redemption ever has to do with names—written by grace into the book of God. The word *exodus* comes from the Greek and means "the way out."

Between Genesis and Exodus the patriarchal family became a nation numbering between two and three million. In Genesis 15:13–16, God plainly told Abraham that four hundred years would elapse between the *promise* of Canaan as an inheritance and the *possession* of Canaan as an inheritance.[1] Abraham was also told in advance that his people would be afflicted in a strange land.

Three distinct movements advance the drama of redemption as seen in Exodus:

I. An Enslaved People Are Saved (chaps. 1–12)
   A. God Develops His Man (chaps. 1–4)

B. God Displays His Might (chaps. 5–11)
C. God Declares His Mind (chap. 12)
II. A Saved People Are Separated (chaps. 13–18)
A. Complete Separation (chaps. 13–14)
B. Conscious Separation (chap. 15)
C. Contented Separation (passim.)
D. Continual Separation
1. Marah: A Lesson on Following
2. The Manna: A Lesson on Feeding
3. Rephidim: A Lesson on Fighting
E. Convincing Separation (chap. 18)
III. A Separated People Are Sanctified (chaps. 19–40)
A. The Foundation of Sanctification (chaps. 19–24)
B. The Focus of Sanctification (chaps. 25–27; 30–31)
C. The Function of Sanctification (chaps. 28–29)
D. The Failure of Sanctification (chap. 32)
E. The Fulfillment of Sanctification (chaps. 33–40)

I. AN ENSLAVED PEOPLE ARE SAVED (CHAPS. 1–12)

With a great world empire for a stage; with Pharaoh and his court, Moses as the prophet, Aaron as the priest, and a nation of several million slaves for a cast; with Calvary as a background and the world for an audience, God wrote in Exodus the story of redemption. Alongside the ebb and flow of history, alongside Israel's historic emancipation from Egyptian slavery, the story of the crossing of the Red Sea, and the subsequent experiences in the wilderness, there runs another story. This phenomenon is quite common in the Bible. God often uses the history of a person or a people to illustrate deeper truth. The actual historical events of the exodus mirror, on a gigantic scale, the three great principles of *salvation, separation,* and *sanctification,* which lie at the heart of the gospel.

A. God Develops His Man (chaps. 1–4)

God never leaves Himself without a man. This is marvelously made manifest in the book of Genesis. Satan had his man, Pharaoh, seated on a throne, high and lifted up, wielding death as a weapon, the extermination of enslaved Israel as his goal. He was that "strong man" of whom Jesus spoke keeping his goods (Matt. 12:29).

But where was God's man? He was there, but God had to develop that man. Hence one of those mysterious periods when God remains strangely silent. The man was there, though, standing in the shadows, awaiting God's call.

Before long his name would be a household word—Moses!

An old country preacher found himself confronting a group of theological students from the nearby liberal theological seminary. Old Jimmy, though untutored, was more than a match for them. He happened to make mention of Moses. At once the leader of the group pounced. "Surely sir," he said, "you don't mean to tell me you believe in Moses?"

Jimmy Hodsen was ready for him. "Surely, young man," he said, "you don't mean to tell me you *don't* believe in Moses? Don't you know that Moses is mentioned by *name* no less than 290 times in the book of Exodus alone? He is likewise mentioned 79 times in Leviticus, 124 times in Numbers, 38 times in Deuteronomy, and 56 times in the book of Joshua, as well as 4 times in the book of Judges, 43 times in the books from Samuel to Nehemiah, and 37 times in the Gospels. Why, young man, Moses is referred to at least 640 times in the Old Testament and 719 times in the Bible altogether.

"But you don't believe in Moses! Why man! To get rid of Moses you would have to tear your Bible to shreds. I should like to know what you intend to use as a Bible. And what about the Lord Himself? He believed in Moses. Doubtless you want to get rid of Him. God have mercy on those who trust you to be their spiritual guide."

The life of Moses, Israel's "kinsman-redeemer," divides into three periods, each of forty years—forty years learning to be somebody as the adopted son of Pharaoh's daughter; forty years learning to be nobody as an exiled fugitive in the backside of the wilderness; and forty years learning obedience to the will, the way, and the Word of God.

The first forty years of Moses' life were spent in the court of Pharaoh, where he became versed in all the wisdom of the Egyptians. Then God's call came. Moses' first move was disastrous. Wishing to show the Hebrew slaves in Goshen that he was one of them, he struck a blow for God—or so he thought. The would-be missionary became a murderer.

For the next forty years Moses, a wanted fugitive, roamed the wide wilderness as a shepherd. Added to all the skills he acquired in Egypt's schools, Moses learned the art of pastoring a flock.

B. God Displays His Might (chaps. 5–11)

Armed with might and miracle, Moses, accompanied by his brother Aaron, stood before Pharaoh. He delivered a demand from the living God of the Hebrew slaves: "Let my people go!"

Pharaoh sneered: "I know not the Lord, neither will I let the people go" (see 5:2).

Moses' response was to rain down judgment after judgment, miracle after miracle. Flies! Frogs! Blood! Boils! Lice! Locusts! Darkness! Disease! Pharaoh seesawed back and forth. Moses was adamant. The issue of salvation swung in the balance. There could be no compromise.

C. God Declares His Mind (chap. 12)

The miracles of Moses, as mighty and as many as they were, did not achieve the salvation desired. It was not until the tenth and last miracle that deliverance came. God spoke. He secured Israel's redemption by means of the shed and applied blood of the Passover lamb. "When I see the blood, I will pass over you" (v. 13).

The lamb was taken and examined to make sure it was without blemish. It was kept, then on the appointed day, it was killed. It was the final act in the unfolding drama of redemption. All pointed far away, to Jesus, the One that John the Baptist proclaimed to be "the Lamb of God, which taketh away the sin of the world" (John 1:29; see also 1 Cor. 5:7). Israel looked forward by faith to Calvary; we look back to the cross.

That night the power of the enemy was broken, and a sin-enslaved people were free.

II. A Saved People Are Separated (chaps. 13–18)

Even before the contest with Pharaoh was over, God told Moses he was to lead the people across the Red Sea into the wilderness. Moreover, there was to be no going back to Egypt. The old way of life was to be left behind forever. In the waters of the Red Sea, Israel died, as it were, to Egypt, and Egypt's hold over Israel was completely broken (chaps. 13–14).

On the wilderness side of the sea, Moses lifted up his voice in song—the first song in Scripture. Only a redeemed people can truly sing. Salvation and song go together. When a person is saved and knows it, when he becomes fully conscious that he has passed from death unto life and is separated from the old way of life—then he can sing (chap. 15)!

The most direct route from Egypt to Canaan was up along the coastline of the great sea. God, however, took His saved people all the way down, around the Sinai peninsula. There were many things for this newly redeemed people to learn before they would be able to come to grips with the giants of Canaan. Truly, "The longest way round was the shortest way home."[2]

And what lessons they learned! They were put under the blood, baptized unto Moses in the cloud and in the sea, and gathered around the table in the wilderness. They drank water from the riven rock, they had war with Amalek, and came to Mount Sinai, where they spent a year learning how to live a redeemed life.

God was at work weaning His people away from the wisdom and ways of this world. The way God dealt with Israel in the wilderness is the way God deals with us in the world.

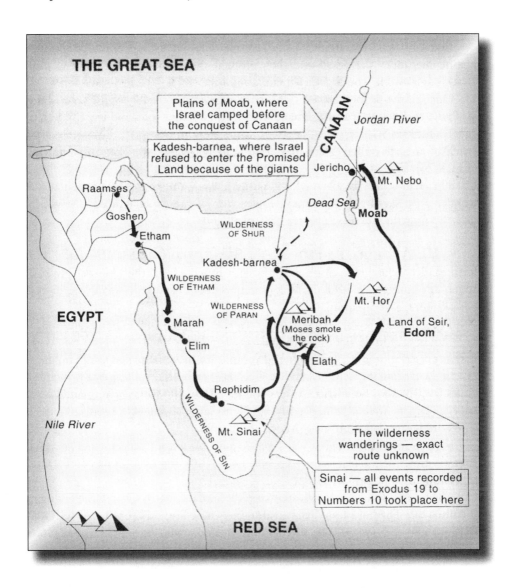

God was very thorough in separating His redeemed people from their old way of life. That separation started even while they were still in the midst of the enemy. Under the ninth plague, for instance, God plunged all of Egypt into abysmal darkness—but gave Israel light throughout all the Goshen ghetto. It was a sobering sign.

It was sobering, too, when word was received that the Egyptian cavalry was thundering down upon them. God simply put Himself between His people and the foe. To get at them, the enemy first had to get past Him.

Israel also was separated from the Egyptian lifestyle by baptism. God first put His people under the blood and then brought them through the water (1 Cor. 10:2). Later on He would gather them around the table.

Once all the people stood on resurrection ground, the Holy Spirit says, "Thus the LORD saved Israel," and in their content, "then sang Moses and the children of Israel" (14:30; 15:1).

Day after day there were new lessons to be learned—lessons in following (15:23–26), in feasting (16:15), and in fighting (17:8).

Then came the day when Moses' father-in-law came to see for himself all the wonders of a saved and separated people. He was utterly convinced. "Now," he said, "I know that the LORD is greater than all gods" (18:11).

III. A SEPARATED PEOPLE ARE SANCTIFIED (CHAPS. 19–40)

Sinai marks a change in God's dealings with Israel. There, the Law was given to Israel, and under the most terrifying circumstances. The Law was given in two parts—moral and ceremonial.

The moral law reveals to saint and sinner alike that the human heart cannot produce holiness of itself. Foolishly, though, the Israelites promised to keep the whole Law as graven in stone. The people had yet to learn their frailty and God's holiness.

In the closing segment of Exodus, God sets before us certain divine principles, God's law, rules for holy living. It was composed of 613 separate commandments, which, in turn, were summarized in the Ten Commandments (Exod. 20:1–17). The Lord reduced them to two (Matt. 22:35–40).

Keep in mind that the law was given to a people already redeemed. The moral laws were intended to teach a saved people how to live. It took a whole year for God to thoroughly indoctrinate His people.

The utter failure of the people to keep the moral law necessitated the giving of the ritual law. The Lord Jesus lived an absolutely holy life and kept the law fully and flawlessly. So then, in His life He demonstrated moment by moment that God's law could be kept—a condemnation for one and all.

The magnificent ritual law all pointed to Christ, particularly to His death. The rituals required under the ceremonial law are presented to us largely in the form of types, shadow pictures. So while the law as a standard remains in effect, the law as a system was abolished at Calvary when Jesus tore the temple veil in two (Matt. 27:51).

Exodus ends with a twofold description of the tabernacle. The tabernacle was built according to a divine blueprint, handed down from heaven. The law spoke of God's precepts, but the tabernacle spoke of God's presence. He had come to tabernacle with His people, to pitch His tent among them. When the tabernacle was finished and furnished God moved in.

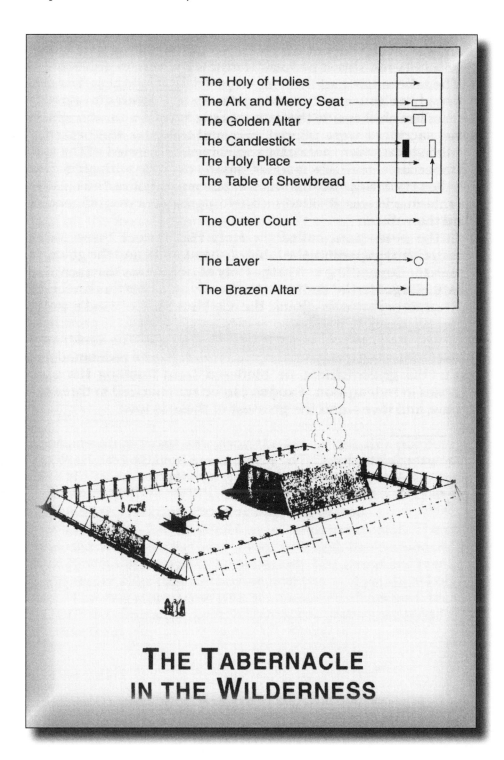

The Holy of Holies

The Ark and Mercy Seat

The Golden Altar

The Candlestick

The Holy Place

The Table of Shewbread

The Outer Court

The Laver

The Brazen Altar

THE TABERNACLE IN THE WILDERNESS

A large part of Exodus is devoted to a description of the tabernacle (chaps. 33–40). Some fifty chapters in the Bible relate to this important structure. The tabernacle was to be the focal point of the national life of Israel in the wilderness. The tribes encamped around it in an orderly fashion, and the life of the nation was lived in direct relationship to the tabernacle. Every part of the tabernacle spoke of Christ, the true gathering center of His redeemed people (Matt. 18:20).

The tabernacle resembled a compound containing three courts. The first was a large curtained enclosure with a wide gateway hung with curtains of gorgeous color. Just inside the gateway was the brazen altar on which animal sacrifices were offered. Beyond the altar sat the brazen laver containing water for the various washings demanded of the priests.

The inner tabernacle, or tent, was made of boards overlaid with gold and resting on sockets of silver. Over these boards were draped four different coverings of various materials. The tent was divided into two parts by a magnificent curtain called the veil.

The outer part of the tent, called the Holy Place, housed three pieces of furniture: the lampstand, the table of shewbread, and the golden altar of incense. Beyond the veil, in the Holy of Holies, rested the sacred chest known as the ark. Its golden cover was called the mercy seat, because resting on the mercy seat was the Shechinah cloud, the visible token of God's presence among His people.

Nothing of the entire tabernacle or its furnishings was left to the imagination or ingenuity of man. Every peg and pin, every curtain, cord, and color of the tabernacle was to speak of Christ. When at last it was finished, God took up His abode behind the veil, upon the mercy seat between the cherubim. Then the glory of God filled the whole place. It is a fitting climax to a book that deals with redemption.

CHAPTER 4

LEVITICUS

Provisions for Holy Living

The book of Exodus tells how God gets His people out of Egypt. Leviticus tells how God gets Egypt out of His people. Leviticus stands in the same relation to Exodus as the Epistles do to the Gospels.

All the sinner needs to know is that a Lamb has been provided, blood has been shed, salvation is available. The saved sinner needs to know very much more than that. Exodus is expounded in Leviticus; the Gospels are expounded in the Epistles.

The whole of Leviticus, and the first ten chapters of Numbers, come between the first day of the first month and the twentieth day of the second month in the year following that of the exodus.

Leviticus begins with God speaking to Moses "out of the tabernacle" (v. 1). This is in contrast with God's previous words to Moses midst shaking rocks and roaring flames and blanching terror.

In Leviticus, monumental truths are embodied in vivid symbols. All the demands for various offerings, for highly symbolic feasts and fasts, and for strict rules in procuring cleansing or in terminating a period of consecration—all applied, of course, to a people wedded to a divinely ordained religion. These rituals, which were *types* in the Old Testament, have become *truths* in the New Testament. Mostly they pointed to Jesus, were designed as a species of prophecy, concealed in the Old Testament but revealed in the New.

Like the other books of the Pentateuch, Leviticus is linked to its predecessor by a conjunction. This invites us to put Leviticus into perspective by comparing it with Exodus. Exodus has to do with *sinners*; Leviticus has to do with *saints*. Exodus

45

shows people *the way out*; Leviticus shows them *the way in*. In Exodus we have God's approach to us; in Leviticus we have our approach to God. Exodus shows us our *union* with Him; Leviticus shows us our *communion* with Him. In Exodus we see how we can be *delivered from Satan*; in Leviticus we see how we can be *dedicated to God*. God thunders from Sinai in Exodus; He speaks from the tabernacle in Leviticus.

Leviticus is a book of worship. The key to the book is found in the very first verse: "And the Lord called unto Moses and spake unto him out of the tabernacle." No other book in the Bible contains so many actual words of God. No less than eighty-three times in Leviticus statements are prefaced by a reference to the fact that God is speaking. That alone should draw us to this book. We observe in passing that the Holy Spirit is not once named in Leviticus, although He is referred to in all the other books of the Pentateuch. The reason is that everything in Leviticus refers to Christ, and the Spirit's work is to glorify Him.

I. The Way to God (chaps. 1–10)
   A. The Sacrifices of the People (chaps. 1–7)
      1. Requirements (1:1–6:7)
      2. Regulations (6:8–7:38)
   B. The Sanctity of the Priesthood (chaps. 8–10)
      1. Consecration (chap. 8)
      2. Ministration (chap. 9)
      3. Violation (chap. 10)
II. The Walk with God (chaps. 11–20)
   A. A Clean Life Selfward (chaps. 11–15)
   B. A Clean Life Godward (chaps. 16–17)
   C. A Clean Life Manward (chaps. 18–20)
III. The Worship of God (21:1–24:9)
   A. The Family of the Priests (chaps. 21–22)
      1. The Priest's Family (21:1–15)
      2. The Priest's Fellowship (21:16–22:16)
      3. The Priest's Function (22:17–33)
   B. The Feasts of the Lord (chap. 23)
   C. The Furniture of the Tabernacle (24:1–9)
IV. The Witness to God (24:10–27:34)
   A. In the Sphere of Profession (24:10–23)
   B. In the Sphere of Possession (chaps. 25–26)
      1. Times Connected with the Possession (chap. 25)
      2. Terms Connected with the Possession (chap. 26)
   C. In the Sphere of Promise (chap. 27)

I. The Way to God (chaps. 1–10)

A. The Sacrifices of the People (chaps. 1–7)

Five major offerings were required under the law. They set forth aspects of the sacrifice of Christ on the cross. More than five offerings, in fact, were required under the Mosaic Law, but the others were complementary to these five. These five offerings were divided into two main types. The first three were called *sweet savor* offerings; they were fragrant because they set forth Christ's willing devotedness to the divine will. The last two were sin offerings; they typified what Christ has done to obtain forgiveness for men. They can be set forth thus:

- The Preciousness of Christ's Sacrifice
  (The Sweet Savor Offerings—The Godward Side of Calvary)
  * The Burnt Offering—The Fullness of Christ's Devotion
  * The Meal Offering—The Flawlessness of Christ's Devotion
  * The Peace Offering—The Fruitfulness of Christ's Devotion

- The Purpose of Christ's Sacrifice
  (The Sin Offerings—The Manward Side of Calvary)
  * The Sin Offering—Covering the Principle of Sin
  * The Trespass Offering—Covering the Practice of Sin

The Old Testament Hebrew probably only dimly apprehended the typical significance of these offerings. They were to him a very practical provision under the law for the problem of sin's guilt. From earliest times God had insisted on sacrifice as the ground upon which He was to be approached. Every Israelite knew this. Adam, Abel, Noah, and Abraham all had their altars. The time had now come for the sacrifices to be systematized and made an integral part of the Hebrew religion.

The *burnt offering* had to do with worship. All was for God except the skin of the animal, which was given to the priest. Various clean animals—from a pair of pigeons to an ox—could be brought as a sacrifice The bigger the offering the greater the offerer's apprehension and appropriation of Calvary. Special encouragement was given to the poor. True, the poor could afford only the humblest sacrifice, but in the case of the poor, special assistance was given by the officiating priest. All sacrifices pointed forward to Calvary.

The *meal offering* was "a gift to God." It was made of fine flour mingled with oil and must be free from leaven. This offering spoke of the sinless humanity of Christ.

The *peace offering* was "a sweet savor offering." The offerer identified himself with his offering by laying his hand upon its head. Its blood was sprinkled on the altar round about. The thought is that the peace offering points to the peace of Christ, which passes all understanding.

That peace is now actively ours. God and the worshipper have been brought into fellowship. Peace has been established, thanks to the encircling blood of Christ.

The *sin offering* covered error, weakness, and sins of ignorance but not deliberate sin. It dealt with the principle of sin. Everything about the sin offering was intended to bring home to the sinner the enormity and costliness of his sin. He had to learn that he was a sinner not because he sinned; he sinned because he was a sinner. Sin, he discovered, was a radical condition, and it required a radical cure. We do what we do because we are what we are—sinners.

The *trespass offering* had to do with the practice of sin. When, under conviction, the sinner came to the priest, laden with guilt, he made a sudden discovery. Before God would put away the man's sin he had to make full restitution to the one he had wronged. More! He had to add a 20 percent penalty. Only then would God remove the guilt and stain of sin.

B. The Sanctity of the Priesthood (chaps. 8–10)

Where priesthood is introduced in the Bible, as an office, it is for a people already redeemed. There is no priesthood for the world. The priest's function was to represent the people of God. The Lord Jesus alone as the Great High Priest does this to perfection. The priesthood connected with Aaron was only a provisional measure. It was abolished in due time by the better priesthood of Christ.

Israel's first official priest was Aaron, the brother of Moses. Elaborate instructions were given concerning the consecration, robing, office, and functions of Israel's priests. Aaron and Moses were from the tribe of *Levi*, which was later set apart to minister to God in connection with the more secular aspects of the tabernacle service. Only Aaron's sons and descendants, however, could properly be priests. Israel's kings were to be from the tribe of Judah, so no man in Israel could be both a king and a priest. Technically this excluded the Lord Himself from being a priest. Indeed, during His lifetime He made no attempt to intrude into the priestly office. Never once did He seek to enter into the Holy Place of the temple, still less into the Holy of Holies.

Centuries before the birth of Aaron, however, there was a king-priest by the name of Melchizedek, who reigned in Jerusalem (Gen. 14:18–20). Jesus is called a priest "after the order of Melchizedek." Christ's title to priesthood, like that of Melchizedek, has nothing to do with descent from Aaron. His priesthood is superior to that of Aaron in every way. He is a royal priest with an eternal, changeless, unique, and flawless ministry. While the Aaronic priesthood is inferior to that of Melchizedek and, of course, to that of Christ, it does set forth many valuable lessons.

Whenever Aaron is considered alone, he sets forth the priestly ministry of the Lord Himself. Where he is considered in connection with his sons, he sets forth the priestly ministry of the church. Where he is considered in connection with the Levites, he sets forth the priestly ministry of each true believer today.

II. The Walk with God (chaps. 11–20)

Leviticus sets before the redeemed people of Israel the emphatic need for personal cleanliness. The dietary laws of chapter 11 were not only medically sound, they also set forth many valuable spiritual lessons concerning the believer's walk. The same applies to the laws covering births, leprosy, and issues in chapters 12–15.

The Day of Atonement described in chapter 16 was a great day in Israel. The ritual was most impressive. There were great searchings of heart, and sin was symbolically put away from the nation. On this day the high priest was permitted to enter the Holy of Holies in the tabernacle. He went there to sprinkle blood on the mercy seat of the ark of the covenant. The Day of Atonement speaks of the finished work of Christ and his present ministry in the presence of God on behalf of His people. In view of this great provision, Israel was expected to maintain the highest standards of holiness in all its conduct (chaps. 18–20). So are we.

III. The Worship of God (21:1–24:9)

This section begins with a series of regulations concerning the priestly family (chaps. 21–22) and ends with a brief note regarding the furniture of the tabernacle (24:1–9).

Many lessons can be gleaned from the rules regarding the priestly family and especially who could or could not eat of the bread upon the table in the Holy Place. A blind priest, for instance, could partake of the sacred emblem; many of the Lord's people have defective vision and cannot see much glorious spiritual truth. A lame priest could eat. Many have a walk with God that is imperfect. A priest who was improperly developed could eat, for the truth is that many are far from what they should be. Many, however, who were graciously allowed to eat of the sacrament were not allowed to serve the Lord. Their deficiencies barred them from that.

There was one notable exception as to who could eat of the bread among the priestly ranks. If a priest had leprosy he was banished from the table. Leprosy is a type of sin. Sin bars us from fellowship.

It is not difficult to see the spiritual application of all this. Nor is it hard to discern how these regulations can be applied to those who participate at the Lord's Table today.

In like manner, much useful instruction can be gleaned from a study of Israel's annual feasts. Israel's religious festivals were to be days of great joy and of instruction. They were planned by God to constantly remind the people of the great epochs in their history. These festivals were also intended to be public acknowledgment that the Promised Land belonged to God.

The festivals helped, too, in bringing about a sense of national unity—something Jeroboam recognized when he set up the rival ten-tribe kingdom in revolt against the throne of David in Jerusalem. One of Jeroboam's first acts was to organize a new religious calendar in order to break all ties with Jerusalem and the temple.

The festivals commanded under the law were also to serve as object lessons to the children. They were to be occasions when religious instruction could be imparted to the little ones. Seven such annual feasts and fasts were observed, four of them were celebrated in rapid succession at the beginning of the year, the other three took place in succession in the seventh month. The prophetic teaching covered by the first four feasts was all literally fulfilled at Christ's first coming. The remaining three will be just as literally fulfilled by Christ at His second coming. The interval between the feasts in Israel's religious calendar illustrates the time gap between the first and second comings of the Lord.

Here is a brief summary of the prophetic significance of the feasts:

The *Passover Feast* commemorated the deliverance of Israel from Egypt in the days of Moses as recorded in the book of Exodus. It speaks of redemption and typically it stands for "Christ our passover is sacrificed for us" (1 Cor. 5:7).

The *Feast of Unleavened Bread* was closely associated with the Passover. In the Bible, leaven is a symbol of evil, especially of evil doctrine. The Israelites were to put all leaven out of the house, and for seven days they were to eat unleavened bread. First comes redemption and then a separated walk.

The *Feast of Firstfruits* dedicated the harvest to God and marked the beginning of the grain harvest in the land. A sheaf of barley was taken from the field and waved before the Lord. The feast took place on the first day of the week and typifies the resurrection of Christ.

The *Feast of Weeks* (*Pentecost*) took place fifty days (7 x 7 + 1) after the presentation of the wave sheaf, on the first day of the week. Two loaves were presented and waved before the Lord, marking the completion of the grain harvest. In type, Pentecost looked forward to when Pentecost would be "*fully come*" (Acts 2:1) and the Holy Spirit would descend to bring the church into being.

An interval elapsed between the Feast of Pentecost and the *Feast of Trumpets*. The trumpets represented Jehovah's call to Israel, a herald for the ingathering of the exiles. The regathering was in preparation for the two great events to follow almost immediately.

The *Day of Atonement* marked the most solemn occasion in Israel's religious calendar. It was called a day of affliction, and it was a time when the nation's sins were called to remembrance. On this day only, in the whole year, the high priest was permitted to pass beyond the veil and enter into the Holy of Holies in the tabernacle. Two goats were taken, and one, chosen by lot, was slain and its blood sprinkled by the high priest on the mercy seat in the Holy of Holies. The remaining goat (called the scapegoat) had all the sins of the people symbolically laid upon it. It then carried those sins to a "land not inhabited" (16:22). This festival anticipates the time when Israel will be smitten with remorse for the crucifixion of Christ and will nationally repent and turn to Him.

The Feast of Tabernacles was a joyous occasion. The people gathered together for eight days, dwelling in booths and rejoicing in the goodness of God. The first-fruits of the oil and the wine were brought in, and a final thanksgiving was made for the year's harvest. Commemorated also were the wanderings of Israel in the wilderness after the exodus from Egypt (Lev. 23:39–43). It also looks forward to a future era of peace and prosperity, when Jesus shall reign.

In the Old Testament each feast was called a "feast of Jehovah [the LORD]," but in the New Testament they had so deteriorated in the thinking of the people that each was labeled a "feast of the Jews" (John 5:1; 6:4).

THE FEASTS OF ISRAEL					
Month				Festival	
Sacred Year	Civil Year	Jewish	Christian	Day	Event
1	7	Nisan (Abib)	March–April	14	Passover
1	7	Nisan (Abib)	March–April	15–21	Unleavened Bread
1	7	Nisan (Abib)	March–April	16	Firstfruits (barley harvest)
3	9	Sivan	May–June	6	Pentecost
7	1	Tishri (Ethanim)	Sept.–Oct.	1	Trumpets
7	1	Tishri (Ethanim)	Sept.–Oct.	10	Day of Atonement
7	1	Tishri (Ethanim)	Sept.–Oct.	15–21	Tabernacles

IV. THE WITNESS TO GOD (24:10–27:34)

The book of Leviticus closes with a series of chapters dealing with practical issues affecting the testimony of God's people in the world.

A. In the Sphere of Profession (24:10–23)

An interesting incident is recorded here, involving an Israelite who blasphemed God. The man was only half Hebrew—his mother was an Israelite, but his father was an Egyptian. The decree, issued by God Himself, was that the blasphemer was to be stoned to death. He was the first of nine people stoned in Scripture—the last person to be stoned and left for dead was the apostle Paul, who, interestingly enough, also describes himself as having been a blasphemer in his unregenerate days (1 Tim. 1:13). This Old Testament blasphemer was a Danite, a tribe that later took the lead in Israel's fatal plunge into idolatry. A foul mouth ruins a man for witness and betrays the condition of his heart.

B. In the Sphere of Possession (chaps. 25–26)

In this section God enunciated certain times and terms connected with Israel's tenure of the Promised Land. Of considerable interest is the law of Jubilee. Every fiftieth year the land was to be allowed to lie fallow, and all property purchased since the last Jubilee was to be restored to its original owner. The spiritual significance of this is challenging. Picture, though, an Old Testament Hebrew as the day of Jubilee approaches, considering his attitude toward property investment. Each year investment property would decline in value. It would decline, too, in direct ratio to the nearness of the Jubilee. Investing in such material things would grow less and less desirable as the great day of release drew near. Thus, God taught Israel that investment down here should always be viewed in the light of the weightier matters of eternity. By the law of Jubilee, God taught Israel the decreasing value of material things and the folly of covetousness and of a materialistic concept of life. True investment must be made not for time but for eternity.

C. In the Sphere of Promise (chap. 27)

The Israelite was to keep his vows. Promises made to God were to be kept. Thus in Leviticus, God's people were taught the demands and dictates of practical sanctification. God's people are to be a holy people, whether in the home or on the highway, whether in the pursuit of wealth or in the path of worship. At all places, at all times, in their conduct and in their conversation, God's people must regulate their lives according to the highest standards of holiness. This is the theme of Leviticus.

CHAPTER 5

NUMBERS

The Book of Pilgrimage

Numbers! The book is so called from two numberings of the people of God recorded within its pages. The numberings are only two of the many important events recorded in this book. A better title would be "The Wilderness," for that is really what the book is all about. It records the wilderness experiences of God's people. What the wilderness was to Israel, the world is to us. *good*

The book covers a period of about thirty-eight years. Of the twenty-seven chapters that record events after the Hebrew people left Sinai (chaps. 10–36) no less than seventeen (chaps. 20–36) are taken up with the events of the last year.

Like the book of Leviticus before it, Numbers records many of the actual sayings of God. Some seventy-three times in this book God is said to be speaking.

In Leviticus we have the believer's *worship*; in Numbers we have the believer's *walk*. Leviticus has *purity* for its theme; Numbers has *pilgrimage*. In Leviticus we have the believer's *position*; in Numbers we have the believer's *progress*. Leviticus is largely *ceremonial* in character; Numbers is mostly *historical*. Leviticus sets forth our *privileges* as the people of God; Numbers deals with our *responsibilities*. *Faithfulness to God* is the clarion call of Leviticus; *fellowship with God* is the clarion call of Numbers. In Leviticus the spiritual emphasis is on the priests and their *access to God*; in Numbers the spiritual emphasis is on the Levites and their service for men.

Exodus, Leviticus, and Numbers all enumerate various laws of God. Exodus emphasizes *moral* law, Leviticus emphasizes *ritual* law, and Numbers emphasizes *civil* law. Exodus looks at law from the standpoint of the prophet, Leviticus from the standpoint of the priests, and Numbers from the standpoint of the king.

The very first verse is the key verse in Numbers: "And the LORD spake unto Moses *in the wilderness of Sinai,* in the tabernacle of the congregation." First Corinthians 10:1–12 makes it clear that much of Numbers is typological in character.

The wanderings in the wilderness, which occupy our attention in this book, were brought on by Israel's disobedience. God had a way through the wilderness that would have brought Israel into immediate possession of Canaan, but their unbelief at Kadesh-barnea brought upon the people God's displeasure and His discipline. Unbelief always robs us of the present enjoyment of our salvation.

Here is an outline of Numbers:

I. Israel in the Wilderness: The Old Generation (1:1–19:22)
   A. Discipline in the Wilderness (1:1–9:14)
      1. The People Counted (1:1–54)
      2. The People Camped (2:1–4:49)
      3. The People Cleansed (5:1–31)
      4. The People Consecrated (6:1–9:14)
         a. As People (6:1–27)
         b. As Princes (7:1–89)
         c. As Priests (8:1–26)
         d. As Partakers (9:1–14)
   B. Direction in the Wilderness (9:15–10:36)
      1. The Instruments of This Direction (9:15–10:10)
         a. The Vision of the Cloud (9:15–23)
         b. The Voice of the Trumpet (10:1–10)
      2. The Incident of This Direction (10:11–28)
      3. The Influence of This Direction (10:29–32)
      4. The Invocation of This Direction (10:33–36)
   C. Discontent in the Wilderness (11:1–13:33)
      Criticizing:
      1. The Present Life of Faith (11:1–9, 31–35)
      2. The Perfect Love of God (11:10–25)
      3. The Prophetic Light of Others (11:26–30)
      4. The Personal Leadership of Moses (12:1–16)
      5. The Promised Land of Canaan (13:1–33)
   D. Death in the Wilderness (14:1–16:50)
      In answer to:
      1. Prayer (14:1–45)
      2. Presumption (15:1–41)
      3. Pride (16:1–40)

    4. Persistence (16:41–50)
  E. Despair in the Wilderness (17:1–19:22)
    1. A Good Reason for It (17:1–18:32)
    2. A Gracious Removal of It (19:1–22)
 II. Israel on the Way: The New Generation (20:1–36:13)
  A. Recalling the Past (20:1–29)
    1. Its Memories (20:1)
    2. Its Methods (20:2–13)
    3. Its Mistakes (20:14–22)
    4. Its Ministries (20:23–29)
  B. Redeeming the Present (21:1–27:11)
    1. Practical Victory (21:1–35)
    2. Positional Victory (22:1–24:25)
    3. Personal Victory (25:1–18)
    4. Potential Victory (26:1–27:11)
  C. Reviewing the Future (27:12–36:13)
    1. The Leadership of Israel (27:12–23)
    2. The Laws of Israel (28:1–30:16)
      a. Various Offerings (28:1–29:40)
      b. Verbal Obligations (30:1–16)
    3. The Land of Israel (31:1–36:13)
      a. Compromise (31:1–32:42)
        (1) How Forgetful They Were (31:1–54)
        (2) How Foolish They Were (32:1–42)
      b. Commentary (33:1–49)
      c. Commandments (33:50–36:13)
        (1) Possession (33:50–56)
        (2) Partition (34:1–35:5)
        (3) Protection (35:6–36:13)
          (a) Of the Innocent (35:6–34)
          (b) Of the Inheritance (36:1–13)

One simple way of remembering the content of the book of Numbers is to memorize the geographical movements it describes. The three main movements are:

1. from Sinai to Kadesh-barnea (chaps. 1–12);
2. from Kadesh-barnea through the various wilderness wanderings and back to Kadesh-barnea (chaps. 13–19);
3. from Kadesh-barnea to Jordan (chaps. 20–36).

I. ISRAEL IN THE WILDERNESS: THE OLD GENERATION (1:1–19:22)

A. Discipline in the Wilderness (1:1–9:14)

God is a God of order. One of the things that impresses itself on our minds as we read through Numbers is that Israel, a nation of two or three million people, was no mob in the wilderness. Israel comprised an orderly camp spread out according to divine decree, around the tabernacle. Each person had his proper place among the people of God. All things were done decently and in order.

First, the people were *counted*, beginning with the fighting men. Pedigree was the determining factor in this. Only true Israelites were allowed to fight the battles of the Lord. Next the Levites were counted. There were three families of Levites: the Gershonites, Kohathites, and Merarites, each family being descended from one of the sons of Levi.

The handling of the tabernacle and its furniture was entrusted to these Levites. When the princes of Israel gave their dedicatory offerings of wagons and oxen for the transportation of the tabernacle, an unusual division of these was made by Moses. He did not divide the six wagons and twelve oxen equally between the three families of Levi. The Kohathites received none at all. The reason is clear when it is seen that God entrusted to them the transportation of the ark, the table, the candlestick, the altar, and the vessels of the sanctuary. These sacred objects were to be carried *by hand*. We need to remember that machinery may have its place in the service of God, but the real work is done by hand.

Then the people were *camped* as shown in the illustration "The Camp of Israel."

Each person in the camp was assigned his proper place. All were encamped around the tabernacle, which was placed in the very center of everything. This reminds us that God has a place for each of us in His plan. Corporately, as His people, we each take our place with Jesus "in the midst" (2:17).

Next the people were *cleansed*. In this section are the laws regarding leprosy. The leper was to be put "outside the camp" (see 5:3), excommunicated from the rest of God's people. Leprosy, in the Bible, is like no other disease. It was regarded by the Jews as "the stroke of God," and it is always a picture of sin. Gehazi and King Uzziah are both outstanding examples of leprosy as discipline for sin. No leper could take his place among God's people until his leprosy was cleansed and his cleansing confirmed by the priest. Only three lepers were cleansed in the Old Testament. Interestingly enough, one was Moses and another was his sister Miriam. The only other leper cleansed was a Gentile, Naaman the Syrian. The ritual for the cleansing of the leper was highly symbolic of Christ's death and resurrection. Only through our identification with *that* can we be made fit for the place where God meets with His people.

THE CAMP OF ISRAEL

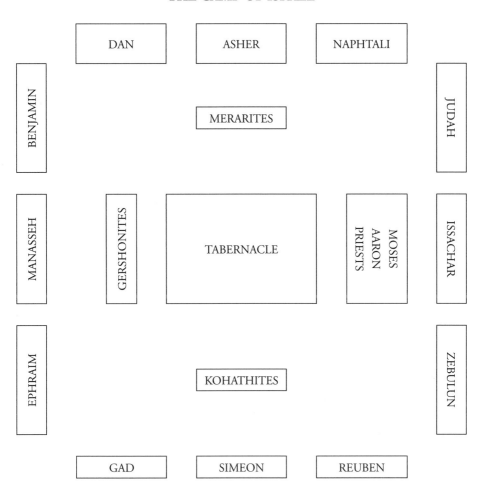

Then the people were *consecrated*. In this chapter we have teaching concerning the Nazarite vow. The Nazarite was a person who, for one reason or another, made a special vow of consecration to God. Certain distinguishing marks set the Nazarite apart from the rest of God's people. He was not to cut his hair; he was to drink no wine; he was forbidden to touch any dead body, even that of his nearest and dearest. The long hair of the Nazarite showed that his appearance was on the altar. He stood out from all others. No one would have any trouble knowing that he was a consecrated man—it showed. His abstinence from wine, the common drink of the day, proclaimed that his *appetites* were on the altar. His separation from all that spoke of death, even in his closest relatives, proclaimed that his *affections* were on the altar. God was to come before even the Nazarite's family, even at a time when human relationships and domestic duty might make legitimate demands upon him.

The ritual connected with the conclusion of his vow is no less constructive. The Nazarite was to bring to the altar a burnt offering, a sin offering, a peace offering, a meal offering, and a drink offering. All this was a confession of his natural sinfulness and of his glaring shortcomings. His sincere consecration came short of what God required. Only the Lord Jesus really lived a truly consecrated life.

The Nazarite then had to cut off the long hair, which had grown during the period of his vow, and burn it. Otherwise he might have been tempted to keep it as a souvenir. Never would he be able to bring out the long locks to show to his grandchildren and say, "See this hair? Twenty years ago I took a Nazarite vow . . ." God wants us to keep our consecration up-to-date. Samuel, Samson, and John the Baptist were the only lifelong Nazarites in Scripture. Jesus never took a Nazarite vow. He was sinless and holy and had no need for vows.

B. Direction in the Wilderness (9:15–10:36)

Valuable lessons can be gleaned here about God's guidance. The most important is in connection with the Shechinah glory cloud. That fiery, cloudy pillar was the chief means God used to lead Israel through the wilderness. Normally the Shechinah cloud rested on the mercy seat in the Holy of Holies in the tabernacle. From there it overshadowed the whole camp. When it was time to move, the cloud arose and moved forward. The tribes, in their proper order, struck camp and followed where it led.

All guidance as to movement was therefore *conscious* guidance—there was not a man, woman, or child who did not know, at any given time, that he was where God wanted him to be. It was *conspicuous* guidance—there could be no mistake. When the cloud moved they moved, where it went they went, when it stopped they stopped. It was *continuous* guidance, for the cloud led them every step of the way. That did not mean that the Israelites always had an easy path, free from troubles and trials, but it did mean they could rest assured they were in the place God wanted them to be.

Guidance today can be just as certain. The means of guidance, however, is spiritual rather than visual.

C. Discontent in the Wilderness (11:1–13:33)

A better title for Numbers might be "The Book of Murmurings." From the time the people left Egypt until the time they finally forfeited their right to enter Canaan, they complained. They complained about the manna. They criticized when the prophetic gift was manifested by others. Aaron and Miriam criticized Moses for his marriage to a foreigner. Finally the people criticized the Promised Land itself.

Kadesh-barnea is a significant place in Hebrew history. There, the people who had come up out of Egypt by an act of faith so thoroughly disbelieved God as to make their entry into the land an impossibility. They trusted God to bring them *out of Egypt* but failed to trust Him to bring them *into Canaan.* The report of the spies concerning the giants and the walled cities so undermined their faith that the passionate pleadings of Joshua and Caleb went unheeded. Unbelief won the day.

There is a solemn and practical lesson in all this. Many believers, it seems, trust God to save them from the penalty of sin but fail to trust God to save them from the power of sin. All their lives they live in defeat and discouragement. They never enter into their "Canaan" of peace, prosperity, and power. All their days they wander, as it were, in the wilderness, coming short of God's best for their lives.

D. Death in the Wilderness (14:1–16:50)

First, there was death *in answer to prayer.* At Kadesh-barnea the people wept and murmured against Moses and Aaron. "Would God that we had died in the land of Egypt! or would God we had died in this wilderness!" they cried in their dread of the Canaanite giants (14:2). God immediately answered their prayer: "Your carcasses shall fall in this wilderness" was His sobering judgment (14:29).

Then there was a death *in answer to presumption.* Chapter 15 records the incident of a man who was so careless of his spiritual responsibilities under the law that he profaned God's Sabbath. He deliberately went to work on the day of rest. He was caught gathering sticks and arrested. Moses was not certain of his ground, so he asked the Lord what he should do. The offense seemed minor; it was the infraction of a ceremonial rather than a moral law. God, however, took a serious view of the matter and instructed that the man be put to death for the sin of presumption.

Then there was death *in answer to pride,* which was manifest in the rebellion of Korah, Dathan, and Abiram. Korah was the first cousin of Moses and Aaron. Soon after the judgment at Kadesh-barnea, Korah led a rebellion against the leadership of Moses and the priesthood of Aaron. He and his fellow conspirators were exposed and executed in a most startling way; the earth yawned open and swallowed up the rebels. Thus God solemnly taught His people that it is a serious thing to challenge God-ordained leaders.

Next there was death *in answer to persistence.* No sooner was one rebellion dealt with than another broke out (16:41–50). The whole camp was up in arms against Moses and Aaron, who, because of the death of Korah and his followers, were accused of murdering the Lord's people. God's answer was swift. A plague broke out in the camp and was only stayed when Moses took the place of mediator between the people and God.

E. Despair in the Wilderness (17:1–19:22)

The priestly authority of Aaron, challenged by Korah, was now to be divinely endorsed. God commanded each one of the heads of the tribes to bring a rod inscribed with his name. Aaron's name was written on the rod for the tribe of Levi. The rods were placed in the tabernacle overnight. By next morning, the rod with Aaron's name on it had come to life, had budded, and blossomed, and brought forth almonds. This astonishing confirmation of Aaron's priestly role was memorialized by the preservation of Aaron's rod inside the sacred ark of the covenant.

These extraordinary happenings brought home to Israel the enormity of their sin: "Behold, we die, we perish, we all perish," they said in despair. "Whosoever cometh any thing near unto the tabernacle of the LORD shall die; shall we be consumed with dying?" (17:12–13). The people now went too far in the opposite direction.

To offset their despair, God ordained the sacrifice of a red heifer in the wilderness and established a unique, once-for-all ritual of cleansing—another of those Old Testament reminders of the sufficiency of the atoning work of Christ.

II. ISRAEL ON THE WAY: THE NEW GENERATION (20:1–36:13)

We come now to the second numbering and to the events that were linked with it. The people now to be numbered were not the same as those numbered before. This is a new generation, the generation about to inherit the land. A gap of thirty-seven and one-half years occurs between chapters 19 and 20 of Numbers.

A. Recalling the Past (20:1–29)

First we see Moses recalling the past with its memories, its methods, its mistakes, and its ministries. The death of Miriam must have brought a flood of *memories*. Miriam was Moses' sister, the courageous, faithful girl who had watched over him as a babe when he was hidden in the bulrushes. Her death severed a very dear tie for Moses and Aaron—one of the very few people remaining who remembered the old days in Egypt.

The *methods* of the past are recalled when Israel murmured again over the lack of water. The first time that happened, Moses was told to *smite* the rock; this time he was told to *speak* to the rock, but in anger and with hasty words, he smote the rock again. God, in grace, allowed the water to flow, but He punished Moses. He told him he would not lead Israel into Canaan.

Many important lessons are linked with this. How serious a matter is a lost temper! How solemn a matter it is to speak angrily to the people of God! In terms of the type, there are other lessons to be learned. The "rock" was a picture of Christ. God allowed His Son to be smitten *once* so that the waters of blessing might flow, but He is never to be smitten again. Now we need only speak to Him. Moses spoiled that type. Then, too, Moses represented the law, and the law cannot get us into "Canaan" and all that Canaan represents.

The *mistakes* of the past are recalled, the time when the Edomites refused Israel's request that they be allowed to pass peaceably through their country on the way to Canaan. The Edomites were kin to the Israelites, being descended from Esau, Jacob's twin brother. This time Israel did not flee precipitously as once before or fight presumptuously as on a previous occasion. They recalled the mistakes of the past and avoided them. Instead they quietly followed the Lord's leading and left God to deal with Edom in His own good time and way.

The *ministries* of the past were recalled by the death of Aaron, Israel's first high priest. We read, "And Moses stripped Aaron of his garments"—how *solemn!* What a reminder of the temporary nature of the Aaronic priesthood—"and put them on Eleazar his son, and Aaron died there"—how *sad!* For Moses it was the severing of another link with the past. He must have been overwhelmed with loneliness—"in the top of the mount"—how *sweet!* Aaron finished well. He finished on the mountaintop, on high ground—"and Moses and Eleazar came down from the mount"—how *sublime!* God buries His workers but His work goes on (20:28).

B. Redeeming the Present (21:1–27:11)

These chapters ring with a new note of victory. From now on, despite setbacks, the children of Israel move forward.

We note an incident of *practical victory*. Arad the Canaanite fought against Israel. He was utterly destroyed by a people walking in obedience to the Lord.

But then came a relapse. The morrow after a great victory is always a time fraught with danger for God's people. The Israelites began to murmur against the manna, bread from heaven, that God had miraculously provided as sustenance in the wilderness. "Our soul loatheth this light bread," they said (21:5).

Instant punishment followed. A plague of fiery serpents attacked the camp. It is a dangerous thing to despise God's Word, that wondrous bread from heaven. It makes possible an attack from the serpent. God's answer was a brazen serpent, lifted high upon a pole, and the clear gospel call, "Look and thou shalt live!"—an incident to which the Lord referred Nicodemus (John 3:14–16).

Then came another resounding victory. This time it was over Sihon, king of the Amorites and over Og, king of Bashan. It was Israel's first taste of victory over the giants that had so terrified them years before at Kadesh-barnea.

We note an incident of *positional victory* (22:1–24:25) in the remarkable story of Balaam. Balaam was from the Euphrates and a hireling prophet—what we would call nowadays a psychic. He was commissioned by Balak, king of Moab, to curse the children of Israel. Balak was terrified because of Israel's victorious advance. He decided to resort to the occult world for aid. Balaam was quite willing to oblige— for a price. He tried to curse God's people four times. Each time God changed his curse into a blessing. The seer actually foretold Israel's glorious future. The king of Moab was beside himself with rage.

The reason for Balaam's failure was simple. He was taken each time by Balak to a new location on some height overlooking the Hebrew camp. That meant that the prophet was seeing the people from God's perspective. He was seeing them from above, seeing them in all the perfection of God's finished work with them. They were blessed! They could not be cursed. This was positional victory.

We note an incident of *personal victory* (chap. 25). Then came the devilish advice that Balaam gave to Balak: "You cannot curse them, my lord king, so why not corrupt them. Then their own God will smite them. You cannot overcome them with the men of Moab; why not try the women of Moab?"[1] The New Testament calls this "the doctrine of Balaam." It describes any attempt to unite the church with the world.

Israel fell for it. The people became embroiled with the women of Moab and the corrupt and false worship of Moab's god Baal-peor. Then Phinehas, a grandson of Aaron, distinguished himself by leading a sweeping purge of all who had been involved in this "whoredom," as the Holy Spirit so graphically describes it.

We note also the anticipation of *potential victory* (26:1–27:11). There was a second numbering of the people, now in anticipation of the impending conquest of Canaan.

C. Reviewing the Future (27:12–36:13)

Three major emphases are found in this closing section of the book.

1. The Leadership of Israel (27:12–23)

God told Moses that he would not be the one to take Israel over Jordan. It was a bitter disappointment. Moses had brought them out, he had brought them through, but he could not bring them in. God explained, "Ye rebelled against my commandment in the desert of Zin, in the strife of the congregation, to sanctify me at the water before their eyes" (27:14). Moses had smitten the rock when God had told him to speak to it. He had lost his temper and called God's people "ye rebels." Rebellion in Moses was as serious as rebellion in the people, even though it was not expressed in the same way. God expects more, too, from those who have served Him for many years than He does from one not so long in the path. Our failure to "sanctify" God in the eyes of the lost and of weaker brethren is a serious thing.

Moses bowed his head. His first words showed his true stature: "Let the LORD, the God of the spirits of all flesh, set a man over the congregation . . . that the congregation of the LORD be not as sheep which have no shepherd" (27:16–17). His first thought was for his flock. He was a true shepherd of the sheep. God's response was to appoint Joshua as Moses' successor, a man Moses had trained. Moses was to formally lay his hands upon Joshua in the sight of priest and people so that there might be an orderly transfer of power.

2. The Laws of Israel (28:1–30:16)

An emphasis was placed on their *various offerings*. Special emphasis, though, was placed on the great annual celebrations of Passover, firstfruits, and tabernacles, but also with emphasis on the daily, weekly, and monthly offerings to be given regularly and systematically to the Lord. Day by day, week by week, month by month, year by year, Calvary was to be kept publicly and prominently in the forefront of all their thinking. It must needs be so, for as the hymn writer says,

> Tell me the story often
> For I forget so soon;
> The early dew of morning
> Has passed away at noon.
> —A Katherine Hankey,
> "Tell Me the Old, Old Story"

Then there was an emphasis on their *verbal obligations*. Commands were given on the importance of keeping vows and promises made to God. Again, we are so prone to forget.

3. The Land of Israel (31:1–36:13)

The first section deals with *compromise* (31:1–32:42). The incident with Midian illustrates how *forgetful* we are (chap. 31). The Midianites evidently had joined with Moab, especially in seeking to corrupt the children of Israel (chap. 25). When God delivered the Midianites into Israel's hands, they took the women as spoil and were roundly rebuked by Moses. These were the very women who had led them astray and caused the plague.

Another incident involves the tribes of Reuben and Gad and half the tribe of Manasseh. They wanted their inheritance at once, on the wilderness side of Jordan. How *foolish* we are (chap. 32). Their choice was world-bordering, and they were the first tribes to be carried away into captivity in the days of the Assyrians. It never pays to see how close we can get to the world. We need to get over Jordan.

The second section is *commentary* (33:1–49). In this chapter Moses recites the long, dreary list of the places the Hebrews had wandered in the days of its punishment for their sin at Kadesh-barnea. It was another way of reminding Israel of the high cost of disobedience and backsliding.

The final section contains *commandments* (33:50–36:13). In the light of Israel's readiness to compromise with Midian, Moses stated the law of *possession* (33:50–56). They would be allowed to continue in the Promised Land only if they thoroughly cleansed it of the Canaanites. Failure here would be disastrous. There were to be no half-measures with the foe; he was too crafty and corrupt.

Then came the law of *partition* (34:1–35:5). Detailed instructions were given for the division of the land between the tribes and the provision of special cities in each tribe for the Levites. By placing Levites in each tribe, some measure of assurance was given that spiritual things would be kept before all the people.

Finally came the law of *protection* (35:6–36:13). The provision of cities of refuge assured protection of the *innocent* (35:6–34). In the case of involuntary manslaughter the offender could flee to one of these cities, there to be protected from "the revenger of blood" (v. 19). He was to remain in the city of refuge until the death of the high priest, at which time he was granted amnesty and protection from the avenger. The six cities set apart for this purpose were so placed that they were readily accessible to all Israel on both sides of Jordan.

The final protection was of the *inheritance* (36:1–13). Laws were enacted to ensure that tribal territory remained within the tribe and that family holdings were protected against transfer, for any reason, into wrong hands. It was Naboth's appeal to this law that so frustrated wicked King Ahab and led to Naboth's murder (1 Kings 21).

Looking back over the book of Numbers, there is one phrase which sums it all up: *trust and obey.*

CHAPTER 6

DEUTERONOMY
The Book of Remembrance

Deuteronomy! What a name for a book! The Jews of Alexandria who translated the Bible from Hebrew into Greek gave the last book of Moses that cumbersome name. It is derived from two Greek words, which together mean "The Second Law." For in Deuteronomy we have the second giving of the Law, or rather, we have an exposition of the Law by Moses for that second generation of Israelites who were about to venture into Canaan.

John Bunyan, in the second part of *Pilgrim's Progress*, tells how Christiana and her boys, having belatedly set off to follow Christian on his pilgrimage to the Celestial City, come within sight of that dreadful valley where, some time before, Christian had so desperately fought with the fiend Apollyon. Responding to a question put by young Samuel, Mr. Greatheart, the companion of Christiana and her boys, replies,

> Your father had that battle with Apollyon at a place yonder before us, in a narrow passage just beyond Forgetful Green. And indeed, that place is the most dangerous place in all these parts.

In one of his books, F. W. Boreham relates that battle to the book of Deuteronomy and suggests that, in view of the nature of Deuteronomy, a better title would be "The Dangers of Forgetful Green." (In Bunyan's day a "green" was a public park, or grassy plain in the center of a town or village.) The book of Deuteronomy consists of a series of addresses by Moses designed to warn the Israelites, whom he was soon to leave, of the dangers of forgetfulness. "Beware lest ye forget," he said again and again. "Thou shalt remember." These two warnings run like a refrain from page to page of Deuteronomy.

"Take heed to thyself, and keep thy soul diligently, lest thou forget the things which thine eyes have seen" (4:9). "Take heed unto yourselves, lest ye forget the covenant of the LORD your God" (4:23). "And remember that thou wast a servant in the land of Egypt" (5:15). "Then beware lest thou forget the LORD, which brought thee forth out of the land of Egypt, from the house of bondage" (6:12). "And thou shalt remember all the way which the LORD thy God led thee these forty years in the wilderness" (8:2). "Beware that thou forget not the LORD thy God, in not keeping his commandments" (8:11). "But thou shalt remember the LORD thy God: for it is he that giveth thee power to get wealth" (8:18). "Remember, and forget not, how thou provokedst the LORD thy God to wrath in the wilderness" (9:7). "Remember what the LORD thy God did unto Miriam" (24:9). "Remember what Amalek did unto thee by the way" (25:17).

God's title for the book is found in the opening statement—"These be the words . . ." The book comprises a series of speeches made by Moses to the children of Israel. They were about to begin the conquest of Canaan, a conquest in which he himself was to have no part. He had brought the vast Hebrew host out of Egypt and across the desert sands to the plains of Moab and the banks of Jordan. The city of Jericho stood sentinel on the farther side. The people were to be given a second chance. Moses gazed longingly across that little strip of water. He was a man under sentence of death. He had brought the people *out*, he had brought the people *through*, but he could not bring the people in.

Moses represented the Law. In him was summed up and personified the principle of works. Because he embodied the Law, represented it, clothed it in flesh and blood, Moses could no more take people into Canaan than a system of good works can take a person to heaven. Moses could not give the people victory and rest in the promised land of Canaan. Similarly, a system of self-effort cannot give a believer victory and rest in the heavenlies today. A new Man representing a wholly different principle must lead the people into rest.

Events recorded in Deuteronomy took place in the eleventh month of the fortieth year. The last fifteen chapters of Numbers correspond to this book (Deut. 1:3). That last fortieth year was a sad and eventful one. In the first month, Miriam died (Num. 20:1); in the fifth month, Aaron died (Num. 33:38); at the end of the month Moses himself died and was mourned for thirty days (Deut. 34:5–9). A new generation now stood poised to enter into the Promised Land. The mantle of Moses was passed on to Joshua, God's chosen successor to Moses.

Before Joshua could begin his great work, however, the people needed to be confronted one more time with all the tremendous demands and dictates of God as summed up in the Mosaic Law. The law is God's schoolmaster to bring us to

Joshua foreshadows Christ (handwritten)

Christ; the law was Israel's tutor to bring them to Joshua. Thus Moses rose up, before passing forever from the scene, to lay down the law one more time. Joshua would then step into his shoes and do that which Moses and the law could not do—bring the people into the Promised Land.

Moses laid down this time with a brand new emphasis. Since Moses first met God at the burning bush, he had come to know Him in a much more intimate and personal way. He had learned that God is not only a God of *government*, He is also a God of *grace*; He is not only a God of law, He is also a God of *love*.

Moses struck this new note in Deuteronomy. God is not revealed as a God of love in the laws of Exodus, Leviticus, and Numbers. This concept is developed for the first time in Deuteronomy. The word "love," it is true, occurs once or twice elsewhere in the books of Moses, but it is a lonely stranger in those other books. It takes up its home as a welcome guest in the book of Deuteronomy. This "second law" tells us that "God is love."

know God of love (handwritten margin note)

Deuteronomy teaches us that behind all God's ordinances and edicts and implacable demands for holiness beats a heart of love. At Sinai the thunders rolled, the mountain shook, the trumpets pealed. There were dire warnings. There were leaping flames. There was a voice that spoke and that made the masses shake. Behind it all beat a longing, loving heart.

God struck a new note through it all: "Because he *loved* thy fathers, therefore he chose their seed after them, and brought thee out in his sight with his mighty power out of Egypt" (4:37). There was more: "Now, Israel, what doth the LORD thy God require of thee, but to fear the LORD thy God, to walk in all his ways, and to love him" (10:12). That is the book of Deuteronomy. Law! But law lifted high, lifted right out of the realm of duty to the lofty realm of desire. It is not, however, love at the expense of law. It is love robed in light, walking hand in hand with law.

Here is an outline of Deuteronomy.

I. The History of Israel: The Backward Look (chaps. 1–3)
  A. The Journey Reviewed: Horeb to Kadesh (chap. 1)
    1. Trekking to Kadesh (1:1–19)
    2. Trembling at Kadesh (1:20–45)
    3. Tarrying at Kadesh (1:46)
  B. The Journey Resumed: Kadesh to Beth-Peor (chaps. 2–3)
    1. Conquering the Land East of Jordan (2:1–3:17)
      a. Victory over the Giants Possible (2:1–23)
      b. Victory over the Giants Proven (2:24–3:17)
    2. Contemplating the Land West of Jordan (3:18–29)
      a. Moses Speaks to Israel (3:18–20)
      b. Moses Sees the Inheritance (3:21–29)

II. The Holiness of Israel: The Inward Look (chaps. 4–11)
    A. Moses Speaks about the Law (chaps. 4–6)
    B. Moses Speaks about the Lord (chaps. 7–8)
    C. Moses Speaks about the Land (chaps. 9–11)
III. The Heritage of Israel: The Forward Look (chaps. 12–30)
    Laws concerning:
    A. Purity in the Land (chaps. 12–14)
    B. Property in the Land (chap. 15)
    C. Piety in the Land (16:1–17)
    D. Positions in the Land (16:18–18:22)
    E. Protection in the Land (chaps. 19–20)
    F. Persons in the Land (chaps. 21–25)
    G. Priorities in the Land (chap. 26)
    H. Permanence in the Land (chaps. 27–30)
IV. The Hero of Israel: The Upward Look (chaps. 31–34)
    A. Moses the Statesman (chap. 31)
    B. Moses the Singer (chap. 32)
    C. Moses the Seer (chap. 33)
    D. Moses the Saint (chap. 34)

Deuteronomy begins with the *historical*, moves on to the *judicial*; points us to the *prophetical* and concludes with the *biographical*. God would have us take four looks. Not only at this book, but also at our own lives.

I. THE HISTORY OF ISRAEL: THE BACKWARD LOOK (CHAPS. 1–3)

The first three chapters of Deuteronomy deal with recent history. History is important. The first seventeen books of the Old Testament and the first five books of the New Testament are all books of history. Of the sixty-six books of the Bible, twenty-two are history books—a third of the Bible.

Moses begins by taking the Hebrew people back to Kadesh-barnea, to the great watershed of their spiritual history, to the place where they came to a great divide. Israel had marched out of Egypt. Behind them was a country desolated and spoiled as never before in its long, illustrious history. The cloudy pillar had led the people across the Red Sea, down around the rim of Sinai, and on to Kadesh-barnea.

It was there that the people first heard about the giants. "The sons of the Anakim are there!" they were told. At Kadesh-barnea unbelief decided the day. The disbelieving, defiant, and disgruntled people had been condemned to wander in the wilderness for forty years—redeemed, but shut out from rest. For them it was, henceforth, the question of a saved soul, but a lost life.

Now the tribes had come back to Kadesh-barnea. Note, it was a new generation that stood there. The nation was about to be given a second chance to enter the land. Moses hammered home the lessons of the past.

He told them that victory *could* be theirs. The Moabites, the Edomites, and the Ammonites, three nations near of kin to Israel, had met and mastered those giants without any of Israel's spiritual resources. If Moab, Edom, and Ammon could conquer giants, certainly Israel, the people of God, led by the Lord, could conquer them, too.

Victory had been theirs was Moses' second point. The Israelites themselves had conquered Sihon the Amorite, as well as Og, king of Bashan. Both these kings had been of the same cursed race—both were *Nephilim*.

God brings us to our spiritual Kadesh-barnea, too, to our places of failure, where unbelief had won the day. The giants are still there. God, however, loves to give us another chance. He would have us take the backward look, underline the fact of past failure, and then go on to victory.

II. THE HOLINESS OF ISRAEL: THE INWARD LOOK (CHAPS. 4–11)

These chapters probe behavior. We cannot possess all that God has for us unless we are willing to order our lives in a way that pleases Him. This is the great theme of this section of Deuteronomy.

First, Moses spoke to his people about *the law*. He reminded them of how it came, what it contains, and whom it concerns. God's standards were high and holy and the law itself was given amidst scenes of sobering solemnity. The law itself neither saved nor sanctified but it did stand as an awesome expression of God's holiness and as a reminder of man's sinfulness.

Moses spoke next about *the Lord* and in so doing lifted the question of right behavior to a different and higher plane. Israel was to behave as God decreed, not because of the law's demands but because of love's desires. It is part of the genius of the Bible that it centers things not in precepts but in a Person, not in a legal code but in the living Christ. Moses summed it up in a statement of singular beauty and power: "The LORD did not set his love upon you, nor choose you, because ye were more in number than any people . . . but because the LORD loved you" (7:7–8). He chose you because He loves you! What could be added to that as an incentive for holy living?

Next, Moses spoke about *the land*. There was a principle to be recognized (chap. 9), a past to be remembered (chap. 10), and a power to be realized (chap. 11). He says, "Not for thy righteousness, or for the uprightness of thine heart, dost thou go to possess their land: . . . Understand therefore, that the LORD thy God giveth thee not this good land to possess it for thy righteousness; for thou art a stiffnecked people" (9:5–6). The land was being given to them solely on the ground of grace. The application of this truth to us is self-evident. Heaven is not ours because we deserve it. Neither our self-righteousness, nor our respectability, nor our religiousness can earn us God's salvation. The inward look tells us why.

III. THE HERITAGE OF ISRAEL: THE FORWARD LOOK (CHAPS. 12–30)

This is a long section. Its primary interpretation belongs to Israel, not to us today. It details the conditions under which God would permit the nation to possess the Promised Land. All sorts of conditions are covered, but the great thrust was that Israel's sojourn in Canaan would depend on their behavior. If the people abided by the law of God, He would bless them, but if they abused their privileges and broke His laws, He would eject them to wander fearful and homeless in the world.

This section contains those fearful curses that caused Paul to speak of "the curse of the law" (Gal. 3:13). God solemnly warned Israel that disasters would most certainly come if the people forsook His law. The nation would be cursed with *disease*, with *drought*, with *defeat* in battle, with *deportation*. "And the LORD shall scatter thee among all people, from the one end of the earth even unto the other; and there shalt thou serve other gods. . . . And among these nations shalt thou find no ease, neither shall the sole of thy foot have rest: but the LORD shall give thee there a trembling heart, and failing of eyes, and sorrow of mind: and thy life shall hang in doubt before thee; and thou shalt fear day and night, and shalt have none assurance of thy life: in the morning thou shalt say, Would God it were even! and at even thou shalt say, Would God it were morning!" (28:64–67).

The history of the Jews for the past two thousand years has been one long commentary on this prophecy. There is hardly a country that has not harbored the Jews. They have sought asylum in nation after nation, settled down, prospered, grown great, invoked the envy of their Gentile neighbors, been discriminated against, persecuted, and driven back out. Anti-Semitism is a worldwide disease, one that is always endemic in the world and one that at times becomes epidemic.

We read through these great speeches of Moses and marvel at his eloquence. This, we recall, is the man who once excused himself from divine service with the plea, "I cannot speak" (see Exod. 4:10).

IV. THE HERO OF ISRAEL: THE UPWARD LOOK (CHAPS. 31–34)

The last four chapters of Deuteronomy focus on Moses himself. We see him as a statesman, a singer, a seer, and a saint. With true statesmanship he made his preparations for the transfer of power upon his death. Then he burst into song, into that great hymn known as "the song of Moses," now sung in heaven along with "the song of the Lamb." Then, like the dying Jacob, Moses cast his eye prophetically down the long future ages of Jewish history and spoke of the future of the tribes.

His words ended, this great hero of the Hebrew people turned his face toward Mount Nebo. There he was given a view of the Promised Land, the land he was never to possess and upon which his feet would never stand until summoned to stand there for a few moments with Elijah and the Son of God. Finally he yielded himself up into the arms of God, died with the smile of God upon him, and was buried by the angels in an unknown, hidden grave. "And Moses," we read, "was an hundred and twenty years old when he died: his eye was not dim, nor his natural force abated" (34:7).

Thus ends the book of Deuteronomy and thus closes the Pentateuch. We close our survey of Deuteronomy by borrowing the words of that mysterious pagan psychic, Balaam of Mesopotamia: "Let me die the death of the righteous, and let my last end be like his!" (Num. 23:10). Balaam never made it; Moses did; so may we.

CHAPTER 7

JOSHUA

From Victory unto Victory

Moses was dead. For forty phenomenal years he had championed the cause of the children of Israel, emancipating them from hopeless bondage in Egypt. He had done the impossible. He had not only freed millions from slavery and the sentence of death, he had humbled to the very dust the greatest empire of his day.

"Let my people go!" That was God's demand (Exod. 5:1).

"I know not the Lord," said Pharaoh, "neither will I listen to what He says" (see Exod. 5:2). The exodus from Egypt seems to have taken place about the year 1440 B.C. Possibly, then, the pharaoh of the oppression who denied the sovereignty of God was the dynamic Thutmose III. The pharaoh had appealed to the multiplied gods of Egypt. God smote them down. By the time Moses was through with them, the gods of Egypt were exposed, shattered, empty, and defeated. Plague after plague reduced Egypt to a shambles. The country was in a state of ruin from end to end. The liberated Hebrew slaves marched out of Goshen's ghetto, laden down with spoil.

Now Moses was dead. He had been their liberator and their leader. He had brought them out of Egypt, across the desert sands, and right up to the border of Canaan. Now he was dead. He had brought them out. He had brought them through. But he could not bring them in. His mantle had passed on. Joshua had it now.

The book of Joshua occupies a strategic place in the Old Testament. Like the book of Acts in the New Testament, it is a book of transition. Like the book of Ephesians, it portrays the wealth, the walk, and the warfare of God's people down here. It can be set in contrast with Deuteronomy: Deuteronomy expounds the prospects of victory in Canaan; Joshua expounds the possession of Canaan.

73

Joshua was born a slave in Egypt. He had lived through the wandering that had marked Israel's experiences in the wilderness. He had been tutored by Moses. He had led the armies of Israel. He had spied out the Promised Land. He and Caleb had brought back the minority report. The land was ripe for conquest. It was a land "flowing with milk and honey" (Exod. 33:3).

Joshua's name means "Jehovah the Savior." In the Greek it would be rendered "Jesus." Indeed, in several places in the KJV New Testament, the name of Joshua is actually rendered as "Jesus" (Acts 7:45; Heb. 4:8).

Joshua conquered Canaan. He failed, however, to bring the people into Canaan rest. Only the true Joshua (Jesus) can give us real rest. It is possible to be truly saved but never to enter into all that God has for us in Christ.

Before surveying this book we need to note Joshua's three strategic blunders. First, he failed to gain possession of the coastline of Canaan. He left five major cities in the hands of the Philistines (Ekron, Ashdod, Ashkelon, Gath, Gaza), and two even greater cities in the hands of the Phoenicians (Sidon, Tyre). As a result the entire coastal strip north and south from Carmel remained an enemy. Israel was oppressed by *Philistine rule* until David came and by *Phoenician religion* until after the Babylonian captivity. The Philistines and Phoenicians made any effective rest in Canaan a virtual impossibility.

Then Joshua made a serious blunder in signing a treaty with the Gibeonites. The city of Gibea remained within the boundary of Israel for many years. On one occasion an entire tribe (Benjamin) was practically annihilated as a result of Gibeonite vileness.

Finally, Joshua failed to complete mopping-up operations. Pockets of paganism remained dotted here and there, holding remnants of the Canaanites. They kept paganism—along with its debaucheries and dreadful cruelties—alive and vigorous in Israel. God had commanded the extermination of the Canaanites. Joshua failed to obey. In time Israel became apostate.

I. Claiming the Land (chaps. 1–5)
   A. Faith Believes the Bible (chap. 1)
   B. Faith Counts the Cost (chap. 2)
   C. Faith Makes a Move (chap. 3)
   D. Faith Strengthens Its Stand (chap. 4)
   E. Faith Pays the Price (chap. 5)
II. Conquering the Land (chaps. 6–11)
   A. Facing Major Foes: Jericho (chap. 6)
   B. Facing Minor Foes: Ai (chaps. 7–8)
   C. Facing Moderate Foes (chap. 9)
   D. Facing Multiplied Foes (chaps. 10–11)

III. Colonizing the Land (chaps. 12–24)
  A. Declaring the Spoils of Victory (chap. 12)
  B. Dividing the Spoils of Victory (chaps. 13–21)
    1. Statutes of Liberty (chaps. 13–19)
    2. Statements of Equality (chap. 20)
    3. Standards of Justice (chap. 21)
  C. Dedicating the Spoils of Victory (chap. 22)
  D. Defending the Spoils of Victory (chaps. 23–24)

Joshua teaches us that there can be no shortcuts to a life of victory. We are in enemy territory. Victory is assured only when we trust and obey, when we watch and pray. God's answer to the flesh in the life of a believer is not Pentecost, but Calvary.

I. Claiming the Land (chaps. 1–5)

A. Faith Believes the Bible (chap. 1)

"The Lord spake unto Joshua" (v. 1). What was it that separated Moses from everyone else? God spoke to him—face to face, God to man, heart to heart. Now God spoke in like manner at various times to Joshua. It all begins there. "Faith cometh by hearing, and hearing by the word of God" (Rom. 10:17).

What a relief it was when, suddenly, the voice of God rang through. The Hebrew people were camped on the east bank of Jordan. The Canaanites, with their giants and their cities and towering fortifications, lay ahead. The tribes of Israel were unseasoned in war. They had played the coward the last time they were faced with the conquest of Canaan. Moses was dead.

But God was very much alive.

So the book of Joshua begins with this encouraging note: "The Lord spake unto Joshua." Just as he had spoken to Moses. Joshua had a fresh word from God. Everything begins with what God said: "This book of the law shall not depart out of thy mouth; but thou shalt meditate therein day and night, that thou mayest observe to do according to all that is written therein: for then thou shalt make thy way prosperous, and then thou shalt have good success" (v. 8).

Nobody has ever had a victorious life as a believer who has neglected the daily quiet time. All backsliding, all defeat begins when time is no longer set apart each day to see what God has to say. We must get to know the Book and know it better than we know our professional journals, our school textbooks, our newspapers and magazines, or whatever it is we read.

B. Faith Counts the Cost (chap. 2)

Joshua now sent a couple of spies into Canaan to assess the strengths and weaknesses of the foe. We can make one of two mistakes. We can *underestimate* the strength of the foe. The believer has three enemies—the world, the flesh, and the Devil. The great goal of the world is to pour us into its mold, offering us its pleasures, its power, its praise. If its smile does not seduce us, it will try its scowls, seeking to paralyze us with its wrath. The world is the external foe.

The great goal of the flesh is to defile us. It plays upon our lusts and longings. The flesh is the internal foe.

The great goal of Satan is to devour us as a roaring lion. He is our diabolical foe, and he has enormous power. But he is no match for the Holy Spirit. Satan has countless legions of fallen angels and demons to work his will, but God draws lines beyond which they cannot go. Nonetheless, we must not underestimate the enemy.

We can, however, *overestimate* the strength of the foe. All our enemies ultimately have to deal with God. Our task is to take God at His word. Regardless of Satan's minions—be they principalities, or powers, or rulers of this world's darkness, or wicked spirits in high places—our victory is assured. "If God be for us, who can be against us?" (Rom. 8:31).

Joshua's two spies came back with a glowing report. God had already put His fear into them.

The two spies, having found refuge in the house of Rahab, listened with astonishment to what she had to say: "I know that the LORD hath given you the land, and that your terror is fallen upon us, and that all the inhabitants of the land faint because of you. For we have heard how the LORD dried up the water of the Red sea for you, when ye came out of Egypt; and what ye did unto the two kings of the Amorites, that were on the other side Jordan, Sihon and Og, whom ye utterly destroyed" (2:9–10).

C. Faith Makes a Move (chap. 3)

But now Jordan must be crossed. Jordan in the Bible is constantly set before us as a type of death. Everything about the river pictures death. It was called "the descender" by the Jews because it plunges down from the snow-covered heights of Hermon, through a wild and desolate land, to bury itself forever in the depths of the Dead Sea. Before Israel could conquer Canaan, the people must first cross Jordan; they must pass through death.

They had first learned this lesson when they came out of Egypt. There, they had to come through the waters of the Red Sea. The New Testament says they were "baptized unto Moses in the cloud and in the sea" (1 Cor. 10:2). It was an unforgettable experience, which, when the unredeemed Egyptians tried to copy, led to their death. The Red Sea and the Jordan both picture the death, burial, and resurrection of Christ.

Israel might have entered Canaan forty years earlier in the power of their Red

Sea experience. Had they done so, they would not have had to repeat their coming through the waters. Unbelief kept them out of Canaan for the life span of a whole generation. So, before Canaan could be theirs, they had to learn again, in a practical way, the lesson of the Red Sea. They had to go through Jordan. There can be no conquest of our Canaan, no entering into our possessions in the heavenlies, until we appropriate our identification with Christ in His death, burial, and resurrection (Rom. 6).

D. Faith Strengthens Its Stand (chap. 4)

This chapter records a critically important ceremony. Two distinct memorials were erected, each one constructed of twelve stones—one for each tribe of Israel. The one set of stones was buried in the Jordan; the other was set up at Gilgal. In this twofold act, faith took its stand, confirming publicly the move it had recently made.

Twelve stones were taken from the wilderness—the scene of Israel's wanderings, carnality, and defeat. These stones were buried deep in the bed of the Jordan. The forty years of wilderness wanderings were thus symbolically put in the place of death and buried out of sight. They were never to be seen again. In their place, twelve stones were taken from the bed of the river, carried over to the other side, and set up as a permanent memorial at Gilgal. There they stood, a permanent reminder of the new position Israel now gained through "death, burial, and resurrection." They were to be, as the Spirit of God said, "a testimony to all the people of the earth" (see v. 24). No other nation or people ever had an experience like that. It was unique; it belonged to Israel alone.

The two ordinances Christ left with His church teach us similar truth. What was taught Israel symbolically, in the ordinance of the buried stones and the memorial pillar, is taught to us spiritually in the rite of baptism and the ordinance of the Lord's Supper. In baptism we proclaim our death with Him; at the Lord's Table we proclaim His death for us.

E. Faith Pays the Price (chap. 5)

Israel must now take its stand on resurrection ground. They must act on the basis of revealed and known truth. Throughout their wilderness wanderings the tribes had neglected a certain truth. It was a painful truth, but it had to be taught and its truth obeyed. The people had neglected the great Abrahamic covenant seal of circumcision.

They overlooked this basic requirement of their faith. God hadn't. Israel must learn that before God would allow them to draw the sword on the foe, they must bring the knife to bear upon themselves. The flesh must be dealt with. The walls of Jericho were not going to fall before a disobedient people.

So, at Gilgal, the neglected rite of circumcision was administered to all males in the congregation. Faith paid the price. And a sharp, unforgettable lesson it was.

Now Israel was ready for victory at last. But first they must observe the Passover. God spread a feast of remembrance in the wilderness, in the presence of their enemies. Thus spiritually fortified, the people of God could go forward, confident that no foe could daunt them.

II. CONQUERING THE LAND (CHAPS. 6–11)

Looked at from the standpoint of military strategy, Joshua's campaigns in Canaan were simple and sound. First he drove a wedge into the heart of the country, dividing his foes and making it impossible for them to create a united front. Then Joshua turned his armies south, smashing a budding coalition centered at Jerusalem. After that he marched north in time to crush another coalition being formed there. In three swift, major campaigns he completely conquered the land.

A. Facing Major Foes: Jericho (chap. 6)

At the outset of any new venture of faith, God invariably lets his people come face to face with some major obstacle. Failure at this point would spell failure everywhere.

We all have our Jerichos—a long, entrenched evil habit, a circle of godless companions, a temperamental weakness, what God calls "the besetting sin," a tyrannical boss, an unsaved fiancé. Whatever it is, there it stands, right across our new resolve, to stumble us, to bring to naught our new life of victory.

God had a fail-proof plan for dealing with Jericho. He would deal with it Himself. Joshua went out to see for himself what he would be up against at Jericho. It certainly was a formidable foe. At that critical moment Joshua became aware that he was no longer alone.

"And it came to pass, when Joshua was by Jericho, that he lifted up his eyes and looked, and, behold, there stood a man over against him with his sword drawn in his hand." At once Joshua challenged him: "Art thou for us, or for our adversaries?" he said. He dismissed the sword, unafraid. He took a firm stand against this probable foe. He was not about to compromise. Instantly all doubts were settled. "Nay; but as captain of the host of the LORD am I now come" was the reply (5:13, 14). Instantly Joshua enthroned God as Lord in his life.

The order of battle was set out for him. Day after day he marched his men around the towering walls of Jericho. It doubtless was an odd way to wage a war. He was not called to bring up great battering rams or lofty scaling ladders. All he had to do was march around the city, trumpet in hand. He was to trust and obey. People must have thought it a silly way to fight a foe. Then it happened. "By faith the walls of Jericho fell down" (Heb. 11:30).

That is how to deal with our foe, our major foe.

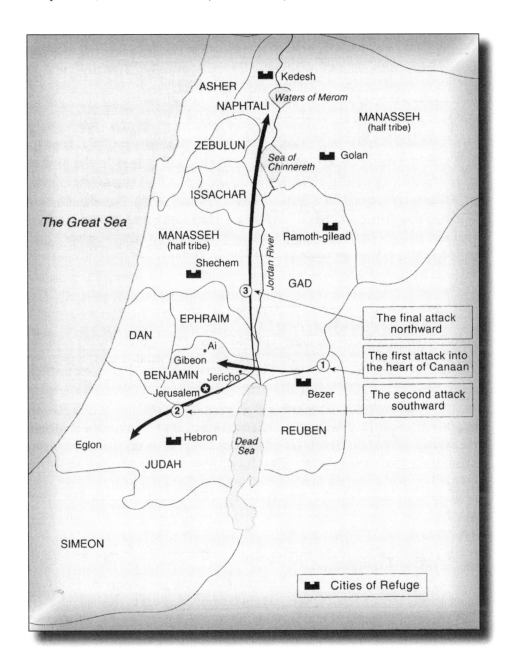

B. Facing Minor Foes: Ai (chaps. 7–8)

After Jericho came Ai and an utter, devastating defeat. The first temptation after a great spiritual victory is to imagine that, somehow, we won the victory through our own prowess and effort. The next temptation is to think that we can act in independence of God, especially when the matter before us seems small and insignificant. This is what happened at Ai. It was a case of having confidence in the flesh. "It is only a little city," they said. "We can handle places like Ai" (see 7:3). As a result, they came face to face with a bitter and humiliating defeat.

Had Joshua prayed before launching his attack on Ai, he would soon have discovered that there was sin in the Israelite camp. A man named Achan had stolen some of the spoil of Jericho, every stick and stone of which had been dedicated to God. The secret sin of this individual affected the position of the corporate body of God's people. Until it was exposed and confessed and judged and put away there could be no further progress. God's battles are fought along spiritual lines, not natural ones. That is why it is so important that we have a daily quiet time. God speaks to us from His Word. He shows us sin in our lives, sin that needs to be confessed and cleansed so that the Spirit might remain ungrieved.

C. Facing Moderate Foes (chap. 9)

This time it was a case of deception, and again, it was a matter of acting independently of the Word of God. God's Word, indeed, seemed to cover this case, but had Joshua sought guidance he would soon have discovered that the enemy was taking advantage of God's own Word to trap him.

The background is important here. Deuteronomy 20:15–16 laid down guidelines for making treaties with other nations. There must be no compromise with the foul Canaanites. Regarding far-off nations, however, those not so thoroughly debauched as the Canaanites, some terms could be offered. The Gibeonites came pretending to have traveled from a vast distance, seeking a treaty with Israel. They exhibited what looked like foolproof evidence—moldy bread, rent wineskins, worn out shoes. They came with a believable story: when they left home their bread was hot from the oven, their wineskins and shoes were brand new.

On the strength of Deuteronomy 20:15–16, Joshua made the league for which they asked—only to discover the moment it was signed that the Gibeonites were among the next tribes due to be conquered by Israel. It was a costly mistake. God made Joshua honor his treaty. True, he reduced the Gibeonites to serfdom but there they remained, a pocket of raw paganism in the midst of the people, and a source of future trouble. May the Lord deliver us from lightly entering into what look like legitimate enough engagements but that turn out to be costly mistakes. Let us bear this in mind—God will make us honor commitments we have made; marriage to an unsaved person, for example, or a bad business deal that has gone sour. Just because we realize our mistake does not mean that God will absolve us of its natural consequences. Beware of Gibeon.

D. Facing Multiplied Foes (chaps. 10–11)

On two distinct occasions Joshua had to face the massed might of the enemy. In both cases he was called upon to trust and obey the Word of God. The manner in which victory came, however, was strikingly different in each case.

On the first occasion, Joshua had to face a southern coalition centered at Jerusalem. His victory this time illustrates the *providential* side of a spiritual victory. We read, "The LORD cast down great stones from heaven . . . they were more which died with hailstones than they whom the children of Israel slew" (10:11). And we read, "And the sun stood still, and the moon stayed, until the people had avenged themselves upon their enemies" (10:13).

In other words, on this occasion the victory was supernatural. God stepped in and swept away all opposition with a display of mighty, omnipotent power. That is the way it is sometimes. We all know of drunken men made permanently sober, the very taste for alcohol being removed; of men hopelessly addicted to drugs being so thoroughly cleansed by the Holy Spirit that the habit drops away like last year's leaves before the budding spring. Like the sun standing still in the heavens, the Lord stands yonder in the heaven of heavens until every spiritual power hostile to God in a man's or a woman's soul is laid low.

But other cases are quite different. In time, Joshua had to face another coalition, another powerful accumulation of hostile and deadly foes. This time there were no miracles at all. It was hard slogging all the way. Joshua's victory this time illustrates the *personal* side of a spiritual victory. All down through chapter 11 we read that Joshua and Israel smote their foes with the edge of the sword. "[Israel] smote them, and chased them . . . they . . . smote the king" (11:8, 10). It was hard, hand-to-hand combat every step of the way. God was still for them, and God was still with them, but now there were no more signs and wonders. They had matured; they didn't need them. They knew now that victory was in the sword (the Word).

We know of men and women afflicted with some besetting sin, longing and praying for instant, complete deliverance—deliverance that never comes. What is wrong? Do they lack faith? Had God ceased to be God? Is there sin in the life, some wrong motive? No! It is simply that, in these cases, God expects His child to become proficient in the use of "the sword of the Spirit"; then, in the power of God's Word, to smite and smite and smite the foe. There has to be a daily struggle with the foe until, at last, after a long, arduous struggle, victory is gained.

In this day and age, now that we have a completed Bible, God points us to His Word and to its application to the life of the believer. Opening ourselves to God and His Word may be a harder way to win victories, but this is the way to true spiritual maturity.

III. Colonizing the Land (chaps. 12–24)

There is much of interest in this section of the book. The land was divided by lot among the tribes of Israel. Other factors also entered into the division, such as the capacity of the holder, rights of conquest, petition, and faithfulness. Most space in the narrative is devoted to the inheritances of Judah and Joseph (Ephraim and Manasseh). Cities of refuge were set apart to deal with murder and manslaughter. The Levites, who had no actual tribal inheritance, were given scattered cities among the tribes. In this way the spiritual influence of this tribe could be felt throughout the entire nation. Forty-eight such cities were given to the Levites.

When the fighting was over, two and one-half tribes (which had chosen their inheritance east of Jordan) were allowed to return home. They built an altar, an act that almost brought about civil war. They hastily explained that it was intended to signify their solidarity with the other tribes.

Joshua's last words in chapter 24 are important in view of the failure that followed, as recorded in the book of Judges. Joshua's solemn closing sermon (for that is what it was) can be summed up in a single sentence: All the ground gained will be lost if we fail to watch and war against the foe, for there is no discharge in this war, no shortcuts, no permanent deliverance. That is, until we get to Glory. Or until the Lord returns.

CHAPTER 8

JUDGES

The Folly of Forsaking God

It is an axiom of Bible study that we may look for the key to any book in its opening paragraphs. It is usual for the Holy Spirit to hang the key, as it were, by the *front* door. With Judges, He hangs the key not by the front door but by the back door. It is when we read the last verse of the book that we put our finger on the inspired statement that unlocks its story. "In those days there was no king in Israel: every man did that which was right in his own eyes" (21:25).

Mark that statement well, for it is one of the most terrible indictments of fallen human nature that is found in the Bible. It does not say that every man did that which was *wrong* in his own eyes, but that every man did that which was *right* in his own eyes. The result was an age of Hebrew history blacker with moral pollution and darker with religious apostasy than almost any other age. The whole book of Judges becomes one great volume inspired of God to expound the Holy Spirit's verdict of fallen man—"There is none that doeth good, no, not one" (Rom. 3:12). For here, *every* man was doing what he thought right. As we would say today, he was doing his own thing. And in so doing, the aggregate of Hebrew behavior during this four hundred year epoch outraged and incensed the living God time after time after time.

The book of Judges is a sad sequel to the book of Joshua. In Joshua the "heavenlies" are typified, in Judges the "earthlies." Joshua rings with the shout of victory; Judges echoes with the sobs of defeat. In Judges we go round and round—rebellion, retribution, repentance, and restoration. Then the same cycle all over again, some six or seven times.

The book of Ruth, together with the last five chapters of Judges, forms a kind of appendix to the book of Judges, highlighting the moral and spiritual conditions of the whole period.

I. Israel's Wars (1:1–2:5)
   A. The Tribe of Judah (1:1–21)
      1. The Promise of Initial Victory (1:1–18)
      2. The Peril of Incomplete Victory (1:19–21)
   B. The House of Joseph (1:22–2:5)
      1. The Promise of Initial Victory (1:22–26)
      2. The Peril of Incomplete Victory (1:27–2:5)
II. Israel's Woes (2:6–16:31)
   A. The Summary of the Period (2:6–23)
   B. The Survey of the Period (chaps. 3–16)
      1. The Experienced Man: Othniel
      2. The Exasperated Man: Ehud
      3. The Exhorted Man: Barak
      4. The Exercised Man: Gideon
      5. The Execrated Man: Abimelech
      6. The Excommunicated Man: Jephthah
      7. The Exceptional Man: Samson
III. Israel's Ways (chaps. 17–21)
   A. Religious Perversion (chaps. 17–18)
   B. Moral Pollution (chaps. 19–21)

During the period covered by the book of Judges, Israel is seen in subjection to

1. The Mesopotamians (3:8–11)
2. The Moabites, Ammonites, and Amalekites (3:12–30)
3. The Canaanites (chap. 4)
4. The Midianites (chaps. 6–7)
5. The Ammonites (10:6–32)
6. The Philistines (chaps. 13–16)

The various judges who are mentioned in the book are

1. The Elders (2:7–23)
2. Othmel (3:1–11)
3. Ehud (3:12–30)
4. Shamgar (3:31)
5. Deborah (chaps. 4–5)
6. Gideon (chaps. 6–8)
7. Abimelech (chap. 9)
8. Tola (10:1–2)

 9. Jair (10:3–5)
10. Jephthah (10:6–12:7)
11. Ibzan (12:8–10)
12. Elon (12:11–12)
13 Abdon (12:13–15)
14. Samson (chaps. 13–16)

To get a better picture of the period of the Judges, see the chart on the next page. Some of the periods probably overlapped.

I. Israel's Wars (1:1–2:5)

This section is a recapitulation of Israel's failure to possess the possessions given to them by God. It consists of a summary of the wars of the tribe of Judah and the wars of the tribes of Joseph. It tells also of initial victory fading off rapidly into complacency, compromise, and carelessness.

Solemnly and repeatedly Israel had been warned by Moses to make no league with the inhabitants of Canaan. Regarding the Amorites, their iniquity was now full. Their religious, moral, and social habits were utterly vile, and they had polluted the land with the abominations. Their gods were demons and their religious practices filthy. The worship of Ashtoreth was the special sin of the Canaanite nations. It entailed idolatry of the most revolting form in which immorality was elevated to an act of worship. All virtues were surrendered. "To go a-whoring" was far more than a figure of speech.

Israel was instructed to remove this moral cancer from the land. In its place they were to set up the pure worship of Jehovah and be a witness to all mankind of the true and living God. Instead, they "forsook the Lord God of their fathers, which brought them out of the land of Egypt, and followed other gods, of the gods of the people that were round about them, and bowed themselves unto them, and provoked the Lord to anger" (2:12).

The early victories of Israel were not carried through to final triumph. One reason was because the "iron age" was dawning in Canaan, and the Israelites felt themselves unable to cope with the military hardware of their foes. But more important, yet forgotten, was the fact that "the Lord of hosts" was the true Captain of their salvation. Israel surrendered. Soon compromise ended in complicity, and Israel sank to the level of the nations she had been destined to replace.

Baal and Asherah of the Canaanites; the gods of Syria, Zidon, Moab, and Ammon; and Dagon, the god of the Philistines—all these Israel served in turn. Behind the grotesque idols of wood and stone were the real gods of Canaan—evil spirits. Idolatry in any form is inspired by demons (Lev. 17:7; Deut. 32:17; 1 Cor. 10:19–22) and invariably results in degradation.

THE PERIOD OF THE JUDGES

The Enemy	Subjection	Deliverer	Peace
Mesopotamians	8 years	Othniel	40 years
Moabites Ammonites Amalekites	18 years	Ehud Shamgar	80 years
Canaanites	20 years	Deborah Barak	40 years
Midianites	7 years	Gideon Abimelech, the usurper Tola Jair	40 years 3 years 23 years 22 years
Ammonites	18 years	Jephthah Ibzan Elon Abdon	6 years 7 years 10 years 8 years
Philistines	40 years	Samson	(20 years)
Total:	111 years		279 years*

* This total does not include Samson's twenty years, which overlapped with the forty-year Philistine oppression. In addressing the Sanhedrin, Stephen summarized this period: "And after that he gave unto them judges about the space of four hundred and fifty years, until Samuel the prophet" (Acts 13:20). We can arrive at that figure thus:

Years of subjection	111 years
Years of rest	279 years
The ministry of Eli	40 years
The ministry of Samuel	20 years
Total	450 years

Again and again God allowed Israel to taste the bitter fruits of idolatry. The nations that Israel had failed to drive out grew stronger and subdued them, and cruel, evil, and ruthless tyrants oppressed them. Terrible times of hardship, privation, and woe followed hard upon each period of national apostasy.

II. Israel's Woes (2:6–16:31)

We now see the fruit of Joshua's three political mistakes. His failure to obey God and utterly exterminate the foul Canaanite tribes now had to be paid for by Israel. In chapter 2 we have a *summary* of the period. In chapters 3–16 we have a *survey* of the period.

A. The Summary of the Period (2:6–23)

Time and again God raised up deliverers, "judges" as they were called in this book. Nowadays we would probably refer to them as strongmen. Yet they were not strongmen, after all, in today's sense of the word, because God's strongmen are never counted for much by this world's standards.

They seem to have been a somewhat unusual crowd of nobodies. There was Othniel, a younger brother; Ehud, a left-handed man; Deborah, a woman; Shamgar, who had but an ox goad; Gideon, going to war with a lamp and a pitcher; Jephthah, an outlaw; and Samson, whose greatest victory was with the jawbone of an ass!

Indeed, the whole period seems to sum up the words of Paul to the intellectual, worldly wise, carnal, gifted, and boastful Corinthians: "God hath chosen the foolish things of the world to confound the wise; and God hath chosen the weak things of the world to confound the things which are mighty; and base things of the world, and things which are despised, hath God chosen, yea, and things which are not, to bring to naught things that are: that no flesh should glory in his presence" (1 Cor. 1:27–29).

B. The Survey of the Period (chaps. 3–16)

The book of Judges, for the most part, is the story of seven men.

1. The Experienced Man: Othniel

With God, the punishment is always suited to the crime. Israel had been called to be a witness to the nations against the follies and vileness of idolatry. The founding father of the race, Abraham, had been called out of Mesopotamia for that very purpose. In response to the revelation of the true and living God to his soul, he had renounced his pagan gods and become a living testimony for God in the earth. He left Mesopotamia, the place where all idolatry had its origin, and set out for the Promised Land.

Now Israel had gone back to idolatry. God therefore raised up an oppressor, Cushan-rishathaim, king of Mesopotamia. His name means "black, double wickedness." Mesopotamia represents the world; its prince represents the prince of this world. Egypt, Assyria, and Mesopotamia are all used in the Bible to represent the world in its entrenched enmity against God. Egypt is the world and its *culture*—a seemingly brilliant place filled with wisdom and learning and skill. Assyria is the world and its *cruelty*—a place where the most vicious atrocities are committed as part of a planned policy. Mesopotamia is the world and its *creeds*—a place where idolatry and religious error reign supreme.

If Israel must worship idols, then Israel must be brought into servitude to the prince of this world. Thus for eight years they served Cushan-rishathaim, king of Mesopotamia. In New Testament language, they were handed over to the prince of this world, to Satan himself, for chastening.

Deliverance was wrought by Othniel, the experienced man. He was nephew and son-in-law of Caleb, the conqueror, and had already won victories against Israel's foes. Now "the spirit of the Lord came upon him," and the Lord delivered Israel through his ministry (3:10). We have already met this man; his name means "the lion of God." He is the hero of a mighty conflict in the south country, at which time he took a city named Kirjath-Sepher, "The City of the Book." That is the way to victory over the world and its prince. There has to be found a man who knows the Book and who points toward the Lion of God—an experienced man who has already proven for himself the need of the Book and the Lion. Happy is the nation that has men like these in its midst.

The world today desperately needs Othniels, men living in personal victory and who are able to lead first the church and then the nation back to the Book and back to God's great Lion, back to Christ.

2. The Exasperated Man: Ehud

Israel's second bondage was to Eglon, the fat and repulsive king of Moab. The Moabites were blood relatives of Israel, and they represent those who profess connection with God's people but who have no contact with God Himself. Moab could say, "We are kinsmen; why should there be enmity between us?" Thus he could come in and gradually take possession.

Moab was ruled by Eglon, an enormous mountain of a man, bulging all over with great gobs of fat. He is the *very* embodiment of the flesh. He and the Moabites came over into the territory of God's people as far as Jericho. Jericho is another of those lesser biblical mirrors of the world. Called "the city of the palm trees," it stands for the world in its fragrance and attractiveness. It was the *very* first enemy God's people had to overthrow on their entrance into Canaan. Moreover, it was a city under the curse of God.

So here we have Moab, professing kinship with God's people, insinuating himself into the sphere that belongs to God's people—but making his headquarters in the world. And the Israelites go along with all that. They are now ruled by the flesh. It suggests to us what has happened in the church. It has been taken over by and large by those who profess Christianity but who have no relationship with Christ, and who are governed by a great deal of carnality.

This time God raised up an exasperated man—a man who had taken about all he could take of that kind of thing. Ehud was a Benjamite. The name Benjamin means "son of my right hand." The Lord Jesus, of course, is the Son of God's right hand. That is exactly where He sits right now. But Ehud, the Benjamite, significantly enough, was a left-handed man! In the Bible the right hand is the hand of power and the left hand is synonymous with weakness. So here is a Benjamite who is left-handed. What does it mean?

We have a perfect standing before God in Christ—the One who is at God's right hand, but our state is something else. We have no power of our own. Our own right hand is useless. We, in ourselves, are poor, powerless, left-handed men. That is exactly what God wants in us! God says, "My strength is made perfect in weakness" (2 Cor. 12:9). So Ehud, the left-handed man, speaks to us of our own utter inability to do anything about the flesh.

But he was exasperated, fed up with the rule of Eglon. So he took a dagger, or a sword with two edges. It was a cubit long—the measure from the elbow to the fingertip. He came up on Eglon when he was indulging himself in his summer pavilion, and said, "I have a message from God unto thee" (3:20). Then he took that sword and buried it up to the hilt in the flesh of that fat, repulsive king.

Translating the type, he took "the sword of the Spirit which is the Word of God," drove it into the flesh as far as it would go, and slew all that the flesh stood for. That is God's answer to the flesh. God's answer is not an ecstatic experience; it is the Word of God applied in convicting power to the very seat of carnal power in our lives. God's answer to the flesh is death—death made possible by the Bible, which is described as "quick [living], and powerful, and sharper than any twoedged sword" (Heb. 4:12).

3. The Exhorted Man: Barak

Some people need constant exhortation before they are willing to do anything for God. They belong to the Lord's people, they know their place, but they refuse to do anything. They need to be exhorted. Barak was such a man, and God used a godly woman to exhort him.

In Deborah we see a woman taking the lead in the things of God because there was no man willing to do so. God never leaves Himself without an instrument—if He cannot find a man, He will find a woman. We note, however, that Deborah did not overstep the bounds of propriety. She did not mobilize an army and lead it into battle, but she knew the way of victory and knew how to exhort a man who had leadership potential to take his rightful place.

This time the enemy was the Canaanite. The Canaanite, whom God had ordered to be completely destroyed, now rose up to be Israel's oppressor. The Devil well knows how to resurrect defeated foes. Perhaps there is an area in life where once we had complete victory. We thought the thing was over and done with forever, but it has reared its head again. That is what happened to Israel—it found itself dominated by a foe that once had been conquered. The Canaanites were led by Sisera who, with nine hundred chariots of iron, seemed invincible. Israel was paralyzed by those chariots of iron, so for twenty years Sisera "mightily oppressed the children of Israel" (4:3). How could they ever overcome so mighty a foe? Already they had forgotten their history, forgotten how God had dealt with Pharaoh and all his chariots—until Deborah and Barak came along. Deborah exhorted Barak to take his place of leadership. And so he did—in a half-hearted kind of way. He said, in effect, "I'll go if you come and hold my hand" (see v. 8).

God gave a mighty victory that day. He simply sent rain. "The clouds also dropped water," sang Deborah later (5:4). That was all! Rain! And Sisera's vaunted chariots were bogged up to the axles in mud, wholly immobilized, and their occupants an easy prey for Israel's archers and infantry. Satan may resurrect old foes, old heresies, old once-conquered habits, but it is an easy thing for God to overthrow them for us if we will listen to what He has to say.

4. The Exercised Man: Gideon

Now it was the turn of the Midianites to oppress Israel. Like the Moabites, the Midianites were blood-kin of the Israelites—the descendants of Abraham through Keturah, his second wife. Their penetration into Israel was deeper far than that of the Moabites. Moreover they were inveterate enemies of God's people. It was Midianites who carried Joseph down to slavery in Egypt. It was Midianites who joined with Balak to summon Balaam to curse Israel.

Pouring into the land, they swarmed everywhere, like locusts. Their chief object was to seize the food supply of the people of God and to keep it for their own ends. Thus the Midianites represent the world in another of its forms—the world as the destroyer of that which feeds God's people—the world coming into the church to cut off the people from the truth of God's Word. Any liberal theologian or cultic teacher is symbolized by Midian. They rob people of the truth of God's Word.

Gideon first appears on the scene when he was threshing wheat in a winepress—to hide it from the Midianites. He was determined to have at least some gleanings for himself. He was an exercised man, picturing those who glean something from the Word, determined that no enemy is going to deprive them of at least their share in the Word of God. That is the kind of man God can use—the man who at all costs sees to it that he feeds his own soul and those of his family on Christ in the Word. So the first time we meet Gideon, he is an exercised man.

Then he put things right at home by casting down the grove and the altar of Baal, which his father had set up in his own back yard. The word translated "grove" is the word *asherah*. It does not mean an enclosure of trees at all but refers to an image, a particularly vile and offensive image dedicated to the goddess of love. In short, it was a pornographic object. That Gideon's father should have erected one in his back yard shows how backslidden Israel had become. God said, "Cut it down" (see 6:25). One wonders what lewd and unclean things are allowed in some believers' homes. Nowadays many books—some being popular best-sellers—are unfit to read; many television programs are lewd and suggestive and even pornographic. Yet some professing Christians allow them a place in their homes. No wonder the Holy Spirit is grieved.

As soon as Gideon had his own family affairs in order, God could use him. He mobilized an army of thirty-two thousand men, but at once God told him he had too many. Too many? When the Midianites were as countless as locusts? A paltry thirty-two thousand men too many?

Too many! God will not share His victories with a host of carnal and cowardly Israelites.

First Gideon had to rid himself of those who *feared*—twenty-two thousand men resigned. That left Gideon with ten thousand men—still too many. Gideon next had to get rid of those who *faltered*, those who were not desperate enough for victory, those who would allow their own comforts to intrude. The army was taken to the brook to drink. Those who were so sold out to the idea of victory that they would stay only to snatch a handful of the precious water were kept. The rest were dismissed. The water represents the necessities of life, and God is looking for men who will be content with just what they need. Those who go in wholeheartedly for luxuries and adornments—who make them their absorbing occupation—will be left behind in the day of victory. Their affections are in the wrong place. Gideon's army was now reduced to a mere three hundred men, sometimes referred to as "God's Ironsides." With these three hundred men, the Lord led Israel to a stunning victory over the countless hosts of Midian. Gideon was the exercised man.

5. The Execrated Man: Abimelech

Gideon had many sons, and one of them had a craving to be king. He wanted to lord it over the people of God. His name was Abimelech, which means "the father of a king," suggesting perhaps how the idea of becoming king first found lodging in his mind. Abimelech was the fruit of polygamy. He should never have been born. As soon as his father was dead, he massacred sixty-nine of his father's other sons and would have slain the remaining one if he could have caught him.

Thus, callous of all but his ambitions, he imposed himself on Israel as a self-appointed king. His heart eaten up with pride and self-importance, he was no fit ruler for God's people. He came to a swift end, one that was an example of God's poetic justice. He died when he was hit on the head by a rock thrown at him by a woman! No more ignominious end could be imagined for a proud Israelite deluded by ideas of his own importance.

God has His own way. He knows how to abase those who would lord it over the people of God and who usurp a leadership to which they are not called and for which they are not qualified.

6. The Excommunicated Man: Jephthah

Jephthah was the man cast out by his brethren. They said to him, "You don't belong in the family and we want nothing to do with you. We are not going to have fellowship with you, out you go" (see 11:2). So they excommunicated him. They did it on what they considered were sufficient grounds, but their action was cruel and uncalled-for. Jephthah had done nothing to warrant excommunication. His brothers, however, considered there was something suspicious about his birth, and on those grounds refused to recognize him as a legitimate member of the family.

Jephthah was not discouraged, though he did not forget this cavalier treatment. Instead, he turned the period of his rejection to good account. He learned how to live victoriously in Canaan, despite the oppressions and the apostasies he saw on every hand. Moreover, he taught the secret of victory to others. He gathered about him a band of vagabonds—"vain men" they are called in the English of the King James Bible (11:3). The word means "broken" or "bankrupt men." Jephthah took these men and transformed them into a band of victorious believers. He did not sit and sulk or run all over the country castigating his brethren, or embitter his soul with angry murmurings! Instead, he learned to live victoriously. Thus he was ready in the hour of great need, which soon came upon Israel.

About this time Israel was sold into the hands of the Philistines and the Ammonites who "vexed and oppressed the children of Israel" for eighteen years (10:8). Once again Israel cried to the Lord, but this time the Lord allowed them to go on reaping the harvest of their folly for a little longer. Then He put His hand on Jephthah, and the Spirit of the Lord came upon him. The elders of Israel were forced to turn to the very man they had vilified and excommunicated! In humility, with many apologies for their treatment of him years ago, they came and asked the excommunicated man to come back into the fellowship—to come back, moreover, as their leader and their judge. And so he did—and once more God delivered His people.

7. The Exceptional Man: Samson

Everything about Samson was exceptional. He was exceptional in his birth, in his upbringing, in his unusual anointing of the Holy Spirit, in his strength, in his victories—even in his defeat and downfall—and in his final triumph.

There are times when God raises up exceptional men—men of exceptional grace like George Müller and men of exceptional gift like Charles Spurgeon. The history of the church is really the history of a succession of such exceptional men. Yet often, in their generation, few people recognize their true genius.

Samson's brethren did not recognize his. The elders of Judah wanted to bind this extraordinary man, pour him into their narrow mold, make him hew to their defeatist, pacifist line. The Philistines were the great enemy in those days, and Samson's exploits were rocking the boat. He was causing too much trouble, upsetting the status quo. Israel's weak-kneed elders, fearing reprisals from the foe, wanted Samson to keep the peace. But Samson, while allowing himself to be bound, was made of sterner stuff. Under a mighty infilling of the Holy Spirit, he broke *every* unscriptural and unsanctified limitation his brethren would impose upon him.

But alas for Samson! This man who no man could conquer was soon enslaved by his lusts and by his fondness for the opposite sex. His death was a gory sunset, full of splendor, indeed, and with the promise of a better tomorrow. Samson was, indeed, the exceptional man. Of the seven references in Judges to the Spirit of the Lord, no less than four occur in connection with Samson. Of the twenty-three references in the book to the angel of the Lord, no less than thirteen are found in chapter 13 in connection with the birth of Samson. Of all the judges, only Samson was a Nazarite. Yet this exceptional man wasted his great gifts and mighty fillings of the Spirit. He abused both the gifts of God and the grace of God and died in captivity. Yet, in his death, he wrought more than he ever accomplished in his life. He dealt the enemy of God's people a blow from which they scarcely recovered before Samuel was upon them and then David, who put an end to their pretensions forever.

III. Israel's Ways (chaps. 17–21)

The last five chapters of Judges and the little book of Ruth are an appendix to the main section of Judges. They show the moral and spiritual conditions that prevailed in Israel throughout the entire period covered by the book.

They tell the story of *religious perversion* (chaps. 17–18). It is the story of a man named Micah who deliberately set up an idol in his home in defiance of the second commandment. He should have known better, of course. His very name means "who is like Jehovah?" But that is what he did. Then he found a wandering Levite and consecrated him to be the priest of this new religion of his, putting the Levite on his payroll to ensure his loyalty. Soon after, the Levite defected to become the priest of the tribe of Dan, whose warriors stole Micah's solid silver idol and who offered the Levite a raise in pay. The Levite's name is given as Jonathan, the son of Gershom, the son of *Manasseh* (18:30). Scholars are agreed that this is a deliberate corruption of the text. It should read, "the son of Gershom, the son of *Moses.*"

That is how rapidly religious perversion took over in Israel. The very grandson of Moses became a committed idolater, prostituting his office as a Levite to promote a false religion just for the sake of a salary. The Jews, outraged at such a slur on the name of Moses, deliberately changed the name of his grandfather from "Moses" to "Manasseh."

The final chapters tell of *moral pollution* (chaps. 19–21). Idolatry having inserted a man-ordained priest of a corrupt, idolatrous faith between the soul and God, the next step is moral degradation. The whole story of these chapters is of the vilest corruption, centering in Gibea and resulting in the decimation of one of the tribes of Israel.

We see a man, one who is supposed to be consecrated to God, given over to carnal appetite, acting in stubborn self-will, participating in wild parties, being trapped by a pack of filthy Sodomites, and surrendering his concubine to their lusts. He then takes a savage and appalling way of making his grievances known to the other tribes. One would think the scene was set in Sodom rather than in Israel.

These were the spiritual and moral conditions that prevailed throughout the period of the Judges. It is no wonder God allowed their enemies to rule over them.

And what is the abiding lesson of this book? That when "lust hath conceived, it bringeth forth sin: and sin, when it is finished, bringeth forth death" (James 1:15). Yet God is ever gracious. He has a Great Deliverer waiting, mighty to save, if only we will forsake our sins and turn wholeheartedly to Him.

CHAPTER 9

RUTH

The Virtuous Woman

W ho can find a virtuous woman?" wrote King Lemuel, "for her price is far above rubies" (Prov. 31:10). "All the city of my people doth know that thou art a virtuous woman," said the noble Boaz to Ruth, the alien woman from the land of Moab (Ruth 3:11).

Never judge a book of the Bible by its bulk! Some of the most pungent books of the Bible are the shortest. Jude, for instance, has only one chapter, but where in all the world can we find such a devastating exposure of apostasy and the vile sins it makes possible in society?

Philemon has only one chapter—but this is the book that dealt the deathblow to slavery.

Or consider Ecclesiastes. This book is not very long, but nothing has ever been written to compare with its devastating exposure of worldliness.

Jonah has only four short chapters. But what a revelation of pride and prejudice, broken on God's anvil!

So, too, with the book of Ruth.

This book is really an appendix to the book of Judges. The book of Judges has three appendices—one dealing with the moral pollutions that existed in Israel during that period, one dealing with the religious apostasy that prevailed during the same period, and the third (the book of Ruth) dealing with the spiritual faithfulness of some, even in that dark period in Israel's history. The book shows that God never leaves Himself without a witness. The darker the times, the more definite the testimony.

The book of Ruth is one of the most beautiful stories ever told. The climax toward which the whole book moves is the birth of a babe in Bethlehem. It provides the vital link between the days of the Judges and the coming of David. The romance is woven around the story of a prodigal family and a kinsman-redeemer, around a Gentile woman and a high-born Hebrew of the princely line of Judah.

The book of Ruth is the story of redemption. It tells how one who was a stranger to the commonwealth and covenants of Israel, dwelling afar off in heathen darkness, was introduced to one who became her kinsman-redeemer and her lord.

The book divides into three parts:

I. The Backsliders (chap. 1)
   A. The Sudden Change (1:1–5)
      1. Moving to Moab (1:1–2)
      2. Marriage in Moab (1:3–4)
      3. Misery in Moab (1:5)
   B. The Second Chance (1:6–13)
   C. The Simple Choice (1:14–17)
II. The Believer (chaps. 2–3)
   A. Ruth in the Field of Boaz (chap. 2)
      1. The Greeting of Boaz (1:22–2:4)
      2. The Glance of Boaz (2:5–7)
      3. The Goodness of Boaz (2:8–9)
      4. The Grace of Boaz (2:10–14)
      5. The Gift of Boaz (2:15–23)
   B. Ruth at the Feet of Boaz (chap. 3)
      1. What She Decided (3:1–5)
      2. What She Desired (3:6–9)
      3. What She Demonstrated (3:10–11)
      4. What She Discovered (3:12–18)
III. The Bridegroom (chap. 4)
   A. The Property (4:1–4)
   B. The Person (4:5–12)
   C. The Posterity (4:13–22)

The typical significance of the book of Ruth has been recognized from earliest times. The meaning of the names, for instance, the presentation of Boaz as the kinsman-redeemer, and the role played by Ruth all suggest that beneath the surface of this historical incident lie deeper truths.

The book of Ruth is one of the *Megilloth*, or Festal Rolls, one of which was read at each Jewish festival. Ruth was read at the Feast of Pentecost.

I. THE BACKSLIDERS (CHAP. 1)

There were four of them. There was Elimelech, the head of the family, the man charged by God with the spiritual welfare of his wife and children. He paid the penalty of his backsliding by dying in Moab, far from the people of God. There was Naomi, his wife, who went along with the decision of her husband, and who paid the price by losing her joy in the Lord. There were the two boys, who fell in step with their father and who never were restored to the Lord. Such is the high cost of backsliding. Of the four involved, only one ever made it back into the fellowship of God's people. The others died in their sad condition.

A. The Sudden Change (1:1–5)

The story begins with the ominous words, "Now it came to pass in the days when the judges ruled, that there was a famine in the land." A famine in the Promised Land was always a mark of divine displeasure. The constant neglect of God by the people who professed His name called for punishment. God simply turned off the rain. The crops withered in the fields; the cattle died along the roads; people were reduced to starvation. Hunger, misery, and death went hand in hand.

At this point, we see Elimelech taking the first downward step.

1. Moving to Moab (1:1–2)

Turning his back upon Bethlehem, Elimelech "went to sojourn in the country of Moab" (v. 1). Probably he had no intention of staying there. Few backsliders ever intend to make permanent shipwreck. The difference between a backslider and an apostate comes into focus right here: a backslider *rationalizes* what he is doing, trying to justify it and square it with his conscience. An apostate *repudiates*, root and branch, the truth of God, which once cast light upon his soul. Elimelech was not an apostate; he was a backslider. We see him moving to Moab. Thus, his circumstances, instead of being the spur to drive him closer to God, became the spur that drove him away from God.

Moving to Moab is bad. The next step was worse.

2. Marriage in Moab (1:3–4)

The two sons married pagan women—women who had no knowledge at all of the true and living God, no knowledge of the Bible, no grasp of spiritual things, no concern about the mind and heart and will of God, no knowledge of His salvation, no concern about His people. Such a marriage God could not bless.

Throughout the Bible, God warns against the marriage of a believer with an unbeliever. Occasionally, in His grace, He does overrule such a marriage. Usually it remains singularly unblessed. In the case of these two boys, the pair of them died before they could bring any sons into the world to cement them in their pagan way of life.

Next comes the result of moving to Moab and marriage in Moab.

3. Misery in Moab (1:5)

The Lord loves us too much to allow us to become really happy in a backslidden condition. We read of Naomi that "the woman was left of her two sons and her husband" (v. 5). She was now in Moab, out of touch with God's people, a lonely widow in a foreign land in a day and age when widows had no pension and no protectors, and were looked upon as unlucky and unwanted. So there was a sudden change—a change from the land of promise to the land of Moab, and from the place of blessing to a place under the specific curse of the Law.

B. The Second Chance (1:6–13)

Here is another difference between a backslider and an apostate. God leaves the apostate alone. He lets him go his own way. He abandons him to the consequences of his choice. But He pursues the backslider.

Naomi now was given a second chance to make good, to bring her life into line with God's will. She heard good news from home. Things were better among God's people, the famine was over, the Lord was blessing back there in Bethlehem. A great longing sprang up in her heart to get back into fellowship with God's people, to enjoy the good things that were happening there where God had put His name.

She broke the news to her daughters-in-law, Orpah and Ruth. She was going to leave Moab forever, and get back to the place of blessing. Her testimony was *very* sad. "I am a barren old woman," she said. "My life has been rendered fruitless by my years in Moab. I am not only a barren old woman, I am a bitter old woman. The hand of the Lord has gone out against me" (see vv. 12, 13). Indeed, later on she was still more specific. She changed her name from *Naomi*, which meant "pleasantness," to *Marah*, which meant "bitterness" (v. 20). Backsliding always robs a believer of the best of both worlds in the end. It leaves him ruined and wretched.

Naomi's depressing testimony had the effect of driving Orpah back into paganism. She and Ruth had evidently both shown signs of interest in spiritual things. Both had expressed a desire to join Naomi on her pilgrimage back to Bethlehem, both had manifested a desire to learn more about God and His people. Naomi discouraged them. She told them that if they came with her they could say "goodbye" to any chance of ever getting married again. No godly Hebrew would, after all, marry a Moabite woman. They would be condemning themselves to widowhood for the rest of their days.

What a depressing, carnal, and worldly attitude! Still, there it was—Naomi herself, out of touch with God, could be only a negative, depressing influence on those who were showing the initial signs of interest in the things of God. What a thing to have on her conscience to the end of her days—the bad testimony, the wrong impression she had given to Orpah and to Ruth.

Thus, in the story of the backslider, we have considered the sudden change and the second chance. Now we move to phase three.

C. The Simple Choice (1:14–17)

The two pagan Moabite women now stood at the greatest of all life's crossroads. They were face-to-face with the greatest single decision ever to confront a human being in this life—the decision of what they would do with Jehovah—what they would do with Jesus, as we would put it today.

Orpah made the *worldly choice*. She kissed Naomi good-bye and went back into paganism, back to the demon gods of her people, back into the dark, and her name is blotted out of God's book. Naomi's blighted testimony had been only too effective. The eternal damnation of Orpah stands written, at least in part, to Naomi's account.

But Ruth made the *wondrous choice*. "Entreat me not to leave thee," she said, "whither thou goest, I will go; . . . thy people shall be my people, and thy God my God" (v. 16). She decided for Christ—then and there. She had no idea where it all would end, but she made her wondrous decision, that the true and living God should henceforth fill her life. It was the parting of the ways.

II. THE BELIEVER (CHAPS. 2–3)

The focus of the story now moves on as we watch in these two chapters the growth of a soul in the knowledge of God. Ruth arrived at Bethlehem still largely untaught about the way of life of the people of God. She had made her decision, and it had changed the whole direction of her life. But there was much she had to learn.

She had to learn that, for her, the purposes of God all centered in the person of Boaz, the kinsman-redeemer. While she had already made the life-transforming decision for Christ, so to speak, she still knew nothing at all about the fullness of God's plan of salvation. Thus, these next two chapters tell us how she came to know Boaz and how she came to yield herself unreservedly to him. All that Boaz was to Ruth, that—on a more spiritual, higher, and loftier plane—the Lord Jesus is to us. In chapter 2 we see her in his field; in chapter 3 we see her at his feet. It is the growth of a soul in the knowledge of God.

A. Ruth in the Field of Boaz (chap. 2)

Boaz appears nine times in this chapter, for the life of the believer has a new center. Once everything centered around self, now it centers around the Redeemer.

1. The Greeting of Boaz (1:22–2:4)

In chapter 1 there is no mention of Boaz at all, Ruth had never even heard his name, had no idea that such a man existed. Her decision for God was a hazy, untaught, groping kind of thing at best. God, of course, credited her with all the blessings and benefits of the gospel—but she herself had so much to learn! She really knew nothing about the one who was to be her redeemer. But from now on, it is Boaz, Boaz, Boaz, all the time.

First, we have his greeting. Ruth did the right thing by coming to the place where God could bless and by seeking at once to be useful. She went out to glean. She knew little or nothing about the people of God, but she determined that she would get busy doing the kinds of things they were doing. She found her way to the harvest field and followed the reapers. She sought to govern her life by the principles of the Word of God as she knew it (Lev. 19:9–10; 23:22; Deut. 24:19) and as it related to her.

Then Boaz came, and for the first time Ruth's eyes fell upon the one who was to be her kinsman-redeemer. The very first words she heard him speak directed everyone's thoughts to the covenant God of Israel. "The LORD be with you," he said to his reapers. "The LORD bless thee," they said in response (v. 4).

2. The Glance of Boaz (2:5–7)

The keen eye of Boaz took in the whole harvest field. He spoke to the servant who was set over the reapers—to "the lord of the harvest"—indeed—"Whose damsel is this?" (v. 5). He had noticed Ruth and had singled her out from all the others working for him in the great harvest field. He noticed her, this poor, pagan woman from the cursed land of Moab, this woman who had made her great decision and was now gleaning, doing what little she could, in his field. How like our Redeemer! He notices us, takes in each and every one of us. He loves individual people, not just the masses; He loves us one by one, each one as a separate, needy human being. He seeks me out to love me just as if I were the only person in the universe.

3. The Goodness of Boaz (2:8–9)

Boaz came and talked to Ruth, and set before her four things he desired for her. How her heart must have thrilled—to think that he, a prince of the house of Judah, a mighty man of wealth, he who had all things, who had need of nothing, he who commanded whatever he wanted, who had the love and respect of thousands, that he should stoop down in the harvest field to talk to her, the pagan woman from Moab who had made her decision for the living God. He told her what he desired for her, and what he said revealed the goodness of the man.

"Go not to glean in another field." That was *separation*—she was not to wander away.

"Abide here fast by my maidens: Let thine eyes be on the field that they do reap." That was *sanctification*—she was to be set apart for him and his work.

"Have I not charged the young men that they shall not touch thee?" That was *security*—he threw his mantle of protection over her.

"When thou art athirst, go unto the vessels, and drink of that which the young men have drawn." That was *satisfaction*—all her needs would be cared for by him. Thus Boaz made every provision for her. He set her heart at rest, thrilled her soul with his goodness, set in motion all the dynamics of his influence and power to keep her in the ways of God.

4. The Grace of Boaz (2:10–14)

Overwhelmed that Boaz should show such an interest in her, despite her past, despite the fact that she was a Moabite and therefore under the curse of the Law, Ruth cried out, "Why have I found grace in thine eyes, that thou shouldest take knowledge of me, seeing I am a stranger?" (v. 10). To which Boaz simply replied that he knew all about her. He knew how she had come to put her trust beneath the wings of the God of Israel.

5. The Gift of Boaz (2:15–23)

She had come to glean in his field, to have a share in his work, to do what little she could in the harvest field. But nobody can ever do anything in the harvest field that the Lord does not acknowledge as having been done for Himself, and reward accordingly. Thus Boaz sent Ruth home that night laden down with good things, with all that she could carry away. We are told that Boaz instructed his servants to leave "handfuls of purpose" for Ruth (2:16), and that she gleaned "about an ephah of barley" (v. 17). When giving instructions to the Israelites as to how much manna each man should gather, God said, "an omer for every man" (Exod. 16:16). Later we are told "an omer is the tenth part of an ephah" (v. 36). Ruth came away with ten times what she needed! She came in empty and went away full. Nobody can ever out give God!

Thus we find Ruth, in chapter 2, in the *field* of Boaz.

B. Ruth at the Feet of Boaz (chap. 3)

Now we see Ruth—her heart warmed toward Boaz, that mighty man of wealth, that glorious, princely man—being brought into the closest possible relationship with him.

1. What She Decided (3:1–5)

When she arrived home that night, having gleaned to such purpose in the field of Boaz, she told Naomi all that had happened, how she had met this man, how kind he had been, how he had shown grace toward her. And Naomi immediately began to speak to her about Boaz. Up until now she had never mentioned him; now she tells Ruth more and more about this mighty man of wealth and what God's Word had to say about such a one as he. She taught Ruth to seek a closer relationship with Boaz, the kinsman-redeemer. It was well enough to be the recipient of his grace, to have received his gifts, but she must know him better than that. She must get to know him as a wife knows a husband—she must be willing to give herself to him, to be his and his alone. She must live for him and become his in the deepest, truest sense of the word.

It is with the utmost deliberateness that the Holy Spirit likens the relationship between Christ and His church to the marriage relationship. The one is a chosen type of the other. When we first come to Christ we might have a very hazy notion of what we are doing. We really want to be saved from our sin and from a lost eternity, to have the damning record of guilt and sin and shame expunged forever from the account and have a home in heaven and peace with God. But once we are saved, then we must give ourselves more fully, more completely, with a broader, deeper, more mature knowledge, to the Lord Jesus Christ.

Naomi urged this upon Ruth. Cleansed and clothed, she must go to Boaz and tell him all this. And Ruth said, "All that thou sayest unto me I will do" (v. 5). That was her decision. It is wonderful to make the initial decision for Christ; it is even more satisfying to make that deeper commitment that leads to fruitfulness and lasting joy.

2. What She Desired (3:6–9)

She came that night to Boaz and "did according to all that her mother-in-law bade her" (v. 6). She put herself at his feet. She asked him to take her and make her his very own before God and man. She wanted to belong to him and him alone. She wanted him to fulfill all the law's demands for her, and own her before the whole world. She desired to be his! She wanted her whole life, henceforth, to revolve around him. She wanted to serve him—not just in the harvest field, in a general kind of way as so many others did—but in that special, unique way that is reserved for those who love with all their heart and mind and soul and strength. This is what consecration is all about. It is giving ourselves to the Lord Jesus, body and soul, mind and heart, now and forever. As the little chorus puts it,

> Now I belong to Jesus
> Jesus belongs to me;
> Not for the years of time alone—
> But for eternity.
>
> —Norman J. Clayton

In the Old Testament story, that is what Ruth wanted in her relationship with Boaz. In the New Testament fulfillment, that is what we should want in our relationship with the Lord Jesus.

3. What She Demonstrated (3:10–11)

She demonstrated unimpeachable conduct and an unimpeachable character. Boaz gave her the highest compliment that could have been paid to a woman who had been reared a raw pagan. He said, "All the city of my people doth know that thou art a virtuous woman" (v. 11). Later on, the book of Proverbs would say, "Who can find a virtuous woman? for her price is far above rubies" (31:10). Ruth is, in fact, the only woman in the Bible who is actually called "a virtuous woman."

Her stay among the people of God had been brief. She had been in their midst for hardly more than a few days. Yet already her testimony was such that God's people had nothing but the highest praise for her. And Boaz himself (who stood to her in exactly the same relation that the Lord Jesus stands to us) bore witness to the impact her conduct and character had made on all who had come to know her.

What higher honor could a person have than that? To have the Redeemer Himself, and all the redeemed people, bear witness to the transparent purity of our testimony.

4. What She Discovered (3:12–18)

Ruth discovered her relationship both to law and to grace. She discovered, for one thing, that the law of God had its claims. Those claims were "holy, and just, and good" (Rom. 7:12) and they could not be set aside. Between her and Boaz stood the law. Much as she might long after this closer relationship with him, much as he himself might desire it, not even he, mighty man of wealth that he was, prince of the house of Judah that he was, not even he—especially he being who he was and what he was—could lay aside the claims and demands of the law. There the law stood, like a fearful barrier between them.

There was a nearer kinsman. The law had to be kept. If the outworking of that law kept them forever apart, then so be it! The claims of the law must be met if their relationship was to be honorable and possible at all. But with this dark prospect laying its shadow on Ruth's heart, there came a word of encouragement. Boaz would do what he could. He would take up the demands of the law himself; he would fulfill them in such a way that Ruth and he could be together, in the smile of God's love, forevermore. Which brings us to the closing chapter of this lovely story.

We have taken a look at the *backsliders*, and we have taken a look at the *believer*.

III. THE BRIDEGROOM (CHAP. 4)

Now the story closes with a long look at the *bridegroom*. The last chapter tells us how Boaz met the demands of the law, which stood between him and the one upon whom he had set his heart. It has three movements:

A. The Property (4:1–4)

First thing the next morning, Boaz hailed the nearer kinsman. We do not know who he was or why he had a prior claim in the matter of Ruth. He represents the claims of the law upon our lives—the law that stands between us and Christ, the demands of which must be met. But who was he, this nearer kinsman? He was a brother of Boaz, probably an older brother, son of the same father, but having a different mother. On the surface he had a purer pedigree than Boaz,[1] and a prior claim upon Ruth.

The first order of business was the property: "Naomi, that is come again out of the country of Moab, selleth a parcel of land, which was our brother Elimelech's" (v. 3). The land-laws of Israel demanded that property be kept in the family; it was not to be sold to an outsider. If offered for sale, the other members of the family, in order of priority, had the right to redeem it. The older brother had no compunction at all about acquiring more property. He at once agreed to take up his option.

Things were looking bad for Ruth. The law was already asserting itself, making its claims known, demanding its rights, requiring its pound of flesh. But Boaz knew what he was about. He was now going to take a step that would forever satisfy and silence the law's demands.

B. The Person (4:5–12)

The focus shifts from the property, although it was not some inconsequential parcel of land that belonged to Elimelech. It was that parcel of land that belonged specifically to Mahlon and Chilion, the two sons of Elimelech who had inherited the property upon the death of their father. So far as the property of Chilion was concerned, there was no problem, it was unencumbered. But Mahlon's property was different. He had left a widow (a *Moabite* widow!) who was a rightful claimant to the property. The only way that property could be acquired was by marrying the widow of Mahlon, and this, too, the law required.

Instantly the older brother backed off. Marry a Moabite? Impossible! Never! The curse of God rested on the Moabites. He would mar his inheritance; he would defile his pedigree. It simply could not be done—at least by him. And in this he showed the basic weakness of the law. The law applied to good people; it could not redeem a people it had cursed. The refusal of that other brother to redeem Ruth exposed the law's jugular vein.

Boaz instantly took advantage of it. He himself would redeem both the person and the property. He would bring in a higher principle than law. He would introduce the principle of love, and love would win through. Love would fulfill all the demands of the law. He himself, Boaz, the mighty man of wealth, would meet all its demands and pay the price of Ruth's redemption. He would take care of it all, no matter at what cost to himself. Thus,

> Love found a way to redeem my soul,
> Love found a way that could make me whole;
> Love led my Lord to the cross of shame,
> Love found a way! Oh, bless His holy name!
>   —Avis N. Christiansen and Harry D. Loes

There, on the cross of Calvary, the Lord Jesus paid the price of our redemption, and paid it in full. There He met the very last demand of the law. There He took the "handwriting of ordinances that was against us, which was contrary to us" (Col. 2:14), and took it out of the way, nailing it to His cross. He paid the price, paid it in full, paid it in blood. Never again can the law's demands be raised against us. He has satisfied its very last claim and has taken away all that stood between Him and making us His own.

But let us remember this: the kinsman-redeemer in the book of Ruth, in fulfilling the law's demands, redeemed both the *person* and the *property*. This is exactly what the Lord Jesus has done. On the cross of Calvary, He purchased our redemption, bought our persons, we are eternally saved the moment we put our faith and trust in Him. That alone would be wonderful. But there is more! He has also redeemed our property—this poor old world in which we live, this world that sprang so fair from the Creator's hands, stamped as it was with God's approval. "It was very good," is the way the Bible puts it (Gen. 1:31).

When Adam sold himself into sin, he pawned his vast estates as well. So the whole world, as Paul puts it, "groans and travails" (see Rom. 8:22). The world itself is under the curse. There is waste, wilderness, and war everywhere we look. There are howling deserts, savage beasts, poisonous snakes, natural disasters, blight and decay, pestilence and death. But it is all going to be changed. Jesus is coming again. He is going to set up a millennial kingdom—it is part of redemption. The lion will lie down with the lamb; the desert will blossom as the rose; swords will be beaten into plowshares. The redemption of our *property* is as much a part of Calvary as the redemption of our *persons*.

So Boaz redeemed both. The one was inseparable from the other under the law. Finally, the focus turns to the future.

C. The Posterity (4:13–22)
The family tree is given, reaching back to Pharez, the son of Judah, bringing

in Boaz, embracing the son that was born to Boaz and Ruth, and continuing on in anticipation of David. Matthew picks up the line and carries it on to Jesus. From Boaz and Ruth was a posterity, a living link with Christ. Little did Ruth realize, when she made her great decision down there in Moab, that it would lead her directly to Christ Himself, that she would have such a living, wondrous, glorious link with Him!

CHAPTER 10

1 SAMUEL

Israel Comes of Age

From judges to priests

Like the book of Acts in the New Testament, the first book of Samuel is a book of transition, a book of change. The long period of the judges, lasting some four hundred years, with its unsettled government, religious apostasy, and social problems, was about to end. For the most part, the judges were soldiers, "strong men," as we would call them today. They had their day, and their sun set with Samson. Now a new kind of judge was to take their place, a sacerdotal judge, a priest. Forty years sufficed to show the failure of that kind of rule as, under Eli, the corruption of the priesthood rose to appalling heights.

Then Samuel came. He was not a political judge, nor yet, strictly speaking, a priestly judge; he was a prophet judge. But with Samuel the days of the judges were over. The theocracy was replaced by the monarchy, Eli and Samuel replaced by Saul and David. So 1 Samuel is a book of transition. It was always God's intention to give Israel a king. As far back as Genesis 49, Jacob had prophesied, "The scepter shall not depart from Judah, nor a lawgiver from between his feet, until Shiloh come; and unto him shall the gathering of the people be" (v. 10). In the Mosaic Law instructions were given as to who could or could not be a king, and restrictions were placed upon such a king. The great sin of Israel in 1 Samuel was anticipating the purpose of God and insisting on the king of their choice instead of waiting for the king of God's choice.

In the books of Samuel the long period of national disorder came to an end. Samuel crowned two of Israel's kings—Saul, the people's choice, and David, God's choice.

First Samuel is the story of four men: Eli, Samuel, Saul, and David. Their stories are interwoven so that the story of Eli overlaps that of Samuel, the story of Samuel overlaps that of Saul, and the story of Saul overlaps that of David. A note of failure runs through the book, as the office of the priests sank to an all-time low during the days of Eli and his evil sons. Saul, Israel's first king, failed dismally. Samuel was a prophet and, as such, stood apart from both kings and priests and exercised authority over both—the appearance of a prophet in Bible times always signified failure. But Samuel, great as he was, failed too, for his sons did not walk in his ways, giving rise as much as anything to the popular demand for a king. The failures of these men make all the brighter the luster of the Lord Jesus, who, as Prophet, Priest, and King, alone brought perfection to each of the offices.

The book can be divided into two parts. In the first part we witness *the dying theocracy*. A theocracy is that kind of government where people are ruled directly by God. The nation of Israel is the only nation that has ever had a true theocratic form of government. Its failure is a sad commentary on the sinful nature of man. The dying theocracy is brought into focus around the stories of Eli, an established priest, and Samuel, an energized prophet.

The second part sees *the dawning monarchy*. The people's clamor for a king was blunt. They wanted to be "like all the nations" (8:5). The surrounding nations were governed by kings; they had no king. Politicians, priests, and prophets were all very well but the disorders and failures were deplorable and intolerable. What was needed, they thought, was a strong central government, an establishment where power was passed on generation after generation in an orderly fashion and, above all, a visible throne around which the tribes could rally.

They wanted a king. They wanted to be like the other nations. They had been chosen to be *unlike* the other nations, to be a people governed directly by God, but they wanted to be like everyone else. The mere existence of a monarchy did not, however, guarantee good, strong, capable, or fair government. A study of neighboring monarchies would have proved that. No matter! A king they wanted and a king they would have. So a king they *would* have. Their demand for a king was a rejection of God. Not a dethronement of God; God can be rejected but He cannot be dethroned.

God gave them their king. He gave them two kings, Saul and David. Saul was given to underline *their mistake* in this matter, and David was given to underline *God's mind*. Thus, as we study the stories of these two men, we must mark well the tragedy of Saul and the training of David. Saul turned out to be Israel's scourge; David turned out to be Israel's savior.

God's ideal form of government is not a democracy nor a republic. It is not government of the people, by the people, and for the people. That is man's ideal form of government, the best that man can produce. God likens it to a vain mixture of iron and clay.

God's ideal form of government, the kind of government yet to be imposed on this planet during the millennium, remains a theocratic monarchy—government of people by God through His Son. God's ideal form of government is an absolute dictatorship with all power vested in the person of the Lord Jesus Christ. The Old Testament prophets surpass themselves in describing the world as it will be like when that form of government is imposed in a day soon to dawn.

    I. The Dying Theocracy (chaps. 1–7)
       A. Eli: The Established Priest
         1. His Failure as a Priest (1:9, 13; 2:27–36)
           a. No Spiritual Vitality
           b. No Spiritual Vision
           c. No Spiritual Values
         2. His Failure as a Parent (2:12–17, 22–25)
           His sons were:
           a. Unregenerate
           b. Unrestrained
           c. Unrepentant
       B. Samuel: The Enlightened Prophet
         1. His Mother
         2. His Ministry
           Samuel was there:
           a. When the Wars of God Were to Be Fought
           b. When the Word of God Was to Be Taught
           c. When the Will of God Was to Be Sought
   II. The Dawning Monarchy (chaps. 8–31)
       A. The Tragedy of Saul (chaps. 8–15)
         1. He Was an Impressive Man
         2. He Was an Impatient Man
         3. He Was an Impenitent Man
       B. The Training of David (chaps. 16–31)
         1. In the Country
         2. In the Camp
         3. At the Court
         4. In the Cave

So, then, 1 Samuel is a book that marks the transition from the theocracy to the monarchy.

I. THE DYING THEOCRACY (CHAPS. 1–7)

It was God's intention that the nation of Israel be a visible testimony of Him to other nations. This testimony was to be most evident in Israel's form of government—a government of the people by God Himself. The theocracy failed, not because God failed, but because Israel failed. Nowhere does Israel's failure come into sharper focus than in Judges and in the first book of Samuel.

A. Eli: The Established Priest

The book opens with a man named Eli in charge of national affairs. Somehow or other, Eli occupied the office of the high priest of Israel, the highest and most sacred office in the land. We do not know how Eli came to be Israel's functioning high priest. He was not in the direct line of high-priestly succession. His occupancy of the office is yet another indication of the disorder of the times. The book sets before us Eli's conspicuous failure along two lines—as a priest and as a parent. No doubt the traits that made him a failure in the one area made him a failure in the other.

1. His Failure as a Priest (1:9, 13; 2:27–36)

His failure in this area is underlined in three characteristics he lacked.

a. No Spiritual Vitality

We read, "Now Eli the priest sat upon a seat by a post of the temple of the LORD" (1:9). That is, he was marked by a complete lack of exercise in spiritual affairs. While the nation was going to wrack and ruin about him, he was content to take his ease.

We meet Eli three times. Once we see him propped up against one of the pillars of the tabernacle, once he is in bed, and once he is sitting on a seat by the wayside—he fell off that seat and broke his neck. He is the only priest in the Old Testament we see sitting down. Old Testament priests were to stand and to minister actively and energetically. Theirs was an unfinished work. In Eli's day there was urgent need for a dynamic, virile high priest. Eli, however, was content to take his ease. He was soon to be rudely shaken out of his lethargy and complacency.

b. No Spiritual Vision

Eli was taking things easy one day when he saw a woman in the courtyard of the tabernacle. Her shoulders were shaking and her mouth was moving, but no sound was coming. He concluded she was drunk, and sharply rebuked her. This broken-hearted woman was not drunk; she was pouring out her soul in prayer. Yet Eli said she was drunk. He had no spiritual vision. It was typical of the man.

The Holy Spirit comments on the basic spiritual problem of that day: "The word of the LORD was precious in those days," He says, "there was no open vision" (3:1). People were ignorant of the Bible. In an added comment, the Holy Spirit says of Eli that "his eyes began to wax dim, that he could not see" (3:2). His physical blindness matched his spiritual blindness. He was supposed to be the spiritual leader of Israel but he had no vision of spiritual things himself.

c. No Spiritual Values

"[Thou] honourest thy sons above me," said God (2:29). Eventually, stirred on to do so by pressure from God, Eli did remonstrate with his sons for their vile behavior. But his rebuke was mild and meek and it in no way matched the outrageous nature of their crimes. They deserved to be put to death. Someone has well said,

> When barren Hannah, prostrate on the floor
> In heat of zeal and passion did implore
> Redress from heaven—critic Eli thought
> She had been drunk, and checked her for her fault.
> Rough was his censure, and his word austere—
> Where mildness should be used, we're oft severe.
>
> But when his lustful sons, that could abuse
> The house of God, and ill God's offerings use—
> Appeared before him, his indulgent tongue
> Compounded rather than rebuked the wrong.
> He dared not shoot for fear he wound his child!
> Where we should be severe, we're oft too mild.
>
> —Francis Quarles

Eli's sense of values was all mixed up. "[Thou] honourest thy sons above Me." God will not have that.

2. His Failure as a Parent (2:12–17, 22–25)

The Holy Spirit underlines three things about Eli's sons, three things they were but should not have been.

a. Unregenerate

They are described as "sons of Belial," and it is said of them that they "knew not the LORD" (2:12). They wore the garb of priests and occupied the position of priests, but they were actually children of the Devil. God says so.

It is not always a man's fault if his children are unregenerate. Dr. Culbertson, when he was president of Moody Bible Institute, once said, "God has no grandchildren." There is many a godly parent who has an ungodly child. Being born into the family of God is not a matter of descent but of decision.

It is not always a man's fault that he has unsaved children. I knew a man years ago who did pioneer missionary work in the Yukon Territory. He left behind him many converts and a trail of blessing. He was one of the godliest men I ever knew. He was staying in our home one day on his way back to the north when he said, "Let's take a walk." We walked together along the banks of the Frazer River that flowed not far from our home. He linked his arm in mine.

"John," he said, "I have an unsaved son. He is a good son, has an excellent job, is dutiful, and polite, and kind. But he is unsaved. I have asked God many times to save him. He has used me to lead others to Christ, but I cannot reach my son. What do you think of that?"

I looked into the noble face of this godly man, so many years my senior. "What do you think of it?" I countered.

"Well," he replied with a smile, "I have no doubt that God will one day save my son. In fact, He has assured me He will. One day when I was praying about this, God said to me, 'Charles, I will have your son. But in the meantime I *want* you to have an unsaved son. It will keep your heart tender toward others who have unsaved sons.' That," he concluded, "is why I have an unsaved son."

But in Eli's case the fact that his children were unregenerate is noted along with his other faults. They were "sons of Belial," they "knew not the Lord," yet they were functioning as priests.

b. Unrestrained

They were well known for their lustful appetites and vile passions. They used their priestly occupation to cloak their vile behavior and to minister to their evil desires. Eli had never restrained them when they were young. Now, he who would not restrain them could not restrain them—not even though God sent a prophet to him demanding that he put his house in order.

Some time ago, a columnist in one of Chicago's daily newspapers received a letter from a distraught mother. She said, "My son is seventeen years of age. He will not listen to a thing I say. He's in with the wrong crowd; he's in trouble with the police. What can I do?" The columnist's answer was brutally frank—"Shrink him down to seventeen months and start all over again." How many wish they could.

But even in this, we "sorrow not, even as others which have no hope" (1 Thess. 4:13). The columnist's advice was cold comfort for that mother. How can anyone shrink a boy back down to seventeen months? The gospel assures us that God can! In fact, it demands, as the very starting place for the Christian experience, not a reduction in age but a new birth altogether! We need to besiege the throne of grace for those wayward children, that God will perform a spiritual miracle in their hearts and lives.

Eli's children were not only unregenerate, they were unrestrained. Even when they were grown men, responsible for their own behavior, Eli made excuses for them and sought to protect and shield them from the consequences of their wickedness. That is a great mistake, one of the traps into which parents fall. They try to shield their grown children from the natural penalties of their wicked behavior; they bail them out again and again, give them money, subsidize their godless lifestyles. Thus their wayward, even wicked children do not feel the brunt of the consequences of their godless ways. Shielding them is a mistake. Eli made that mistake.

c. Unrepentant

Finally they were confronted with the hard evidence of their shocking behavior. They were told as from God Himself that they must repent. They were by now so hardened in their godless lifestyle that the Holy Spirit records, "Notwithstanding they hearkened not" (2:25). This is what brings down upon people the judgment of God. It is not that they are sinners; that is born and bred into the very warp and woof of our being. It is that we will not repent when confronted with the hard, cold evidence of our sin.

Thus we have set before us the established priest, Eli, and his dismal failure both as priest and as parent. From now on in Israel, God will rarely use the office of the priest to speak to the people. The priesthood had failed and, since Eli would not set his house in order, God did it for him in sweeping judgment. He said, "There shall not be an old man in thine house. And thou shalt see an enemy in my habitation. . . . All the increase of thine house shall die in the flower of their age. . . . Thy two sons, Hophni and Phinehas; in one day they shall die, both of them" (2:30–34). And it happened just as God had warned.

The story turns next to Samuel.

B. Samuel: The Enlightened Prophet

He bridged the gap between the priests and the kings, and founded the prophetic order in Israel. He was the last of the judges and the first of the prophets. It was Samuel who founded the famous "school of the prophets" in Israel—a kind of theological seminary where young men could be trained in the Scriptures even though many of them could never minister as priests.

God spoke to Israel at various times through prophets, priests, and kings. The prophetic order was higher and holier than that of the king, and took precedence over that of the priest. Thus we find prophets countermanding edicts of kings and offering sacrifices as though they were priests even though they might not have belonged to the priestly family of Aaron or the royal family of David. Prophets ranked above all others.

Samuel was Israel's king-maker—first finding Saul and anointing him, then finding David and anointing him. Henceforth, whenever a message needed to be delivered to Israel, God found a prophet to deliver it.

Samuel ranks in Scripture as one of God's giants. His influence lay not in his military exploits, not in his diplomatic skill, and not in his political acumen, but in his unswerving integrity and loyalty to God. He ranks with Abraham and Moses as men raised up by God to provide leadership for Israel.

1. His Mother

The Holy Spirit tells us his mother was a godly woman, Hannah by name. Driven to desperation because she was unfruitful, she besieged the throne of God, promising that if God would give her a son she would give him right back to God.

And so she did. When her little boy was born, she called him Samuel, "asked of God"—as though to constantly remind herself of her pledge, lest she should fall into the sin of Eli and put her son before God. We can marvel at the magnificent faith of Hannah. She took her little boy to Eli, of all people, to the man who had accused her of being drunk, to the man whose own sons were a public scandal in Israel. She said, "Here is my little boy. I have given him to God. I don't know any other way to give him to God except to give him to you. You train him to be a man of God" (see 1:28).

She must have upheld that little boy in prayer night and day. As she had besieged the throne of God for the *gift* of that son, so now she besieged that throne even more vehemently for the *growth* of that son. Over her whole life can be written just that one sentence that she uttered to Eli when she brought the boy to him: "For this child I prayed" (1:27).

A most significant statement records the way she and her husband brought that little boy to Eli. We read that they "slew a bullock, and brought the child to Eli" (1:25). That is, in an Old Testament way, they claimed the sacrifice of Calvary and the sheltering power of the shed blood of Christ for that little boy now to be entrusted into such a home as that of Eli.

Those prayers and that sacrifice paid off, for "Samuel grew, and the Lord was with him, and did let none of his words fall to the ground. And all Israel from Dan to Beersheba knew that Samuel was established to be a prophet of the Lord" (3:19–20).

2. His Ministry

We always found Samuel there, when God needed a man in those dark and far-off days.

a. Samuel Was There When the Wars of God Were to Be Fought

Samuel was no Samson, but he knew how to lead the people of God to victory. Indeed, he was better than Samson. Samson was a loner but Samuel taught others how victory could be won in their lives. And his victories were more permanent and of a more spiritual nature than those of Samson. We read, "And the hand of the LORD was against the Philistines all the days of Samuel" (7:13). He was never found wanting when the wars of God were to be fought. We always find him standing for the truth—right in the forefront of the battle. That was his ministry!

b. Samuel Was There When the Word of God Was to Be Taught

We read, "And Samuel judged Israel all the days of his life. And he went from year to year in circuit to Bethel, and Gilgal, and Mizpeh, and judged Israel in all those places. And his return was to Ramah; for there was his house; and there he judged Israel; and there he built an altar unto the LORD" (7:15–17).

Samuel was not a priest. Strictly, only a priest could offer sacrifices and then only upon the altar in the court of the tabernacle. But Samuel was a prophet. The emergence of a prophet in Israel always signals a time of apostasy and backsliding. The priesthood had failed, so God raised up a prophet to preach the Word of God to the nation and apply it to the consciences of the people. Since teaching God's law to the people meant giving them considerable instruction about the sacrifices and offerings, and since the priests had lost the confidence of the people, and the sacrificial system had been abused and had fallen into disrepute, Samuel did not hesitate to offer sacrifices himself. The Word of God needed teaching. Samuel was there. It was his ministry.

c. Samuel Was There When the Will of God Was to Be Sought

It comes out again and again in his history. Samuel was a man addicted to prayer, ever seeking God's face in order to discern His will. Here are some examples: "And the children of Israel said to Samuel, Cease not to cry unto the LORD our God for us, that he will save us out of the hand of the Philistines" (7:8).

When Israel demanded a king, we read, "But the thing displeased Samuel. . . . And Samuel prayed unto the LORD" (8:6).

After Saul was chosen to be king, Samuel said to the people, "God forbid that I should sin against the LORD in ceasing to pray for you: but I will teach you the good and the right way" (12:23).

When the Lord told Samuel that Saul had been set aside, the Holy Spirit records, "And it grieved Samuel; and he cried unto the LORD all night" (15:11).

If King Saul had seen Samuel as we see him, a man of God, a spiritual giant, he would have been ruled by him and would never have lost his kingdom. When the will of God was to be sought—Samuel was there. It was his ministry!

II. THE DAWNING MONARCHY (CHAPS. 8–31)

Samuel formed the living link between the theocracy and monarchy. It had always been God's intention to eventually give Israel a king—in His own time and way. Israel's impatience forced the issue, so God gave them the kind of king they deserved—Saul. Afterward, in accordance with His own divine plan and purpose, He gave them the king He had intended to give them all along—David.

A. The Tragedy of Saul (chaps. 8–15)

It is difficult to sum up in a few words the many chapters that deal with Saul, especially since the story of Saul is so closely intertwined with the stories of Samuel and David.

1. He Was an Impressive Man

Saul was a giant, towering head and shoulders above all the people. He had the physical form of a leader of men, of a king. Samuel and all Israel were impressed by Saul's massive girth. It was too bad that he had such a small soul. It is no wonder that later on, when Samuel was similarly impressed by the physical appearance of Eliab, the son of Jesse, and David's older brother, that the Lord said, "Look not on his countenance, or on the height of his stature; because I have refused him: for the LORD seeth not as man seeth; for man looketh on the outward appearance, but the LORD looketh on the heart" (16:7).

Saul was an impressive man, not only in his great size but in his initial, seeming humility and in his God-given gifts of the Spirit. God is not small-minded and mean. He gave Saul every chance to succeed, even gave him the kind of heart he needed to rule. He gave Saul the heart of a king. He gave Saul, too, a taste of the prophetic gift. But there was nothing to the man; he was like a hollow tree, all outward show.

2. He Was an Impatient Man

Saul lost his kingdom for an act of impatience. When the Philistines were massing on his borders and his army was wasting away, Saul could not wait for God to act. Samuel had promised to come and bless him and intercede for him with God so that victory would be his, but Samuel was delayed and Saul could not wait. He took matters into his own hands and sacrificed an offering himself—and so lost his crown. He failed to see that Samuel's delay was a test, designed of God to see whether Saul had the stuff in him to wait upon God and not to rush in, in the energy of the flesh.

The president of a certain mission board employed this very method to test potential candidates for the mission field. The young person would be told to arrive at the president's home for an interview at a specific time. The candidate would come, would be shown into a small room by a receptionist, and would be left there for half a day. The test was to see if he had the patience necessary for the mission field—to see what his spirit was like under delay and neglect. This is what God did to Saul. Saul failed—he was an impatient man.

3. He Was an Impenitent Man

But he had a worse—far worse—characteristic. It came out first in his sin with Amalek. He had been told by God to deal judicially with this hereditary foe of Israel. He was to spare nothing. God gave Saul a great victory, but he disobeyed God and spared the Amalekite king and the best of the Amalekite cattle. For this he was set aside by God finally and forever. Samuel indignantly repudiated Saul's pretense that he had saved the cattle in order to sacrifice them to God. He called his sin "rebellion" and likened it to witchcraft—a significant thing in the light of Saul's final end. "To obey is better than sacrifice" (15:22) was Samuel's cutting word. Instead of repenting, Saul asked Samuel to help him keep up appearances.

But Saul's impenitence reached fearful heights when he was confronted with David. He hated David and was intensely jealous of him. He recognized that David would one day sit upon his throne, and he persecuted David from one end of the kingdom to the other, never ceasing in his long-range objective to get rid of David by fair means or by foul.

It is here that the basic difference between Saul and David surfaces. David sinned about as badly as Saul ever did, but whereas Saul remained impenitent, David threw himself prostrate on the floor before God, and with bitter tears implored for forgiveness.

Saul's impenitence climaxed just before his last battle. Samuel was dead, and God no longer spoke to Saul. Finding heaven's door barred to him, Saul went and knocked at the door of hell. He consulted a witch, dabbled in the occult, and received immediate sentence of death from beyond the grave. Impenitent to the last, he died by suicide the next day.

The dynasty that dawned and played out in the tragedy of Saul flickered out. But in the shadows, out there among the hills and the hedges, ever only a heartbeat away from the throne, was a man after God's own heart—David. In David it was ordained to raise up a throne, which will one day be occupied by David's Son and Lord—Jesus, the Son of God.

B. The Training of David (chaps. 16–31)

We trace the fortunes of David, the beginnings of which are woven throughout the second half of 1 Samuel. We see David in the *country*, in the *camp*, in the *court*, and finally in the *cave*.

David was God's ideal king. He was a shepherd, and God's purpose for kingship in Israel was the king preeminently as shepherd. All the kings of Judah are measured by David.

Saul was a herder of mules; David was a keeper of sheep. Saul was used to driving, David to leading. The first time we see Saul, he had just lost his father's mules and had not the slightest idea where to find them; the first time we see David, he was keeping his father's sheep and was willing to give his life for his flock.

1. In the Country

We first meet David living quietly in the will of God, doing his duty, minding his sheep, fighting off the wolves and the lions and the bears. He was happy in the Lord, spending his days beside still waters and green pastures, and his nights out on the hills, as "the door of the sheep." He kept his harp and his heart in tune. He had it in mind to praise the Lord come what may, and he had a heart to write half the book of Psalms.

2. In the Camp

The long-smoldering war between Israel and the neighboring Philistines broke out at last, but Israel was defeated before the battle even began. The Philistines had Goliath of Gath—a giant, standing ten feet tall. Israel had Saul—a giant, too, but no match for Goliath. But David came and slew the giant because he had something Saul did not have. Saul had the position, David had the power; Saul had girth, David had God. His spectacular victory over the Philistine giant secured for David a warm place in the affections of all the people, won him the firm friendship of Jonathan, Saul's son and heir, and earned him the growing suspicion and hatred of Saul.

3. At the Court

In time, David was summoned to court to play on his harp in the hope that the music might charm the king out of his demented moods. For Saul, having done despite unto the Spirit of grace, was now oppressed by evil spirits. His courtiers hoped that David's music might coax their king into a better frame of mind. But David's presence only infuriated the king, for he saw in him a rival for the throne. Saul tried many times to get David killed—in one way or another. Saul tried on no less than twenty-four different occasions to get rid of David. But David "behaved himself wisely." Again and again the record stands—"David behaved himself wisely in all his ways; and the LORD was with him" (18:14).

4. In the Cave

David became a fugitive from Saul, with Saul's bloodhounds ever on his trail. More than once David had Saul in his power, but he refused to retaliate against his enemy. After all, Saul was still "the Lord's anointed." God would deal with him in His own time and way. Though he was hunted like a partridge on the mountains,

David attended the school of God, and he learned his lessons—the chief of which was patience. Impatience had been Saul's downfall; it would never be David's.

In the country, God molded David's *character*; in the camp, God manifested David's *courage*; at the court, God marked David's *conduct*; in the cave, God matured David's *convictions*. Thus every circumstance of David's life was made to minister to him to prepare him for the day, in the will of God, when he would come at last to the throne.

Thus, woven into the tragedy of Saul is the training of David. And woven into the story of the training of David is the story of scores of others, men and women, whose lives are transformed because of their contact with him.

One could profitably study the stories of Jonathan, David's friend; of Joab, David's tough and unscrupulous general; of Abner, who spent his life fighting David but came over to him at last; of Barzillai, who took such a bold stand for David but backed out of following him all the way; of Shimai, the man who cursed David; of Ahithophel, David's Judas; of Abishai, David's priest; of Ittai, a Philistine from Gath who cast in his lot with David; of Absalom, David's prodigal son; of Michal, Saul's daughter, who married David but lived with somebody else; of Abigail, who enthroned in her heart David as lord; of Bathsheba, who sinned with David; of Uriah, who read David a lesson in loyalty; of Nathan, David's fearless prophet; of Zadok in whom David restored the high priesthood to its rightful heirs.

Preeminently, David is a type of Christ. To David came the outcasts and the outlaws, those in debt and in distress. He received them, changed them, associated them with himself, made them the backbone of his kingdom. What David did for them, great David's greater Son will do for us if we will come to Him.

CHAPTER 11

2 Samuel

King David

The two books of Samuel are one book in the Hebrew Bible. The Hebrew scholars who, centuries before the birth of Christ, translated the old Hebrew Bible into Greek decided to divide Samuel into two books. That translation thereafter became what is known as the Septuagint version of the Bible. It wasn't such a bad idea, for in that way we have a book devoted entirely to David.

David was, after all, Israel's greatest king. More is written about David and by David in the Bible than any other person except Jesus. He appears constantly in the historical books; he wrote half the book of Psalms; he is mentioned by name in both the first and last chapters of the New Testament. It is somehow fitting that we should have a whole book devoted to him.

Second Samuel begins with a poem and ends with a plague; it begins with deception and ends with devotion; it begins with war and ends with worship. It begins with a lamentation by David over his lifelong enemy, King Saul, and over his lifelong friend, Jonathan the son of Saul. This ancient song was written three thousand years ago by a young man just turned thirty years of age. It shows us just what kind of man David really was—a man who did not forget his friends and who could gloriously forgive his foes.

David came to a kingdom rent by civil war and with its affairs in total confusion, both at home and abroad. Israel's ancient enemies triumphed all along the frontiers while tribal jealousies kept the Hebrews at loggerheads among themselves. David subdued the foreign foes of Israel, united the tribes, cleared Jerusalem of the last lingering remnants of the Jebusites, and made it Israel's capital. He planned for the temple, led a great revival in religious affairs, pioneered a renaissance of Jewish culture, put the nation's records in order, and founded a deathless dynasty. No wonder there is so much about him in the Bible. No wonder those seventy long-bearded Alexandrian sages decided, when they came to the book of Samuel, to give David a book to himself!

    I. The Patient Years (chaps. 1–4)
       A. The Downfall of the House of Saul (chap. 1)
       B. The Defiance of the House of Saul (chaps. 2–4)
   II. The Prosperous Years (chaps. 5–12)
       A. David's Coronation (chap. 5)
       B. David's Convictions (chap. 6)
       C. David's Covenant (chap. 7)
       D. David's Conquests (chap. 8)
       E. David's Compassion (chap. 9)
       F. David's Critics (chap. 10)
       G. David's Crime (chaps. 11–12)
  III. The Perilous Years (chaps. 13–24)
       A. The Trouble with His Kinsmen (chaps. 13–19)
         1. The Lust of Amnon
         2. The Lawlessness of Absalom
       B. Trouble with His Kingdom (chaps. 20–24)

I. THE PATIENT YEARS (CHAPS. 1–4)

It was over seven years before the whole house of Israel crowned David king over all the tribes. These were the patient years. His old enemy, Saul, was dead, having committed suicide on the field of battle. The tribe of Judah had proclaimed David king at once, but the other tribes were not so sure. Who was this fellow David, anyway? Was he not a fugitive from justice? Was he not just a successful brigand? Why should David be king? David might well have taken on the quarrelsome tribes in battle and forced himself upon them, but that was not David's way because that was not God's way. David preferred to wait, and the record of his period of waiting takes up the first four chapters.

A. The Downfall of the House of Saul (chap. 1)

The house of Saul was centered in that self-willed, weak-kneed giant, Saul himself. When Saul fell, his house fell. And, by all natural codes of conduct, David should have flung his hat in the air, out there on the Judean hills. But he didn't. He idealized King Saul and eulogized him. He said, "Saul and Jonathan were lovely and pleasant in their lives. . . . Ye daughters of Israel, weep over Saul." (1:23–24).

What a thing for David to say about a man who had for years used half his army to hunt David down in order to hang him up to some tree—and all without cause! What a thing to say about a friend who professed to love him once but who refused to give up any of his comforts in order to help him in his need! "Saul and Jonathan were lovely and pleasant in their lives . . . they were swifter than eagles, they were stronger than lions" (1:23). This is the love that covers a multitude of sins, the love that suffers long and is kind, the love that many waters cannot quench. This is the love of God shed abroad in a human heart.

Chapter 1 tells of the downfall of Saul's house. It also records that interesting story of the way in which David dealt with a man who tried to profit from Saul's death.

B. The Defiance of the House of Saul (chaps. 2–4)

"Now there was long war between the house of Saul and the house of David: but David waxed stronger and stronger, and the house of Saul waxed weaker and weaker" (3:1).

Saul had a general named Abner. He knew a good thing when he saw it. As soon as Saul was dead, Abner decided to run the kingdom himself but he needed a front man, so that everything would look legal. Saul's rightful heir was Jonathan, but Jonathan had died in that fateful battle on Mount Gilboa. The right of succession should have gone to Jonathan's son, Mephibosheth, but Mephibosheth was lame in both his feet. Abner knew that Israel would not fight long for a king like that—not against such a notable warrior as David. So Abner ignored Mephibosheth and settled on one of Saul's other sons—Ishbosheth. Abner made Ishbosheth a puppet king and rallied the tribes around him.

Still David waited, but while he had refused to take up arms against Saul, upstarts like Abner and Ishbosheth were a different matter. So there was a long, desultory crisis in the land that lasted over seven years. The powerful tribes of Judah owned David as king; the other tribes owned Ishbosheth. From time to time, tempers flared and a skirmish took place, but David, who could out-general Abner any time, made no attempt to seize the kingdom from Ishbosheth by force. David waited for the situation to resolve itself, knowing that neither Abner nor Ishbosheth had the force of character to last, and that God had, long since, given the throne to him. So David waited, and finally, after seven and one-half years, the two conspirators squabbled between themselves, and Abner came over to make his peace with David. The patient years were over.

David was about sixteen when he was first anointed in secret by Samuel; he was now thirty years old. All in all, he had waited fourteen years for God to give him the throne, and not once had he taken matters into his own hands or tried to seize it for himself.

II. The Prosperous Years (chaps. 5–12)

Each of the events in this section is chronicled in a single chapter, except David's crime; two chapters are assigned to that.

A. David's Coronation (chap. 5)

David was anointed king three times altogether—first secretly by Samuel when he was a teenage lad, then by the tribe of Judah upon the death of Saul, now by all the tribes.

In this, as in so many other ways, the story of David is intended to teach us lessons regarding our relationship to the Lord Jesus. God has already secretly anointed Him. Up there in the glory land He has crowned Him King of Kings and Lord of Lords—a family affair, a secret crowning, witnessed only by those who were present when our Lord came back home from the field of this world. News of that coronation, however, has leaked out. It is recorded in Hebrews 1. Satan, though, has a vested interest in running the kingdom for himself. As King Saul dedicated all his talents, influence, and resources to keep David off the throne and to persecute those who acknowledged David's claims, so the Evil One has wrought mightily this past two thousand years to usurp the throne-rights of God's rightful King and keep this world in rebellion against its Lord.

As David was ultimately acknowledged by the whole house of Israel and openly, joyfully crowned, so one of these days the Lord will return and reign. The nation of Israel, which for so long has opposed Him and rejected Him, will at last see that He is indeed the Lord's anointed and their rightful and legitimate King. That day has not yet come.

It was a turning point for Israel when they finally crowned David. Instantly, new life was infused into the nation. Jerusalem was captured and made the true center of the kingdom. Hiram, king of Tyre, the most powerful mercantile kingdom on earth, hastened to submit to David. The Philistines, who for years had trampled Israel under foot, massed against David and were overthrown.

It will be a turning point for Israel, too, when that nation at last acknowledges Jesus as Lord. No longer will Jerusalem be trodden down of the Gentiles. The nation will take on new life, all its foes will be overthrown, and Jerusalem will become the capital of the whole world.

But there was another anointing of David. There was that anointing he received at the hands of his friends. While the rest of the nation refused for seven long years to own David as king and chose rather to have Abner and Ishbosheth—anybody except David—the house of Judah owned him. Judah crowned David king in the face of the opposition of all the world, and David never forgot it. During the time of his rejection, Judah accepted him and gave him his rightful place.

Thus it is with our Lord. He has been secretly crowned in heaven; he will one day be publicly crowned on earth but, in the meantime, we have a choice. We can side with those who reject Him or we can be like those valiant men of Judah. In the face of the opposition of the world, of family, perhaps, and friends, we can say, "King of my life, I crown Thee now; Thine shall the glory be."[1] If we take our stand with Him today and accept Him as Savior and Lord, we will never regret it. It might cost us something, for it is the unpopular choice; but we will think that cost but a pittance on that great coronation day soon to dawn. As the hymn writer puts it,

> Our Lord is now rejected,
> And by the world disowned,
> By the many still neglected,
> And by the few enthroned,
> But soon He'll come in glory,
> The hour is drawing nigh,
> For the crowning day that's coming by and by.
> —Daniel W. Whittle,
> "The Crowning Day"

B. David's Convictions (chap. 6)

The most sacred religious object in the nation was the ark of God. This was a wooden chest, overlaid with gold. It was covered by the golden mercy seat and the cherubim and it contained a pot of manna, Aaron's rod, and the unbroken table of the Law. For many years the ark had been neglected. It belonged in the Holy of Holies in the tabernacle where it served as God's throne, but it lay forgotten in Gibeah.

No sooner was David firmly in control of affairs than he decided to give the ark its rightful place. It must come up to Jerusalem. David realized that the true gathering center of Israel was not his throne but God's. David's goal of bringing the ark to Jerusalem was accomplished at length after a very bad start when he tried to do God's work in man's way—with disastrous results. But at length the ark arrived in Jerusalem amid great public rejoicing and to the strains of Psalm 24, Psalm 68, and Psalm 132. It was on this occasion that Michal betrayed her true nature.

Michal was Saul's daughter, David's wife. By nature, she was far more daughter of Saul than wife of David. She took great exception to David's enthusiasm and excitement over spiritual things. She saw David rejoicing with all his heart because God was being given His proper place, and she curled her lip in disdain. Then, when David came home from the service with his face radiant and his heart full, with a spring in his step and a song on his lips, she met him with biting words of criticism. It ruined their marriage. With her acid tongue she poured poison all over her husband's zeal for God, and from then on they were married only in name. For marriage must be of the spirit as well as of the flesh, and Michal's spirit was out of tune with David's.

C. David's Covenant (chap. 7)

We all appreciate it when somebody thinks of us and does something for us. And so does God. Now that David was king, he wished to do something for God, and he decided to build a house for Him in Jerusalem, a temple the like of which the world had never seen.

The Lord appreciated David's desire, but refused to allow David to do what was in his heart. David was a man of war; God's house must be built by a man of peace, so David's son Solomon should build that house. David could accumulate the materials for it, but his son should build it. Moreover, God would accept David's thought for the deed, and He would show David how much He appreciated it by building David a house instead. David should found a house, a dynasty, which would never pass away. The royal line of David would continue until it produced the Messiah—He who would be David's Son and David's Lord—at once both the Root and the Offspring of David. From David's royal line the Christ of God Himself would come, and in Him the throne of David would be established forever and ever.

David was overwhelmed! He had learned a great lesson—that it is impossible to outgive God. David's thought had been genuine and sincere, pure and unmixed. He had no thought of giving something to God so that God would be obliged to give something back to him—not like Jacob, who had made just such a deal with God—"You give me one hundred percent and I'll give you ten percent" (see Gen. 28:20–22). David had simply wanted to give to God a spontaneous expression of his genuine love for Him.

And God responded in a way that left David simply overwhelmed.

D. David's Conquests (chap. 8)

It was inevitable that David—who in those days was a man so much in touch with God—should be invincible. David's enemies soon realized that they were dealing with a man in touch with God. One by one, the Philistines, the Moabites, the Syrians, and other persistent enemies of Israel were conquered. David was all-victorious in those days.

E. David's Compassion (chap. 9)

His foes were all defeated. David had united the warring tribes; he had given his kingdom a capital city, which was practically invulnerable; he had rallied the nation to his standard; he had taught his people how to live victoriously—and now finally he was at peace. What could he do next?

He remembered Jonathan, the son of Saul. Saul had been his bitterest foe; Jonathan had been his very best friend. For Jonathan's sake, he would show kindness to someone of the house of Saul—not just human kindness, but what the Bible expressively calls "the kindness of God" (9:3). David wished to show the world for all time how God can forgive an enemy and bless beyond the bounds of measure.

He was reminded about Mephibosheth, the poor, fugitive son of Jonathan, lame in both his feet, and hiding in far-off Lodebar. He sent for him, extended his grace toward him, brought him to himself, exalted him, gave him vast estates, restored that which he took not away, sat him at his table, and adopted him into the family circle as one of the king's own sons. That was David's compassion.

The whole lovely story is a parable of the way the Lord deals with men. We thought ill of Him, harbored in our thoughts lies and slanders about Him. We were born in the ranks of those who persecuted Him to the very death. Now He is exalted on high and seated on His throne, and He reaches out His hand to us and sends His messengers after us. They find us in our exile, far from God, and they bring us to Him. He overcomes our doubts and our reluctance, forgives us, lifts us on high, restores our lost estate, adopts us as His very own, sits us at His table, and shows us the kindness of God.

F. David's Critics (chap. 10)

David next wanted to extend his kindness and grace further afield. When the king of the children of Ammon died, David said, "I will show kindness unto Hanun the son of Nahash, as his father showed kindness unto me. And David sent to comfort him by the hand of his servants" (v. 2). But this was a different story. Nahash refused David's overtures of grace. He chose the part of abysmal folly and offered David the greatest insult one oriental king could ever give to another. He took David's ambassadors, shaved off one-half of their beards, hacked off their robes, leaving them looking ridiculous and exposed, and sent them back with an insulting message.

Now David was a very great saint in those days, but he wasn't stupid. He knew it was as much as his throne was worth to put up with an insult like that. The Ammonites had spurned his grace; very well, they must face his wrath. David consoled his messengers and bided his time. When there was no sign of remorse from Hanun but instead the Ammonites made common cause with the Syrians, David acted. He sent his armies pouring over the frontiers to teach his enemies a lesson they would never forget, and a fearful, full, and formidable lesson it was.

God is gracious, loving, and kind. His first overtures to the soul are always in grace. He sends His messengers with words of peace. God is love, but He is also holy. It would be as much as His very throne was worth to permit vile and sinful men to mock His messengers with impunity—to treat the gospel as garbage. He will not act in a hurry, even when His good intentions are refused and His overtures of kindness are ignored and insulted. He gives space for repentance, time for a change of heart. But if that is not forthcoming, then God, being holy and righteous, acts toward rebellion, insult, and sin as His holiness and righteousness demands—in wrath.

The high tide mark in David's story has now been reached. Two sad chapters follow.

G. David's Crime (chaps. 11–12)

"And it came to pass, after the year was expired, at the time when kings go forth to battle, that David sent Joab . . . and [they] besieged Rabbah. But David tarried still at Jerusalem" (11:1).

Now comes the sad story of David's sin with Bathsheba, the wife of one of David's most faithful warriors; the even sadder story of his arranged murder of the woman's husband, Uriah the Hittite, to clear the way for his own marriage with the woman; and the yet sadder story of a long nine-month period when David played the hypocrite, administering judgment on others while harboring in his soul secret, capital sins of his own.

Nothing is told us of this period, but from some of the psalms we learn of the bitter remorse and agony that ate at David's soul, and also of the terrible physical affliction that overtook him.[2] But outwardly he did nothing. What could he do? Condemn himself to death? That was what the law demanded on two counts—adultery and murder. David, caught now in a terrible net, just went on, passing judgment on others, and excusing himself for his sins.

Then God acted. He sent Nathan the prophet with a parable and a flashing sword of judgment that brought David down from his throne in an instant and down on his face before all his court, crying to God for forgiveness and mercy. That is why David was a man after God's own heart (1 Sam. 13:14). When Saul was convicted of his sin, he simply wanted to keep up appearances and pretend nothing was wrong. When David was convicted of sin, he repented in dust and ashes, and wrote Psalms 6, 32, 38, 51, 102, 130, and 143—but especially Psalm 51. "I have sinned! I have sinned!" cried David. "The LORD also hath put away thy sin," said Nathan (12:13). But then followed the sentence. The guilt of his sin was removed; David would never have to answer for that at the judgment bar of God. But the human and temporal consequences of his sin remained, and these would pursue him down the remaining years of his life, as the remainder of 2 Samuel shows. Sin, from start to finish, is a costly business, and especially sexual sin. That always brings temporal woe.

III. THE PERILOUS YEARS (CHAPS. 13–24)

David emerged from this tragic chapter in his life a greatly weakened individual. The inevitable consequences of his behavior now began to gather force. They followed him like bloodhounds all the rest of the way until at last he crossed over the last Jordan himself and came to that land of fadeless day, where we are delivered, as believers, not only from the penalty and power of sin but also from the pursuit and the very presence of sin.

As we briefly survey the story of these perilous years, we see that David had trouble of two kinds.

A. The Trouble with His Kinsmen (chaps. 13–19)

The consequences of his sin hit him where it would hurt the most—in his family circle.

1. The Lust of Amnon

What a shameful story! Here was passion stalking, naked and unashamed, and inflicting itself on an innocent victim—Tamar, the daughter of David and the full sister of Absalom. What did David do when he heard what had happened? What could he do? How could he inflict the death penalty demanded by the law of Moses on Amnon for his sin when he himself had committed a similar sin not so very long before? So justice in the kingdom went not only blind but gagged. The heartache in David's soul over this flagrant act of lawlessness was matched only by the fury in the heart of Absalom when he saw what had been done to his sister and realized that David intended to hold back judgment in the case. Thus, trouble led to trouble. The lust of David's son Amnon led directly to the next step.

2. The Lawlessness of Absalom

When Absalom saw that his father refused to act against Amnon for his abominable sin, he took the law into his own hands and murdered Amnon in cold blood. What did David do when he heard what had happened? What could he do? How could he inflict the death penalty on Absalom for calculated, premeditated murder when he had been guilty of the same sin himself? So now justice went not only blind and gagged, but bound hand and foot.

But worse was to follow. Absalom fled into exile and there he remained for three years. At the end of that time, through the diplomacy of Joab, David's general, Absalom was granted amnesty and came back home. There, he began to plot against his father, and gradually stole away the hearts of the men of Israel. There followed a dangerous rebellion. David, driven from his throne, fled into the Judean hills, so long familiar to him from his old outlaw days. Then Absalom publicly shamed the women of David's house in an exhibition of lust unsurpassed for public vileness in the whole Old Testament. Then he led his army into the field to catch and kill his own father. Thanks to Joab's military thoroughness and God's faithfulness, Absalom's army was defeated and the traitor slain. But oh! the scar it left on David's soul. His lamentation still rings down the ages: "O my son Absalom, my son, my son Absalom! would God I had died for thee, O Absalom, my son, my son!" (18:33). Many of David's psalms reflect his experiences and inner spiritual exercise at this time.

But David had trouble with more than his kinsmen.

B. Trouble with His Kingdom (chaps. 20–24)

The remainder of the book tells us about that. There were further wars, there were rebellions, there was a famine, there was a pestilence. There was peril (chap. 20) and perplexity (chap. 21) and praise (chaps. 22–23) and pestilence (chap. 24). Truly sin is an expensive business.

But the book ends on a prophetic note. The terrible plague that decimated the nation was stayed at last when David took the place of mediator and stood between the avenging angel and the suffering people. The incident took place on the threshing floor of a Jebusite by the name of Araunah. In a typical act of worship, David bought the place—lock, stock, and barrel. He made a down payment of fifty shekels of silver and later bought the whole area (about six acres) for six hundred shekels of gold (1 Chron. 21:25). And it was there that later Solomon built the temple. Thus 2 Samuel leaves David—leaves him where it found him, even after all his sin—a man after God's own heart.

CHAPTER 12

THE POWERS THAT BE
ARE ORDAINED OF GOD

The history of Israel cannot be properly understood apart from some knowledge of the surrounding world empires. The family of Jacob became a nation in Egypt. The northern kingdom was, in its later years, under constant threat from Assyria. This cruel nation was a terror to all of its neighbors and eventually was permitted by God to bring judgment on Israel, carrying the ten tribes into captivity. The southern kingdom had Babylon to fear, and eventually Judah, too, tasted servitude. The Babylonian Empire was succeeded by the Persians, under whom the captivity came to an end. Later the Persians fell before the Greeks under Alexander the Great, and in time the Romans mastered the known world. Before considering the decline of the Hebrew monarchy, then, some consideration must be given to Assyria, Babylon, and Persia. This will be done through a brief summary of the various kings of each of these empires, showing how they relate to the Bible story.

    I. Threats to Israel: Assyria
       A. Tiglath-pileser III (745–727 B.C.)
       B. Shalmaneser V (727–722 B.C.)
       C. Sargon II (722–705 B.C.)
       D. Sennacherib (705–681 B.C.)
       E. Esar-haddon (681–669 B.C.)
       F. Ashurbanipal (669–633 B.C.)
    II. Threats to Israel: Babylon
       A. Nebuchadnezzar (605–562 B.C.)

B. Evil-merodach (562–560 B.C.)
C. Neriglisar (560–556 B.C.)
D. Labashi-Marduk (556 B.C.)
E. Nabonidus (556–539 B.C.)
F. Belshazzar (553–539 B.C.)
III. Threats to Israel: Persia
A. Cyrus the Great (550–530 B.C.)
B. Darius the Mede (539–525 B.C.)
C. Cambyses II (530–521 B.C.)
D. Smerdis (Gaumata)
E. Darius I Hystaspes (521–486 B.C.)
F. Xerxes (486–464 B.C.)
G. Artaxerxes (Longimanus) (464–423 B.C.)
H. Darius III (Codomanus) (336–331 B.C.)

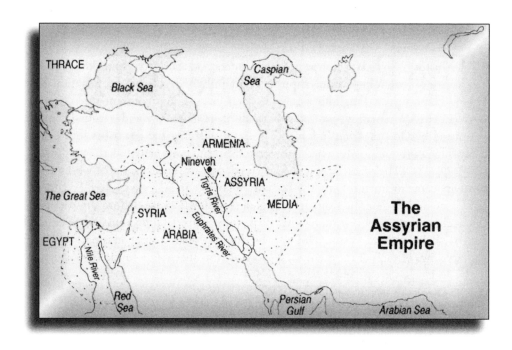

I. Threats to Israel: Assyria

A. Tiglath-pileser III (745–727 B.C.)

Tiglath-pileser III came to the throne of Assyria about the time of the death of

Jeroboam II of Israel. He lifted Assyria from a decline that had made the ambitions of Jeroboam II possible, and made Assyria the foremost empire of the day. Early in his reign he was proclaimed king of Babylon. His Babylonian name was Pulu, and it is as Pul that he is known in the Bible (2 Kings 15:19). His westward advances overshadowed the reigns of Pekahiah, Pekah, and Hoshea of Israel and the reigns of Uzziah, Jotham, and Ahaz of Judah. It was Pul to whom Ahaz, king of Judah, fool-ishly appealed for help against the Syro-Israel league that plagued him. Israel was put under heavy tribute, her kings being little more than puppets of Assyria. Ahaz of Judah aped his Assyrian "protector" and dragged his people low.

B. Shalmaneser V (727–722 B.C.)

Hoshea, the last king of Israel, listening to vain Egyptian promises of help, failed to pay tribute to Shalmaneser V (Tiglath-pileser's successor). Hoshea hereby brought about the siege of Samaria.

C. Sargon II (722–705 B.C.)

Samaria held out for three years and was finally overthrown by Sargon II in 722 B.C. The terrible deportation of the Israelites followed. Hezekiah of Judah also felt the weight of Sargon's hand. Having raised Assyria to new heights of prestige, Sargon then fell in battle. Isaiah walked the streets of Jerusalem "naked and bare-foot" as a sign that Assyria would conquer Egypt and Ethiopia, and as a warning to any who might be tempted to look in that direction for help (Isa. 20:2–6).

D. Sennacherib (705–681 B.C.)

Revolts broke out against Assyria on the death of Sargon II. Judah, under Hezekiah, threw off the Assyrian yoke completely. At this time, too, Merodach-baladan, pretending to congratulate Hezekiah on the recovery from his sickness, sought to win Judah into a great confederacy secretly formed against Assyria (Isa. 39). Isaiah the prophet sharply rebuked Hezekiah for showing his treasures to the Babylonian envoys. Hezekiah's revolt against Assyria is described three times in the Bible (2 Kings 18:13–19:37; 2 Chron. 32:1–21; Isa. 36–37). Sennacherib was a fiendishly cruel and inhuman ruler, given to incredible atrocities. He died a violent death at the hands of his own sons.

E. Esar-haddon (681–669 B.C.)

One of the greatest of the Assyrian kings, Esar-haddon extended Assyrian power to Egypt and was the first Assyrian king to bear the title "king of the kings of Egypt." He is mentioned prophetically in Isaiah 19:4, and Ezra also speaks of him (Ezra 4:2). This was the king who carried Manasseh of Judah into captivity (2 Chron. 33:11).

F. Ashurbanipal (669–633 B.C.)

Ashurbanipal continued his father's policies and resumed the unfinished task of subjugating Egypt. He is referred to in Nahum 3:8–10. The restoration of Manasseh to the throne of Judah was probably in line with the Assyrian policy of keeping the road to Egypt open. The handwriting was on the wall for Assyria, however. Already the Medes were gathering their strength, and by 625 B.C. the Babylonians had joined the Medes. The Assyrians were driven out of Babylonia in 625 B.C. by Nabopolassar, father of Nebuchadnezzar. In 614 B.C. he joined with the Medes to capture Asshur, and in 612 B.C. he destroyed Nineveh. The slackening of the Assyrian hold made possible the reforms of King Josiah of Judah.

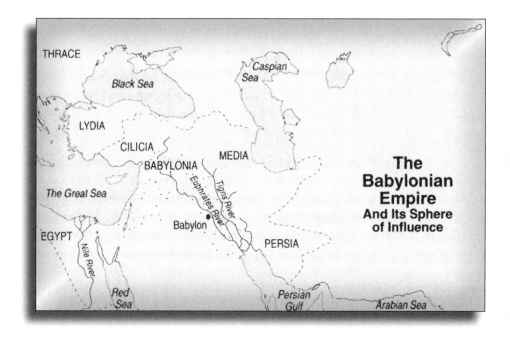

II. THREATS TO ISRAEL: BABYLON

A. Nebuchadnezzar (605–562 B.C.)

Nebuchadnezzar was a strong military leader. In one of the most important battles of history he destroyed the armies of Egypt at Carchemish on the Euphrates in 605 B.C. Having driven Pharaoh-nechoh out of Asia, Nebuchadnezzar returned to Babylon to take over the throne upon the death of his father. He invaded Judah and besieged Jerusalem three times, subjugated the last three kings of Judah, and terminated the

Hebrew monarchy. Jerusalem was at last given over to Gentile domination. In 586 B.C. Nebuchadnezzar besieged Tyre, the siege lasting thirteen years. The Babylonians failed to get any spoil from the city, however, for the citizens withdrew to an island half a mile from shore, leaving the invader with the ruined remains of the old city. Ezekiel foretold this siege of Tyre (26:7–12), and then, after its fall, he recorded that Nebuchadnezzar's army obtained no spoil and promised that Egypt would be given to Nebuchadnezzar in payment (Ezek. 29:18–20). The book of Ezekiel should be read against the background of Nebuchadnezzar's various military campaigns.

B. Evil-merodach (562–560 B.C.)

Evil-merodach is known principally for his kindness to Jehoiachin in the thirty-seventh year of his captivity (2 Kings 25:27–30). As a result of palace intrigue, Evil-merodach was murdered by his brothers.

C. Neriglisar (560–556 B.C.)

No important events took place in Neriglisar's reign. He campaigned in Cilicia in an attempt to stem the rising power of the Lydians.

D. Labashi-Marduk (556 B.C.)

Only a boy when he came to the throne, Labashi-Marduk had reigned only nine months when he was murdered. Power then passed to a new dynasty.

E. Nabonidus (556–539 B.C.)

Nabonidus was a very superstitious man, and neither a great statesman nor a good general. During much of his reign he did not even live in Babylon. His son Belshazzar acted as regent in Babylon while Nabonidus was campaigning in Syria and northern Arabia. After the death of Nebuchadnezzar, the Babylonian alliance with the Medes was broken off. Nabonidus had many enemies, and revolts broke out in various parts of the empire. He stirred up the animosity of many Babylonians who resented his reforms.

F. Belshazzar (553–539 B.C.)

During Belshazzar's dissolute regency, the Babylonian Empire fell before the Medes and Persians. The Babylonian Empire had lasted about seventy years, approximately the time of the seventy-year captivity of the Jews.

III. THREATS TO ISRAEL: PERSIA

A. Cyrus the Great (550–530 B.C.)

Until 550 B.C., the Persians were subject to the Medes. Cyrus the Great

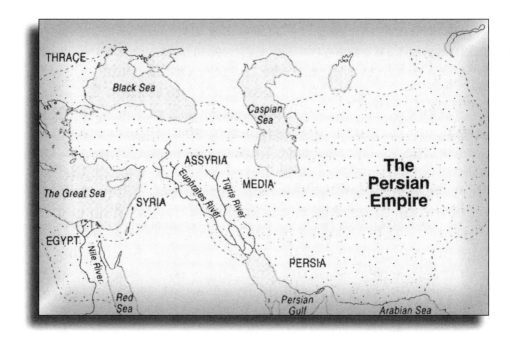

succeeded his father as king of the small Persian kingdom of Anshan in 559 B.C. Soon afterward he rebelled against the Medes, and in 550 united the Medes and Persians under his rule. He conquered Babylon in 539, and made Persia a world power that eventually stretched from east to west for three thousand miles. He permitted the Jews to return to Palestine, a fulfillment of Isaiah 45:1–7, and to rebuild the temple.

B. Darius the Mede (539–525 B.C.)

Darius was made king over Chaldea after the capture of Babylon by the army of Cyrus the Great (Dan. 5:31; 9:1). He reigned part of one year, at least, before Cyrus took over (Dan. 6:28). Probably he held the kingdom in trust for Cyrus, who was still campaigning in other parts.

C. Cambyses II (530–521 B.C.)

D. Smerdis (Gaumata)

This king reigned for only seven months. He is thought to be the Artaxerxes of Ezra 4:7.

E. Darius I Hystaspes (521–486 B.C.)

The building of the temple in Jerusalem had come to a standstill when he came to the throne. Darius, however, permitted the work to go on (Ezra 5–6). The prophets Haggai and Zechariah prophesied during his reign, and the temple was completed.

F. Xerxes (486–464 B.C.)

This is the king Ahasuerus who married Esther, who became queen in 478 B.C. He was a cruel, vindictive, sensual, and fickle man famous for his wars with Greece. He was roundly defeated at sea by a much smaller Grecian fleet at the famous battle of Salamis. A year later the Greeks defeated the land forces of this Persian tyrant. He was murdered eventually by a courtier.

G. Artaxerxes (Longimanus) (464–423 B.C.)

This king was very favorably disposed toward the Jews, even allowing Nehemiah to go up to Jerusalem to rebuild its walls. He is mentioned in Ezra 7:1 and Nehemiah 2:1 and 5:14. Later still, he permitted Nehemiah to become governor of Jerusalem (Neh. 5:14; 13:6).

H. Darius III (Codomanus) (336–331 B.C.)

This last king of Persia was defeated by Alexander the Great, first at Issus in 333 B.C., and then at Arbela in 331 B.C. He was murdered by his servants, and the scepter of world empire passed from Asia to Europe.

CHAPTER 13

1 AND 2 KINGS

Israel Faces the Sunset

A word needs to be said about the division in our Bible of Samuel, Kings, and Chronicles into two books each. Some justification can be seen in the case of the two books of Samuel, since second Samuel deals with the reign of David. It is more difficult to justify the division of the books of Kings and Chronicles. They are treated as one book in the Hebrew canon, as given in the manuscripts and early printed editions of the Hebrew text. These books were first divided the way we now have them by the translators who produced the Septuagint version of the Old Testament Scriptures.

On the surface the division seems to be somewhat arbitrary. In the case of the books of Kings, for instance, the division comes in the middle of the reign of Ahaziah and the ministry of Elijah. The reason for this seems to have been purely utilitarian. Scrolls were probably more or less of equal length. Greek takes up approximately a third more space than Hebrew. One scroll would be filled up before all of the book of Kings was translated. This would account for the poor division of the book. The same would apply to the other books.

For the sake of this survey, we shall treat the books of Kings and Chronicles as two books instead of four.

The two books of Kings record the meridian splendor of Solomon's reign and the slowly lengthening shadows that crept across the monarchical phase of Hebrew history. The twelve tribes were united and were ruled from a single throne for one hundred and twenty years, with Saul, David, and Solomon each reigning forty years. With the death of Solomon, ten tribes broke away from the throne of David to set up an independent kingdom to the north. This kingdom, known as Israel, was eventually ruled from Samaria by various dynasties, all the kings of which were bad, although some were worse than others. The tribe of Benjamin remained true to Judah and the throne of David. Combined, these two tribes comprised the southern kingdom, known as Judah, which was ruled from Jerusalem by the heirs and successors of David. Some of Judah's kings were good, but most were bad.

In the biblical account of the kings of Judah and Israel, the narrative alternates between the two kingdoms. It should be observed that the ministries of many of the prophets fall within this period, but these prophets will not be surveyed in particular until later in this volume.

In the chart below, the good kings of Israel appear in bold type. Dates are based on *The Chart of Old Testament Kings and Prophets*, by John C. Whitcomb.[1] Some of the dates of regencies and prophets are uncertain.

THE KINGS OF JUDAH AND ISRAEL

Dates (B.C.)	Hebrew History		Prophets	Other Events
	The United Kingdom			
1051–1011	Saul			
1011–971	David			
971–931	Solomon			
	Judah	**Israel**		
931–913	Rehoboam			
931–910		Jeroboam		
913–911	Abiram			
911–873	**Asa**			
910–909		Nadab		
909–886		Baasha		
886		Elah		
885		Zimri		
(885–880)		Tibni		
885–874		Omni		
874–853		Ahab		
?–852			Elijah	
873–848	**Jehoshaphat**			

THE KINGS OF JUDAH AND ISRAEL

Dates (B.C.)	Hebrew History		Prophets	Other Events
853–852		Ahaziah		
852–841		Jehoram	Elisha	
848–841	Jehoram (called Joram)			
841	Ahaziah			Married Athaliah— daughter of Ahab and Jezebel
841–835	Athaliah			
841–814		Jehu		
835–796	**Jehoash** (called Joash)			
830–815?			Joel	
814–798		Jehoahaz		
798–782		Jehoash		
796–767	**Amaziah**			
(793–782)		(Jeroboam II regent with Jehoash)		
(790–767)	(**Uzziah** regent with Amaziah)			
785–775			Jonah	
782–753		Jeroboam II		
767–739	**Uzziah** (called Azariah)			
765–755			Amos	
755–715			Hosea	
753–752		Zechariah		
752		Shallum		
752–742		Menahem		

THE KINGS OF JUDAH AND ISRAEL

Dates (B.C.)	Hebrew History		Prophets	Other Events
(750–739)	(**Jotham** regent with Uzziah)			
745–727				Tiglath-Pileser III
742–740	Pekahiah			
740–732	Pekah			
739–731	Jotham			
739–690?			Isaiah	
736–700			Micah	
(735–731)	(Ahaz regent with Jotham)			
732–722	Hoshea			
731–715	Ahaz			
727–722				Shalmaneser V
722		Fall of Samaria		
722–705				Sargon II
715–686	**Hezekiah**			
705–681				Sennacherib
(695–686)	(Manasseh regent with Hezekiah)		.	
686–642	Manasseh			
645–620?			Nahum	
642–640	Amon			
640–609	**Josiah**			
635–625?			Zephaniah	
627–575			Jeremiah	
620–610			Habakkuk	
612				Fall of Nineveh
609	Jehoahaz			
609–597	Jehoiakim			
609–585?			Obadiah	

THE KINGS OF JUDAH AND ISRAEL

Dates (B.C.)	Hebrew History		Prophets	Other Events
605				Battle of Carchemish
605–562				Nebuchad-nezzar
605–536			Daniel	
597	Jehoiachin			
597–586	Zedekiah			
593–558?			Ezekiel	
586	Fall of Jerusalem			
550–530				Cyrus
539				Fall of Babylon
538	Decree of Cyrus			
538–512?	Zerubbabel			
536	Temple begun			
530–521				Cambyses
521				Smerdis
521–486				Darius I Hystabses
520–496			Zechariah	
520–516			Haggai	
520	Temple resumed			
516	Temple finished			
486–464				Xerxes
478	Esther becomes queen			
473	Feast of Purim			
464–423				Artaxerxes
458–443	Ezra			
445–415?	Nehemiah			
435–415			Malachi	
423–404				Darius II

The two books of Kings record the triumphs, tyrannies, and troubles of Israel's and Judah's kings. For, as we shall see, "uneasy sleeps the head that wears a crown!"[2] In the books of Kings, the history is written from the human standpoint, from the viewpoint of the prophets. These books were written before the Babylonian captivity and record the events that led up to that national disaster.

This long period can be divided into three parts. The *years of strength*, which were unequalled in the history of the Jewish people, occurred when Solomon reigned in pomp and pageantry.

The *years of struggle* are characterized by all the ups and downs to be expected when a wise king is followed by a weak king or by a wicked king or by a wishful king. Round and round the cycle goes—triumph and tragedy! Victory and defeat! Revival and relapse! Glory and shame!

Finally, the *years of storm* arrive. Tiny Judah stands alone with the tempest rushing in from the east—held back by God, indeed, for a hundred years, but gathering strength and unleashed at last in all its fury.

I. The Years of Strength (1 Kings 1:1–12:19)
   A. David (1:1–2:11)
   B. Solomon (2:12–11:43)
   C. Rehoboam (12:1–19)
II. The Years of Struggle (1 Kings 12:20–2 Kings 17:41)
   A. The Commencement of the Period (1 Kings 12:20–2 Kings 9:29)
      1. The Rift (1 Kings 12:20–14:31)
         a. Jeroboam and *Israel* (12:20–14:20)
         b. Rehoboam and *Judah* (14:21–31)
      2. The Rivals
         a. Judah
            (1) Abijam (15:1–8)
            (2) Asa (15:9–24)
         b. Israel
            (1) Nadab (15:25–31)
            (2) Baasha (15:32–16:7)
            (3) Elah (16:8–14)
            (4) Zimri (16:15–22)
            (5) Omni (16:23–28)
            (6) Ahab (16:29–22:40)
         c. Judah
            (1) Jehoshaphat (22:41–50)
         d. Israel
            (1) Ahaziah (1 Kings 22:51–2 Kings 1:18)

For centuries, Israel had been a *theocracy*—that is, government was invested in God. There had been no visible head for the nation, though God had spoken and acted through various men raised up from all walks of life: a Moses, a Joshua, a Gideon, a Samuel—a prophet, a priest, a judge. But, like anything else in which man has a part, the theocratic form of government failed. So God gave Israel a king.

The two books of Kings record the long story of the dismal failure of the *monarchy*—tried and tested as it was over more than half a millennium. The period begins with Solomon in all his glory and ends with Zedekiah—broken, blinded and banished, bruised under the heel of a foreign, invading power.

This checkered story can best be surveyed by highlighting in brief the narratives of the more salient kings. We might coin a catchphrase for each of them:

   1. Solomon and His Worldly Ways
   2. Rehoboam and His Foolish Friends
   3. Jeroboam and His Absolute Apostasy
   4. Ahab and His Wicked Wife
   5. Jehoshaphat and His Criminal Compromise
   6. Jehu and His Pious Platitudes
   7. Joash and His Peer Pressure
   8. Uzziah and His Pompous Pride
   9. Jeroboam II and His Political Power
  10. Ahaz and His Public Panic
  11. Hezekiah and His Triumphant Trust
  12. Manasseh and His Pagan Policies
  13. Josiah and His Religious Revival
  14. Jehoiachin and His Meddling Mother
  15. Zedekiah and His Godless Guidance

1. Solomon and His Worldly Ways

Solomon was born and bred in the hothouse atmosphere of harem intrigue. His father was David, his mother was Bathsheba, whose sin with David had caused a national scandal in Israel. He was very young when he came to the throne; Eusebius says he was twelve, Josephus says he was fifteen; certainly he could not have been more than twenty. He was chosen by God to be king—a choice heartily endorsed by David.

Because Solomon was a younger son, his being chosen created a constitutional crisis in Israel and the threat of civil war. It established one important fact regarding the throne of David, however, and the messianic line to Christ—it settled the fact that the throne of David and the messianic line did not necessarily belong to the oldest son of the reigning king.

Solomon's first act was to execute Joab for high treason. Though Joab had been David's general, it was an execution long overdue. Joab's hands were stained with the blood of more than one man in his struggle for power. Nor did Joab's open disrespect for David do anything to mitigate the sentence. He died calling out for sanctuary at Israel's high altar, crying for a mercy he had never shown to those who had stood in his path.

The nation soon got the message—Solomon might be little more than a boy, but he was every inch a king and well knew how to handle those who might be tempted to challenge his right to the throne.

Twice God appears to this youthful king. Conscious of his extreme youth, Solomon pleaded not for wealth, not to be a warrior, but for wisdom to rule well the people of God. God gave him that wisdom but, as with all spiritual gifts, its usefulness hinged upon obedience to God's will. When Solomon turned away from God, his wisdom became earthly, sensual, and devilish. It was not until his later years that he groped his way back to God and wrote the book of Ecclesiastes, one long dirge of warning and regret.

He made two serious mistakes that tarnished all the glamour and glitter of his prosperous and opulent reign. He married the daughters of pagan kings from surrounding countries, hoping to cement the frontiers of his realm and in so doing acted in defiance of God's will. Then he turned a blind eye to the growth of paganism in his country, promoted and fostered by his heathen wives. More! He stooped to paganism himself, imagining, perhaps, that there was good in all religions.

For him to imagine that all religions had some good in them meant that the light that was in him had to be turned into very gross darkness indeed. Of what value was it for Solomon to build the temple when he also built pagan shrines? Of what value was it for Solomon to be Israel's most able adjudicator and adminis-trator when all his enterprises and successes tended at last to the complete secular-ization of his realm? Thus Solomon made shipwreck of his life and of his kingdom.

A prophet was sent to tell him his kingdom would be rent asunder. Ten-twelfths of the kingdom would be given to one of his court officials. Of the twelve territorial tribes, only two would remain true to the throne of David. But for David's sake (not out of respect for Solomon, who had abused both the grace of God and the gifts of God) the disaster would not fall until after Solomon's death. Thus came an end of Israel's brief venture into empire.

2. REHOBOAM AND HIS FOOLISH FRIENDS

Upon the death of Solomon, matters in Israel came swiftly to a head. Solomon had driven his people too hard. He had been a slave driver of a king more than he had been a shepherd. The system of public conscription and onerous taxation was more than people could bear. Headed by Jeroboam, ten of the tribes, the vast northern section of the kingdom, demanded that Rehoboam redress the situation. Rehoboam, Solomon's son and successor, was a fool. He spurned the advice of the wise old men who had counseled Solomon and hailed the advice of his young drinking buddies who, in effect, told the king that he should show the protesting northern tribes just who was boss. As a result, the ten tribes broke away.

The northern kingdom, known as Israel, was made up of ten tribes and ruled ultimately from Samaria; the southern kingdom, known as Judah, was made up of two tribes and some scattered immigrants from the north, and ruled from Jerusalem. Both nations had nineteen successive kings on their thrones. The northern kingdom of Israel lasted for about two hundred years; the southern kingdom of Judah lasted about three hundred and fifty years. The nineteen kings of the northern kingdom came from no less than seven different dynasties; the nineteen kings of the southern kingdom all belonged to one dynasty—all were descended from David. The kings of Judah varied—some were good and some were bad; all the kings of Israel were bad.

Rehoboam, having lost the northern tribes, was warned by God not to try to force them back under his rule. During his reign, too, Egypt directly interfered in Judah's affairs so that Rehoboam had enough trouble on his hands from that quarter to prevent him from launching disastrous expeditions against his rival in the north.

3. JEROBOAM AND HIS ABSOLUTE APOSTASY

Jeroboam, who founded the northern kingdom, was an utterly worldly man. He inaugurated his reign by setting up two rival centers of worship to offset the spiritual influence of Jerusalem—one at Dan and the other at Bethel. Consecrating two golden calves as objects of worship, he instituted a new priesthood and a new religious calendar. And he died under the judgment of God.

As the kings of Judah are measured against the yardstick of David, so the northern kings are measured by Jeroboam "the son of Nebat, who made Israel to sin" (1 Kings 22:52). That was God's estimate of this man. All the kings of Israel followed in his steps.

4. AHAB AND HIS WICKED WIFE

Ahab was Israel's worst and most wicked king. He hitched his wagon to a star—and what a baneful, dreadful star it was. As if all his other sins were not bad enough, he crowned them all by marrying Jezebel, a Sidonian princess devoted to the filthy cult of Baal. She became the real power behind the throne. Even the pretense of worshipping Jehovah was now thrust aside. Baal worship, with its horrible rites and lustful practices, was installed instead, and the State became the armed persecutor of the faithful remnant of believers in the land. An army of eight hundred false prophets and priests, supported by the throne, swarmed everywhere. It was at this time that Elijah appeared, God's prophet to challenge the apostasy of the day.

5. JEHOSHAPHAT AND HIS CRIMINAL COMPROMISE

While Ahab was reigning in Israel, Jehoshaphat was on the throne in Judah. We can call him the wavering king. While he loved God, he seemed fascinated by Ahab and Jezebel. Instead of steering well clear of the wicked pair, he, like a moth, foolishly drew closer and closer to the flame. In the first place he allowed himself to be drawn into Israel's border wars with Syria, for which he was roundly rebuked by the prophet: "Shouldest thou help the ungodly, and love them that hate the LORD?" (2 Chron. 19:2). But worse! He married his son to the daughter of Ahab and Jezebel and thus paved the way for Judah to become infected with the same fearful apostasies that were ravaging Israel.

It is a principle with God that He never leaves Himself without a witness. Indeed, the more degenerate the times, the more definite the testimony. Thus woven into the story of Ahab is the stirring story of Elijah and the almost as spectacular story of Elisha. Elijah strode across the stage like an avenging deity. Calling down fire on his enemies, he took on single-handedly the entire religious and political establishment of the northern kingdom. He towered so high above all those who ever followed him in the prophetic ministry that just two names are needed to sum up the spiritual life of the Old Testament: the names of Moses and Elijah—Moses standing for the law and Elijah for the prophets.

After the translation of Elijah to heaven, Elisha picked up his mantle along with a double portion of Elijah's spirit (Elijah performed eight miracles, Elisha sixteen), and he continued where his friend and master had left off.

Thus, although apostasy had fastened firmly on Israel and was now about to invade Judah, God raised up Elijah and Elisha, two great witnesses, to demonstrate with a whole string of miracles that He and He alone was the true and living God.

6. Jehu and His Pious Platitudes

It was Jehu who put an end to the fateful dynasty of Omri, which had ripened into such rottenness with Ahab. Jehu, Ahab's general, had his ambitions set aflame when one of Elisha's disciples secretly anointed him as Israel's next king. Jehu acted with decision and dispatch. He led a military coup against the rotten Jezebel government and then massacred the Baal worshippers with Machiavellian cunning. But once he was firmly on the throne, with the kingdom of Israel prostrate at his feet, he showed his own contempt for Jehovah by pursuing the godless policies of Jeroboam, Israel's first king.

7. Joash and His Peer Pressure

It was only through the courage of the high priest in Jerusalem that Joash even lived to sit upon the throne. His father, Judah's king, like most kings in those days, had a large family. His chief wife, Athaliah, was the daughter of Jezebel, and was, if possible, viler than her mother.

When the father of little Joash died, Athaliah seized the throne of Judah and massacred anyone who might have a claim to it. Joash escaped by being hidden in the temple by Jehoiadah the priest. When the time was ripe, this godly priest staged a rebellion against Athaliah, slew her, and installed the young boy Joash as king.

Joash ruled well and walked in the ways of the Lord as long as Jehoiadah lived, but once Jehoiadah was dead, Joash turned his back upon God, bowed to the pressure of his peers, and turned to idolatry. Second Chronicles greatly adds to our knowledge of this king's wickedness. Second Kings contents itself with cutting short his story, abbreviating his name from Jehoash to Joash, and recording his murder.

8. Uzziah and His Pompous Pride

Uzziah was the grandson of Joash and a very capable man. During his reign, Judah recovered much of the territory it had lost to surrounding hostile tribes in previous reigns. He broke Israel's stranglehold, smashed the Philistines, imposed tribute on Ammon, and fortified Jerusalem. The Spirit of God comments on his life that "he was marvelously helped, till he was strong" (2 Chron. 26:15). But then pride took over. Intolerant of any rivals, he violated one of the strictest provisions of the Mosaic Law—that which kept church and state separate—and intruded into the temple to function as a priest. He was immediately smitten with leprosy under the stroke of God.

Sometimes Uzziah is called Azariah. Using different names for the same person is not uncommon in the Bible, especially when the names have the same or similar meanings.

9. Jeroboam II and His Political Power

Like Uzziah of Judah, this northern king extended the boundaries of his kingdom.

During his reign of forty-one years—far longer than any other northern king—he smashed the Syrians who had, for so long, plagued his people. Jeroboam was the last king of Israel in the north ever to reign with any semblance of divine authority. After his death, all his successors were mere adventurers, most of whom ascended to the throne over the murdered body of his predecessor. Jeroboam II was an evil king, and during his reign the writing prophets began their ministry. His kingdom, while outwardly prosperous, was marked by the spiritual and moral corruptions that brought forth the scathing denunciations of Amos. His reign was the last flicker of the royal candle in Israel before it was finally gutted out by the advancing Assyrian hordes.

The coming of the Assyrians to world empire was an event filled with horror and woe for the world. The nations in the area were no match for the formidable Assyrian war machine. Those who refused to submit to Assyrian rule were ruthlessly invaded and, once captured, treated with great cruelty. Israel and Judah lay right in the path of Assyrian imperial ambitions.

The few remaining kings of Israel found themselves constantly and increasingly threatened by Assyria. They were a sorry lot, and under their ineffective, backstabbing attempts at government, the domestic and foreign affairs of the northern kingdom simply fell apart. Samaria was taken after a three-year siege, and subjected to the unspeakable horrors of Assyrian reprisals. Those who were left of the ten tribes, when the Assyrian butchers were through, were hauled off into captivity and dispersed far and wide throughout the vast Assyrian domains.

10. Ahaz and His Public Panic

Ahaz had at court one of the sagest and most spiritual men of all time—the great prophet Isaiah—but he ignored him and went his own idiotic way. This foolish king was obsessed by the alliance of Israel and Syria against him, and he allowed himself to be caught up in the desultory Syrio-Ephraimitic war. Isaiah told him not to worry, that neither Syria nor Israel would last, but Ahaz would not listen. Instead he did the most foolish thing a man could ever do—he invited the Assyrian wolf to come in and keep the peace in the local chicken coop. He asked Assyria to intervene in Middle East affairs and protect him from his two petty neighbors. It was like asking the Russians to come and keep the peace in the Middle East today. After the collapse of Samaria and the deportation of the northern tribes, Judah found itself facing the overwhelming military might of Assyria at first hand. Ahaz had thus dragged Judah down and put it under the unbearable yoke of the Assyrian overlord.

11. Hezekiah and His Triumphant Trust

As the dust of Samaria's collapse began to settle and the screams and cries of the dying, the tortured, and the prisoners began to fade, we see godly King Hezekiah sitting upon his somewhat shaky throne, assisted and encouraged by that prince of prophets, the great prophet Isaiah. He had inherited a political and religious mess from his father Ahaz. His first act was to strike a blow at the idolatry that polluted his land. Then he gathered his people together to celebrate the first Passover Feast that had been kept in the kingdom for many a long year. Indeed, the historian declares, "Since the time of Solomon the son of David king of Israel there was not the like in Jerusalem" (2 Chron. 30:26). It was a national reminder to Judah that all hope for the nation and for the individual, that all true redemption, stemmed solely from the shed blood of God's true Lamb.

Hezekiah first bought off Assyria, then, encouraged by Isaiah, he dared to defy the superpower to the north in God's name. On behalf of this king, God worked two of the most notable miracles in the Old Testament. Once he was free of the Assyrian menace, Hezekiah set about arranging and transcribing the Old Testament Scriptures and adding a psalm or two to them himself. At the end of many Old Testament books, three capital letters occur, which no transcriber has seen fit to omit. They are the letters HZK—thought to represent the name Hezekiah. As Hezekiah's scribes completed the transcribing of the various books, Hezekiah would inspect them and add his royal signature. One delights to picture this dear man, the son of one of Judah's most wicked kings and the father of one of Judah's most wicked kings, diligently poring over the sacred Scriptures in his efforts to steer a reluctant nation back to God.

Only five more kings were to sit upon the throne of David. Then the Babylonian deportation would put an end to the kingdom. Of the five, four were utterly ungodly. But God, in His sovereignty, assured that the sacred writings were properly codified, canonized, and copied for posterity before these disastrous reigns began. To this day we owe a lasting debt of gratitude to this godly king for his care and concern for the sacred Scriptures, as well as for some of the notable psalms he wrote and added to the Hebrew hymnbook.

The two great events in Hezekiah's life were his miraculous recovery from a terminal illness (a recovery that assured him a further fifteen years of life—a somewhat doubtful blessing for Judah, considering that it was during those years that Manasseh was born) and the miraculous overthrow of the invading Assyrian army before the walls of Jerusalem.

12. MANASSEH AND HIS PAGAN POLICIES

How is it that the best of fathers sometimes have the worst of sons, and that sometimes the worst of fathers have the best of sons? Ahaz was the worst of fathers, yet he reared Hezekiah, who was the best of sons. Indeed, so good was Hezekiah that one of the rabbis has declared that Hezekiah was undoubtedly the Messiah. Hezekiah was the best of fathers, but he reared the very worst of sons. It would have been better for Judah had this godly king died of his sickness rather than recover and father Manasseh.

Manasseh was not only the most wicked king ever to disgrace the throne of David but he reigned the longest. He reigned for fifty-five years—so long that his pagan but popular policies and his enthusiastic support of every form of idolatry and vice so steeped the nation in vileness that it never recovered. The Holy Spirit's comment on this man's life was that he "hath done wickedly above all that the Amorites did" (2 Kings 21:11). Yet such is the grace of God that, as we read in the parallel record in 2 Chronicles, God actually saved this man's soul.

He was taken prisoner by the Assyrians and carried away to Babylon. There he was converted, and soon afterward he was restored to his throne, at which time he tried to undo some of the damage he had done. Such is the goodness, the patience, the kindness of God. This, perhaps, explains why Manasseh reigned so long. God is longsuffering, not willing that any should perish, willing to lengthen out His grace as He reaches after lost men.

But Manasseh's late reforms in the eventide of his life made little impression on Judah. As Mark Anthony said over the dead body of Caesar, "The evil that men do lives after them, the good is oft interred with their bones."[3] Thus it was with Manasseh. He had taught his people wickedness so well that they were left untouched by his repentance, regeneration, and reforms.

13. Josiah and His Religious Revival

Manasseh was followed on the throne by his son Amon, who sought to reinstate the idolatries under which he had grown up. He lasted only two years, when he was murdered in the palace by some of his servants.

The throne was taken by Josiah, the last of Judah's godly kings. But by now the Babylonians were rising fast to empire. Isaiah had long since died; the prophet Jeremiah had taken his place, and his sob-choked words of doom hung like a pall over Jerusalem. Urged on by the prophet, Josiah attempted reform. He cleaned all the rubbish and all the idols from the temple and repaired it. He discovered a copy of the Law and assembled the people and read it to them. He reinstituted the Passover. He did everything a mortal man in love with God could do to bring revival to his people—and he failed. The best he achieved was a temporary reformation.

Prophet after prophet came and went—in vain. The spiritual law of hardening was already at work.

The death of Josiah was a national tragedy, the result of his meddling in an affair he would have done well to leave alone. Pharaoh-necho of Egypt was marching to the Euphrates, hoping to curb the growing power of Babylon. Josiah tried to stop him at Megiddo and was slain. The Egyptians went to the Euphrates, there to be thrashed at Carchemish by the Babylonians, who thus became virtual masters of the world. Henceforth the handwriting was on the wall for Judah, as first Egypt and then Babylon kept a busy hand in her affairs.

14. JEHOIACHIN AND HIS MEDDLING MOTHER

Josiah's son Jehoahaz lasted only three inglorious and evil months. Pharaoh-necho deposed Jehoahaz and put his brother Eliakim on the throne, changing his name to Jehoiakim. For eleven years this man muddled along, bringing Judah back into its former evil ways.

Nebuchadnezzar invaded Judah and put the country under tribute, generously allowing Jehoiakim to continue on the throne. There followed a few more sad years, during which this evil king restored all the apostasies and immoralities of Manasseh. Then he rebelled against Nebuchadnezzar and came to an ignominious end.

His son Jehoiachin came to the throne, reigning ingloriously for three months and ten days. His name is often shortened to Jeconiah and sometimes, contemptuously, to Coniah. For his apostasies, God laid a curse upon him. "Write ye this man childless," He said (Jer. 22:30). The expression does not refer to his natural descendants, because he had seven sons. The prophet was using poetic language to bar any of Jehoiachin's descendants from sitting on David's throne. From then on, the direct line to Christ must come from elsewhere. As we know now, God went right back to the beginning, bypassed all the royal line through Solomon, and brought His Son into the world through Nathan, one of David's other sons, and traces the line from Nathan to Mary.

Many of Jehoiachin's disastrous policies seem to have been instigated by his mother Nehushta, the daughter of an influential Jerusalem prince. Her meddling brought on the second Babylonian invasion.

15. ZEDEKIAH AND HIS GODLESS GUIDANCE

Zedekiah was the last Old Testament king of the Jews. During his reign, the final deportation to Babylon took place, and the final destruction of Jerusalem and the temple transpired. The judgment was long in coming, but when it came it was thorough, just, and on time. It fell for three reasons. First, the Jews had denied the biblical basis of their national *society*. Their social structure was based upon a weekly Sabbath, a yearly Sabbath, and a Jubilee Sabbath. For centuries the people ignored these Sabbatic laws. Second, the Jews had denied the biblical basis of their national *sovereignty*, which hinged upon their independence of other nations and their dependence upon God. Their country stood astride the great trade routes of the Middle East—astride the natural path of any invading army from north or south or east. Only God could and would defend them. They abandoned God; in the end God abandoned them. Third, the Jews had denied the biblical basis of their national *spirituality*. They were to shun idolatry like the plague. They were to be a testimony to all peoples of the nature and character of the true and living God, who had befriended them and given them so much. Instead, they sank lower than the heathen themselves. Judah became a Sodomite society, and God will never allow the nation to prosper that tolerates such sin.

The last days of Judah were characterized by international intrigues. The weepings and warnings of Jeremiah were ignored, and in their desperation the kings of Judah looked for alliances that might save them from destruction. But Assyria was no more, and Egypt was a broken reed.

The Babylonians were coming to full power. In 605 B.C., the first Babylonian invasion took place, and another followed early in the year 597. Nebuchadnezzar, the Babylonian king, installed Zedekiah as a puppet king and retired from the scene. Ignoring Jeremiah and listening instead to evil counsel, Zedekiah rebelled against his master. Back came Nebuchadnezzar to sack Jerusalem, burn the temple in 586 B.C., deport much of the population of Judah to Babylon, and thus bring an end to the monarchy.

The "times of the Gentiles" had begun. From that day to this, Jerusalem has been almost entirely under Gentile control and will remain so until Jesus comes to reign. The present-day control of Jerusalem by the Jews is only a temporary matter. When the Antichrist comes, he will seize the city and sack it, and it will be subjected to earthquake, persecution, and war.

CHAPTER 14

1 AND 2 CHRONICLES

Second Thoughts

The books of Chronicles are not a mere repetition of the books of Kings. The books of Kings give us history from the viewpoint of the prophets, Chronicles from the viewpoint of the priests. The books of Kings give us history from the human standpoint, Chronicles from the divine standpoint. The former show man ruling, the latter show God overruling. The revival under Hezekiah, for example, is given in three verses in Kings but in three chapters in Chronicles.

The Companion Bible has this helpful comment on the books of 1 and 2 Chronicles: "These books belong to quite another part of the Old Testament, and do not follow in sequence on the books of Kings. They are, according to the Hebrew Canon, the conclusion of the Old Testament; and the genealogies here lead up to that of Matthew 1:1 and the commencement of the New Testament. They end with the ending of the kingdom; and the question of Cyrus, 'Who is there' (2 Chron. 36:23) is followed by the answer, 'Where is he?' (Matt. 2:2), and the proclamation of the kingdom by the rightful King and His forerunner. It begins with the first Adam and leads on to the 'last Adam.' It deals with the kingdom of Judah because Christ was proclaimed as the successor of David."[1]

The books of Chronicles were written after the captivity in Babylon was over. The returned remnant found themselves back in the land of promise with a monumental task before them. Their cities were heaps of rubble, their temple was gone, the land was desolate and in ruins. Ancient enemies were hostile still, and many Jewish people were indifferent to their emancipation, preferring a life of luxury in Babylonia and Persia to the rigors of pioneering under these conditions.

Most devastating of all, the throne of David was gone. The returning remnant under Zerubbabel had a commission to build a temple, not a throne. The books of

Chronicles were written to interpret to the people the meaning of their history in the light of the present and the future.

THE THINGS THAT REMAINED

First, although the *throne* of David was gone, the *line* of David was still intact. From Adam to Zedekiah, as the Chronicles proved, God had never allowed that line to become tangled, broken, or lost. Through all the long ages, God had pursued His purpose. Through days bright with promise and days dark with apostasy God had remained true to His plan. It was inconceivable that the thread could be broken now. The throne of David was a divine institution. The line of David had never become extinct and never would until at last the Messiah Himself, so long promised by the prophets, should come and reestablish and sit upon the throne.

Second, a new temple had been raised on the ruins of the old. The writer of Chronicles shows that the temple had occupied an important place in the history of God's people. If David had given Judah a scepter, Solomon had given Judah a sanctuary. The one was as important as the other. Tenderly the writer of Chronicles keeps in mind the fortunes of the temple. *Conceived* in the mind of David, *constructed* under the guidance of Solomon, *contaminated* by some of the kings, and *cleansed* by others, and at last *consumed* in the fires that demolished Jerusalem, the temple is never far from the center of the story.

Third, the writer of Chronicles proves that all Israel's troubles stemmed from apostasy. Skillfully he gives the testimony of history. Looking back over the past, the people of God could see, in the sharp perspective of history, exactly where apostasy had brought the nation. The book of Chronicles is a philosophy of Hebrew history from the divine viewpoint. It is a clear warning to the people never again to forsake the temple and the worship of the living God.

THE SCOPE OF CHRONICLES

The title "Chronicles" was given to these two books in the fourth century by Jerome. It is a good name. It chronicles history over a vast scope of time—from Adam down to the decree of Cyrus in 536 B.C., which permitted the exiled Hebrew people to return to Palestine and rebuild their ancestral home. In other words, it represents a period of not less than thirty-five hundred years. It covers the longest period of any of the books of the Bible.

Beginning with David and going through to Zedekiah, it relates the history of twenty-one kings and also the inglorious reign of Queen Athaliah, the usurper. In Chronicles, the kings of Israel are mentioned only occasionally in passing. The same number of kings sat on the thrones of Israel and Judah; the kingdom of Judah, however, lasted 136 years longer than the kingdom of Israel. This relative longevity was one effect on the history of their nation imparted by the half-dozen God-fearing kings of Judah.

The human author of the book seems to have been Ezra the scribe. Chronicles is evidently a compilation, a selection of material from existing documents, and the author leaves us in no doubt that it was done with great care. He names no less than twelve different sources from which he drew information. It was also done under the unerring revelation and inspiration of the superintending Holy Spirit. The collection and editing of this material was done with a specific end in view. When we compare the Chronicles with the books of Samuel and Kings, we discover that Ezra has indeed been selective. There are identical passages, there are outright omissions, there are additions. We naturally want to know what Ezra's great objective was in putting this compilation together. After all, the Jews who chose to remain in Babylonia and elsewhere and the Jews who elected to pioneer the rebuilding of the homeland all had the books of Samuel and Kings already. Why did they need another history book?

A study of the books of Kings and Chronicles reveals the following:

DIFFERENCES IN KINGS AND CHRONICLES	
Kings	**Chronicles**
• Was written before the captivity • Was written from the standpoint of the prophets • Embraces the history of the northern kingdom • Is compulsive—written in the dust and din and distraction of the time and place	• Was written after the captivity • Was written from the standpoint of the priests • Ignores the history of the northern kingdom • Is contemplative—written in the quiet and calm of a library, far from the sounds and scenes involved

In other words, *Kings* gives us the *facts* of history; *Chronicles* gives us the *philosophy* of history. Kings tells us *what* happened; Chronicles tells us *why*. Chronicles, with its emphasis on the temple, its servants, its singers, its services, with its passionate hatred of idolatry, is designed to show the *theocratic nature* of Israel's calling and election as a nation; to show that God must be owned and obeyed as God; that only thus can the nation prosper; that all else is a denial of its being and leads to disaster.

    I. The Chronologies of Judah's Kings (1 Chron. 1:1–10:14)
       A. Preexilic Names (1 Chron. 1:1–8:40)

    1. The Primeval Line (1:1–23)
      a. Before the Flood (1:1–4)
        (1) Adam to Noah
      b. Beyond the Flood (1:5–23)
        (1) The Japhetic Nations (1:5–7)
        (2) The Hametic Nations (1:8–16)
        (3) The Semitic Nations (1:17–23)
    2. The Patriarchal Line (1:24–33)
      a. Sons of the Faith (1:24–28)
        (1) Shem to Abraham
      b. Sons of the Flesh (1:29–33)
        (1) Ishmael and His Sons (1:29–31)
        (2) Keturah and Her Sons (1:32–33)
    3. The Promised Line (1:34–54)
      a. The Fathers of Israel (1:34)
      b. The Foes of Israel (1:35–54)
        (1) Esau and the Edomites
    4. The Protected Line (2:1–55)
      a. The Lineal Ancestors of David (2:1–12)
        (1) Israel to Jesse
      b. The Lesser Ancestors of David (2:13–55)
        (1) Jesse and Caleb
    5. The Princely Line (3:1–8:40)
      a. The Royal Family (3:1–24)
        (1) David to Zedekiah
      b. The Related Families (4:1–8:40)
  B. Postexilic Notes (1 Chron. 9:1–10:14)
    1. The Foreword (9:1)
    2. The Faithful (9:2–34)
      a. Jerusalem and Judah's Sons (9:2–9)
      b. Jerusalem and Jehovah's Servants (9:10–34)
        (1) The Priests (9:10–13)
        (2) The Levites (9:14–34)
    3. The Footnote (9:35–10:14)
      a. King Saul's Family (9:35–44)
      b. King Saul's Fall (10:1–14)
II. The Chronicles of Judah's Kings (1 Chron. 11:1–2 Chron. 36:23)
  A. The Throne of David (1 Chron. 11:1–29:30)
    1. His Coronation (11:1–12:40)
    2. His Consecration (13:1–17:27)

a. Events Relating to Bringing the Ark to Jerusalem (13:1–16:43)
b. Events Relating to Building the Temple in Jerusalem (17:1–27)
3. His Conquests (18:1–20:19)
4. His Conceit (21:1–30)
5. His Concerns (22:1–29:30)
    a. For the Sanctuary (22:1–28:18)
      (1) Preliminary Orders (22:1–19)
      (2) Preparatory Organization (23:1–27:34)
      (3) Personal Offerings (28:1–18)
    b. For His Successor (28:19–29:30)
B. The Temple of Solomon (2 Chron. 1:1–9:31)
1. Solomon's Wisdom (1:1–13)
2. Solomon's Wealth (1:14–17)
3. Solomon's Works (2:1–8:6)
    a. The Building of the Temple (2:1–7:22)
    b. The Beautification of the City (8:1–6)
4. Solomon's Ways (8:7–9:31)
C. The Testimony of History (2 Chron. 10:1–36:23)
1. The Decline of Judah (10:1–36:21)
2. The Decree of Cyrus (36:22–23)

A survey of this great portion of Scripture will be best accomplished by looking at five different topics: incomplete registers, inspired religion, incompetent rulers, inconclusive revivals, and increasing rebellion.

1. INCOMPLETE REGISTERS

Chronicles begins with lists of names. Most of us never get past the first chapter when it comes to reading this book! Getting enthusiastic about the first nine chapters of Chronicles is like trying to get excited about reading the telephone book. It's even harder if you're marooned, a total stranger in a city where you don't know a soul, and where the only reading matter in the motel room is the telephone directory.

So what? Who cares? What is the point and purpose of all these names? Well, we know why the lists of names are in the telephone book, but why are they here, in the Bible? Why are there so many of them? Why nine chapters of names?

In the first place, God delights to write names into His Book—and we should be very glad that He does.

We must put ourselves in Ezra's shoes. He had a ministry particularly to that little remnant of hardy souls who had braved the hazards and dangers of the wilderness, the backbreaking toil of reconstruction, the bitter hostility of the Samaritans and others, in order to raise a new nation from the rubble of the past. But they were a discouraged crowd. They had come back under mandate of the king of Persia, but they were just a tiny dependency, a puny province in a vast empire. The Persian Empire stretched from the frontiers of Greece to the borders of India, from the Danube to the Nubian deserts—three thousand miles long and between five hundred and one thousand miles wide. It embraced an area of some two million square miles. In this huge empire, tiny little Judah was a mere smudge on the map.

Under agreement with the king of Persia, a handful of Jews had returned to build a national home on the sacred soil of Palestine. Their difficulties were enormous; but worse than that, they were a mere province in a vast Gentile world. Jerusalem was still under Gentile lordship despite the gallant show of independence. Once the first thrill of the return had worn off and the harsh realities of pioneering and opposition took hold, people began to have second thoughts.

As we have noted, Ezra's first aim was to show that, although the throne was gone, the royal line of David was intact. Hence the genealogies. But these registers are incomplete. Certainly, they trace the messianic purpose from Adam through Noah, Shem, Abraham, Isaac, Jacob, Judah, David, and Solomon to Zerubbabel. But what then? The registers are incomplete; they come to an end before the coming of the promised Messiah.

It is with a stroke of genius that the scribes who collected the Old Testament canon and who arranged it in the order in which the books are found in the Jewish Bible put *Chronicles last!* In the Hebrew Bible the book of Chronicles is not found in the historical section. It does not follow in sequence after the book of Kings. Rather, it concludes the Old Testament. The genealogies in Chronicles lead up to the genealogy in Matthew 1, which opens the New Testament. The Jew reading his Bible comes to this *incomplete register*. He turns to Matthew 1 and finds it completed there.

Down through the four hundred silent years between Malachi and Matthew, the royal line runs on—hidden from the eyes of men, ever preserved by the hand of God. It runs on and on until it exhausts itself in *Jesus of Nazareth*, the one and only rightful *King of the Jews*.

So, while this is a book of incomplete registers, their very incompleteness is a challenge. It is a challenge to cross the great divide and move on from the Old Testament to the New, from the kings of Judah to Him who is and ever will be *King of Kings* and *Lord of Lords*.

2. INSPIRED RELIGION

Chronicles is also a book of religion. We are, in fact, impressed with the amount of space devoted to the temple and its affairs in this book. And so many chapters are devoted to David. Why? Because David *conquered the empire* and *conceived the temple*. In David the messianic purposes of God found a new and sharper focus than ever before in Hebrew history. So many chapters, too, are devoted to Solomon. Why? Because Solomon *consolidated the empire* and *constructed the temple*. It was the greatest and most far-reaching event of his life.

David threw his influence, his insights, and his income behind the vision of a temple in Jerusalem, which would serve as a national focus for the Hebrew faith. Solomon translated David's dreams into massive blocks of stone, fitted with computer precision into an edifice greater than any of the heralded wonders of the world. David accumulated the treasure needed, Solomon activated the talent needed. So a temple was built, which stood there in Jerusalem for about three hundred and sixty years. It was God's plan that the temple should become the center of Israel's national life; instead it was soon neglected, even by Solomon. When the ten tribes set up a rival kingdom in the north, they took immediate steps to make the temple obsolete in the religious thinking of the northern kingdom.

Ezra records the fortunes of the temple during the remaining years. There were times when zealous kings tried to bring the temple back to where it belonged as the focal center of worship of the true and living God. Its smoking altar again pictured for the nation the great scene one day to be enacted on Calvary when God's beloved Son would become "the Lamb of God, which taketh away the sin of the world" (John 1:29).

But, for the most part, the temple was polluted with idols and pagan altars. Its purpose was forgotten, its courts fell into disrepair, a grieved Spirit left it a mere empty shell. And then the Babylonians came and burned it down.

Chronicles is a book of inspired religion—religion centered in a temple and in a sacrifice neglected and ignored by this chosen people, to its peril and to its doom.

3. Incompetent Rulers

Chronicles is also a book of wicked rulers. The book, though, ignores the evil kings who followed one another on the throne of the northern kingdom in Samaria. Nothing much could be expected of them. One and all, they followed in the ways of "Jeroboam the son of Nebat, who made Israel to sin" (1 Kings 22:52). It is a formula of apostasy appended to the name of each and *every* northern king.

David was the yardstick by which God measured the behavior of each successive king of Judah, which is why the book of Chronicles spends so much time on David. For despite his faults, falls, and failings, David was Israel's ideal king. He was a shepherd at heart; but he was also a soldier, a psalmist, a statesman, and a saint. He loved God, and not even his glaring sins could obscure that fact. The great burden of this book seems to be, "Oh! If only we could get back to David! If only the golden days of David could be restored. If only the kings of Judah not only sat on David's throne but ruled with David's heart."

One or two of them almost did. But most of them missed the mark entirely and many of them made no attempt at all to be like David, "a man after God's own heart" (see 1 Sam. 13:14). The gold standard of kingship was set forth in some of the chapters dealing with David's reign, then each king was silently and secretly weighed in that balance. And, for the most part, each king was found wanting. Except for one or two, all had departed from the gold standard to rule with the paper currency of waywardness or with the spurious coin of outright wickedness.

Solomon, for example. Solomon, with all his flair and showmanship, Israel's most splendid and spectacular king. Solomon with his wit and wisdom, his worship and his wealth; Solomon with his wives and worldliness and later shameful wickedness. Solomon with his magnificent buildings and with his magnanimous broadmindedness, and with his ultimate miserable backslidings. Solomon, whose early piety can only be matched by his later profligacy. Solomon, who built the empire to its greatest extent and who tore it to shreds with his own follies. Solomon, who built the temple in seven years and who then took nearly twice as long to build himself a palace. Solomon, who inaugurated his reign with a fantastic burnt offering and the longest prayer in the Bible; and who all but ended his days groveling at the cruel, vulgar, and filthy shrines he had built for his hundreds of pagan wives.

Consider, too, Rehoboam the Fool, who had a kingdom handed to him on a golden plate and a group of courtiers bequeathed to him as well—wise old men who had grown old in the wisdom of Solomon. Rehoboam, who spurned it all like an early George III because he thought that the "Divine Right of Kings" meant the right to tax unmercifully, unscrupulously, and unjustly those over whom he ruled. And who lost more than three-quarters of a kingdom in a bitter war of independence fought by those who resented him and his taxes and his tax collectors and all.

There was Jehoshaphat the Waverer, who thought he could curry favor both with God and man, and who tried to hold on to God with one hand and wicked Ahab of Israel with the other.

There was Athaliah the Foul, dread daughter of Jezebel, queen consort to the throne of Judah, who seized it for herself and baptized her reign with the massacre of all but one of the rightful claimants to David's throne.

There was Jehoash the Ungrateful, who owed an everlasting debt to a faithful priest for preserving for him both his scepter and his skin—and who paid his debt by making a martyr of that good priest's son.

There was Uzziah the Proud, who beat down Judah's foes with the edge of the sword and restored some of the faded and long-forgotten glories of the past to David's throne—and who then, like Lucifer, thought he could ascend his throne above the stars of God and rule as both king and priest, and who died a leper for his pains.

There was Ahaz the Fool, who founded his political insanities on seeking to befriend two sworn enemies at the same time, and who showed his scorn of God by refusing to accept a sign offered to him in God's name by Isaiah, the prophet.

There was Manasseh the Pagan, whose reign was baptized in filth at its beginning and in failure at its end.

There was Jehoiachin the Bad, whose chief claim to fame lies in that he managed, in three and one-half months, to do something no other king of Judah ever did—call down a curse from heaven upon the royal line to the Messiah through Solomon.

There was Jehoiakim the Bold, who tore up Jeremiah's prophecies with a penknife only to have them rewritten by the prophet with an added chapter containing a fearful personal judgment for the king himself.

There was Zedekiah the Faithless, who has the honor of being the king who presided over the final dissolution of the kingdom of Judah—the fruit of his own stubborn refusal to heed the inspired Word of God delivered through the mouth of the prophet Jeremiah.

No wonder the book of Chronicles seems to cry out for another David. And God, who breathed out the impassioned plea of this book, and who inspired the pen of that ready scribe, at last sent that second David—great David's greater Son, and all the rest of the Bible has to do with Him!

Incomplete registers, inspired religion, incompetent rulers! But there's more.

4. Inconclusive Revivals

Chronicles tells of half-accomplished reforms. There are a number of them in this book—at least eight—mini-revivals, most of them, it's true. There were two major revivals, one under Hezekiah, the friend of the prophet Isaiah, and one under Josiah, the friend of Jeremiah. But none of them had lasting effect. The nation never really saw a true spiritual awakening after the death of David. The two greatest revivals, after all, were revivals in the souls of the two kings who led them. They never touched the political leadership of the nation nor the rank and file of the common people. As soon as their sponsors were dead, back the people went to their old evil ways. Revival, after all is said and done, cannot be planned and organized and promoted by men, no matter how great and godly and sincere the men might be. Revival comes down from God.

The United States has seen a spiritual awakening or two in its time. And so has Britain. According to the historian W. E. H. Lecky,[2] who will not be suspected of any undue bias toward Christianity, Britain was saved from the bloodbath of the French Revolution, not by its superior system of government and not by the vigilance of its ships of the line, but by the spiritual awakening under the Wesleys. It was the revival under John and Charles Wesley that brought people to God and then purged the land of its moral and religious and political wrongs. Judah never saw a revival like that.

There is a lot of Christian activity in our day. There are some fine churches and Christian organizations doing a great deal of noble and commendable work and expending vast sums of money, effort, and skill in seeking to win souls to Christ. But we do not see revival. Ezra saw Judah's history as dotted with inconclusive revivals—not really revivals at all.

5. INCREASING REBELLION

Last of all, Chronicles is Judah's history in the light of rebellion. Of course! When a nation or an individual refuses to respond to the spiritual influences the Holy Spirit brings to bear, the result is always worse, blacker, and more hardened rebellion.

Ezra underscored the increasing rebellion of Judah. The people refused to repent, even when the northern kingdom of Israel was swept away in the Assyrian flood. "And the LORD God of their fathers," he says, "sent to them by his messengers, rising up betimes, and sending; because he had compassion on his people, and on his dwelling place: but they mocked the messengers of God, and despised his words, and misused his prophets, until the wrath of the LORD arose against his people, till there was no remedy" (36:15–16).

What was he doing, this faithful scribe, with his inspired pen, as he underlined again and again the stubborn rebellion of Israel against the Holy Scriptures and against the Holy Spirit? He was hammering at the conscience of that little returned remnant. "Don't rebel against God again!" was his plea. "As you look at the dreadful desolation of Jerusalem; as you rummage in the rubble of the temple, remember—rebellion lies at the root of all your national woes, rebellion against God and His Word." And did they heed? Not for long! God sent them one more prophet, Malachi by name. The last word in his prophecy was that ominous word "curse" (Mal. 4:6). It's the word that chronologically ends our Old Testament.

For God sent His Son into the world, at last; the One toward whom the incomplete registers pointed, the One called for by all those incompetent rulers; the One whose coming was at the heart of that inspired religion; the One yearned after in all those inconclusive revivals. And what did they do with Him, this people whose history was marked by increasing rebellion? They crucified Him. They called down, with their own lips, the curse of God upon themselves, and handed Him over to the Gentiles to be crucified.

CHAPTER 15

EZRA

The Godly Scribe

The captivity of Judah took place in three stages. In 605 B.C., Nebuchadnezzar first invaded the land and took away Jehoiakim and the leading nobles including Daniel. In 597 B.C., a second Babylonian invasion took place, and King Jehoiachin was carried away into captivity, together with most of the people of importance, including Ezekiel and the ancestors of Mordecai. In 586 B.C., the final destruction of Jerusalem took place. Zedekiah, the king of Judah, breaking his oath of allegiance to Nebuchadnezzar, entered into an alliance with Egypt to throw off the Babylonian yoke. The Babylonians came back, besieged Jerusalem and terrible scenes took place. At last the city was sacked, the temple burned, and the final deportation effected. The land began to make up for its neglected Sabbaths.

The return of the remnant at the end of the captivity was likewise in three movements. About the year 538 B.C., Cyrus the Persian issued the decree that gave the Jews liberty to return to Jerusalem and rebuild the temple. Led by Zerubbabel, a small group responded. In 458 B.C., a further group returned under the leadership of Ezra. This return was a whole generation later than the first. Then in the year 445 B.C., Nehemiah, a high official in the Persian court, was given permission to return to rebuild the walls of Jerusalem.

Two "exodus" movements occurred, then, in Old Testament history. The first was from Egypt to Canaan and the second was from Babylon to Canaan—with almost a millennium lying between the two events. Both these exiles and returns were the subject of prophecy, the first in Genesis 15:13–14, and the second in Jeremiah 25:11–12; 29:10–11.

Before looking at the books that deal with the return of the remnant, it will be helpful to see the entire period as a whole.

Cyrus the Great entered Babylon on October 29, 539 B.C. Following his policy of state, he encouraged the Jews to return to Palestine and rebuild their temple (2 Chron. 36:22–23; Ezra 1:1–4). The first movement back to the homeland was led by Zerubbabel, the son of Shealtiel (his Babylonian name was Sheshbazzar). As the firstborn of the exiled King Jehoiachin, Zerubbabel gives us an important messianic link between David and Joseph (Matt. 1).

Zerubbabel's contingent returned in 538 B.C. Included among the pioneers were Joshua the high priest and a goodly number of the priests, Levites, and heads of the tribes of Judah and Benjamin. Their first concern was to build an altar to the Lord on its old site and to restore the daily sacrifices (Ezra 2:1–3:3). Next they laid the foundations of the new temple in April or May 536 B.C. This work was helped by financial aid given by the Persian king. There was great rejoicing as the foundations of the temple were laid, although some of the older ones wept at the vanished glory of Solomon's temple (Ezra 3:8–13).

Work on the temple had not proceeded far before the Samaritans asked to have a share in the work. They were refused and henceforth did everything in their power to hinder and harass the builders. In their spite, the Samaritans hired lawyers to misrepresent the Jews at the Persian court. This brought the work to a halt so that no further progress was made during the remainder of the reign of Cyrus nor during the reigns of Cambyses and Smerdis (Ezra 4).

Zerubbabel does not seem to be entirely blameless in this stoppage for the difficulties could have been surmounted, and during the long sixteen-year suspension the settlers had no hesitation about building elaborate houses for themselves (Hag. 1:2–4).

On August 29, 520 B.C. Haggai began to exhort the Jews to resume work on the temple. His ministry was so effective that the Jews, under Zerubbabel and Joshua, began to work again on the temple. At this time, too, Zechariah began his ministry. As the work on the temple proceeded, Tattenai, a Persian governor, wrote to Darius I to challenge it. Darius made a search of the state records and found the decree of Cyrus in the library at Ecbatana and at once ordered the governor Tattenai to help the Jews in every way and to give them financial support. This was one time when "the law of the Medes and Persians, which altereth not" worked in the Jews' favor (Dan. 6:8).

In 519 Joshua the high priest was crowned by the prophet Zechariah. The highly symbolic ceremony looked forward to the day when the Messiah would unite the offices of priest and king in His own person (Zech. 6:9–15).

In 518 B.C. a delegation of Jews came down from Bethel to Jerusalem to ask the priests and prophets if it was needful to continue mourning and fasting over the destruction of Jerusalem. This became the occasion for an important message from the Lord through Zechariah (chaps. 7–8).

CHRONOLOGY OF THE REBUILDING OF THE TEMPLE			
Kings of Persia	**Important Events**	**Prophets**	**Work on Temple**
Cyrus 550–530	Entered Babylon 539 Cyrus's Decree 538 Zerubbabel 538		Temple foundation laid 536
Cambyses 530–521			
Smerdis 521			
Darius I Hystapses 521–486	Joshua priest 519	Haggai 520 Zechariah 520	Work resumed 520 Work finished 516
Xerxes 486–464	Deposed Vashti 483 Married Esther 478		
Artaxerxes 464–423	Ezra returns 458 Nehemiah leaves Persia 445 Nehemiah arrives in Jerusalem 444		

Work on the temple had now advanced to its completion. It was dedicated with much rejoicing in 516 B.C. in the sixth year of Darius. From the time the temple was finished in 516 until the time Ezra appears in 458, some fifty-eight years elapsed. The long and prosperous reign of the mighty Darius I Hystapses had come to an end. He had ruled the mightiest empire the world had ever seen—from the Grecian Archipelago in the west to Persia in the east. It comprised some two million square miles, Judah being an insignificant province.

Darius died in 486 B.C. and was followed on the throne by Xerxes, the king who deposed Vashti and then in the year 478 married Esther. In 464 B.C. Xerxes was succeeded by Artaxerxes I in whose reign Ezra and Nehemiah led more Jewish colonists back to the land of their fathers.

In 458 B.C., Ezra, under mandate from Artaxerxes, led the second group of exiles back. It should be remembered that since the book of Ezra describes both the return under Zerubbabel (chaps. 1–6) and the return under Ezra (chaps. 7–10) a period of fifty-eight years divides the two sections of the book. In other words, a period of fifty-eight years is covered between Ezra six and seven, and a period of eighty years between Ezra one and seven.

Twelve years after Ezra's expedition, Nehemiah was also given permission by Artaxerxes to go to Jerusalem. His commission in 445 B.C. was to rebuild the walls of Jerusalem. He was given a cavalry escort for the journey and letters of introduction to the various Persian governors along the way. He was also appointed governor of Judea. He arrived in Jerusalem in 444 B.C. in the twentieth year of Artaxerxes' reign and threw himself into the work with tireless energy. Despite the discouragements that faced him and the determined opposition of his enemies, he was able to complete his monumental task in just fifty-two days.

The wall being built, attention was next given to the instruction of the people, and a great religious revival followed. After governing Jerusalem for twelve years, Nehemiah returned to Persia about the year 433 B.C. Later he asked for a further leave of absence (Neh. 13:6) and returned to Jerusalem, where he seems to have ended his days.

I. The First Revival (20 years; 538 B.C.): God Used a Prince
    Emphasis: Divine Sovereignty in Revival (chaps. 1–6); there are six movements marked by the following:
    A. Waking (chaps. 1–2)
    B. Worshipping (3:1–4)
    C. Working (3:8–13)
    D. Warring (chap. 4)
        1. Subtle Opposition (4:1–3)
        2. Straightforward Opposition (4:4–24)
    E. Witnessing (chap. 5)
    F. Winning (chap. 6)
II. The Further Revival (1 year; 458 B.C., 58 years later): God Used a Priest
    Emphasis: Human Sanctity in Revival (chaps. 7–10)
    A. The Man (chap. 7)
    B. The Movement (chap. 8)
        1. Ezra's Perfect Trust in God
        2. Ezra's Precautionary Trust in Man
    C. The Mistake (chaps. 9–10)
        1. Confessed (9:1–10:2)
        2. Corrected (10:3–44)

Zerubbabel was a descendant of David and the only person of royal blood to return at this time. Daniel's great age and his enormous influence and importance in Babylon doubtless hindered him from joining this second exodus.

It is likely that the young Zerubbabel was well-known to the aged Daniel. It may well be that Zerubbabel's hopes for an end to the exile and his own desire to lead a return to the Promised Land were first fired by Daniel. Many Jews had long since accommodated themselves to the exile. The vast Persian Empire was a great place to do business! Zerubbabel was not impressed by that kind of thing. "What about the Promised Land?" he would demand.

One can picture a conversation between the eager young man and the revered old prophet Daniel.

"Zerubbabel, I have been reading the words of the late Jeremiah and have been much in prayer. It seems to me that the captivity must end. The Scriptures say so, but how? That's what perplexes me. The time is at hand but I see no signs."

We can see the youthful prince Zerubbabel lean forward with an eager face. "You mean, my lord Daniel, that the prophet Jeremiah predicted an end to the captivity?"

"That is so, my son," says the prophet Daniel, "and the time is at hand."

"Perhaps, my lord, you should show the prophecy to the emperor."

"It is a worthy thought, my son. I will ask the Lord about it."

The godly prophet is about to move away, but he has caught fire to the imagination of the young man. The young Zerubbabel rises from his seat and hurries after the departing man of God.

"My lord! Tell me—do you think that Cyrus will restore the kingdom to Israel?"

"He has to restore it in some degree, my boy. The Scriptures say so and the Scriptures cannot be broken."

"My lord, I am Zerubbabel. I stand in direct line to the throne of David. Do you think the emperor will give the kingdom of Judah to me?"

We can see the aged prophet look with fresh interest at the eager young man.

"My son, your father is Pedaiah. Your mother is the widow of Shealtiel, through whom you have legal title to the throne of David. But you will never sit upon that throne, my son. Your grandfather Jeconiah was the last of his line ever to be named a king. The prophet Jeremiah has said so."

"Then I cannot be king even though Cyrus restores the kingdom to Israel?"

"No, my son. When Cyrus restores the Promised Land to Israel it will not be a kingdom he restores, only a dependency. The kingdom has failed until the coming of Christ. But, my boy, if you cannot be a king, you can be a leader among our people, a spiritual prince and a great man. I shall pray to this end that God will make you, Zerubbabel, a leader of the people of Israel in these momentous times."

And so it came to pass that when Cyrus the Persian made his historic decree, Zerubbabel, a prince of the house of Judah, obtained favor in the sight of the king. He was appointed the first governor of the reborn land of Israel and was invested with the power to lead back to the Promised Land the first group of pioneers. And

Joshua, the high priest, became the religious leader. The story of it is recorded by Ezra the scribe. For the book of Ezra is not the book of Ezra alone, it is the book of Zerubbabel the prince as much as it is the book of Ezra the priest.

The actual number of Jews who responded when Cyrus signed his edict was very small. There were only thirty-three family groups, together with four groups of priests and some Levites. In all, only about fifty thousand people wanted to go back to Palestine—a very small remnant indeed when one considers that thousands upon thousands of Jews were scattered far and wide throughout the new Persian domain.

One reason the response was small related to the journey itself. It was long and hazardous, the path filled with perils. There were some 700 miles to be covered, with the repatriate traveling daily for about five months.

Moreover, the majority of Jews preferred the land of plenty to the land of promise. Babylon looked good to them. Revival is disturbing, upsetting, life-changing. Perhaps that is why history records so few.

The first contingent to return was led by Zerubbabel. About eighty years later the priest-scribe Ezra led an even smaller group back. The book of Ezra is concerned with these two movements among the Jewish exiles, with the narrative moving straight from the return under Zerubbabel to the return under Ezra. The historical gap is ignored.

I. THE FIRST REVIVAL (20 YEARS; 538 B.C.): GOD USED A PRINCE

Emphasis: Divine Sovereignty in Revival (chaps. 1–6)

Of the six movements to be discerned in these six chapters, the first can be summed up by the word *waking*.

A. Waking (chaps. 1–2)

Israel outside of the Promised Land was outside the place of blessing. Before God could make good His promises to this people, He had to bring them back to the place where He could bless them. They had to get back to Canaan. The tragedy was that so few responded.

The first movement was one of waking—the waking up of at least some to respond to this historic movement of God in history. We read, "Then rose up the chief of the fathers of Judah . . . all them whose spirit God had raised, to go . . ." (1:5). There were plenty of people willing to give money when they saw God at work. We read, "And all they that were about them strengthened their hands with vessels of silver, with gold, with goods . . . with precious things willingly offered" (1:6). God makes note of that as He makes note of any gesture made toward Himself, but He reserved His blessing for those who went. So there was a *waking* movement. We note that God devotes almost a whole chapter to writing down the names of those who responded to the Spirit's call. God will not allow their names to be forgotten. God always honors those who honor Him.

The second movement can be summed up in the word *worshipping*.

B. Worshipping (3:1–4)

When God begins to revive a human heart, true worship is always the result. "From the first day of the seventh month," we read, "began they to offer burnt offerings unto the Lord" (3:6). Of the five different types of offering that were commanded under the Mosaic Law, the burnt offering was the one that spoke particularly of worship. It was all for God, an expression of personal appreciation to God for His kindness and His love. We also read that they kept the Feast of Tabernacles. Again, there were seven feasts, which by edict of the Mosaic Law were to be kept annually, but the great Feast of Tabernacles was the happiest of them all. The burnt offering brought joy to the heart of God; the Feast of Tabernacles brought joy to the heart of men. Thus revival resulted in worship.

The third movement is summed up in the word *working*.

C. Working (3:8–13)

"Now in the second year of their coming unto the house of God in Jerusalem, in the second month, began Zerubbabel . . . and Joshua . . . to set forward the work of the house of the Lord . . ." (v. 8). Worship is always followed by service. God's work goes forward. The house of the Lord was rebuilt. We read, "And all the people shouted with a great shout, when they praised the Lord, because the foundation of the house of the Lord was laid" (3:11). Then we read, "And the noise was heard afar off" (v. 13). It was not long before the world took note that something was happening among the people of God. You cannot keep revival a secret!

The next step follows logically. Working was followed by *warring*.

D. Warring (chap. 4)

The revival among the people of God soon ran into opposition from the world.

1. Subtle Opposition (4:1–3)

At first the opposition took the form of *proffered help*. This kind of opposition is difficult to detect and difficult to defeat. How do you turn down proffered help from a seemingly well-meaning but unsaved and unsanctified individual? But nothing will stop a spiritual movement faster than accepting help from those who are not moved by the Spirit of God. The Lord does not need the world's money, manpower, methods, mentality, or management. Zerubbabel was wise enough to detect the danger of accepting unsanctified help. At the risk of deeply offending those who wanted to do God's work without first getting into God's family, the leader of the movement declined the offered help.

This resulted in the second kind of opposition.

2. Straightforward Opposition (4:4–24)

It took the form of *persistent hindrance*. The unsaved threw off all pretense and did everything in their power to oppose the revival of God's people. No tactic was too base or despicable. And it looked as if they were successful. We read, "Then ceased the work" (4:24). But not for long! The next movement in this work of revival can be summed up by the word *witnessing*.

E. Witnessing (chap. 5)

"Then," we read, "the prophets, Haggai . . . and Zechariah . . . prophesied unto the Jews that were in Judea and Jerusalem in the name of the God of Israel. . . . Then rose up Zerubbabel . . . and Jeshua . . . and began to build the house of God . . . and with them were the prophets of God helping them" (5:1–2). The opposition did not stop. Indeed, it became more vehement and vocal than ever, but God's people simply left the opposition to God and went on with the work.

Revival, in other words, was now guided by the inspired Word of God. It is easy for a new movement of the Spirit of God to be taken over by the sensationalists. It must be anchored not to emotion but to truth. So we see that this new work for God was both guided and guarded by the Word of God. Haggai and Zechariah were sent along to give the warrant of God's Word to what was happening among God's people. The Bible will save us from pseudo-revival and from false emotionalism and from Satanic delusion. Any so-called work for God *must* square with what God has to say in His Word.

The last movement in this first revival can be summed up by the word *winning*.

F. Winning (chap. 6)

The work of the temple was finished. God's house had been raised again out of the ruin and rubble of over seventy years. "And they builded, and finished it," we read, "according to the commandment of the God of Israel, and according to the commandment of Cyrus, and Darius, and Artaxerxes king of Persia" (6:14). Thus, men ruled, but God overruled in the affairs of His people. Three kings on earth and one in heaven, the King eternal, immortal, invisible, were all involved in these happenings. And the will of that great eternal King was done on earth as it is in heaven. Human hatred, scorn, hindrance, and intrigue might ebb and flow, but nothing could hinder what was evidently a work of God.

Human nature remains, however, human nature. Even such a great revival as this, such a historic movement of God upon the stage of human history—even that could not last. No revival has ever lasted. Within a generation was needed a fresh visitation of the Spirit of God.

Hundreds of churches and Christian organizations attest to the fact that a *movement* that ceases to move becomes a *monument*. So we move on from Ezra 6 to Ezra 7, remembering as we do that we pass over about fifty-eight years. To this interim period belongs the story of Esther. In this period were fought the great battles of Marathon, Thermopylae, and Salamis. In the distant East occurred the deaths of Confucius and Buddha. The Holy Spirit ignores all the secular side of things and brings us to another movement.

II. THE FURTHER REVIVAL (1 YEAR; 458 B.C., 58 YEARS LATER): GOD USED A PRIEST

Emphasis: Human Sanctity in Revival (chaps. 7–10)

This time we observe just three simple steps. The Holy Spirit focuses on the man, the movement, and the mistake.

A. The Man (chap. 7)

The man God chose to use was the man who later sat down, under the inspiration of the Holy Spirit, and chronicled for us the story of this book. The man was Ezra, Israel's high priest. His pedigree is traced right back to Aaron, Israel's first high priest, underlining for us one of the basic lessons of this book.

No permanent work can be done for God that does not find its ultimate center in God's Great High Priest. God's Great High Priest today is the Lord Jesus Christ. No religious movement can prosper that does not give Him the central place; everything must be traced back to Him. God has no plans, no programs, no promises, no prospects for this earth that are not centered in the person and work of His beloved Son.

Nearly sixty years had elapsed since Zerubbabel—under the inspiring preaching of Haggai and Zechariah—put the final capstone on the revival God had used him to lead by finishing the temple in Jerusalem. But sixty years is a long time in human history. A generation passes away, another generation takes its place and waxes old and prepares to hand over to the grandchildren. Spiritual realities, purchased at high cost by the grandparents, very often come cheap and easy to the grandchildren. It is not often that the third generation has the fervor and the fire of the first for a rediscovered spiritual truth or a tremendous spiritual awakening. It has become history.

In Israel, in the Promised Land, spiritual truth had worn thin. The Scriptures had been much neglected, and the people were occupied largely with material things. Much that had been purchased so dearly by the grandparents was taken for granted. It was time for a second work of grace. So God found a man, Ezra by name, a man addicted to the book of God. Ezra determined to make that book the center of his life and he did so along three lines. Ezra prepared his heart to "*seek* the law of the LORD, and to *do it*, and to *teach*" it (v. 10). In other words, he decided to ponder the Word of God, to practice the Word of God, and to preach the Word of God. So God put His hand upon Ezra and used him. He became a second Moses to the Hebrew people and led the further revival of those stirring times.

B. The Movement (chap. 8)

Ezra's move from Babylon to Jerusalem was not an isolated move. He took others with him. And, again, God delights to write into His Book the names of those who responded to this second moving of the Holy Spirit. We note, too, that this great movement was spearheaded by a number of influential people in the community, each of whom not only responded to the tug of eternity in his own soul but each one of whom had an impact on those they normally influenced. This was a movement of the Spirit of God that attracted men gifted to lead.

Not all revivals are like that. Indeed, God has said that "not many mighty, not many noble, are called" (1 Cor. 1:26). But occasionally the upper classes do respond. During a period of revival years ago, one titled lady said she was thankful to God for one single letter of the alphabet, the letter "M." She was glad, she said, that God had said not *many* noble, instead of not *any* noble.

The movement led by Ezra attracted men of influence and these, in turn, attracted others. An evidence of the outright sincerity of the people who responded is indicated in the great fast Ezra called before the group left for the Promised Land. He explained it like this: "that we might afflict ourselves before our God, to seek of him a right way for us, and for our little ones, and for all our substance" (v. 21). They brought the matter of their *footsteps*, their *families*, and their *finances* to God in earnest prayer. Then, in bold faith, they refused the escort the king wished to provide for them. "For I was ashamed," says Ezra, "to require of the king a band of soldiers and horsemen to help us against the enemy in the way: because we had spoken unto the king, saying, The hand of our God is upon all them for good that seek him; but his power and his wrath is against all them that forsake him" (v. 22).

Ezra had been witnessing to the king about the greatness of God, and he was not about to water down that witness just for the sake of an armed escort. But if Ezra had a perfect trust in God, he had only a partial trust in men. A very large offering had been donated to help forward the work of God. Ezra was a spiritual man; he was also a sensible man. The two do not always go together. Like a wise man, he carefully weighed the treasure to those who were to transport it and let them know it was to be weighed again at the other end. He did not say, "Well, brother, you look like an honest man. You take this." He acted in a businesslike way, which removed temptation from one and all.

C. The Mistake (chaps. 9–10)

Times of spiritual awakening always result in the exposure of sin. The people who had been born in the land after the first revival had soon lost sight of a basic spiritual truth—often one of the first spiritual truths to be abandoned in the wake of a revival. They lost sight of the truth of separation from the world. When Ezra came, the breath of a further revival conviction set in. Ezra says, "The princes came to me saying, The people of Israel, and the priests, and the Levites, have not separated themselves from the people of the lands, doing according to their abominations. . . . And when I heard this thing, I rent my garment" (9:1, 3). Ezra had not been poking and prying into affairs. The Spirit of God had. The result was conviction and confession of sin.

As a result the people sought to get right with God, and the unholy alliances that had been formed with the ungodly were dissolved. The pain, the cost, the heartache notwithstanding, the people broke off the liaisons they had formed with the world. It was the price of continuing revival.

Ezra saw that quite clearly, which is why he insisted that at all costs the people cut loose from their worldly entanglements and separate themselves solely for God. It was the price of revival. It is the price God still demands.

CHAPTER 16

NEHEMIAH

God's Statesman

Aftcr thc Pcntatcuch, the historical books of the Old Testament begin with Joshua and end with Nehemiah and Esther, and span a period of about one thousand years. To equate the nation of Israel under Nehemiah with the nation under Joshua would be like comparing England under William the Conqueror (1066) with England under Winston Churchill (mid 1900s).

A thousand years is a long time in any nation's history. During that vast millennium the prophets spoke, the psalmists sang, the sages raised their voices. During that millennium Egypt passed away as a world power and so did Assyria and Babylon. During that millennium the great men of the heathen nations appeared—Confucius and Buddha, Hesiod and Herodotus, Pericles and Plato. During that period the great men of Israel appeared, Moses died, Joshua conquered Canaan, David reigned, Solomon came and went with all his glory, Isaiah and Jeremiah, Ezekiel and Daniel prophesied and preached with passion and power.

Nehemiah now comes on the scene, twelve years after Ezra went to Jerusalem to effect his reforms. Zerubbabel went to Jerusalem under decree of Cyrus the Persian in 538 B.C. Ezra went eighty years later, and Nehemiah twelve years after that. Zerubbabel went to bring about *religious* reforms; Ezra went to bring about much needed *moral* reforms; Nehemiah went to bring about *political* reforms. Zerubbabel was a prince of the house of Judah, Ezra was a priest of the family of Aaron and a scribe, Nehemiah was a nobody—that is, his ancestry is unknown. All we know is that he was the son of one Hachaliah and the brother of Nanani—and that does not tell us anything at all.

We know he was the king's cupbearer. The king was Artaxerxes Longimanus, who reigned over the Persian Empire for forty years. The king's cupbearer, in oriental courts, was usually a man chosen for his handsome appearance and for his attractive personality. His task was to taste the wine before it was passed to the king. He was a man greatly trusted, a man with frequent access to the royal presence and, consequently, a man of great influence. Oriental cupbearers were always persons of rank and importance.

Such a man was Nehemiah. A careful study of Nehemiah's character as it is revealed in his words and deeds indicates a man of deep religious conviction, unafraid of hard work, fearless in the face of danger, and a zealous patriot—a fact all the more amazing when it is remembered that he was born in captivity and had never seen Palestine. He was, moreover, a man of wisdom and integrity, marked by generosity and unselfishness, focused energy, and one not bashful, either, about asserting physical force where he thought it would help or where his passions were aroused. Such was Nehemiah.

With personal attributes like that he did not have to rely upon a family tree to give him status and standing in the halls of the Hebrew great. Without the work he effected in Jerusalem, it is doubtful if the struggling, fledgling, pioneer state could have survived—despite the noble work of Zerubbabel and Ezra and the prophets Haggai and Zechariah.

We need to remind ourselves of the political situation that faced the newborn nation of Israel when Nehemiah arrived in Jerusalem. In the twelve years between Ezra's return to the Promised Land and the arrival of Nehemiah, great changes had taken place. The Syrian satrap had so successfully defied his royal master, the Persian emperor, that Artaxerxes Longimanus had been forced to concede to his satrap's own conditions for peace. This is the first sign we have of internal decay within the mighty empire of Persia. Deprived, thus, of royal support, Ezra's position as governor of Judea became untenable. The Samaritans stepped up their harassment of the state, the walls of the city remained unbuilt, Ezra ceased to be governor, and the people were in great affliction and under constant reproach. The Arabs, Israel's enemies then as now, had moved their hostile camps close to Jerusalem. Sanballat and his allies seemed to be all-powerful. Priests and people alike had gone back to their foreign wives.

When Nehemiah was first exercised about going to the Promised Land, the restored remnant had been back there for over ninety years. Zerubbabel and his pioneers had passed away, and another generation had taken their place. Conditions were very bad. Some of the poorer Jews had been forced to mortgage themselves to their wealthier compatriots. The temple had been rebuilt on a much inferior scale, but already neglect of the Sabbath was a common thing. Nehemiah heard about it all from Hanani, his brother.

At this point we need to get before us an outline of the book of Nehemiah.

I. The Work of Construction (chaps. 1–6)

These chapters have to do with Nehemiah's arrival in Jerusalem and with the subsequent building of the broken walls of the city. Nebuchadnezzar's armies had done a thorough job of demolishing the defenses of Jerusalem. A century and a half of neglect had reduced those once-mighty walls to heaps of rubble overgrown with shrubs and weeds and trees.

A. The Sad Tidings (chap. 1)

It would seem that Nehemiah's brother had been living in Jerusalem; for how long we do not know. But, along with others, he was sent up to the Persian capital, probably by Ezra, to bring information about the condition of the Jews in the pioneer state. The fact that Hanani's brother, Nehemiah, was one of the few men who had the ear of the king was probably why he was sent. He brought with him a tale of woe.

Nehemiah's first act did not involve rushing off to the king and trading upon his position as the king's cupbearer. That might have been the "sensible" thing to do; it was certainly not the spiritual thing to do, and Nehemiah did the spiritual thing. He had the ear of the king, but more important, he had the ear of God. He fasted and prayed before the God of heaven. He knew only too well that the best way to get things done on earth was to get God's will from heaven. He presented his case to a greater King than Artaxerxes Longimanus. He fasted and prayed, in fact, for four months (1:1–2:1).

We say, "Four months! What a waste of time!" Not so. Nehemiah knew enough about Eastern despots to know how much hung upon a throw of the dice. He would prefer to wait for God to move the heart of the king and give him the natural opening to speak of Jerusalem, Judea, and the Jews rather than risk everything by catching the king in a wrong mood.

B. The Simple Testimony (chap. 2)

Four months of fasting and prayer left their mark upon Nehemiah's face. One day, as he was serving wine to the emperor, the king suddenly noticed.

"Nehemiah! What's the matter? You look sad!" (see v. 2). That was a capital offense in those days—to look sad in the presence of the king. Nehemiah confessed he was afraid; nevertheless, this was the opening for which he had been praying.

"Let the king live forever," he cried, "why should not my countenance be sad, when the city, the place of my fathers' sepulchers, lieth waste, and the gates thereof are consumed with fire?" (v. 3). It was a simple testimony, but effective. The king's interest was evident.

"For what dost thou make request?" he asked (v. 4).

Nehemiah tells us what happened next. He says, "So I prayed to the God of heaven. And I said unto the king, If it please the king, and if thy servant have found favor in thy sight, . . . send me unto Judah, unto the city of my fathers' sepulchers, that I may build it" (vv. 4–5).

Notice that "So I prayed to the God of heaven. And I said unto the king . . ." That is what Guy King[1] calls "a sky telegram" and what my father used to call "the upward glancing of the eye." We can be quite sure that when Nehemiah says that he prayed to the God of heaven, there in the presence of the king, with the whole business of empire suspended so that he might make his request, his prayer was not half an hour long. He sent up a sky telegram. "Now's the time, Lord!" "Speak through me, Lord!" Something like that. But remember, that sky telegram was backed by four solid months of persistent prayer.

The king at once granted Nehemiah's selfless request. Think of what he was giving up—the most influential and coveted post in the empire—to go hauling stones and bricks in far-off, beleaguered Palestine. It would be as though Benjamin Disraeli, the brilliant Jewish Prime Minister of England in the heyday of Britain's far-flung empire, were to have resigned his office to go and dig ditches with a handful of Jews of Palestine.

He arrived in Jerusalem with letters signed by the king. His arrival infuriated two men. One was an unsavory character by the name of Sanballat, said by Josephus to be the satrap of Samaria, and the other was a toady named Tobiah, called "the servant," probably a kind of secretary to Sanballat. These two men were greatly grieved because "there was come [to Jerusalem] a man to seek the welfare of the children of Israel" (v. 10).

Nehemiah rested up for three days after his strenuous journey, then, by night, he surveyed the dimensions of the task by taking a ride around the broken walls of the city. As a result, he called a conference of the leading people of the city. He set before them a twofold plan for reviving the people of God, and for restoring to its former influence and grandeur the place where God had put His name.

The first plan involved *work*. "Let us rise up and build," he said (v. 18). The Samaritans heard about it and roared with laughter.

The second plan involved *witness*. The Samaritans, having mocked Nehemiah and "these feeble Jews" (4:2), next challenged Nehemiah's authority. They accused him of inciting rebellion against the king. He disdained to answer their slanders. "The God of heaven," was all he said, "he will prosper us" (2:20). So, whether to the king on the throne, the people of the land, or the enemies at the gates, Nehemiah's simple testimony was the same. He testified to the God of heaven.

C. The Strenuous Task (chap. 3)

Chapter 3 gives us some idea of the dimension of the overwhelming task. Nehemiah, however, was a clever and capable organizer. He divided the wall into sections, each section running from one gate to the next. Each section was assigned to a different work party; all sections were to be built simultaneously. It was imperative that the work be carried out with the utmost urgency and expedition so that the enemies might not have enough time to organize too formidable a resistance. There were forty-two different work parties, and each worked on the section of the wall nearest to where he lived. This was good psychology and it worked.

The book of Nehemiah stands in the Bible as a permanent rebuke to those who imagine that any kind of organization of God's work is wrong. Spirituality plus organization plus hard work all played a part in Nehemiah's success. And successful he was. The work was finished in fifty-two days—just seven and one-half weeks! Indeed, from the time he received his mandate from Artaxerxes to the time he completed the main part of his work, only six months elapsed. It just shows what can be done when God's people are a praying people and a planning people and a productive people.

D. The Successive Tests (chaps. 4–6)

It all sounds so easy in the summary in chapter 3, just as when missionaries come home with glowing accounts, sometimes, of great successes on the field. But nothing goes on for God in this world that Satan does not actively oppose, and he is a resourceful foe. If one tactic does not succeed in stopping the work, he'll try another. So the next three chapters tell of the various types of opposition with which Nehemiah had to contend.

There was opposition from *without*—scorn, force, and guile. There was opposition from *within*—rubbish, fear, and greed. "What do these feeble Jews?" taunted the foe. But when they saw that scoffing failed to hinder the work, they resorted to more active means.

1. The Enemy Without (chap. 4)

Mutual enemies became mutual friends in opposing the work. Sanballat and Tobiah and the Samaritans teamed up with Arabs, Ammonites, and people from former Philistine territory around Ashdod. All joined forces against the Jews. Nehemiah's answer was to arm the workers. We are reminded of Oliver Cromwell's famous dictum: "Trust in God and keep your powder dry."[2] Ridicule, rubbish, and resistance all failed to daunt Nehemiah.

2. The Enemy Within (chaps. 5–6)

There was *greed* (chap. 5). Some of the more wealthy Jews were exploiting their weaker and poorer brethren, and this came closer to wrecking the work than anything. If Satan cannot destroy a revival by opposition from without, he will try to wreck it from within by stimulating the natural selfishness of the human heart— even the heart of the brother in Christ.

Then there was *guile* (chap. 6). The enemy tried to persuade Nehemiah to come down off the wall for a conference. "I am doing a great work," he replied, "why should the work cease, whilst I leave it, and come down to you?" (6:3).

Thus it is that the first seven chapters set before us the great work of *construction*. But rebuilding the bulwarks against the foe was only part of Nehemiah's task.

II. The Work of Consecration (chaps. 7–10)

This was an even more important work. A revival is only as strong, after all, as the work it accomplishes in the hearts of men and women. We can do all the building we want, but if the heart is not right, then nothing will last. So Nehemiah joined forces with Ezra the scribe to ensure that a work of lasting grace be done in the hearts of the people. There were three steps in this work of consecration.

A. The Beloved Congregation (chap. 7)

Here the names of God's people are written into God's Book. God's chief concern in this world is people. We must never get so taken up with the program that we overlook the people.

B. The Bible Conference (chap. 8)

We are told how it was *convened* and how it was *conducted* and how it was *concluded* and how it was *continued*. The emphasis was placed on the public reading of the Word of God. Any revival not solidly based on Bible doctrine is suspect from the start. Revival is usually an emotional time. Hearts are stirred, consciences are ripped open, sins are confessed, tears are shed, joy fills the heart, wrongs are righted. There is a great deal of emotion, but emotionalism is no solid basis for a continuing work. Indeed, unless the work is undergirded by the Word of God it will soon lead to unscriptural excess.

So Nehemiah brought in the Bible teacher. "And Ezra," we read, "opened the book in the sight of all the people" (v. 5). "So," we are told, "they read in the book in the law of God distinctly . . . and caused them to understand the reading" (v. 8).

C. The Bitter Confession (chaps. 9–10)

The people assembled, under deep conviction of the Holy Spirit brought about by reading the Word of God, to search their hearts in God's presence. They humbled themselves before God as the great God of *creation*, the God who made everything from stars to seas.

They humbled themselves before God as the great God of *covenant*, the God who chose Abraham and made him an unconditional promise. They prayed to the God who put up with the sins and apostasies of Abraham's descendants for generation after generation with unwearied patience. "Neither," they cried, "have our kings, our princes, our priests, nor our fathers, kept thy law, nor hearkened unto thy commandments" (9:34).

The bitter confession ended with a plea and a pledge. "We are in great distress," they cried. "And because of all this we make a sure covenant, and write it; and our princes, Levites, and priests, seal unto it" (9:37–38). And sign it they did. And Nehemiah copied the names of those signers into the tenth chapter of his book.

Such was the period of consecration. God had spoken through His Word. His Word had searched the souls of men. Men had come under conviction, and they pledged that henceforth they would order their lives according to the demands and

dictates of God's Word. That is revival. Revival is not thrills and chills and bab-
bling and boasting. Revival is getting right with God—individuals, communities,
a whole nation. It is what the world needs to see today.

III. THE WORK OF CONSOLIDATION (CHAPS. 11–13)

Sensible steps were taken to consolidate the great spiritual gains that had been won.
We are told, first, how this work of consolidation began.

A. How It Was Commenced (11:1–12:26)

There are two distinct emphases in this section.

1. Responsiveness (11:1–36)

The first thing Nehemiah did was to make sure the city of Jerusalem was popu-
lated. A census was taken, then one person out of every ten was chosen by lot to
take up residence in the new city. So deep and effective was the work of consecration that those who were thus chosen "willingly offered" (11:2) to accept their new
status. And the people of the land applauded this public-spirited move. It was no
doubt a costly move. It would mean giving up homes and businesses in other parts
of the country, and there is no hint of financial remuneration. One of the first
evidences of a true work of the Holy Spirit in a person's life is sacrifice of material
advantage, and unselfishness.

2. Responsibility (12:1–26)

There follows a fresh listing of the priests and Levites, to emphasize the importance God placed on spiritual leadership among His people. God's people are
consistently viewed in their relation to one another and to God-ordained elders and
leaders. God places no premium on a spirit of independence and self-will.

The unwary reader needs to be warned of a fault in the chapter divisions of
the Bible here. Between verses 26 and 27 of chapter 12, there is a break of several
years. It is a pity that those who divided the Bible into chapters and verses did not
recognize this and give us a new chapter. Between these two verses, after the great
revival and the initial work of consolidation, Nehemiah kept his promise to his
royal master in Persia and went back to make report to his king. We are not told
how long he stayed there but it was evidently long enough for the revival to have
lost its hold on the people. The text passes over this period of Nehemiah's absence
from Jerusalem, passing directly from telling us how the work of consolidation was
commenced to telling us how the work of consolidation was finished.

B. How It Was Completed (12:27–13:31)

The walls of the city were finally dedicated. The temple worship was put back into good order and then Nehemiah turned his attention to the serious lapses of godly order that had crept in during his absence.

He discovered, for instance, that the sanctuary was being defiled by the high priest, Eliashib. He was somehow related to that archenemy of Israel, Tobiah the Ammonite, and had so far degraded his office as spiritual leader of God's people as to make room in one of the temple chambers for some of Tobiah's "stuff." The indignant Nehemiah tossed the stuff out of the temple and ordered the chamber to be cleaned.

Just as bad, if not worse, the high priest had permitted one of his grandsons to marry the daughter of Sanballat the Horonite in direct defiance of God's Word. The indignant Nehemiah chased the young priest off the premises.

More, he found the Jews desecrating the Sabbath, turning God's day of rest into another day for business. He put a speedy end to that.

Then he found that, after all they had learned of God's will, the Jews had actually once again contracted marriages with the ungodly. Nehemiah angrily seized some of the offenders by the hair and pulled it out by the roots! Nobody had any doubts as to where Nehemiah stood when it came to the honor and glory of God.

Many are the lessons that can be learned from this book. Let us conclude with one—perhaps the grandest statement that fell from the lips of this vigorous and dedicated servant of God. When his enemies urged him to leave what he was doing, come down, and parley with them, he replied, "I am doing a great work . . . why should the work cease while I leave it and come down to you?" (6:3) We pass over the centuries and stand upon Golgotha's brow. The Satan-inspired leaders cried to the dying Christ, "Come down from the cross" (Matt. 27:42). He said nothing. Their taunt had been answered long ago: "I am doing a great work . . . why should the work cease while I leave it and come down to you?"

CHAPTER 17

ESTHER

God's Providence

The book of Esther is one of the two books in the Bible named after women. Ruth was a Gentile woman who married a Jew; Esther was a Jewish woman who married a Gentile. The events recorded in the book of Esther took place between the books of Ezra and Nehemiah.

GOD'S NAME HIDDEN IN THE LAND OF EXILE

The book describes events that took place at Susa, the principal Persian capital. The actors are either Persians, or Jews of the dispersion. No mention is made of Palestine, Jerusalem, the temple, the law of Moses, or general Hebrew history. The Persian king is mentioned many times in the book, though God is not mentioned at all. None of the titles for God in general use among the Jews are to be found, neither Elohim nor Jehovah nor Shaddai nor Adonai.

This is all the more remarkable considering that the Persian king is mentioned 192 times in 167 verses. His kingdom is referred to 26 times and his name, Ahasuerus, is given 29 times.

God had warned His people that if they forsook Him, He would hide His face from them (Deut. 31:16–18). Here this threat was fulfilled. But even though He was hidden from them He was still working for them. Satan was at work, through Haman, to exterminate the chosen people and thus prevent the birth of the Christ. God was likewise at work to frustrate Satan's scheme. But God's work was secret—therefore His name (Jehovah) is hidden secretly in the book.

This secret hiding of God's name in the book of Esther is not evident in the English Bible. In the Hebrew Bible it is found in the words:

1. All the wives shall give (1:20).
2. Let the king and Haman come this day (5:4).
3. This availeth me nothing (5:13).
4. That there was evil determined against him (6:7).
   In the Hebrew Bible these words appear as acrostics in which are exhibited the name JEHOVAH.
   There is another such hidden acrostic:
5. Who is he and where is he (7:5)?
   This acrostic exhibits the divine title "I AM" rather than the name JEHOVAH.

GOD'S PEOPLE COMFORTABLE IN THE LAND OF EXILE

Half a century earlier, the Persian king Cyrus had issued a proclamation permitting the Jews to return to Palestine. That proclamation was a direct fulfillment of prophecy (Isa. 44:28; Jer. 25:11–12; 29:10). Not a Jew should have remained in Persia, "not a hoof should have been left behind" (see Exod. 10:26).

Comparatively speaking, however, not many of the Jews responded to God's great movement in history, opening the door for them to return to the Promised Land. Not more than about fifty thousand went, followed in the days of Ezra by about six hundred more. Most of the captives had been born in Babylon. Conditions were congenial there, and they were well settled, accepted, and influential. Why trade their comforts for the rigors of pioneering in Palestine? They had it too good in Babylon. (A similar situation exists with American Jews today.)

To a people that had largely ignored His activity on their behalf, God remained largely concealed.

GOD'S PEOPLE THREATENED IN THE LAND OF EXILE

The book of Esther describes a crisis that arose in Hebrew history in the days of the mighty Xerxes. The successive verses in the book can be described according to the stages of that crisis.

    I. How the Plot Was Formed (chaps. 1–3)
      A. The Might of Ahasuerus (chaps. 1–3)
      B. The Marriage of Esther (2:1–20)
      C. The Ministry of Mordecai (2:21–23)
      D. The Malice of Haman (chap. 3)
   II. How the Plot Was Fought (chaps. 4–5)
      A. The Cry of Israel (4:1–3)
      B. The Convictions of Mordecai (4:1–14)

THE STORY OF ESTHER

Esther lived in Persia in the days of the mighty Xerxes. This king is known to history as a tyrannical despot, imperious in temper, ruthless in the exercise of his power, grandiose in his schemes and ambitions, abandoned in his sensuality. During his reign, the Jews of the dispersion were threatened with total extermination through the machinations of Haman, one of the emperor's chief ministers of state. Haman was angered because a Jew named Mordecai refused to pay him the homage of bowing to him as he passed by. In revenge, Haman plotted the public execution of Mordecai on a special gallows, and planned a sweeping purge of all the Jews in the vast Persian domain. His plot almost succeeded.

Haman's anti-Semitic bloodlust is by no means unique to history. Pharaoh attempted to stamp out the Jewish people when they were in bondage in Egypt in the days of Moses. In more recent times, Hitler tried to do the same thing in Europe. But God has His hand upon the Jewish people, and He has His own high purposes to work out with them. Satan's attempts to thwart the birth of Christ by annihilating the Jews failed. His subsequent attempts to wreak his vengeance on them have been terrible, but he has never succeeded in eradicating them. The Jews remain a gulf stream in the ocean of mankind, and cannot be assimilated or exterminated by the Gentiles. They will yet occupy that lofty place in world affairs that God has planned for them.

In Esther there are no miraculous interventions by God to prevent Haman's plot from coming to fruition. Instead there is an outworking of events by natural sequence, God behind the scenes, checkmating each of Haman's moves. God does not have to work miracles in order to bring to naught the schemes of men. Look at what happened. Esther became queen, Mordecai rendered the king a great service, which went unnoticed at the time although it was worthy of great reward. The king could not resist the beauty, courage, and pleas of Esther. On the most critical night in the story, the king was unable to sleep and learned of Mordecai's service. Haman was forced to play the part of a slave to Mordecai in a public exhibition of the king's regard for this Jew. Then the arch plotter was trapped at Esther's banquet and hanged on the very gallows he made for Mordecai, and the Jews throughout the empire were delivered from their plight. The timing and sequence of the events are no less remarkable than the events themselves. To this very day the Jews annually keep the Feast of Purim in remembrance of the deliverance Esther wrought from the plot of Haman the Agagite.

With the book of Esther the historical portion of the Old Testament comes to a close. Looking back over the unfolding of this history, we see divine providence overruling in the affairs of men, even in their darkest hours. Behind the scenes God rules. James Russell Lowell puts it thus in "The Present Crisis":

> Careless seems the great Avenger: history's pages but record
> One death-grapple in the darkness 'twixt old systems and the Word.
> Truth forever on the scaffold, wrong forever on the throne,
> Yet that scaffold sways the future, and behind the dim unknown
> Standeth God within the shadow, keeping watch above His own.

But this historical survey by no means exhausts the significance of the book of Esther. Just as in Exodus and Ruth, the obvious facts of history cover a hidden message of salvation.

Esther has four main characters. First there is the *king*. He represents the unsaved, unregenerate man, ignorant of God, motivated and totally controlled by worldly principles.

The second, *Mordecai* the Jew, provides salvation and therefore represents the Savior.

The third, *Haman*, is the villain whose lineage leaves no doubt who he represents. He was an Agagite, a man directly linked with Amalek and Esau. He represents the enemy.

Finally is *Esther*, the one who knows and loves Mordecai (the savior) and who bears witness of the truth to her husband, the king.

To bring out the spiritual lesson in the book of Esther, we shall employ a somewhat different outline, one that emphasizes the king.

    I. The King as a Resentful Man (chaps. 1–3)
       A. His Sinful Ways (chap. 1)
       B. His Second Wife (chap. 2)
       C. His Stubborn Will (chap. 3)
    II. The King as a Restless Man (chaps. 4–6)
       A. How the Lord Arrested the Silent Believer (chaps. 4–5)
       B. How the Lord Aroused the Sinful Unbeliever (chap. 6)

III. The King as a Responsive Man (chaps. 7–10)
    A. A Monumental Fall (chap. 7)
        1. Haman Exposed
        2. Haman Executed
    B. A Manifest Faith (8:1–2)
    C. A Marvelous Future (8:3–17)
    D. A Memorial Feast (chaps. 9–10)

The book opens with the king, who is ignorant of God and His salvation. He struggles as God deals with his heart, finally surrenders, hands everything over to Mordecai the savior, and thereafter brings blessing to others.

I. The King as a Resentful Man (chaps. 1–3)

The king (known here as Ahasuerus but in secular history as Xerxes) has just suffered two great defeats. His navy was sunk at Salamis and the Greeks decimated his armies at Thermopylae, thus thwarting his life's ambition of conquering Greece. He has just learned there are limits to his imperious will and to his insatiable wishes and wants. God has drawn the line and flung him back for trying to cross it.

The king, of course, did not know that *God* thwarted him. He only knew he was prevented from having something he wanted.

A. His Sinful Ways (chap. 1)

The disappointed king threw an enormous feast for leading members of the Persian ruling class. The six-month feast was to be a magnificent affair and a tribute to the king's pomp and power. After a week of drinking and carousing, the king decided to liven up his party by showing off his wife Vashti, an exceedingly good-looking woman. With rare courage, Vashti refused to exhibit herself to gratify the wishes of her drunken husband.

The enraged king divorced her, and covered his willful action with a farcical manipulation of the law. We see a man ruled by worldly pride, worldly pleasure, worldly passions, and worldly policy.

B. His Second Wife (chap. 2)

He chose her as arbitrarily and arrogantly as he did everything else—by holding a beauty contest throughout the Persian Empire. The judges would choose Miss Babylon, Miss Egypt, Miss Syria, and so on, and bring these beauties to the king. Then he would choose Miss World, who would become his new wife and queen.

We are not told how Esther, a lovely Jewess, got caught up in all this. Perhaps she had no choice. But she won the contest and became the king's new wife and Persia's queen.

All this time Esther retained in her heart a love for Mordecai, the man cast in this book as her savior. Actually Esther's older cousin, Mordecai had brought her into his family after she was orphaned, on the basis of adoption. She was deeply grateful for all his love and care.

Mordecai also provided salvation for the king. He heard of a plot on the king's life. He told Esther, who told the king, and the would-be assassins were hanged. When Esther told the king about the plot, she brought the name Mordecai to him as the one who had thus provided salvation for him. The king ignored that part of her message, which must have been discouraging for the young woman who wanted her husband to love her savior too.

C. His Stubborn Will (chap. 3)

No sooner did he ignore the message of salvation than Haman is introduced: "After these things did king Ahasuerus promote Haman the son of Hammedatha the Agagite, and advanced him, and set his seat above all the princes that were with him" (3:1).

How significant! Haman, the enemy, was there all the time but he gained real ascendancy over the king once the king ignored the message of salvation. The king listened to Haman's whispers and stooped to his greatest act of wickedness by signing a decree calling for the extermination of all the Jews.

Often those who receive a witness of salvation do not respond immediately. Indeed, instead of responding, they sometimes go from bad to worse, and the enemy gains greater power over them than before. Haman harbored two great hates—the *person* of Mordecai because Haman had no influence or power over him; the *people* of Mordecai, simply because they were Mordecai's people.

II. The King as a Restless Man (chaps. 4–6)

The king became restless; God had begun to deal with him, though he did not know it. The dazzling moment of revelation had not yet come, but it was on the way.

That great moment of awakening in the soul of Esther's husband could not come until something was done in her own heart. For too long she had been content to be a silent believer. True, she once said something to her husband about Mordecai—about the savior—but she had long since given up that kind of thing.

A. How the Lord Arrested the Silent Believer (chaps. 4–5)

We see Esther struggling against the convicting voice of Mordecai, her savior, who was grieved by Haman's growing power and Esther's silence. Esther did what many do when faced with conviction—she tried to silence the convicting voice by giving Mordecai a gift. How often we seek to hush our consciences by giving a large donation to the Lord's work.

Mordecai, however, was not to be thus appeased. Esther had to get involved, she had to tell her husband the truth about what was happening in his life. If she refused, God would raise up somebody else, but she would be forever the loser.

Esther surrendered. She urged God's people to fast and pray and made up her mind that, no matter what the cost, she would speak again to her husband about the things of God. The principle involved in this is simple—God could not do anything about the rebellion in the heart of Esther's husband until He had first done something about the rebellion in the heart of Esther.

B. How the Lord Aroused the Sinful Unbeliever (chap. 6)

The removal of Esther's disobedience cleared the way for God to act directly in her husband's life. The change began that very night. Unable to sleep, the king commanded the court librarian to read to him. Of all the books in the palace library and all the places in that book to begin, the librarian chose the account of Mordecai's role in preventing the king's death.

Such are the ways God overrules in human affairs. Mordecai's great work of salvation had not been forgotten. It had been written in a book and there, in the middle of the night, we see two unsaved men sitting up and one man is reading to the other man of a savior and of a salvation provided for him.

The arrow of conviction pierced the king's heart. All this time he had remained ignorant of the salvation provided for him by Mordecai. Evidently he had forgotten Esther's testimony, and she had long remained silent.

Now the king was convicted. He realized he had done nothing to acknowledge his debt to the one who provided salvation for him.

Note what happened next: Haman reappeared. At that critical moment, as the king is about to make his decision public, the enemy came.

How true to life! How often the soul winner experiences distraction right at the moment of decision. The telephone will ring, the baby cries, or someone imparts a distraction into the conversation—it is the enemy's last-ditch effort.

But he was too late. The king had already made up his mind, and God simply used Haman's intrusion to magnify the savior.

The king knew he must publicly confess his indebtedness to his savior and exalt that one by placing him over all his affairs. He gave his thanks to the one who had provided salvation, but he had no idea of the enormous changes that would take place.

Mordecai never intruded upon the king's sovereign right to decide how to respond to him as the savior. God does not force His salvation upon us, even though He brings us face-to-face with the facts and with our need to respond. The story of salvation is always a blending of the supernatural and the simple, of divine sovereignty and the human right to decide.

In the quietness of his bedroom, in the dead of night, surrounded by unsaved people, the king gave his unknown savior the place that rightfully belonged to him. All the king's affairs soon went under new management.

The story, however, is not yet over. When a person gives the Savior His proper place, it is only the first step to a brand new life.

III. THE KING AS A RESPONSIVE MAN (CHAPS. 7–10)

The story has four closing movements:

A. A Monumental Fall (chap. 7)

One can imagine Esther's delight when she learned that her husband acknowledged his debt to the savior. Her task now was to reveal to him the truth about the enemy and how the enemy had been using him and manipulating him.

First, *Haman was exposed*. His murderous hatred of the person and people of Mordecai was shown to the king, who was astonished when he saw what had been happening in his life. Then *Haman was executed*. He was hanged on the gallows he had prepared for Mordecai—not any old gallows, but *that* one. Besides poetic justice, there is a spiritual principle in this. God's only answer to the enemy is the cross, not just any cross, but the cross of Christ. Romans 6 clearly teaches this. Moreover, all Haman's sons were hanged with him, for the enemy had a prodigious family. Sin, self, and Satan are all dealt with in terms of the cross.

B. A Manifest Faith (8:1–2)

"The king took off his ring, which he had taken from Haman, and gave it unto Mordecai. And Esther set Mordecai over the house of Haman" (8:2). Where once the enemy had ruled, now the savior ruled. People soon noticed the difference. The kingdom knew at once that there had been a dramatic change of management in the king's affairs. There was an immediate change for good and for God.

C. A Marvelous Future (8:3–17)

Esther told the king about the enemy's plot to destroy the people of God. With that baneful influence removed and with the savior in control, the king's heart went out warmly and generously to the people of God. He regretted his former wicked thoughts and directed the full weight of his influence on their behalf.

"The Jews had joy and gladness, a feast and a good day. And many of the people of the land became Jews; for the fear of the Jews fell upon them" (8:17). In New Testament terms, there was a revival.

Wherever the king's sovereignty reached, the impact of the savior's rule was felt, even to the far ends of the earth. Multitudes sought to become one with the people of God, and the people of God were filled with joy.

D. A Memorial Feast (chaps. 9–10)

God did not want the great work of the savior to be forgotten, so a feast of remembrance was instituted so that, from time to time, those who had been saved might remember the one who had provided so great salvation for them.

God wants us never to forget what He has done for us and what we owe to our Savior. That is why we, too, have a feast of remembrance at our Lord's Table.

The story concludes with Mordecai's continued advancement and with his great work being written up in a new book. Such is the story of Esther—a wonderful reminder of New Testament truth beneath the surface of Old Testament history.

PART 2
OLD TESTAMENT POETRY AND PROPHECY

CHAPTER 18

HEBREW POETRY

Music of the Heart

The major poetic forms are dirge, drama, elegy, epic, idyll, lyric, and ode, and many of them are represented in the poetical sections of Scripture. The book of Lamentations, for instance, is a dirge, a song of terrible grief. Psalm 22 is an example of lyrical poetry in which the deep feelings of the heart are bared rather than some outward incident described. Psalms 78, 105, 106, and 136 are odes.

In the West, we have generally liked our poetry to have rhyme and rhythm and a definite swing to it, although not much English poetry conforms to these demands. The blank verse so characteristic of Shakespeare is an example of poetry that does not altogether depend on rhyme.

Hebrew poetry depends on parallelism of thought rather than on the phonetic coupling of words. An idea is stated one way and then repeated in another, and this is done in one of three ways:

1. Synonymous parallelism
2. Antithetic parallelism
3. Synthetic parallelism

SYNONYMOUS PARALLELISM

In this type of poetry the second half of the verse repeats the content of the first half, only in different words, as in the following examples:

He that sitteth in the heavens shall laugh: the Lord shall have them in derision. (Ps. 2:4)

Deliver me, O Lord, from the evil man: preserve me from the violent man. (Ps. 140:1)

Antithetic Parallelism

In this poetic arrangement a thought is stated in the first verse, only to be set out in contrast, or antithesis, in the second, like this:

The young lions do lack, and suffer hunger: but they that seek the Lord shall not want any good thing. (Ps. 34:10)

A righteous man regardeth the life of his beast: but the tender mercies of the wicked are cruel. (Prov. 12:10)

Synthetic Parallelism

In this type of poem a thought is given and then expanded in succeeding lines, each line building on the first, as follows:

And he shall be like a tree planted by the rivers of water,
that bringeth forth his fruit in his season;
his leaf also shall not wither;
and whatsoever he doeth shall prosper.
(Ps. 1:3)

Wisdom hath builded her house,
she hath hewn out her seven pillars:
She hath killed her beasts;
she hath mingled her wine;
she hath also furnished her table.
(Prov. 9:1–2)

Synthetic parallelism can take the form of an introversion or an alternation, sometimes extending over more than one psalm, where, for example, two psalms go together as a pair. The following, taken from *The Companion Bible*, illustrate introversion and alternation. See Psalm 135.

A. The idols (v. 15)
  B. Their fabrication (v. 15)
    C. Mouth without speech (singular) (v. 16)
      D. Eyes without sight (plural) (v. 16)
      D. Ears without hearing (plural) (v. 17)

        C. Mouth without breath (singular) (v. 17)
      B. Their fabricators (v. 18)
   A. The idolaters (v. 18)[1]

In the next example, not only is an illustration of extended alternation given, but this parallelism illustrates how closely united in thought are Psalms 135 and 136.

Psalm 135
A. Exhortation to praise (vv. 1–5)
   B. Creative wonders (vv. 6–7)
      C. Deliverance from Egypt (vv. 8–9)
         D. Deliverance on journey (vv. 12–13)
            E. Gift of the land (v. 14)
               F. Goodness to His people (v. 14)
                  G. False gods (vv. 15–18)
                     H. Praise (vv. 19–21)

Psalm 136
A. Exhortation to praise (vv. 1–3)
   B. Creative wonders (vv. 4–9)
      C. Deliverance from Egypt (vv. 10–15)
         D. Deliverance on journey (vv. 16–20)
            E. Gift of the land (vv. 21–22)
               F. Goodness to His people (vv. 23–24)
                  G. The true God (v. 25)
                     H. Praise (v. 26)[2]

Acrostics were great favorites with the Hebrew poets, who sometimes built their poems so that each verse began with a separate letter of the Hebrew alphabet. The book of Lamentations is built on this principle and so are Psalms 111, 112, and 119.

Poetry can be found in all parts of the Bible. When we speak of the "poetical books," however, we generally mean the books of Job, Psalms, Proverbs, Ecclesiastes, and the Song of Solomon.

It has often been observed that the teaching of these five books is progressive, beginning with the experiences of a renewed heart from the hour that the self is revealed in all its unattractiveness (Job 42:5–6) until Christ becomes all in all (Song 5:16). The subject matter of these books may be summarized in this way.

JOB: THE PROBLEM OF PAIN

There is no greater problem among men than suffering, especially when the sufferer is a child of God and, by all human standards, an outstandingly good man, one, moreover, who is pronounced "perfect" by God. The book of Job gives some basic answers to this age-old problem. The great question that underlies the book of Job is, *Will this man's theology triumph over his experience, or will his experience triumph over his theology?* The basic lesson of the book is do not judge by outward appearances. The many arguments put forward in the book are nearly all wrong because the various speakers are all drawing conclusions from incomplete data. We learn, too, that there are reasons behind seemingly meaningless suffering and that, moreover, God can and does use our adverse circumstances to teach us spiritual lessons.

PSALMS: THE WAY TO PRAY

The book of Psalms was both the Hebrew hymnbook and the Hebrew prayer book. It touches all the chords of human experience and it sounds all the notes of prayer, confession, petition, intercession, adoration, thanksgiving, and praise.

Throbbing through the book is the prophetic, messianic consciousness of the person of the Lord Jesus. Thus the faithful Man of Psalm 1 became the forsaken Man of Psalm 22 so that the filthy man of Psalm 14 might become the forgiven man of Psalm 32.

The psalms are a mine of information, too, about other aspects of Bible prophecy. Not only is much revealed in this book about the two advents of the Lord Jesus, but much detail is given about such matters as the great tribulation, the end-time judgments, and the millennial reign of Christ. The psalms are also a mine of information on the life and times of David, Hezekiah, and other historical figures of the Old Testament.

PROVERBS: THE BEHAVIOR OF THE BELIEVER

Behind the book of Proverbs is the shadow of Rehoboam. Solomon had a fool for a son, and he knew it. Many of the proverbs of Solomon were doubtless written with that fact in mind. Most of the proverbs, however, were wasted on Rehoboam. May they not be wasted on us. They are a veritable handbook on spiritual life, practical psychology, child raising, business ethics, and similar practical topics.

ECCLESIASTES: THE FOLLY OF FORGETTING GOD

Behind the book of Ecclesiastes is the shame of Solomon. Rehoboam had a fool for a father. For Solomon, who set sail in the morning of his reign with all canvass drawing, pennants flying, under a cloudless sky, and laden down with rich gifts from heaven, made shipwreck before nightfall. He forgot God, lived for the world, wrecked the kingdom, did more to destroy the nation than any other man, turned Jerusalem into Babylon, and brought down upon himself the displeasure of God. Ecclesiastes is really his apology for the folly of his life.

The book is in the Bible because it shows us how the wordly minded man thinks, and exposes the total inadequacy of a philosophy of life that leaves out God and ignores the world to come.

SONG OF SOLOMON: THE ART OF ADORATION

This great love song will come into its sharpest focus only when we interpret it in the light of Christ and His church. Solomon wrote over a thousand songs (1 Kings 4:32); this one he calls "the song of songs." It has depths in it beyond anything Solomon ever knew, which is why the Holy Spirit, who inspired it, picks it up and crowns all the other Hebrew poetry with it.

There are numerous approaches to the interpretation of this book. That God is not once mentioned adds a touch of interest to the book and helps emphasize there having to be a deeper significance to it than that which lies on the surface.

CHAPTER 19

JOB

The Problem of Suffering

The book of Job is believed to be the oldest book in the world. He himself was a historical figure and is mentioned as such both in the Old Testament and the New (Ezek. 14:20; James 5:11). Almost certainly he lived before the giving of the law, and some claim he lived before Abraham, placing the book between Genesis 11 and 12. Others have suggested he was one of the sons of Issachar (Gen. 46:13).

The book of Job consists of a prologue, a dialogue, and an epilogue, the dialogue being in poetry and the other parts in prose. Its subject is the problem of suffering, especially as it bears upon the life of a believer. Job should be read in the light of Psalms 37 and 43 and Hebrews 12. Why do the godly suffer, and why is God silent? Job and his friends wrestle with these problems but arrive at no satisfactory conclusion. Not until God speaks is the true answer found, for in such matters human reasoning must ever bow before the superiority of divine revelation.

I. How He Faced Calamity (1:1–2:13)
   Job in the hands of Satan
   A. Job Compassed with Blessings
   B. Job Crippled by Bankruptcy
   C. Job Crushed with Bereavement
   D. Job Covered with Boils
   E. Job Cursed with Bitterness
II. How He Faced Criticism (3:1–37:24)
   Job in the hands of men
   A. Job and the Critics (3:1–31:40)
      1. Eliphaz: The Man with the Exotic Experience

Job was a remarkable man. Some think that at the time the events occurred in this book, the birth of Moses and the penning of the Pentateuch lay perhaps at least a hundred years in the future. Thus, in Job's day not a page of Scripture had as yet been penned. By comparing Scripture with Scripture, though, we gather that Job was probably a son of Issachar, one of the sons of Jacob (Gen. 46:13), and that his three friends were descendants of Esau (Gen. 25:2; 36:10; Jer. 49:7–8).

In any case, Job lived before the Bible was begun and in a period when men's morals were still monitored by *conscience* rather than by *conviction*, by *society* rather than by *Scripture*, by *custom* rather than by *commandment*. All this makes Job's behavior and belief remarkable indeed.

I. HOW HE FACED CALAMITY (1:1–2:13)

A. Job Compassed with Blessings

We have five glimpses of Job as his calamities come upon him. First, we see a man *compassed with blessing*. He has seven sons and three daughters, 7,000 sheep, 3,000 camels, 500 yoke of oxen, 500 she-asses, and a very great household. Indeed, he was the greatest man in the East. In an age when material prosperity was the mark of spiritual blessing, Job excelled. The Old Testament "blessing of the Lord" was "the blessing of the LORD, it maketh rich, and he addeth no sorrow with it" (Prov. 10:22). By that standard alone (and it was by that standard that his friends judged him) Job was a very righteous man.

God, too, owned him to be a righteous man. When Job finished his dialogues with his friends he cataloged his acts of righteousness, and a very impressive list it is. He said he never looked with lust, that he was a father of the fatherless, a friend and helper to the widow, and that no stranger ever escaped his hospitality. Even his farms and fields were given their Sabbath rest—long before Sabbath laws were given to the Hebrew people as part of the Mosaic Law. Unfortunately, Job's catalog of his acts of righteousness savors of self-righteousness (he uses the personal pronouns *I, me,* and *my* 195 times in listing his moral and spiritual assets), but just the same God owned him a righteous man and blessed him accordingly.

B. Job Crippled by Bankruptcy

Then we see Job *crippled by bankruptcy*. His vast fortune was swept away in a series of unprecedented disasters. His oxen and donkeys, while grazing on the nearby hills, were carried off by brigands. Then, during a terrific thunderstorm, lightning destroyed Job's flocks of seven thousand sheep. Next, three bands of Chaldean adventurers swooped down upon his camel caravans, slew his drivers, and made off with all three thousand of his camels and plundered what was left of his vast fortune. Job was bankrupt.

C. Job Crushed with Bereavement

Next we see Job *crushed with bereavement*. Job had seven sons and three attractive daughters. By judicially marrying off his daughters, putting his sons to work, and harnessing his own considerable business acumen, Job doubtless hoped to recoup his losses. But Job, who had lost his fortune, was now going to lose his family, too.

The dreadful news came—his ten much-loved children, all ten of them, were dead. A tornado had struck the home where they were together on a visit and all ten had died in the disaster. Poor old Job! With a broken heart he went into his room, closed the door, flung himself on his face and wept. "Dear Lord, I don't know why! It doesn't make any sense at all! But Lord, You gave and You have taken away. Blessed be Your name" (see 1:20–21). Says the Holy Spirit, "In all this Job sinned not, nor charged God foolishly" (1:22).

D. Job Covered with Boils

Next we see Job *covered with boils*. He had lost family and fortune and he lost his health. He was smitten with a loathsome, disfiguring, painful, and horrible disease. It was agony to sit, stand, or lie upon his bed. From the crown of his head to the soles of his feet he was covered with boils. He writhed in anguish of soul and agony of body. All he had left was his wife.

E. Job Cursed with Bitterness

Finally we see him *cursed with bitterness*. A man who has an understanding, sympathetic, courageous, and spiritual wife to share his joys and sorrows still has something far above the price of rubies. But now Job's wife turned against him: "curse God, and die," she said (2:9). *It was the voice of the Devil.* "He will curse you!" the Devil had said to God (see 1:11); "curse God, and die," said Job's wife. Job told her not to talk like that and reaffirmed his belief in God's integrity, even though he could not understand the reason for God's dealings with him.

That was how Job faced calamity. He triumphed gloriously! His life had become a stage upon which two great protagonists had fought for his loyalty and his soul. All heaven and all hell had watched with bated breath as God and Satan had fought this titanic struggle. Not a spot in the galaxy was of greater interest during this week than the land of Uz, south of Edom and west of the Arabian desert, reaching toward Chaldea, and there was not a created being in the universe being more closely watched and more intensely scrutinized during these days than Job.

And Job triumphed! Satan was defeated and retired from the conflict in confusion. The joy bells rang in heaven as the hosts above burst into the hallelujah chorus. The high halls rang and the echoes of the everlasting hills awoke to roll back the sound! The Devil was so thoroughly beaten that his voice is not heard again in the Old Testament.

Job triumphed! So why did he not get better? The answer is that God intended to use the calamities that had overtaken Job to teach him some truths about himself. Job was taken out of the hands of Satan and placed in the hands of men.

II. HOW HE FACED CRITICISM (3:1–37:24)

A. Job and the Critics (3:1–31:40)

The man who triumphed gloriously over calamity fell flat on his face when criticized by his friends. Much of the criticism was untrue and unfair, but God used it to show Job "the hidden things of darkness" (1 Cor. 4:5) that lurked within his heart, all unsuspected by himself. Job nursed bitterness, pride, sarcasm, anger, impatience, and self-righteousness within his breast, and he did not know it. God was about to reveal it to him by letting him get upset!

When a bottle is upset, what is inside spills out. Upsetting the bottle doesn't determine the contents—it just displays the contents. If there is honey in the bottle, honey will come out; if there is vinegar in the bottle, vinegar will come out.

So along came Job's three friends. We can almost picture Job as he saw them coming. He must have groaned; he knew these men, knew them only too well; they had come to *sympathize*, but they would stay to *sermonize*.

So Job did the only thing he could—try to sit them out. Since oriental courtesy demanded that Job be the first to speak, Job determined not to speak at all. It did not work. Job's friends had a lot to say to him. They simply pulled up their chairs, determined to wait him out. They sat and stared in silence at poor Job for a whole week—they would have stayed for a year. Finally Job could stand it no more and opened his mouth to curse the day he was born.

There were four men now ready to pounce on the unhappy man—three older men: Eliphaz the Temanite, Bildad the Shuhite, and Zophar the Naamathite; and a younger man, Elihu the son of Barachel the Buzite, sometimes called the mediator.

The book is mostly about the things these men said to Job and the things Job had to say to them.

1. Eliphaz: The Man with the Exotic Experience

The first to speak was Eliphaz. Eliphaz was the man with the exotic experience. He liked to talk about spirits and visions. If you had not had his experience, then you evidently had missed out in your spiritual life—or so he thought. He has many spiritual heirs in the church today.

Eliphaz *suggested* that Job must have been a great sinner, otherwise these things would not have happened to him. Here are the kinds of things he had to say:

> Behold, thou hast instructed many. . . . But now it is come upon thee, and thou faintest. (4:3, 5)

> Remember, I pray thee, who ever perished, being innocent? . . . I have seen, they that plow iniquity, and sow wickedness, reap the same. (4:7–8)

> Behold, happy is the man whom God correcteth: therefore despise not thou the chastening of the Almighty. (5:17)

"Job! You should be singing, man! You should be happy! You should be praising the Lord. Come on! Let's have a smile and a song!" Not a very helpful friend. He took it for granted that Job's sufferings were deserved and, with an objectivity we often find so easy to apply to someone else's sorrows, he told Job to be happy because "whom the Lord loveth he chasteneth" (Heb. 12:6).

2. Bildad: The Man with the Clever Clichés

The second to speak was Bildad. Bildad was far worse than Eliphaz. Eliphaz merely *suggested* that Job must have been a sinner. Bildad *supposed* that Job was a sinner. Bildad was the man with the clever clichés. He was the kind of person who has a pat answer, a pet proverb, a pertinent verse for every occasion. His great forte was human tradition. Again, let us look at some samples of Bildad's approach:

> Doth God pervert judgment? . . . If thou wert pure and upright; surely now he would awake for thee, and make the habitation of thy righteousness prosperous. (8:3, 6)

> Can the rush grow up without mire? . . . Whilst it is yet in its greenness, and not cut down, it withereth before any other herb. So are the paths of all that forget God; and the hypocrite's hope shall perish. (8:11–13)

He essentially said, "Job, you are a hypocrite; that is all there is to it. This pious front you used to put on! Did you ever have us fooled! Well, now we know better."

3. Zophar: The Man with the Made-up Mind

The third speaker was Zophar, the man with the made-up mind. He was the kind of person who knows it all, who thinks he has some kind of a monopoly on God. His arguments are based on human merit, and he is quite sure he is a shining example of all that a person ought to be.

This man was callous. He did not suggest nor suppose, he bluntly *said* that Job was a sinner, and he said it in the harshest of terms. We need to look at only one example of his sharp and cutting speech:

> But oh that God would speak, and open his lips against thee; and that he would show thee the secrets of wisdom. . . . Know therefore that God exacteth of thee less than thine iniquity deserveth. (11:5–6)

What a terrible thing to say! "Job, if you were getting what you deserved, you would not only be diseased, you'd be dead—and not only dead but damned. You'd be in hell-fire at this moment!"

We must remember Job had lost his fortune; all his children were dead and buried; he was in physical, mental, and spiritual agony; even his wife had turned against him. Yet this man Zophar was so callous and smug as to make the kind of remark he did.

As for Job, sometimes he responded in anger:

> But ye are forgers of lies, ye are all physicians of no value. O that ye would altogether hold your peace! and it should be your wisdom. (13:4–5)

"You fellows," he said in effect, "if you would keep your mouths shut, somebody might make a mistake and imagine you were wise men, but the moment you open your mouths you betray yourselves."

> But now they that are younger than I have me in derision, whose fathers I would have disdained to have set with the dogs of my flock. (30:1)

Basically, he said, "You fellows, I would not even put your fathers in my dog kennel!" What an insult!

Sometimes Job responded in agony. Several times he came close to making grave accusations against God. He actually did accuse God of cruelty, injustice, and indifference:

Thou knowest that I am not wicked . . . yet thou dost destroy me. . . . Hast thou not poured me out as milk, and curdled me like cheese? (10:7–8, 10)

On one occasion he compared his treatment of the poor, the unfortunate, and the suffering with God's seeming treatment of him. And the comparison is in Job's favor, not God's:

Thou art become cruel to me. . . . Did not I weep for him that was in trouble? Was not my soul grieved for the poor? When I looked for good, then evil came upon me: and when I waited for light, there came darkness. (30:21, 25–26)

Sometimes Job responded in assurance. He exclaimed at one point,

God understandeth! (28:23)

Then came that statement of his that rings out even yet as the most outstanding declaration of faith to be found almost anywhere in the whole Bible:

Oh that my words were now written! Oh that they were printed in a book! That they were graven with an iron pen and lead in the rock for ever! For I know that my redeemer liveth, and that he shall stand at the latter day upon the earth: And though after my skin worms shall destroy this body, yet in my flesh shall I see God. (19:23–26)

In the whole Bible is no greater statement on the physical, bodily resurrection of the believer until we come to the fifteenth chapter of Paul's first letter to the Corinthians! And Job had never seen a single page of Scripture!

B. Job and the Comforter (32:1–37:24)

When Job and his friends had finished—and remember, Job gave as good as he got—then the young man, Elihu, took over. Job had prayed for a "daysman," for someone who could stand between him and God and place his hand upon both and mediate on equal terms his case, someone who being man could understand as a man, someone who being God could understand as God. This young man steps up to Job's bed and says, "Well, here I am—the daysman you were asking for."

"Behold, I am according to thy wish in God's stead: I also am formed out of the clay" (33:6). Elihu bridges the gap between Job and his friends and Job and his God.

Elihu, just the same, left much to be desired as a comforter, a daysman. He pointed to God as the source of true righteousness for helpless, guilty sinners such as Job. He did not console Job as much as he corrected him; he did not love him; he lectured him. "Should [God's recompense] be according to thy mind?" he demanded (34:33).

He warned Job that if he failed to look out, even worse things would happen to him: "Because there is wrath, beware lest he take thee away with his stroke" (36:18).

III. HOW HE FACED CONVICTION (38:1–42:17)

Job was wrong in his overall view of his sufferings, Job's wife was wrong, Eliphaz and Bildad and Zophar were wrong, and Elihu was wrong. None of these people had all the factors. When we read the book of Job, we start with the first two chapters so we know why it all happened. We see Satan's spite and malice at work, and we see God proving Satan wrong. Then we turn to the last chapter and see how it all ended. But Job did not have the first two chapters; nor did he have the last chapter. That is what makes the book so valuable. God usually does not tell us why trials and troubles come upon us; He wants us to trust Him even when everything looks hopeless and black. Nor does God usually give us the assurance that our trials will come to a speedy end. Sometimes they never do in this life. So Job and the others were arguing from incomplete data. They were like men trying to solve an intricate algebraic problem without two key factors in the equation. No matter how brilliant their deductions they were bound to be wrong. How foolish it is to criticize another person!

We notice three things about Job in the hands of God.

A. How He Was Rebuked (38:1–42:6)

First God asked Job a series of questions about the *material* universe—questions designed to expose Job's ignorance and weakness:

Where wast thou when I laid the foundations of the earth? (38:4)

Hast thou commanded the morning since thy days? (38:12)

Canst thou bind the sweet influences of Pleiades, or loose the bands of Orion? (38:31)

Doth the eagle mount up at thy command? (39:27)

Job could not answer a single question. In effect, God was saying to Job, "Job, you have had a great deal to say about things. But you do not know how I do things in the material universe, so how can you possibly know how I do things in the moral and spiritual universe?" In the end, Job cried out: "I abhor myself, and repent in dust and ashes" (42:6).

B. How He Was Released (42:7–10)

We are told that "the LORD turned the captivity of Job, when he prayed for his friends" (42:10). Poor Job had himself tied up in knots. God set him free from his own misery, brought on by his wrong reactions to his critics, when he got down on his knees and prayed for them. "Dear Lord," we can hear his entreaty, "I'm sorry for the things I said to Eliphaz and to Bildad and Zophar. Bless them, Lord, and young Eliphaz, too. Bless them with the blessing of the Lord that maketh rich and addeth no sorrow thereto."

C. How He Was Rewarded (42:11–17)

He was given back his fortune and his family—indeed, he was given double. God evidently keeps accurate books: in chapter 1, Job had seven thousand sheep, in chapter 42 he had fourteen thousand; in chapter 1 he had three thousand camels, in chapter 42 he had six thousand; in chapter 1 he had five hundred yoke of oxen and five hundred she-asses, in chapter 42 he had a thousand of each.

But notice this. In chapter 1 he had seven sons and three daughters and in chapter 42 he had seven sons and three daughters. Now why was that? Why did God give him double his sheep and camels, oxen and she-asses, but the same number of sons and daughters that he had before? God had surely not made a mistake!

Of course not! The point is that Job had lost his camels and his cattle but he had not lost his children. They were dead and buried, but he had not lost them.

The time came when Job died and went to heaven and, in due course, the last of his children died and went to heaven. Then Job stood up in the presence of God and counted up his children and, sure enough, he had fourteen sons and six daughters!

> How good is the God we adore,
> Our faithful, unchangeable Friend,
> Whose love is as great as His power,
> And knows neither measure nor end.
> —Joseph Hart,
> "How Good Is the God We Adore"

CHAPTER 20

THE PSALMS

Hymns of the Hebrews

The book of Psalms was the Hebrew hymnbook. There are five books of psalms, each ending with a doxology, and each more or less corresponding to the five books of Moses.

- Book 1: Psalms 1–41—God's Sovereignty. The first book reflects the book of Genesis, the key thought being man and God's counsels concerning him.

- Book 2: Psalms 42–72—God's Salvation. In the second book the key thought is Israel. This book begins with Israel's cry for deliverance and ends with Israel's king reigning over the redeemed nation. Many of the psalms in this group reflect the teaching of Exodus.

- Book 3: Psalms 73–89—God's Sanctuary. The third book has the sanctuary for its dominant note and therefore parallels Leviticus.

- Book 4: Psalms 90–106—God's Sufficiency. These psalms clearly correspond to Numbers, the fourth book of Moses. This group of psalms begins with one written by Moses and ends with one that recounts Israel's rebellions in the wilderness.

- Book 5: Psalms 107–150—God's Sayings. The fifth book is linked with

Deuteronomy, the prevailing thought being God's Word. The great Psalm 119 occurs in this section, a psalm devoted to the exalting of God's Word.

The first group of psalms, mostly written by David, was probably collected by Solomon, the second group by the Levites descended from Korah, the third group by Hezekiah, and the remaining two groups by Ezra and Nehemiah. If this is so, then the collection and arrangement of the psalms took half a millennium to be completed.

THE VALUE OF THE PSALMS

Many psalms were composed for private and public worship; others were born out of deep experiences of the soul. They include meditations, historical recitals, formal instruction, and passionate entreaties. As such, they are a treasury of thought from which to draw when approaching God in prayer whether congregationally or privately, for in the psalms man's soul is bared. Sin, sorrow, shame, repentance, hope, faith, and love are all expressed, and these topics are universal in scope, timeless in nature, and the very material of which prayer is made.

The book of Psalms is also a collection of 150 hymns that cover the whole range of human emotion and experience. Is it a troublesome experience, a terrifying experience, a triumphant experience, a testing experience, a tragic experience? It is mirrored in the psalms. Is it joy that floods the soul? Is it a sense of justice outraged? Is it happiness, holiness, horror, or hate? Is it gladness or sadness? Is it love or longing or loneliness? Is it passion or is it peace? Is it worship or is it war? Is it frustration or forgiveness or fear?

The psalms reflect it all. From the lower notes of the keyboard of human feeling, we run our fingers up the scale of human experience, up another, another, and yet another. We run our fingers back down again from the high notes to the low. We combine notes. We harmonize high notes and low notes. Often, within a single psalm, the tempo will change, the tone will change, the tune will change. The psalms blend together the deep notes of gloom and the light airy notes of exaltation and joy. Some of the psalms are almost like choruses; we almost wish they could simply be whistled!

Make a joyful noise unto the LORD, all ye lands. Serve the LORD with gladness: come before his presence with singing. Know ye that the LORD he is God. (Ps. 100:1–3)

Others hammer away persistently at the low notes.

O God, the heathen are come into thine inheritance; thy holy temple have they defiled; they have laid Jerusalem on heaps. The dead bodies of thy servants have they given to be meat unto the fowls of the heaven. (Ps. 79:1–2)

CLASSIFICATION OF THE PSALMS

Many of the psalms lend themselves to classification under various titles relating to their general subject matter. There are messianic psalms, penitential psalms, natural and historical psalms, experiential psalms, millennial psalms, didactic psalms, devotional psalms, prophetic psalms, imprecatory psalms, and hallelujah psalms.

For example, Psalms 2, 8, 16, 22, 23, 24, 31, 40, 41, 45, 68, 69, 102, 110, 118 are *messianic*; Psalms 6, 32, 38, 51, 102, 130, 143 are *penitential*; Psalms 8, 19, 29, 33, 104 are *nature* psalms; Psalms 78, 105, 106 are *history* psalms; Psalms 35, 58, 59, 69, 83, 109, 137 are *imprecatory*; Psalms 106, 111, 112, 113, 117, 135, 146, 147, 148, 149, 150 are *hallelujah* psalms; Psalms 2, 16, 22, 40, 45, 68, 69, 72, 97, 110, 118 are examples of *prophetic* psalms; Psalms 46, 72, 89 are examples of *millennial* psalms.

THE AUTHORS

Of the one hundred and fifty psalms, one hundred are directly attributed to various authors, and fifty are anonymous. David is credited with seventy-three, and Asaph, one of David's choir leaders, with twelve. David's era was one of remarkable renaissance in Israel, much like the Elizabethan era in English history. Israel's enemies had been subdued, Jerusalem had become the nation's capital, the ark of God was in its place, Israel's influence was being felt abroad, prosperity had come to the nation, and plans were in hand to build a magnificent temple. These circumstances left their mark on the cultural and religious life of the nation, and more than half the psalms were written during this period.

All but thirty-four psalms have titles. Many have roots deep in Hebrew history, so one good way to study them is to observe the circumstances that gave them birth. For instance, we can compare the following:

Psalm 3—2 Samuel 15–18	Psalm 56—1 Samuel 21:10; 27:4; 29:2–11
Psalm 30—2 Samuel 5:11–12	Psalm 57—1 Samuel 22
Psalm 34—1 Samuel 21:10–22:1	Psalm 59—1 Samuel 19
Psalm 51—2 Samuel 11–12	Psalm 60—2 Samuel 8:13–14
Psalm 52—1 Samuel 21–22	Psalm 63—1 Samuel 22:5; 23:14–16
Psalm 54—1 Samuel 23:19; 26:1	Psalm 142—1 Samuel 22:1; 24:3

CLASSIFICATION OF THE PSALMS

Untitled	111 112 113 114 115 116 117 118 119 135 136 137 146 147 148 149 150
	1 2 10 33 43 71 91 93 94 95 96 97 99 104 105 106 107
Songs of Degrees	120 121 122 123 124 125 126 127 128 129 130 131 132 133 134
Hallelujah	106 111 112 113 117 135 146 147 148 149 150
Imprecatory	35 58 59 69 83 109 137
Prophetic	2 16 22 40 45 68 69 72 97 110 118
Devotional	3 16 28 41 54 61 67 70 86 122 144
Didactic	1 5 7 15 17 50 73 94 101
Millennial	46 72 89
Experiential	3 7 18 30 34 51 52 54 56 57 59 60 63 142
Historical	78 105 106
Natural	8 19 29 33 104
Penitential	6 32 38 51 102 130 143
Messianic	2 8 16 22 23 24 31 40 41 45 68 69 102 110 118

The history of Hezekiah sheds light on a considerable number of psalms born out of the fiery womb of the Assyrian invasion of Israel and Judah. Also Hezekiah seems to have written the fifteen psalms titled "Song of Degrees" (Pss. 120–134). The only other mention of "degrees" in Scripture is when the shadow on the sundial of Ahaz went back ten degrees as a miraculous sign to Hezekiah that he would recover from his sickness. That this group consists of fifteen psalms suggests the fifteen years added to King Hezekiah's life. Five of these psalms are attributed to David and Solomon, the other ten are not named. Probably they have reference to the ten degrees on the sundial. Hezekiah would not need to specifically sign them if they were the songs he calls "my songs" in Isaiah 38:20. The historical record is in 2 Kings 20:8–11.

Many of the psalms originated in times of religious revival as did most of the best hymns in our own hymnbook. Five periods in Hebrew history mark times when God visited His people with a measure of spiritual awakening. These times of revival took place under David, Jehoshaphat, Hezekiah, Josiah, and Ezra. Most of the psalms can be traced to the times when these men lived. The fifty anonymous psalms do not have the same individual character as the signed psalms. They were written to represent the community as a whole rather than the personal experience of the author.

By far the most prolific songwriter in Israel was David, Israel's greatest and godliest king. He wrote seventy-three of the psalms (seventy-five, if we count two psalms that are anonymous in the hymnbook but that are attributed to him in the New Testament).

We can divide David's life into three periods and fit many of his psalms into one or another of these periods:

I. The Period of the Testings
   A. In the Country: As a Shepherd
   B. At the Court: As a Courtier
   C. In the Cave: As an Outlaw
II. The Period of the Triumphs
III. The Period of the Troubles

Let us briefly review these periods.

I. The Period of the Testings

During this period David was a shepherd, a courtier, and an outlaw. We see him either in the country, at the court, or in the cave. Over two dozen psalms flowed from his pen during this period of his life.

A. In the Country: As a Shepherd

We instinctively think of Psalm 23: "The Lord is my shepherd; I shall not want."

But Psalm 19 is a psalm of the shepherd years as well. We can see the youthful David as the sun sinks to its rest across the distant rim of the great western sea. The twilight deepens, and the hand of God reaches out of the sleeve of the night to light the evening stars. The sheep have settled down, and David's fingers roam restlessly across the chords of his ten-stringed lyre. And suddenly the song is born!

> Behold the lofty sky
> Declares its maker God,
> And all His starry works on high
> Proclaim His power abroad.
>
> The darkness and the light
> Still keep their course the same;
> While night to day, and day to night
> Divinely teach His name.[1]

B. At the Court: As a Courtier

David was not popular at court. He was kept there as the king's private musician and his job was to sing the king into a good humor when the black, Satanic moods darkened his mind and heart. The king was jealous and suspicious of him, and there were plenty of sycophants at court only too willing to put a spike in David's wheel. Time and again the king set traps for David and put assassins on his trail. During this period of his life, the psalms David wrote included Psalms 140 and 141. The Old Testament narrative tells us with stark brevity that "David behaved himself wisely" (see 1 Sam. 18:5, 14, 30). Psalm 140, however, tells us what David thought of Saul in those days: "Deliver me, O LORD, from the evil man: preserve me from the violent man" (v. 1). Psalm 141 tells how he had his daily quiet time, from whence his wisdom came. For certainly David's wisdom was not mere natural prudence. He was picking his way through a deadly minefield—one false step and Saul could have him arrested for high treason and hanged out of hand.

David's wisdom stemmed from the same source as ours does—a daily communion with his God:

> My God, accept my early vows,
> Like morning incense in thy house.
> And let my nightly worship rise
> Sweet as the evening sacrifice.
>
> Watch o'er my lips, and guard them, Lord,
> From every rash and heedless word;

> Nor let my feet incline to tread
> The guilty path where sinners lead.[2]

C. In the Cave: As an Outlaw

During two periods, David lived as a fugitive—when as a young man he fled from *Saul*, and when as an older man he fled from *Absalom*. Unless a given psalm specifies so, it is not always easy to identify into which of these two periods the fugitive psalms fall.

Psalm 34, for instance, was written after David's disastrous experience in Gath. We know that, for the title tells us so. Tired of forever running away from Saul, David fled across the border into Philistine country and sought political asylum with the king of Gath. At first he was hospitably received, but then the Philistines discovered who he was. This was the David who had slain their champion, Goliath! At once David's life was in danger. Scared out of his wits, he pretended to be mad and was subsequently tossed out of Gath as a lunatic. Psalm 34 was written as a prayer of thanks to God for delivering him when all seemed lost. For God had been generous. He had not reproached David for his lack of trust and for the loss of his testimony. He had delivered him. With his band of fellow outlaws around him, David bursts into song:

> O sinners! Come and taste His love,
> Come learn His pleasant ways.
> And let your own experience prove
> The sweetness of His grace.
>
> He bids His angels pitch their tents
> Round where His children dwell
> What ills their heavenly care prevents
> No earthly tongue can tell.[3]

One way and another, these fugitive years were turned by David to good account. It was the same when he fled from Absalom. The Hebrew hymnbook would be immeasurably the poorer if David had not had those experiences—or if he had turned them into a chronicle of complaints. David had a happy way of turning his buffetings into blessings.

This can be seen in Psalm 3. The whole nation had arisen against David and swept the handsome and unprincipled Absalom to the throne. David's cleverest counselor, Ahithophel, spurred on by resentful, revengeful rage against David, was soon telling Absalom what moves to make, and his advice was full of craft edged with cruelty. Absalom's troops were soon pouring into Jerusalem and mobilizing for a manhunt in the hills, while David was clambering over the rocks helped by a mere handful of friends. Every step was a prayer. Then, worn out, exhausted, utterly overwhelmed in body and soul, the deposed king found a sheltering cave, flung himself down, and instantly fell asleep. The next thing he knew it was morning. He had slept the whole night through and he felt like a new man. He could see his troubles in a new light. He reached for his harp and began to sing:

> I cried, and from His holy hill
> He bowed a listening ear;
> I called my Father and my God
> And he subdued my fear.
>
> He shed soft slumbers on mine eyes
> In spite of all my foes;
> I woke, and wondered at the grace
> That guarded my repose.
>
> What though the hosts of death and hell
> All armed against me stood,
> Terrors no more shall shake my soul
> My refuge is my God.[4]

David experienced, though, not just the period of testings.

II. THE PERIOD OF THE TRIUMPHS

David reigned through glorious years when the smile of God rested upon him and all his foes fled before him. Some twenty-three psalms seem to have been written during these prosperous and powerful years. One of the greatest of them is Psalm 139, in which David speaks of God's omniscience, omnipresence, and omnipotence. For in those early days of his reign he never lost sight of that. His reign was predicated on the fact that God saw all that he did; that God was ever present, not only with him but with all men; that ultimately all power came to rest in God.

So David sang of God's *omniscience*:

> Lord, Thou hast searched and seen me through;
> Thine eye commands with piercing view
> My rising and my resting hours,
> My heart and flesh with all their powers.

> My thoughts, before they were my own,
> Are to my God distinctly known;
> He knows the words I mean to speak
> Ere from my opening lips they break.[5]

And he sang of God's *omnipresence*:

> Could I so false, so faithless prove
> To quit thy service and Thy love,
> Where, Lord, could I Thy presence shun
> Or from Thy dreadful glory run?
>
> If up to heaven I take my flight,
> 'Tis there Thou dwellest enthroned in light;
> Or dive to hell, there vengeance reigns
> And Satan groans beneath Thy chains.
>
> If mounted on a morning ray
> I fly beyond the western sea,
> Thy swifter hand would first arrive
> And there arrest Thy fugitive.
>
> Or should I try to shun Thy sight
> Beneath the spreading veil of night;
> One glance of Thine, one piercing ray,
> Would kindle darkness into day.[6]

And then, surveying the wonders of his own physical form, David sang of God's *omnipotence*:

> 'Twas from Thy hand, my God, I came,
> A work of such a wondrous frame;
> In me Thy fearful marvels shine
> And each proclaims Thy skill divine.
>
> Thine eyes did all my limbs survey
> Which yet in dark confusion lay;
> Thou saw'st the daily growth they took,
> Formed by the model of Thy book.[7]

But David did not always remember these great truths. He forgot, he sinned, he committed two capital offences, and God smote him in both his kingdom and in his kindred.

III. The Period of the Troubles

Over two dozen psalms are related to David's sins and his consequent sorrow and suffering. For, even here, David's keen sense of spiritual truth was able to wring profit from his losses. Out of his travails and tears he distilled a most fragrant frankincense of penitence and petition and praise, pungent still.

Shall we ever cease to fly to Psalm 32, for instance, when seeking words wherewith to confess our sins and looking for words to assure again our souls of sin forgiven and peace with God?

> Happy the man to whom his God
> No more imputes his sin;
> But washed in the Redeemer's blood
> Hath made his garments clean.
>
> Happy beyond expression, he
> Whose debts are thus discharged
> And, from the guilty bondage free,
> He feels his soul enlarged.
>
> His spirit hates deceit and lies,
> His words are all sincere;
> He guards his heart, he guards his eye
> To keep his conscience clear.
>
> While I my inward guilt suppressed,
> No quiet could I find
> Thy wrath lay burning in my breast
> And racked my tortured mind.
>
> Then I confessed my troubled thoughts,
> My secret sins revealed;
> Thy pardoning grace forgave my faults,
> Thy grace my pardon sealed.[8]

So, one way and another, David wrote half the book of Psalms. Asaph, David's choir director, wrote a dozen. The sons of Korah wrote eleven; Moses wrote one;

two men celebrated for their wisdom, Heman and Ethan, both wrote one, and Solomon wrote two (Pss. 72, 127).

The Psalms, as they are arranged in our Bibles, are in the same order they were in the days of the Lord Jesus. It is worth remembering, when we read the Psalms, that we are reading words known and loved and memorized by Him. It was to the Psalms He turned in the hour of His deepest woe. In the upper room, He and His disciples sang psalms together—and we know exactly which psalms they sang. They sang the Passover Psalms (Pss. 113–118), essentially psalms of praise. At the annual commemoration of the Passover, the Jews sang Psalms 113 and 114 before the meal and before drinking the second festal cup. Then, at the close of the meal, at the time the fourth cup was filled, they sang Psalms 115–118. Close your eyes, picture the Lord Jesus at the head of the table gazing into the wine that spoke so eloquently of His blood soon to be shed, seeing so clearly what the next hours would hold for Him of agony and horror.

Then see Him as He brings His thoughts back to the Passover He was celebrating, His last Passover. A wondrous smile lights up His face. His rich voice raises the tune and rings out the words of Psalm 113:

> Ye servants of the Almighty King,
> In every age His praises sing;
> Where'er the sun shall rise or set,
> The nations shall His praise repeat.
>
> Above the earth, beyond the sky,
> Stands His high throne of majesty;
> Nor time, nor place His power restrain
> Nor bound His universal reign.
>
> Which of the sons of Adam dare,
> Or angels with their God compare?
> His glories how divinely bright,
> Who dwells in uncreated light!
>
> Behold His love! He stoops to view
> What saints above and angels do:
> And condescends yet more to know
> The mean affairs of men below.[9]

So He sang psalms in the upper room. He quoted them on the cross. They were on His lips when He rose from the dead. So when we meditate on the Psalms we are pondering pages dearly loved by our Lord.

Two vital elements characterize the psalms. One is the historical element and the other is the prophetical element. When you are reading the psalms, you are aware that you are reading history. If we derive our understanding of Israel's history solely from the historical books of the Bible, we miss a whole dimension of truth. The psalms reveal to us how the Hebrew people felt about the experiences through which they passed. Any nation passing through a time of crisis has strong feelings about it. We only need to think of the *belligerent* feelings aroused in this country when the Japanese bombed Pearl Harbor or of the *bitter* feelings aroused over the Vietnam War. How did Israel feel when a whole generation was condemned to wander for forty years in the wilderness because of national unbelief? Psalm 90 tells us that. How did Israel feel when uprooted because of apostasy and exiled to far-off Babylon? How did they feel when their captors asked them to sing some of their national songs? Psalm 137 tells us that.

The psalms mention such places as Jerusalem, Zion, Moab, Philista, Bashan, Hermon, Edom, and Tyre. They mention such people as Abraham and Lot and Jacob and Joseph and Aaron and David.

Suppose you were adrift and cast upon a desert island and the only book you had with you was a copy of the Psalms. How much of the Old Testament history could you reconstruct from that one book? Well, for one thing, you could reconstruct a detailed history of the Old Testament from the creation down to the time of David.

Many details in the life of David that are not even hinted at in the historical books can be learned from some of his psalms. After his sin with Bathsheba and the subsequent murder of Uriah, David evidently fell prey to a serious sickness. It can even be inferred from some of the things he and others said that he actually became a leper. This is not recorded in the historical books but it can be discovered in his psalms.

If we are aware that we are reading *history* when we read the psalms, we are also aware that we are reading *prophecy*, for every single psalm has a prophetic note to it. Some psalms are clearly messianic. They foretell the two comings of Christ—His coming to redeem and His coming to reign. Psalms 22 and 69, for instance, both clearly foretell the Lord's death and sketch a graphic picture of death by crucifixion as well as abandonment by God. Psalm 16 prophesies His resurrection; Psalm 68 speaks of His ascension into heaven; Psalm 119 foretells His present ministry as Great High Priest, and Psalms 96, 97, and 98 foretell His return. About fifteen psalms, in fact, are clearly messianic.

But this does not exhaust the prophetic element in the Psalms. Some psalms speak of the Gentile nations and anticipate the time when Christ will reign over all mankind. The greatest of these, probably, is Psalm 2. In that psalm David foresaw the rise of the nations to collective rebellion against God in the last days. He saw their world federation giving belligerent and blasphemous voice to their hatred of God and His Son. He heard the terrible laughter of God at this ultimate expression of the abysmal folly of fallen man. To think that finite, puny, mortal creatures of blood and mud could seriously consider overthrowing the throne of Almighty God! And he heard the Holy Spirit counsel the nations to be wise and make their peace with God's Son while still there was time.

There are *redemptive* psalms and there are *royal* psalms. There are *revengeful* psalms and there are *retrospective* psalms. There are *remorseful* psalms, *religious* psalms, and *rejoicing* psalms.

Do we have trouble knowing how to pray? We should take the psalms and pray them back to God. Do we have difficulty overcoming doubt and depression? We should go and live for a while in the psalms. Do we have a horror and fear of death? The psalms will help us put death where it belongs. Do we have a burden of guilt and shame, a deep awareness of sin? Then we should allow God to speak to us in the psalms.

When all is said and done, however, the book of Psalms is essentially a hymnbook. The best way to survey a *hymnbook* is to turn to its table of contents and see how the compiler has put the book together or, better still, turn to the back of the book and study the topical index.

Here is a suggested topical listing for the Psalms:

BOOK ONE: PSALMS 1–41

1. The Saint and the Sinner
2. Rebels of the World, Unite!
3. David at Mahanaim
4. An Evening Hymn
5. Good Morning, Lord!
6. A Dark Night
7. A Loud Cry
8. Death of a Champion
9. The Fall of the Beast
10. The Lawless One
11. Why Not Run Away and Hide?
12. The Deceitful Man
13. How Long? How Long? How Long?
14. The Depravity of Man
15. A Guest in the Lord's House
16. Satisfied

vv. 73–80 In Good Company
vv. 81–88 A Bottle in the Smoke
vv. 89–96 Settled in Heaven
vv. 97–104 A Scholar and a Saint
vv. 105–112 The Lamp
vv. 113–120 Trusting and Trembling
vv. 121–128 Lord, It Is Time
vv. 129–136 God's Wonderful Word
vv. 137–144 God's Word Is Always Right
vv. 145–152 Crying with the Whole Heart
vv. 153–160 When Affliction Comes
vv. 161–168 Peace in Spite of Persecution
vv. 169–176 A Final Plea
120. The War Lords
121. Safe in the Arms of Jesus
122. A Pilgrimage to Jerusalem
123. Scorned!
124. Clean Escaped!
125. Safe!
126. Free at Last!
127. Building House and Home
128. The Well Being of Home and Nation
129. Israel and Her Foes
130. A Penitential Psalm
131. A Humble Believer
132. God's Promise to David
133. The Unity of the Spirit
134. Without a Cloud Between
135. Worship
136. The Kindness of God
137. Jerusalem, Babylon, and Edom
138. Trusting When Things Go Wrong
139. From Everlasting Thou Art God
140. Deliverance from the Wicked Man
141. The Cunning Plot
142. Down in the Valley
143. Deep Depression
144. A Happy People
145. A Wonderful God
146. God Cares

147. The Goodness of God
148. Praise Him All Creatures Great and Small
149. The Song of the Sword
150. The Hallelujah Chorus

CHAPTER 21

PROVERBS

A Book of Rules

The English-speaking peoples have sprinkled the language with many drops of distilled wisdom:

> A stitch in time saves nine.
> Make hay while the sun shines.
> Look before you leap.
> A penny saved is a penny earned.

We recognize these sayings instantly. They are *proverbs*, pithy sayings that in a few pungent words give the results of years of human experience. Proverbs have fallen out of style somewhat in recent years, but in other ages people often quoted them.

Solomon was very fond of proverbs. He wrote hundreds of them and collected hundreds more. They were stamped from the mint of his keen intellect and passed into the current coinage of human speech. Many of his proverbs have become part and parcel of the general knowledge of the English-speaking world; thus the English-speaking world owes an enormous debt to the Bible—a debt it has very largely forgotten. When we say, for instance, "Spare the rod and spoil the child" (see 13:24 and others), we are paraphrasing from the book of Proverbs. When we speak of "heap[ing] coals of fire" on someone's head we are quoting from the Proverbs (25:22).

Solomon wrote 3,000 proverbs and 1,005 songs (1 Kings 4:32), and was wiser than all the fabled philosophers of his day, his wisdom being a direct gift from God (1 Kings 3:12). He wrote three of the books of the Bible: *Song of Solomon*, presumably when he was young and in love; *Proverbs* when he was middle-aged and his intellectual powers were at their zenith; *Ecclesiastes* when he was old, disappointed, and disillusioned with the carnality of much of his life.

We can readily picture the background against which Solomon wrote his books. His wealth and wisdom were the talk of every kingdom and tribe of his day. His great Tarshish ships plied the trade lanes of the Mediterranean and also found their way down the coastline of East Africa to Arabia and India, so that into Jerusalem flowed the exotic merchandise of the East. Great caravans of camels crossed the deserts, spreading his fame far and wide and returning with riches for the king.

From all over the East men came to hear his wisdom. They talked with bated breath of the godlike judgment that had suggested carving up a living child to share him half-and-half with two women, each claiming him as her own, thus revealing the true mother. His fame reached far south to Ethiopia, from whence came the Queen of Sheba, all the way up the Nile, across the burning sands of Sinai and on up to the hill country of Judah, there to sit at Solomon's feet in undisguised awe. As she turned back toward home at last, it was with an ache in her heart and a confession on her lips. "The half was not told me," she said (1 Kings 10:7).

Not all the proverbs originated with Solomon and not all were edited by him. The wise (22:17), the men of Hezekiah (25:1), Agur (30:1), and King Lemuel and his mother (31:1) all shared in the production of this book.[1] Likely, the "men of Hezekiah" included Isaiah and Micah. Perhaps some later editing was done by Ezra. They are filled with practical wisdom for all ages but, in a special way perhaps, should be taught to our young people.

The book of Proverbs richly repays study, abounding as it does with characters who stand in bold relief drawn by a skillful sage. Dr. Scroggie delineates many of them for us in graphic form.

> [There is] the prating fool, winking with the eye; the practical joker, as dangerous as a madman casting firebrands about; the talebearer; the man who "harps upon a matter," separating chief friends; the whisperer whose words are like dainty morsels going down into the innermost parts of the belly; the backbiting tongue, drawing gloomy looks all around as surely as the north wind brings rain; the false boaster, compared to wind and clouds without rain; the haste to be rich; the liberal man that scattereth and yet increaseth, while others are withholding only to come to want; the speculator holding back his corn amid the curses of the people; the man of wandering life, like a restless bird; the unsocial man that separateth himself, foregoing wisdom for the sake of his own private desire; the cheerfulness that is a continual feast.[2]

The book of Proverbs contrasts "wisdom" and "folly." Six different Hebrew words translated "wisdom" and three different Hebrew words for "fool" are used in this book. Solomon's own son, Rehoboam, turned out to be a fool, so he could not have paid much attention to the wisdom penned by his learned father. In these days of lowered moral standards every young person should be made familiar with the inevitable end of immoral living so clearly pictured in Proverbs. Happy are those teenagers whose parents have drilled them in the Scriptures and taught them those absolute moral standards demanded of all men by God.

In Proverbs, too, we find Solomon's cure for disobedient children, a cure much neglected today (Prov. 13:24; 19:18; 22:15; 23:13; 29:15). Some years ago a columnist in one of Chicago's largest daily newspapers printed a letter he had received from a distraught mother of a rebellious teenage son. In essence she said, "My son is running around with the wrong crowd and breaking my heart. He will not listen to me and defies me to my face. What can I do about it?" Jack Mably's answer was terse and to the point: "Shrink him down to seventeen months and begin all over again." In other words, for this lad the mother's awakening had come too late. "Spare the rod and spoil the child" is the homespun English version of a truth that is deeply embedded in the book of Proverbs.

One fascinating way to study the book of Proverbs is to see its pearls of wisdom strung into the lives of Bible characters. Think, for example, how Proverbs 16:18, "Pride goeth before destruction, and a haughty spirit before a fall," is illustrated in the lives of Asahel, Benhadad, Nebuchadnezzar, Herod Agrippa, and in the histories of Edom and Babylon. See how the first part of Proverbs 10:7, "The memory of the just is blessed," is illustrated in the lives of Elisha, Jehoiada, the Virgin Mary, and Dorcas, and how the second part of the proverb, "but the name of the wicked shall rot," is reflected in the lives of Cain, Balaam, Ahaz, Athaliah, Jezebel, Herod the Great, and Judas Iscariot. Almost all of the proverbs can thus be related to life—not only to the lives of Bible figures but to our own lives and the lives of those around us today.

The book of Proverbs is intended to do for our *daily* lives what the book of Psalms does for our *devotional* lives. Psalms tells us how to worship; Proverbs tells us how to walk. Psalms was the Hebrew *hymnbook*; Proverbs was the Hebrew *handbook*. The one is chiefly concerned with *what I believe*; the other is chiefly concerned with *how I behave*.

The book of Proverbs is quite different from any other book in the Bible. It is not history, or poetry, or rhapsody, or prophecy, or law, or ritual, or story, or dogma. It belongs with the Wisdom literature of the Hebrew people but it differs from the other Wisdom books of Job and Ecclesiastes. It deals with countless topics—wisdom, sin, goodness, wealth, temptation, pride, humility, justice, folly, friendship, idleness, poverty, family life, pleasure, revenge, strife, gluttony, drunkenness, success. Regardless of Proverbs' myriad subjects, an outline of the book can be produced.

   I. The Prologue (1:1–9)
     A. The Purpose of the Book (1:1–6)

B. The Principles of the Book (1:7–9)

II. The Monologue (1:10–29:27)

A. Moral Issues (1:10–9:18)

   1. The Way of Wickedness (1:10–19)

   2. The Way of Wisdom (1:20–9:18)

      a. Wisdom's Plea (1:20–33)

      b. Wisdom's Protection (2:1–22)

      c. Wisdom's Path (3:1–5:23)

      d. Wisdom's Precepts (6:1–35)

      e. Wisdom's Presence (7:1–27)

      f. Wisdom's Patience (8:1–9:18)

B. Miscellaneous Issues (10:1–19:5)

   1. Contrasts: The Lot of the Godly and the Ungodly (10:1–15:33)

      a. Blessings Gained or Lost (10:1–32)

      b. Behavior Good and Bad (11:1–15:33)

   2. Comparisons: The Life of the Godly and the Ungodly (16:1–19:5)

      a. The Right Focus in Life (16:1–33)

      b. The Right Features in Life (17:1–19:5)

         (1) How to Build Contentment (17:1–28)

         (2) How to Build Character (18:1–19:5)

C. Monarchial Issues (19:6–29:27)

   1. Proverbs of Solomon: Edited by Himself (19:6–24:34)

      a. The Favor of the Throne (19:6–11)

      b. The Fury of the Throne (19:12–20:7)

      c. The Fear of the Throne (20:8–30)

      d. The Functions of the Throne (21:1–24:34)

   2. Proverbs of Solomon: Edited by Hezekiah (25:1–29:27)

      a. The King and His Subjects (25:1–27:27)

      b. The King and His Sins (28:1–29:14)

      c. The King and His Sons (29:15–27)

III. The Epilogue (30:1–31:31)

A. The Ideal Life (30:1–33)

B. The Ideal Wife (31:1–31)

The real problem in surveying the book of Proverbs is knowing exactly where to start. The book contains thirty-one chapters and 915 verses, and almost every verse is another flash of concentrated light. But let us begin thus:

I. THE PROLOGUE (1:1–9)

In the first half-dozen verses Solomon sets before us two basic elements:

A. The Purpose of the Book (1:1–6)

He sets forth the goals he had in mind when writing it. The goals relate to four classes of people whom he has in mind. *The seeker* is the ordinary person, the man in the street, if you like, the person of average intelligence—the rank and file of the human race. Solomon's goal for such is that they get to know wisdom, instruction, understanding (v. 2).

The statesman—whether it be the king on his throne, the politician in office, the judge upon the bench—is whom we would call today a public servant. Solomon's goal is to teach them wisdom, but the special kind of wisdom needed by such to guide and guard the ship of state—the wisdom of justice, judgment, and equity (v. 3).

The simpleton is the fool, the person Solomon here calls "the simple." Gullible people will always be around. Solomon has words that will arm them against the con man and the exploiter (v. 4).

For *the scholar*, Solomon wants to add to the learning, the understanding, the wise counsels of the learned. He wants to set before scholars some guidelines for interpretation, whether it be of matters relating to God's Word or man's world (vv. 5–6). That is the purpose of this book.

B. The Principles of the Book (1:7–9)

"The fear of the LORD is the beginning of knowledge: but fools despise wisdom and instruction" (v. 7). For the most part, Solomon teaches by contrast—the contrast between the wise man and the foolish man. The difference between the two will be brought into focus around two basic principles: *reverence for God* and *respect for authority*—the two areas where modern man has lost his moorings. No wonder the nations of the earth are headed on a catastrophic collision course economically, ecologically, socially, culturally, religiously, militarily, politically, and internationally! Modern man has no respect for God and no respect for authority, and as a result, the world is in upheaval. Modern society is like an express train thundering out of control through the night, with throttles wide open, with the engineers engaged in a deadly struggle in the cab, and with a dangerous curve right ahead.

Solomon wants to teach us that "the fear of the Lord is the beginning of wisdom." He will use half a dozen Hebrew words in the writing of this book to bring out the full force of what he means by wisdom. He will use words that mean wisdom, purely and simply; words that mean discernment or discrimination; words that mean prudence or good sense; words that mean shrewdness; words that mean understanding.

Surely that is what the nations need today! They need to elect to office men of wisdom, men who have discernment and discrimination, prudence, understanding, men who can negotiate with shrewdness and moral principle. They need men who have this kind of wisdom because they "fear the Lord" far more than they fear the press, the public, and their peers.

Solomon uses three words for fools in this book. He uses a word that means lax or careless in mental and bodily habits; a word that means dense or stupid—the kind of denseness and stupidity that comes from ignorance of God; and a word that means a vulgar bore. One can sympathize with Solomon as he hammers away with these words of his for he had a fool for a son. It was too bad that he himself failed to live by the principles he so ably enunciates. Poor Rehoboam could see his own father living a life of sensual indulgence and tyrannical privilege, so it is little wonder he paid but scant heed to Solomon's sage sayings. "What you are," he might justly have said, "speaks so loudly I cannot hear a word you say."

Now let us turn to the main part of the book and see how Solomon develops his theme.

II. The Monologue (1:10–29:27)

The first nine chapters of Proverbs are almost a little book on their own. They are fairly easy to analyze because they consist of a series of contrasts between immortal wisdom—personified as a lovely lady, pure and stately and attractive—and sin—personified as an immoral woman peddling her sordid wares for lust and filthy lucre. The person who knows the fear of the Lord in his life will be drawn to the first woman; the fool who despises wisdom and instruction will be ensnared by the second. In summing up these first nine chapters, we might say that they are made up of three issues.

A. Moral Issues (1:10–9:18)

Two principal Hebrew words are used to describe the immoral woman in this section of Proverbs. The first is a word meaning "apostate to a foreign religion"—the kind of religion that employed immorality as an essential part of worship. What Solomon had in mind here was the apostate Hebrew woman gone over to the idolatrous impurities of heathen religion. The other word means a foreign woman of the same sort. There is a reason for using these two words in warning against immoral behavior: all sexual immorality is a sin in the sight of God in heaven, but sexual immorality in the name of religion is an offensive stench in the nostrils of God.

Five warnings against sexual immorality are found in these nine chapters and five contrasting descriptions of wisdom. In these verses we meet the *passionate stranger* whose house is at the top of a steep incline, at the bottom of which is the yawning gulf of the grave itself.

We meet, too, the *persuasive smoothy*, whose lips are like the honeycomb and whose mouth is smoother than oil, but whose feet lead the soul straight down to hell.

We also encounter the *promiscuous seducer*, the adulteress who is like a prowling beast of prey but whose prey is the human soul.

We meet as well the *purposeful streetwalker* out to proposition the simpletons who find her invitations attractive and whose clients are likened to the ox going up the ramp of the slaughterhouse.

Here we also find the *pitiful simpleton*, the idiotic woman who calls to those who pass her house to come and enjoy her delights. "Stolen waters are sweet," she says, "and bread eaten in secret is pleasant." "Her guests," says the Holy Spirit, "are in the depths of hell" (9:17–18).

Today's society is permissive. At one time Western society had widely accepted standards for morals and manners, but no more. In our culture, everything goes. Television and X-rated movies can be blamed for contributing to the breakdown in public morals. On a typical evening, one commercial television network alone aired three shows about police activities—one right after the other. The scenes included a married couple separated on Christmas Eve, a drunk brandishing a broken bottle and menacing people in a bar, a priest killed in a church, a drunken driver, a stripper, a peeping Tom, six other killings, and more than half a dozen woundings.

By the time the average American child has reached the age of eighteen he has spent 20,000 hours before the television set—more time than he spends at school—and in 98 percent of American households owning television sets, he has seen extensive drug and alcohol use, violence, sex, greed, and gambling—a continual wholesale assault on traditional values.

Meanwhile, soap operas are busy brainwashing the mothers of these children. According to the average soap opera, typical American life features abortion, premarital sex, extramarital relationships, blackmail, murder, drugs, wiretapping, and embezzlement.

Violence is so much a part of television that it occurs about five to nine times an hour in prime time, and as often as thirty times an hour on Saturday morning and after-school cartoons. On television, immorality is the rule, not the exception.

No wonder that we have a sex-obsessed culture. One symptom of our sex-crazy society is the Swingers' Club. In a write-up in *Time* magazine, one such club was described (there are at least half a dozen operating openly in Manhattan alone).[3] The proprietor had two hundred couples on hand and a waiting line for lockers. The locker room was, ironically, the only place on the establishment where people were modest. The establishment attracts 6,500 people a month looking for erotic sexual satisfaction, and grosses $90,000 a month. About the only rule enforced is that couples must join and leave any orgy in pairs. Some of the scenes described in the magazine are completely disgusting to a clean-minded person. The tough-looking bouncer in the establishment, whose job it is to enforce the club's few rules, told the reporter, "These are good people. I am more of a shepherd looking after my flock"!

The Supreme Court of the United States has banned the Bible from our classrooms, but it has not banned filth from television or pornography from bookstores or vice from our streets. Our generation thinks vice is manly, and an inviting pigsty—a good place in which to wallow.

How we need to get back to these first nine chapters of the book of Proverbs! The moral standards they espouse are not Christianity, which has a far higher ethic than even that advocated in Proverbs. Rather, these chapters espouse simple basic morality.

Let us not forget that God warns repeatedly in the Bible that He will punish both the culture and the individual who plays fast and loose with morality. In every single one of the five examples Solomon gives, he adds a warning. In four of the five illustrations he says that death and hell await the immoral person, and in the other illustration he says that the immoral person destroys his own soul.

We should read these chapters to ourselves and to our children every day. We should buy the biggest billboards, rent the most heavily traveled intersections in which to erect them, and on those billboards display these proverbs in box-car letters. We should buy up television time and read these chapters over and over and over again to our generation. These are divine precepts. They are warnings against impure behavior.

B. Miscellaneous Issues (10:1–19:5)

From this point, while we have structurally analyzed the book, all a general survey can do is illustrate the kinds of things Solomon covers. A considerable number of proverbs, for instance, relates to *parenthood*. These proverbs deal with parent-child relationships with a heavy emphasis on discipline—especially on the kind of discipline enforced with the rod. Our generation has largely opted against corporal punishment as a means of enforcing obedience and discipline, or of inducing respect. Such lack of enforcement is one reason we have severe behavioral problems on our hands. *Time* magazine says, "A new remorseless, mutant juvenile seems to have been born, and there is no more terrifying figure in America today."[4] It is a generation raised without the rod, raised for the most part without discipline of any kind, and now without any intention of curbing its passions and lusts.

Here are Solomon's views (or rather, the Holy Spirit's views) on parental discipline:

He that spareth his rod hateth his son: but he that loveth him chasteneth him betimes [carefully seeks discipline for him]. (13:24)

Chasten thy son while there is hope, and let not thy soul spare for his crying. (19:18)

Foolishness is bound in the heart of a child; but the rod of correction shall drive it far from him. (22:15)

Withhold not correction from the child: for if thou beatest him with the rod, he shall not die. Thou shalt beat him with the rod, and shalt deliver his soul from hell. (23:13–14)

Not a very popular philosophy today. Other factors figure in teaching a child obedience, of course, but it is hard to see how a Bible-believing Christian can get away from such clear-cut teachings of the Spirit of God.

Other proverbs deal with *prosperity*. We are living in a materialistic age, the conventional wisdom of which is to get rich and to stay rich. Nor are most people too fussy as to how they acquire their wealth. Solomon, who was one of the wealthiest men in the world, has some things to say about prosperity—or rather the Holy Spirit has some things to say to us about it:

Treasures of wickedness profit nothing. (10:2)

Riches profit not in the day of wrath. (11:4)

A good man leaveth an inheritance to his children's children: and the wealth of the sinner is laid up for the just. (13:22)

In the house of the righteous is much treasure: but in the revenues of the wicked is trouble. (15:6)

C. Monarchial Issues (19:6–29:27)

1. Proverbs of Solomon: Edited by Himself (19:6–24:34)

Solomon was a king and a capable and successful administrator. He knew all about diplomacy, politics, and the art of statecraft. His observations on practical government should be a handbook for all in office today. "When it goeth well with the righteous, the city rejoiceth: and when the wicked perish, there is shouting" (11:10). That would be a good text for most city halls. Instead of proclaiming such abominations as a "Gay Rights Week," what society needs are stiff laws against pornography, permissiveness, and perversion, and firm law enforcement to uphold righteousness, morality, decency, and purity.

Here are two more of Solomon's comments on statecraft:

Righteousness exalteth a nation: but sin is a reproach to any people. (14:34)

Every purpose is established by counsel: and with good advice make war. (20:18)

The Bible does not support pacifism. The Christian ethic does not apply to the state in this age; it applies to individuals in the state. The Sermon on the Mount is only for individuals today. Its lofty precepts cannot be nationally and universally enforced until Christ comes to reign. There are times when a nation has to go to war. There are times when a country, for its very survival, has to draw a line with its foes, as Britain and France did with Germany in the matter of Poland, and say, "That's enough. One more move and it's war."

Solomon has more to say about this:

A wise king scattereth the wicked, and bringeth the wheel over them. (20:26)

The king's heart is in the hand of the Lord, as the rivers of water: he turneth it whithersoever he will. (21:1)

The horse is prepared against the day of battle: but safety is of the Lord. (21:31)

That is, a nation's first line of defense is spiritual. If we allow the spiritual life of a nation to be eroded by the forces of evil, then no matter how vast and efficient its military establishment, how far-reaching and effective its alliances, that nation is vulnerable to its foes.

Again and again during World War II, King George VI of England called the nation to prayer. Just after the end of the war, W. E. Vallance wrote a book titled, *The War, the Weather and God*, in which the author demonstrated that God honored those national days of prayer—with one exception. That was when the British government officially ignored the king's call and urged workers, in view of the national emergency, to put in longer hours on the very day the king had requested a day of prayer.

Still speaking as a king, Solomon wrote much in the proverbs about pride, punishment, prudence, poverty, pleasure, and practical and theological piety. Go through the book, for instance, and write down the dozen or more references to the phrase "abomination to the Lord."[5] List the things the Lord detests—a proud look, a lying tongue, a false witness, he that soweth discord between brethren, wicked-ness, a false balance, sacrifices by the wicked, the way of the wicked, the thoughts of the wicked, he that justifieth the wicked, he that turneth away his ear from hearing the law so that even his prayer becomes an abomination to God.

2. Proverbs of Solomon: Edited by Hezekiah (25:1–29:27)

This section draws scores of little word pictures, little illustrations that glow like little sections in a stained glass window. Here are a few examples:

A word fitly spoken is like apples of gold in pictures of silver. (25:11)

The illustration is graphic and refers to a piece of jewelry. Solomon envisions golden fruit in silver salvers—certainly something rare, not common. A word fitly spoken is like that—rare.

As the cold of snow in time of harvest, so is a faithful messenger to them that send him: for he refresheth the soul of his masters. (25:13)

It would be unusual to have a breath of cold air blowing down on the hot harvest fields of Palestine. Reaping the harvest was hot and heavy work, for the hard manual labor had to be done in the burning heat of a subtropical climate. We can imagine what a sudden gust of chilled air would be like! It would be most refreshing. Just so, a faithful messenger is refreshing to his masters. It is hard and rare to find a messenger who will faithfully, and in the proper spirit, present his master's case without intruding his own thoughts. We can find scores of these word pictures. Here are a few:

As the door turneth upon its hinges, so doth the slothful upon his bed. (26:14)

Where no wood is, there the fire goeth out: so where there is no talebearer, the strife ceaseth. (26:20)

A continual dropping in a very rainy day and a contentious woman are alike. (27:15)

A poor man that oppresseth the poor is like a sweeping rain which leaveth no food. (28:3)

III. THE EPILOGUE (30:1–31:31)

The last two chapters are written by a man named Agur and a person called King Lemuel (sometimes, as we have noted, taken to be different names for Solomon himself). The epilogue is in two parts.

A. The Ideal Life (30:1–33)

The writings of Agur are termed "prophecy." Organizing his observations into groups of four, his themes are the *ignorance* of man, the *inspiration* of Scripture, and the *issues* of life.

B. The Ideal Wife (31:1–31)

Solomon began the book of Proverbs by warning against the wanton woman— and he himself had wide experience of such women, with his three hundred wives and his seven hundred concubines. His palace was a veritable Babel of tongues and must have been a hotbed of jealousy, bad temper, and intrigue. In his closing statement in the book, however, he describes the ideal wife—one suspects rather wistfully, as though he had not found such a woman himself. He describes the ideal wife as a *person*, as a *partner*, and as a *parent*, and he says that the price of such a woman is far above rubies.

How can we close this survey of the book of Proverbs? While wisdom is its principal theme, wisdom is, after all, rather an abstract trait. What God has done for us in the gospels is to incarnate that wisdom in flesh and blood in the person of His beloved Son. And it is as if He has said, "*This* is what it's all about—a life lived just like this." And that *incarnate* wisdom can become *indwelling* wisdom when we invite that glorious One into our hearts.

CHAPTER 22

ECCLESIASTES

A Book of Regrets

S olomon began well. His father, David, despite his personal failures, was one of the great saints of the Old Testament. When Solomon first came to the throne he was afraid he could not fill the shoes of his illustrious father. He thus began his reign by opening diplomatic relations with heaven and, as a result, had God's smile beaming upon him. But as the years slipped away, he made many sad and serious mistakes. He entered into political marriages, for instance, with the daughters of pagan kings and allowed these foreign women to import their vile religions into Israel. Gradually his spirituality declined as his Oriental luxury and opulence increased, and as his harem dinned like Babel with more and more strange tongues. Jerusalem became the home of heathendom.

As Solomon lost his vision of the true and living God, he began to degenerate into a common Eastern despot. He multiplied his slaves, ground onerous taxes from his subjects, and at last followed his outlandish wives into the abominable rites of Ashtoreth and worshipped the abomination of the Zidonians, and even engaged in the savage worship of Milcom and Moloch. It is against this background of wisdom and wealth, women and false worship that the books of Solomon should be read.

An old fable tells of a spider that descended from the lofty rafters of a barn on a single thread. He alighted near the corner of a window, anchored his thread, and from it weaved his web. He had chosen a corner of the barn that was very busy with insects, and soon he waxed fat and prospered. One day, in his prosperity, he was surveying his web when he noticed the strand that reached away up into the unseen. He had long since forgotten its significance and, thinking it to be but a stray thread, he snapped it. Instantly his whole world fell.

That is what Solomon did. In his early days he established a vital line of communication with God, a strand that reached away up into the unseen. Then he grew prosperous, became one of the world's great ones, was courted by ambassadors and kings and, in due course, he forgot the meaning of the strand that linked him with the unseen. He broke off communication with heaven—and, before long, his whole world caved in.

Now, as a disappointed, disillusioned old man, conscious of the fact that he had a fool for a son, that he had lost the love of his people, that his prodigal ways had sown the seeds of division and decay into the Davidic kingdom, and that he had done more to tear down the Davidic throne than he had ever done to build it up, Solomon looked back over a misspent life and wrote this book we call Ecclesiastes.

Solomon knew all about the good life. He had tasted of all that this life has to offer. All that wealth can demand, all that wisdom and love of learning can invent or devise, all that fame can bring—Solomon had it all and in full measure. Moreover he had a proud ancestry, a godly father, a rich national heritage, and a personal knowledge of God and His Word.

Solomon tasted to the full all that life "under the sun" can offer, and wrote Ecclesiastes to show that "all is vanity and vexation of spirit." The abiding value of Ecclesiastes is right there. It concludes that only God can satisfy the deepest hungers of the human heart. While much of the book is undoubtedly pessimistic, the last chapter is positive in its note of assurance. Beyond the sun is a living God who can and will fill the hearts of those who will let Him.

Other men have discovered, by hard and bitter experience, some of the truths Solomon records for us in Ecclesiastes. One such man was Cecil Rhodes. He went out to South Africa when still a young man, at a time when Britain was reaching for empire. At the age of twenty-seven he founded the prestigious DeBeers Mining Company, and within eight short years controlled the entire diamond mining industry of South Africa. At thirty-six, he became Prime Minister of the Cape colony. Five years later, he dominated the gold mining industry of the country. His legacy to the British Empire upon his death was Rhodesia (north and south), a vast spread of territory in Africa equal to Germany, France, and Spain put together. He was probably the richest man in the world.

Cecil Rhodes was a personal friend of General Booth, the founder of the Salvation Army, and probably one of the poorest men in the world. The two men were traveling together one day by train. Presently the general leaned across to his friend, tapped him on the knee, and said, "Tell me, Rhodes, are you a happy man?" The magnate looked at the preacher and said, "Me? Happy? Good heavens, no!" He had learned what Solomon learned, that a life lived without reference to God is empty and that power and possessions, position and prestige cannot make a man happy.

It is obvious from Ecclesiastes that Solomon was not a happy man. He was a haunted man, and in this book he introduces us to the ghost that haunted him. It shows up increasingly in chapter after chapter as the book proceeds. The ghost that haunted Solomon is the same ghost that haunts every unregenerate man and every backslidden believer. The name of the ghost is *Death*.

This book is really a sermon in which Solomon takes as his theme "Life under the sun," and discourses on his subject from every angle. Its philosophies, observations, and arguments are typically those of the materialist, the man of the world, and it is from this viewpoint that the book must be studied and understood.

I. The Preacher's Subject (1:1–11)
   A. He States His Text (1:1–2)
   B. He States His Topic (1:3–11)
     There seems to be:
     1. No Purpose in Anything (1:3–8)
     2. No Point to Anything (1:9–11)
II. The Preacher's Sermon (1:12–10:20)
   A. Some of the Things He Had Sought (1:12–2:26)
     Observe:
     1. His Persistent Search (1:12–2:10)
     2. His Pessimistic Summary (2:11–26)
       a. The Barrenness of Life (2:11–16)
       b. The Bitterness of Life (2:17–19)
       c. The Boredom of Life (2:20–26)
   B. Some of the Things He Had Seen (chaps. 3–6)
     He had seen the vanity of:
     1. Time Without Eternity (3:1–11)
     2. A New Leaf Without A New Life (3:12–17)
     3. Mortality Without Immortality (3:18–22)
     4. Might Without Right (4:1–3)
     5. Plenty Without Peace (4:4–8)
     6. Prosperity Without Posterity (4:9–12)
     7. Sovereignty Without Sagacity (4:13–16)
     8. Religion Without Reality (5:1–6)
     9. Wealth Without Health (5:7–20)
    10. Treasure Without Pleasure (6:1–6)
    11. Life Without Length (6:11–12)
   C. Some of the Things He Had Studied (chaps. 7–10)
     He had studied:
     1. Some of Life's Frustrations (chap. 7)

He is cynical about:
  a. The Better Things of Life (7:1–14)
  b. The Bitter Things of Life (7:15–29)
  2. Some of Life's Fallacies (chap. 8)
  a. The Fiction of Being Great (8:1–9)
  b. The Folly of Being Godless (8:10–13)
  c. The Fantasy of Being Good (8:14)
  d. The Frivolity of Being Gay (8:15)
  e. The Fault with Being Gifted (8:16–17)
  3. Some of Life's Failures (chap. 9)
  a. Man's Brief Mortality (9:1–10)
  b. Man's Bitter Moments (9:11–12)
  c. Man's Bad Memory (9:13–18)
  4. Some of Life's Facts (chap. 10)
  According to his observations we can expect:
  a. The Triumph of Folly (10:1–7)
    (1) Over Everything Reasonable (10:1–3)
    (2) Over Everything Right (10:4–7)
  b. The Triumph of "Fate" (10:8–20)
    (1) Over the Laboring Man (10:8–11)
    (2) Over the Learned Man (10:12–17)
    (3) Over the Lazy Man (10:18)
    (4) Over the Laughing Man (10:19–20)
III. The Preacher's Summary (chaps. 11–12)
  A. He Repeats His Complaints About Life (chap. 11)
  He does so by issuing three challenges:
  1. Look Well to Life's Future Prospects (11:1–6)
  Form those prospects if you can!
  2. Look Well to Life's Fleeting Present (11:7–8)
  Fill that present if you can!
  3. Look Well to Life's Frivolous Past (11:9–10)
  Forget that past if you can!
  B. He Relates His Conclusions About Life (chap. 12)
  These conclusions concern:
  1. Man and His Maker (12:1)
  2. Man and His Mortality (12:2–14)

I. The Preacher's Subject (1:1–11)

Ecclesiastes has been called "the sphinx of Hebrew literature with unsolved riddles of history and life." Like Job, Solomon did not have all the answers to life. Moreover he was writing, under divine inspiration, from the viewpoint of a worldly man. The most valuable lesson to be learned from this book is that death is inescapable, and that its shadow falls on everything we do. The worldly man must be haunted by the specter of Saul.

"Vanity of vanities, saith the Preacher, vanity of vanities; all is vanity" (1:2). Life as most people live it is just so much—like the thought behind the word for "vanity"—chasing of the wind. Solomon is going to demonstrate, by observation, by deduction, and from personal experience that a life lived without God is empty, futile, and pointless.

Where did Solomon find the text for his sermon? It had to have a text, otherwise it would merely be a philosophical discourse. Perhaps he found his text in one of his father's psalms. A psalm that would make a particularly apt text for Ecclesiastes is Psalm 39, especially verses 5 and 11:

> Behold, thou hast made my days as an handbreadth; and mine age is as nothing before thee: verily every man at his best state is altogether vanity. Selah. . . . When thou with rebukes dost correct man for iniquity, thou makest his beauty to consume away like a moth: surely every man is vanity. Selah.

Solomon leaves us in no doubt about his topic—life as lived by man "under the sun" (the expression occurs at least twenty-seven times in the book[1]), life that is lived solely for what this world has to offer, life lived without reference to the world to come. His great aim is to demonstrate that there is little point or purpose in anything so long as one's horizons are dominated by the things of time and sense.

II. THE PREACHER'S SERMON (1:12–10:20)

A. Some of the Things He Had Sought (1:12–2:26)

His sermon elaborates on these things. Few people have been so ably equipped as Solomon to write such a book as this. He was a king. He had been born and bred in a deeply religious atmosphere in the land of Israel, and with a father who had a heart and mind to write half the book of Psalms. He was endowed with great natural gifts and was wealthy beyond words. He had been raised to the throne, and by divine decree was able to reign in peace and prosperity nearly all his days. He was endowed with keen insight and a restless, catholic, exploring mind, schooled in the Word of God. He had even been granted two direct communications from God. Such was Solomon. If ever a man could write this book it was he.

The first thing he did was to give himself over to the world of *thought*. He imagined he could find fulfillment in becoming the world's greatest intellectual. The historian (1 Kings 4:30–32) tells us of Solomon's reputation as a man of wisdom.

People came from far distant lands to listen to him lecture on psychology, natural history, and practical statecraft. His wisdom, indeed, became a proverb in the land. But all intellectualism did for him was fill his soul with vexation. Obviously this was a false path to follow.

Then he gave himself over to the world of *thrills* and abandoned himself to the gratification of every sensual indulgence and every form of entertainment the world had to offer. His revelry was unstinted and unrestrained. His ultimate conclusion on this way of life—"It is mad" (2:2). Sensual pleasure leads to satiation and even insanity.

In a reaction against the bitter disillusion of the pursuit of pleasure he decided to try the world of *things*. He went into business and became a great mercantile prince. His mighty Tarshish ships plowed the sea lanes of the world. His caravans reached into distant lands. His warehouses were filled with exotic goods. And he had the Midas touch; everything turned to gold. His annual personal income amounted to hundreds upon hundreds of talents of gold. Even the pots and pans in his kitchen were of gold! But when he was a preeminent success in business, his fame spoken of in all the civilized world, he summed it all up—"I hated life," he says (2:17). It would seem he even considered suicide as a means of ending it all.

B. Some of the Things He Had Seen (chaps. 3–6)

Having failed to find the answer to life's longings in the things he had sought, he began to observe life more carefully. He carefully observed life as it unfolded all around him. He records the vanity of everything he saw—the vanity of time without eternity, of a new leaf without a new life, of mortality without immortality, of might without right, of prosperity without posterity. The list goes on and on. No matter what he observed so carefully, nothing satisfied. Life was empty! Pointless! Vanity!

Typical of his complaints about life is the one he voiced at the very beginning of this search for meaning by means of observation. "[God] hath made every thing beautiful in his time," he said, "also he hath set the world in their heart" (3:11). That "world" literally means "the ages" or, as someone has suggested, "eternity."

The wail wrung from Solomon's empty heart was echoed by the dissolute Augustine before he found Christ: "Thou hast made us for thyself and restless is our heart until it comes to rest in thee."[2] God has engineered the human soul for eternity, and there is nothing big enough under the sun to fill it.

C. Some of the Things He Had Studied (chaps. 7–10)

"I returned, and considered," he says again and again (see 4:1, 4, 15 and others). He carefully weighed and examined all that came to his attention, and he became an undisguised cynic. He became cynical about *well doing*: "There is a just man that perisheth in his righteousness, and there is a wicked man that prolongeth his life in his wickedness" he said (7:15). In other words, what's the use of even trying to be good? He displayed his cynicism about *wisdom*: "I said, I will be wise; but it was far from me" (7:23). He displayed his cynicism about *women*: "I find more bitter than death," he says, "the woman, whose heart is *snares and nets*. . . . Behold, this have I found, saith the preacher, counting one by one, to find out the account: . . . one man among a thousand have I found; but a woman among all those have I not found" (7:26–28). Roaming his harem, listening to the babble of foreign voices that dinned in his ears, aware of the intrigue and plots that went on and of the petty squabbles among his many wives, he groaned because he could not find a single one compatible with himself.

Increasingly, Solomon became obsessed with the fact of death, with the fact that death awaits everybody. It makes no difference whether a person is wise or foolish, good or bad, optimistic or pessimistic, glad or sad, gifted or disabled, each one comes to the same end. Death catches up with them all. We have heard the expression "the fly in the ointment." It comes right out of this section of Ecclesiastes. And, typically, it is a dead fly. For that is the fly in the ointment for every person living solely for this life—sooner or later death will come along and end it all.

III. The Preacher's Summary (chaps. 11–12)

A. He Repeats His Complaints About Life (chap. 11)
With a sigh of despair, Solomon repeats his complaints about life. "All . . . is vanity. . . . Rejoice, O young man, in thy youth; . . . but know thou, that for all these things God will bring thee into judgment . . . childhood and youth are vanity" (11:8–10).

Benjamin Disraeli, the famous Jewish statesman who helped make Britain great—gifted, brilliant, popular, and successful as he was—echoed Solomon's complaint. He wrote, "Youth is a Blunder; Manhood a struggle; Old Age a regret."[3] If a person is going to limit his horizons to this world, to the things of time and sense, then, of course, there is no more to be said.

B. He Relates His Conclusions About Life (chap. 12)
"Remember now thy Creator in the days of thy youth. . . . Let us hear the conclusion of the whole matter: Fear God, and keep his commandments: for this is the whole duty of man" (12:1, 13). At last Solomon lifted his head above the fogs and mists of this world to catch a fresh glimpse of something beyond the sun.

He appeals to youth in particular, urging them to find a better perspective, to get God squarely into the picture, and to live in the light of the fact that, in the end, they will be personally accountable to Him. And they had better not delay, for old age with its infirmities, its set habits, its increasing weakness, its special problems, comes only too soon. In this passage of singular poetic magnificence he describes the sinister approach of old age.

Here, then, is Ecclesiastes. It is a book for modern man, trapped on the tread-mill of life, blinded by humanism and materialism, trying to find answers without God.

One turns away from this sad book and is thankful to discover a glorious answer to life in a magnificent word of the apostle Paul. Paul's answer to the gloom and pessimism of Ecclesiastes rings out from higher ground than was ever occupied by Solomon—in his belated old-age repentance, and in his inadequate conclusions about life. For who, after all, with the best intentions in the world, can keep God's commandments? And faced with a broken law, then what? Listen then to the wonderful words of Paul: "For to me to *live* is Christ, and to *die* is gain" (Phil. 1:21).

That is an answer that escaped even Solomon.

CHAPTER 23

SONG OF SOLOMON

A Book of Romance

To turn from Ecclesiastes to the Song of Solomon is like stepping out of the wilderness into the promised land. It is like the bright shining of the sun after rain.

If one book of the Bible may be said to be more sacred than another, then the Song of Solomon is that book, the very Holy of Holies of Scripture. The man with an impure mind will never understand this book. Under the figure of a bride and a bridegroom is expressed the love of Christ for His own, and the love that each believer has for his Lord. There is no sin, therefore no shame.

There are several important interpretations for this book. The two main positions usually taken differ in their identification of the bridegroom of the song.

According to one interpretation, the bridegroom is Solomon, and the bride a certain Shulamite woman. The Shulamite is seen awaiting the arrival of Solomon and, surrounded by ladies of the court, pouring out her rapture and longing. The king appears and takes her to his banqueting house, where the two lovers commune together. Then the Shulamite again confides in the court ladies, telling what tender regard she has for her beloved. With an overflowing heart she sings of the way in which her loved king found her, wooed her, how all nature awoke to new loveliness, how she lost him, found him again, and would not let him go.

After this, Solomon is seen approaching Jerusalem with his bodyguard, wearing a splendid crown. He addresses the Shulamite with words of love, and to these she responds briefly but with rapturous delight.

Then a cloud passes over the scene. Under the figure of a dream the bride describes a temporary separation of heart from her groom, her misery, her longing, her search for him, and her appeal to her court companions to help her. In response to their questions the Shulamite tells why she loves her beloved so.

Solomon returns and once more the two are united amid words of praise and assurances of love. The bride invites her husband to return with her to the scenes of her maiden life, and they are next seen enjoying the simplicity of country life, exchanging remembrances and confidences. Others are thought of, and the bride's joy reaches out to her kindred.

The song ends with the bride singing and bidding her beloved to hasten to her side. In this view of the song, Solomon is taken to be a type of Christ and the Shulamite a type of the church.

Another view of the song sees three main speakers and several subsidiary speakers. Solomon is seen as representing the world; the Shulamite, the church; and the Shulamite's shepherd-fiancée, Christ. Solomon uses all the dazzle and splendor of his court to woo the girl away from her true love, seeking to get her to become one of his wives instead. In like manner the world is ever seeking to attract away from Christ those who are "espoused" to Him. Solomon is unable to accomplish his goal, however, for the Shulamite resists all his overtures and remains true to her beloved shepherd to whom, at last, she is reunited. This view is expanded below.

In the first view, given above, Solomon is given as a type of Christ in this book. One verse in particular, however, makes it difficult to substantiate that view. In one of his grand offers to the Shulamite, Solomon unblushingly proclaims,

There are [sixty] queens, and [eighty] concubines, and virgins without number. My dove, my undefiled is but one. (6:8–9a)

"I have more women than I can count," he says in what is supposed to be a flattering proposal. "You can be number one." How a statement like that can be made to square with the idea that Solomon is a type of Christ is difficult to say.

Now, of course, Solomon is a type of Christ in Scripture, but in only one way. He is a type of Christ in respect to one aspect of the kingdom. When the Lord Jesus comes back, He will reign first in His *David* character in order to put down all His foes; then He will reign in His *Solomon* character as the Prince of Peace. In *that* respect, Solomon is a type of Christ, and a wonderful type. But in his personal life, in his polygamy, in his lusts and license, in his worldliness and wickedness, Solomon is certainly no type of Christ.

Solomon did more, perhaps, than any other king, to destroy the very foundations of the Hebrew monarchy. True, he built the temple! True, God appeared to him twice! True, in his early days he displayed a marvelous sensitivity to spiritual things. But, to balance all that, we have to read the wail of despair wrung from his heart in Ecclesiastes as he looks back over his wasted, worldly life. He sees Jerusalem about to be handed over to a son who was an arrant fool. He sees the kingdom soon to be divided. He hears the din of Babel in his harem and sees altars to a hundred pagan, demon-gods all about him. He knows he has made shipwreck of his life. When the events described in the Song of Solomon took place, Solomon was already caught in the riptides of lust that eventually threw him on the rocks and shoals of disaster.

Three main figures people this book: the Shulamite, her beloved shepherd, and Solomon. In this book Solomon is cast in the role of the tempter, and he employs all the lure of the world and all the desire of the flesh to persuade the Shulamite to transfer her affections from her beloved to him. Several subsidiary characters appear in the song—the daughters of Jerusalem, the brothers and the mother of the Shulamite, and several citizens of Jerusalem.[1]

In the story, the *shepherd* is a type of Christ, the *Shulamite* represents the believer or the church, *Solomon* is the tempter, and the daughters of Jerusalem are those who have given their affections to Solomon and all that he stands for in terms of sensuality and worldly pomp and power.

I. An Hour of Trouble (1:1–8)
II. An Hour of Temptation (1:9–11)
III. An Hour of Tenderness (1:12–2:6)
IV. An Hour of Truth (2:7–3:5)
  A. The Love of the Shepherd (2:7–14)
  B. The Love of the Shulamite (2:15–3:5)
V. An Hour of Talk (3:6–11)
VI. An Hour of Togetherness (4:1–5:1)
  A. Her Personal Radiance (4:1–5)
  B. Her Passionate Response (4:6)
  C. Her Pilgrim Responsibility (4:7–15)
  D. Her Promised Rapture (4:16–5:1)
VII. An Hour of Testimony (5:2–6:3)
  A. Her Dream of Her Beloved (5:2–8)
  B. Her Description of Her Beloved (5:9–6:3)
VIII. An Hour of Testing (6:4–8:4)
  A. His Flattery (6:4–7:9)
  B. Her Fidelity (7:10–8:4)
IX. An Hour of Triumph (8:5–14)

I. An Hour of Trouble (1:1–8)

As the story opens, the Shulamite has been taken to Solomon's pavilion, where she is kept virtually a prisoner. She is naturally very much alarmed. Into the pavilion come some of those sophisticated women of Solomon's court, who have quite openly given their affections to him. They like him and all that he has to offer of this world's pleasure, position, and pomp. They have overheard the Shulamite talking to herself about her true beloved and are both disdainful and amused. She has been calling for her absent shepherd and expressing her deep longing for him. "Let him kiss me with the kisses of his mouth," she says. "Thy love is better than wine" (v.2). She talks about the sweet fragrance his name distills in her heart. The court women scorn her because her skin has been tanned by the sun, but she has an answer for that: "I am black, but comely," she says (v. 5).

What does worry her is the snare in which she seems to have been caught. She turns her back upon these women. She wants nothing to do with them. Instead, she fills her mind with thoughts of her shepherd. It was an excellent start.

Sometimes we are caught up in circumstances similar to that of the Shulamite, for this world in which we live is no friend to grace, and its great prince has no love for our Beloved, nor do those who gladly take what the deceiver offers of pleasure and prosperity down here. The best antidote to temptation, to worldliness, to the snares of the Evil One, is to fill one's soul with thoughts of Jesus.

George Müller of Bristol used to consider it the first and most important business of the day to get his soul happy in the Lord.[2] For the world is all around us and its prince is full of subtle wiles. We need to constantly and deliberately engage our thoughts to our Shepherd. If we do that, the tempter will lose his power.

II. An Hour of Temptation (1:9–11)

Now comes Solomon into the pavilion in all his glory, making the most of all that pomp and worldly splendor of which he was so fond. What a splendid showing he makes! He is handsome; blessed with his father's good looks and possessed of his mother's seductive charm. He is an imposing, captivating figure, and he carries himself with bold assurance. He is knowing, hearty, witty, worldly wise, and clever, and confident he will soon sweep this simple country girl off her feet and add her to the list of his conquests. His robes are resplendent, his fingers sparkle with gems, his grooming is impeccable, his manners are superb.

His entrance is designed to overpower this simple country girl. He begins at once with flattering words: "I have compared thee, O my love, to a company of horses in Pharaoh's chariots" (v. 9). My! What a magnificent woman you are! You are as graceful, as magnificent as a gold-harnessed horse. He is full of flattery and charm. Because he is wise in the ways of women he will not stay long. All he wants to do on this first appeal is to dazzle and impress, to hint and suggest, and to sow a seed in her soul.

The tempter is very, very clever. He knows how to seduce. He begins by planting a thought in the mind, a desire in the heart. He offers just a taste of his wares at first, no more. He wants to create a thirst, an appetite, to suggest that he alone has what can satisfy, and that it can be ours.

III. An Hour of Tenderness (1:12–2:6)

Solomon, having made his grand entrance, retires almost at once. Off he goes to banquet elsewhere, doubtless pleased with himself for giving that delectable woman something to think about. He will come back later and reap the harvest of what he has sown. But he has forgotten God.

While he is off enjoying himself elsewhere, the Shulamite has a secret meeting with her shepherd. We do not know how the shepherd is able to get to where she is, but love is always resourceful. The two are seen briefly together, telling each other how great is their love. The Shulamite calls the shepherd her "spikenard" (1:12), and depicts him as a bundle of myrrh held close to her heart. The shepherd tells her that she is fair.

It is with true instinct that the Shulamite calls her beloved spikenard and myrrh. Both are plants used in Bible times in connection with death and burial. The Shulamite brings these thoughts to the fore in talking to her shepherd. Spikenard and myrrh!

We must lift all this to the spiritual realm, translate it from the passion and poetry of a human love song to the language of a soul in love with Christ. For is it not the great work of the cross, the Lord's death and burial, which quicken our love for Him, along with thoughts of His triumph over death? No wonder we sing,

> Oh, tell us often of Thy love,
> Of all Thy grief and pain;
> And let our hearts with joy confess
> That thence comes all our gain.
> —James Hutton,
> "O Teach Us More of Thy Blest Ways"

So, then, the shepherd and the Shulamite tell of their love. The Holy Spirit would have us reach out to our Savior and tell Him just what He means to our hearts:

> You are like the apple tree among the wild trees of the wood. I sat down under your shadow with great delight. You brought me into your banqueting house and spread over me your banner of love. (see 2:3–4)

IV. An Hour of Truth (2:7–3:5)

The worldly wise women of Solomon's court now reappear. The shepherd has gone; the Shulamite is alone once more and the world attacks again.

It is not Solomon now, putting forth his charm, it is those who have given their affections to him, those who have tasted of his wares and who have enjoyed them. They now try to seduce the Shulamite.

We are not told just what they said to her; the Holy Spirit draws the veil over that. But they evidently tried to incite wrong feelings in her—that much is evident from what the Shulamite said to them. But they get nowhere. The Shulamite has just come straight from a few precious moments with her beloved, so the suggestions of these sophisticated women strike a most discordant note in her soul. She says, "I charge you, O ye daughters of Jerusalem . . . that ye stir not up [that you do not excite], nor awake my [passions]" (2:7). In other words, "My love is not for *your* beloved; my love is reserved for my own dear shepherd."

Then she goes on the attack, telling these worldly women all about her shepherd and how he came to her in all the fullness of overflowing life—"leaping upon the mountains, skipping upon the hills" (2:8)—and how he wooed her and won her. She told of opposition at home, how once she had sought her beloved, and how the watchmen of the city had tried to hinder her and how she found him again. "I found him," she cried, "whom my soul loveth: I held him, and would not let him go" (3:4).

Surely that's the best way to talk to those who would lead us into paths not pleasing to God and which would cool our passion for Christ! We should simply tell them about Jesus and all He means to us. The world's talk will soon seem vulgar, cheap, and crude.

V. An Hour of Talk (3:6–11)

There is now a change of scene. Solomon has been in the country, now he comes back to Jerusalem with the Shulamite virtually his prisoner. The streets are lined with spectators. Four voices rise above the crowd in eulogy of their worldly prince. They know nothing of the Shulamite and even less of the shepherd. Solomon's worldly glory fills their thoughts.

The first speaker is enraptured with Solomon's *passion*: "Who is this that cometh out of the wilderness like pillars of smoke, perfumed with myrrh and frankincense, with all the powders of the merchant?" (3:6). Powders of the merchant! That suggests passion for sale! Worldly passion! That is what impressed the first speaker about Solomon.

The second speaker is entranced with Solomon's worldly *power*: "[Sixty] valiant men are about [Solomon's litter]. They all hold swords, being expert in war" (3:7–8). Solomon had the outward trappings of power, which is what impressed this speaker.

The third speaker is taken up with Solomon's worldly *pomp*: "King Solomon made a chariot of wood. He made the pillars thereof of silver, the undercarriage of gold, the coverings of purple, the floor paved in a most lovely way by the daughters of Jerusalem" (see 3:9–10). Solomon knew how to make the world glitter and seem most attractive to human eyes.

The last speaker is enthralled by Solomon's worldly *position*: "Go forth, O ye daughters of Zion, and behold king Solomon with the crown wherewith his mother crowned him in the day of his [marriage], and in the day of the gladness of his heart" (3:11). That may well be! But Solomon was fickle in his infatuations. He has long since forgotten that first woman he married and has added many another to his collection since then. Now he aspires to list the Shulamite as his latest conquest.[3]

An hour of talk! It was just the idle chatter of the world, but it gives us a good estimate of Solomon and his worldly show. None of this appealed to the Shulamite, who remains silent, her troubled heart beating for her absent shepherd. The whole parade, with its candid comments, means nothing to her except to increase her longing to be free of it all.

VI. An Hour of Togetherness (4:1–5:1)

The Shulamite, caught up by Solomon's crowd, is now a virtual prisoner in the palace. Outwardly things look black. Her beloved was able to find a way to talk to her in the pavilion in the country, but how could he get through to her now? Her situation seemed hopeless.

But love always finds a way. All the way down this chapter the shepherd and the Shulamite again are alone, sharing deep expressions of devotion and love. "Thou art fair, my love," says the beloved (4:1). "Let my beloved come into his garden, and eat his pleasant fruits," she says (4:16). In other words, "All that I have is thine."

Soon the Shulamite will have to face a far fiercer temptation than the one over which she triumphed in the wilderness. This time of tryst was essential to fortify her against the insistent assault soon to be made upon her by Solomon.

There is no substitute for the daily quiet time with our Beloved if we are to be victors in the rush and tumble battles of life. All backsliding stems from a neglect of the time of tryst. We must guard it well. It is the one vital line of defense against all that the world, the flesh, and the Devil can hurl against us.

VII. An Hour of Testimony (5:2–6:3)

Once more the haughty women of Solomon's court appear. They make a comment about the Shulamite's beloved, but she interrupts them and begins to tell them about him. Her testimony is in two parts.

A. Her Dream of Her Beloved (5:2–8)

In her dream, her beloved had come to her and had knocked at the door of her house, but she had been too lazy to respond. She had made excuses, so he had quietly gone away. Then, realizing what she had done, she ran after him, only to fall into the hands of the watchmen who insulted her.

The dream has a message for us. Our Beloved will never force Himself upon us. If we are too busy, too tired, or too preoccupied to welcome Him, He will quietly leave us to ourselves. This puts us in spiritual peril for it gives the world an opportunity to do us ill.

No wonder the Shulamite was troubled. It was, however, just a dream, after all. She had not really lost her beloved—but it had frightened her just the same.

Now comes the second part of her testimony.

B. Her Description of Her Beloved (5:9–6:3)

She begins to describe her beloved to these worldly women. What a magnificent description it is! His legs like pillars of marble, his hair blacker than the raven's wing, his mouth most sweet. "Yea," she says, "he is altogether lovely. This is my beloved, and this is my friend" (5:16). So eloquent is her testimony that the worldly women are almost persuaded to seek him for themselves. She, however, with the keen insight of love, sees through their motives and refuses to tell them exactly how and where he can be found. This, then, was the time of testimony.

VIII. AN HOUR OF TESTING (6:4–8:4)

Apart from his first brief appearing at the beginning of the book, Solomon has kept himself in the background. Now he sees that he is making no headway, and he decides to load the dice and gamble everything on a single throw.

A. His Flattery (6:4–7:9)

He pours it on! "Thou art beautiful, O my love, as Tirzah" (a delightful region, selected by the northern kings as a royal residence after the division of the kingdom). "[Thou art] comely as Jerusalem, [awesome] as an army with banners" (6:4). The Shulamite shrugs it all off. But Solomon is persistent. He runs his eye up and down her form and unblushingly details all her physical charms.

He does not dare to actually touch her. He can plead and persuade, flatter and cajole, but he cannot force. That is important. The world, the flesh, even the Devil himself can tempt but they cannot compel. If we yield, it is of our own free will, by deliberate choice.

Popes and prelates, princes and peers of the realm might mass themselves against Martin Luther. The beleaguered monk might stand before them bullied and browbeaten, threatened and pressed. They might try to intimidate him, try to buy his silence with the offer of a high place in their ranks, but they cannot force him to recant. "Here I stand," he cries, making the very rafters ring. "Here I stand, I can do no else. So help me God."[4]

So, then, Solomon uses all his considerable powers of eloquence and persuasion to try to seduce the Shulamite from her loyalty to her shepherd.

But his flatteries give way to her faithfulness.

B. Her Fidelity (7:10–8:4)

Her answer is simple and sublime: "I am my beloved's," she says, "and his desire is toward me" (7:10). She does not say, "I am my beloved's and my desire is toward him," but "*his desire is toward me!*" The astonishing wonder of it all is simply this—"his desire is toward me." That was sufficient to make Solomon's grandiose offers seem like worthless trash. And Solomon remains silent; he has no more to say.

IX. AN HOUR OF TRIUMPH (8:5–14)

The story closes with the Shulamite returning home to her family, still firm in her resolve to give herself only to her shepherd. Her constancy, in the face of the fierce temptations that have come her way, wins over her brothers, who had been so hostile to the shepherd at first.

Notice the last two statements in the book—the *last request of the shepherd*: "The companions hearken to thy voice: cause me to hear it" (8:13). Just think of that! Our Beloved says, "You talk to everyone else. Please talk to Me as well!"; the *last response of the Shulamite*: "Make haste, my beloved, and be thou like a [gazelle] . . . upon the mountains of spices" (v. 14). Oh, Lord, come swiftly! Come soon!

Such is the Song of Solomon. Truly a most remarkable book and, incidentally, one in which God is not even once named.

CHAPTER 24

THE PROPHETS

Men Sent from God

The appearance of a prophet was always a sign that apostasy and rebellion were predominant in Israel. The prophets raised their voices in protest against the idolatry, corruption, and blindness of their times, calling the nation back to God. It is a mistake to think that a prophet's primary function was to foretell the future. The prophet did that, of course, but he was first of all a man with a message from God for his own generation, a "forthteller" rather than a "foreteller." Often the prophets were statesmen with both insight and foresight, clearly seeing the end result of the dangerous religious and political experiments of their contemporaries.

The prophets often did not understand some of their own utterances, for the burdens they delivered sometimes had a double fulfillment: an initial and partial fulfillment close to the time the words were uttered, and a later, more complete fulfillment, at a remote date. They usually spoke from the standpoint of their own people, with the Gentiles being mentioned only to the extent that those other nations would come into conflict with, or blessing through, Israel. The themes of the prophets were many and varied, but apart from the initial, immediate, and partial fulfillment of their predictions, their prophecies focused on two future events: the first and second comings of Christ. The prophets themselves probably could not distinguish between these two comings, and often, too, a message would be given, only to be enlarged upon at a later date by either the same prophet or by another.

Three of the prophets directed their messages to Gentile nations: Obadiah, Jonah, and Nahum—the first to Edom and the other two to Nineveh. It often happened that the prophet was unpopular with the people to whom he delivered the message of God, and sometimes he was bitterly persecuted for his preaching, his message being considered subversive to the national interest, and the prophet himself a traitor. The prophets were the moral conscience of their age.

Bible Prophecy Is Unique

The Bible is the only book that challenges unbelief by foretelling the future, staking its authority on the ultimate, certain, and complete fulfillment of its detailed predictions. It has been said that some 109 Old Testament predictions were literally fulfilled at Christ's first coming, and that of the 845 Old Testament quotations that are found in the New Testament, 333 refer to Christ. Some 25 prophecies uttered by various prophets over a period of some five hundred years concern the betrayal, trial, death, burial, and resurrection of Jesus. These were literally fulfilled, although the chances against such fulfillment have been shown to be one chance in 33,554,438. If the law of compound probabilities is applied similarly to all 109 predictions fulfilled at Christ's first coming, the chances that they could accidentally be fulfilled in the history of one person is one in billions.

The following chart shows that the writing prophets belong to three main periods of Hebrew history, either before, during, or after the Babylonian captivity. Since all the writers are grouped mainly around Isaiah and Jeremiah, these two prophets will, in this current survey, be discussed out of their chronological order so that some overall picture of the times can be given. It should be mentioned that Obadiah is placed at the end of the preexilic prophets, although some authorities place him at the beginning. There were other prophets besides the writing prophets, notably Elijah and Elisha, as well as Enoch, Nathan, Micaiah, and Huldah, a prophetess. Moses, Samuel, and David were also prophets. From the days of Samuel schools were set up for the training of prophets, but the Holy Spirit by no means restricted Himself to these schools when calling a man to preach and prophesy in His name.

Background of the Prophets

The political and religious conditions of their times are constantly reflected in the writings of the prophets, so these conditions need to be studied as part of the background of their books. The empires of Egypt, Assyria, Babylon, and Persia overshadow the whole prophetic era; the empires of Greece and Rome color the visions of Daniel. Lesser kingdoms such as Moab, Edom, Syria, Philistia, Ammon, Phoenicia, Elam, and Ethiopia are also pictured on the prophetic page. The power struggles of these nations form the historical background against which the prophets poured out their warnings, their wooings, and their woes. Something should be known of all these nations, especially Assyria and Babylon, the empires that terminated the monarchies of Israel and Judah. Something should also be known of Persia, the nation that brought about the restoration of the Jews to their homeland.

THE WRITING PROPHETS			
Century (B.C.)	Preexilic	Exilic	Postexilic
9th	Joel Jonah Amos Hosea		
8th	Isaiah Micah Nahum Zephaniah Habakkuk		
7th	Jeremiah Obadiah	Ezekiel Daniel	
6th			Haggai Zechariah
5th			Malachi

Assyria

From the reign of Sennacherib on, Nineveh was the capital city of the Assyrian Empire and, as we are told in the book of Jonah, it was a great city. The Assyrians were fiendishly cruel, their kings often being depicted as gloating over the tortures inflicted on conquered peoples. They pursued their wars with the utmost ferocity, uprooting whole populations as a policy of state and deporting them to remote parts of the Assyrian Empire. The leading men of conquered towns were given over to torment and horribly mutilated before being put to death. It is no wonder that fear of Assyria fell on all her neighbors.

Babylon

The Assyrians were succeeded on the world scene by the Babylonians. God gave Nebuchadnezzar a sweeping mandate over the other nations of the earth, including Judah. Nation after nation fell as the invincible Babylonians swept westward. Egypt fell to defeat in the famous battle of Carchemish on the Euphrates in 605 B.C., and with that victory nothing could halt the Babylonian conquerors. Jerusalem fell and the Jews were deported as warned by Jeremiah and his contemporaries. Tyre was

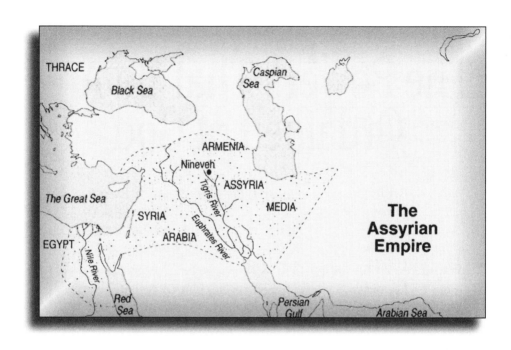

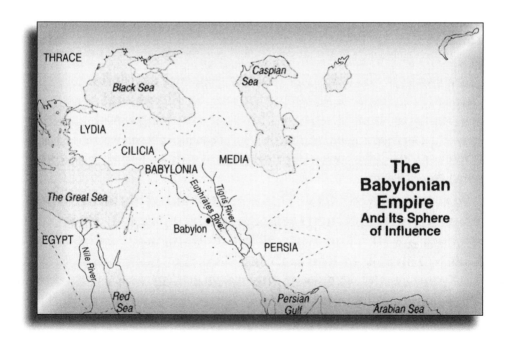

sacked, and Egypt handed over to Nebuchadnezzar by God in payment for this service. Many lesser kingdoms felt the weight of the Babylonian arm, and for about seventy years this empire reigned supreme, the Jews being forced to experience complete captivity to their Gentile captors.

Persia

The Babylonian Empire was ended by the Medes and Persians, with Persia emerging soon afterward as the supreme Gentile power. Cyrus the Great (whose name had been mentioned by Isaiah long before he was born) was a humane ruler, and it was he who issued a decree ending the Babylonian captivity of the Jews. Daniel, carried away to Babylon during the first deportation by Nebuchadnezzar, lived through the entire captivity period and on into the Persian era. He lived to see Judah restored to partial sovereignty and, in vision, saw Persia fall and Greece come into focus, only to fall in turn before the Romans. His piercing eye saw still further into the future than that, for he saw to "the time of the end."

Such were the prophets, and they are unique in the history of the world. Their words still ring with authority as they bring a message for us even today. We shall now look at them one by one.

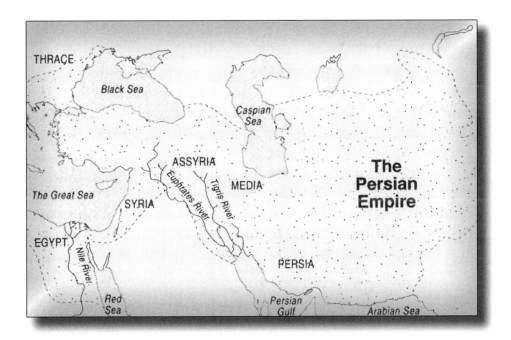

THE PROPHETIC ERA

Judah	Prophets	Israel	World Powers	Prophets
Rehoboam Abijam Asa		Jeroboam I		
		Nadab Baasha Elah Zimri Omri		
Jehoshaphat	Elijah » Elisha »	Ahab Ahaziah	Syria	
Jehoram Ahaziah Athaliah		Jehoram Jehu		
Jehoash	« Joel	Jehoahaz Jehoash		
Amaziah Uzziah	Amos »	Jeroboam II	Assyria	Jonah (Nineveh)
		Zechariah Shallum		
Jotham	Hosea »	Menahem Pekahiah		
Ahaz Hezekiah	« Isaiah « Micah	Pekah Hoshea		
		ASSYRIAN CAPTIVITY 722 B.C.		
Manasseh			Thebes destroyed	Nahum (Assyria)
Amon Josiah	« Zephaniah « Habakkuk		Assyria overthrown 612 B.C.	
Jehoahaz	« Jeremiah		1st Babylonian invasion	Obadiah (Edom)
Jehoiakim Jehoiachin Zedekiah			2nd invasion 3rd invasion	
	« Ezekiel		Persia	Daniel (Babylon)
BABYLONIAN CAPTIVITY 586 B.C.			Cyrus	
Zerubbabel			Darius I	
	« Haggai « Zechariah		Xerxes	
Ezra Nehemiah			Darius II	
	« Malachi			

CHAPTER 25

JOEL

The Prophet of the Plague

Joel is very much an unknown prophet. We do not know who he was, how old he was, where he lived, or even, for sure, when he prophesied. All we know is that his father's name was Pethuel, which doesn't help us very much. We gather from his little memo that he ministered in Jerusalem. As to the time, scholars are divided, but there are sound reasons for the view that he preached at a comparatively early date. He was probably one of the earliest, if not actually the earliest, of the writing prophets. The kinds of sins denounced by Amos and Hosea are not in view; the great world powers of Assyria and Babylon are not mentioned at all, at least by name; the enemies of his people were the Phoenicians and the Philistines, the Edomites and the Egyptians.

Scofield thinks that in his youth Joel may have known Elijah and Elisha, and if true, that casts considerable light upon the prophet and his times. But probably no references are made to time because Joel looks forward, down the long ages to the dim and distant future, to the time of the end and to the events that will usher in "the day of the Lord."

He concentrates on the nation of Judah. The ten-tribed northern kingdom of Israel is not mentioned even once. It is in *Zion* that the alarm is to be sounded. His wrath is stirred against the Philistines, who were troublesome, hereditary foes of his people from their first days in the land, and against the Phoenicians, who were never averse to making money off any Hebrew people the Philistines managed to capture and wished to put up for sale.

Joel's prophecy moves in three circles. He begins with a recent locust plague, which had devastated the land. He enlarges his vision and sees the coming Assyrian invasion—still some time in the future in his day but a veritable human locust plague to be feared and dreaded if ever there was one. Finally he focuses steadily on the end times—although what he has to say earlier about the coming invasion by the Assyrians certainly looks forward, too, to the fearful events of the last days.

His prophecy divides into two major sections. The first emphasis is on *The Day of the Locust* (1:1–14), which occupies the first fourteen verses of chapter 1. Then the prophet takes up his major theme, speaking of *The Day of the Lord* (1:15–3:21).

Before going any further, we need to get a few of the "days" of Scripture into perspective. Regarding *The Day of Man*, Paul, in 1 Corinthians 4:3, says, "But with me it is a very small thing that I should be judged of you, or of man's judgment." The word for judgment here is the word for day, not the usual word for judgment at all. J. N. Darby translates it, "But for me it is the smallest matter that I be examined of you or of man's day." We are living right now in man's day, the day when God is largely silent and when man has so much to say. Any judgment passed on the apostle was merely human judgment. Paul was not nearly so concerned with the opinion of a human court in this, man's day, as in the judgment of that higher Court in a coming day.

Then there is *The Day of Jacob's Trouble.* "Alas! for that day is great, so that none is like it: it is even the time of Jacob's trouble, but he shall be saved out of it" (Jer. 30:7). This will be the day when anti-Semitism reaches its final pitch of fury as the world tries to rid itself of the hated and detested Jew once and for all. This day is referred to in Ezekiel 7:7. The Lord Jesus used the expression the "great tribulation" to describe it (Matt. 24:21). The phrase "the time of Jacob's trouble" takes us back to Genesis 32:24–30. Jacob had just heard that Esau was coming with four hundred men and he was "greatly afraid and distressed" (Gen. 32:7). He cried to God and pleaded "the mercies of God" (see Gen. 32:10). It was a terrible crisis in his life for he was about to get what he deserved. But, had God allowed Esau to smite him, that would have been an end to the future of the children of Israel—the name "Israel" had been given to Jacob just the night before. The great tribulation is the time of *Jacob's* trouble and has nothing whatever to do with the church.

The day of Jacob's trouble will run parallel with *The Day of Christ.* Paul wrote to the Corinthians, "Ye come behind in no gift; waiting for the coming of our Lord Jesus Christ: who shall also confirm you unto the end, that ye may be blameless in the day of our Lord Jesus Christ" (1 Cor. 1:7–8). He wrote to the Philippians, "Being confident of this very thing, that he which hath begun a good work in you will perform it until the day of Jesus Christ" (Phil. 1:6). Paul mentions this day again and again. It is the day when we will be caught up to meet the Lord in the air and will be assembled at the judgment seat of Christ to receive reward and blessing. The judgment seat of Christ has nothing to do with sin; it has everything to do with service. The wood, hay, and stubble of our lives will be burned up; the gold, silver, and precious stones will be displayed. Not quantity but quality will be what counts.

Then we have *The Day of the Lord*. This is the subject of extensive Old Testament prophecy. It is mentioned by name at least eighteen times in the Old Testament (Isa. 2:12; 13:6, 9; Ezek. 13:5; 30:3; Joel 1:15; 2:1, 11, 31; 3:14; Amos 5:18, 20; Obad. 15; Zeph. 1:7; 1:14; Zech. 14:1; Mal. 4:5), and four times in the New Testament (1 Thess. 5:2; 2 Thess. 2:2; 2 Peter 3:10; Rev. 1:10). It overlaps the day of Jacob's trouble, runs on through the Battle of Armageddon and the judgment of the nations, on through the millennium, and to the dissolution of the heavens and the earth in a baptism of fire.

Finally we have *The Day of Our God* (2 Peter 3:12). Paul writes concerning the Lord Jesus of the time "when all things shall be subdued unto him" (1 Cor. 15:28). The sequence of events in this passage is important. Paul writes, "Then cometh the end, when he shall have delivered up the kingdom to God, even the Father; when he shall have put down all rule and all authority and power. For he must reign, till he hath put all enemies under his feet"—that describes the millennium. Paul continues, "The last enemy that shall be destroyed is death. . . . And when all things shall be subdued unto him, then shall the Son also himself be subject unto him that put all things under him, *that God may be all in all*"—that describes the eternal state (1 Cor. 15:24–28).

The "day of God" is the eternal day. Very little is revealed about it in the Bible. We only know that for all the rest of eternity God will be all in all. Peter tells us that the day will be ushered in with the dissolution of the universe and the creation of a new one. He tells us we should be "looking for and hastening unto the coming of the day of God" by holy, godly living (2 Peter 3:12). The thought behind the words "hastening unto" is emphatic. *The Companion Bible* renders it, "Looking for, yes and earnestly looking for, the coming of the day of God." God must have some wonderful things in store!

Joel deals primarily with *The Day of the Lord*, which he mentions five times. It is one of his great themes.

Let us now get the outline of the book before us:

I. The Day of the Locust (1:1–14)
   A. Divine Displeasure Expressed (1:1–9)
   B. Divine Displeasure Expanded (1:10–14)
II. The Day of the Lord (1:15–3:21)
   A. The Day of the Assyrian (1:15–2:32)
      1. A Day of Destruction (1:15–20)
      2. A Day of Darkness (2:1–10)
      3. A Day of Deliverance (2:11–27)

Three brief chapters comprise this book.

I. THE DAY OF THE LOCUST (1:1–14)

Joel begins by asking the old men whether they could ever recall such a national disaster as that which had suddenly come upon the land. The whole country was in the grip of a fearful locust plague. Joel uses four words to describe the locusts—he speaks of the palmer worm, the locust, the cankerworm, and the caterpillar—literally the gnawer, the swarmer (i.e., multiplier), the licker, and the consumer. The force of the Hebrew passage is that what the gnawer leaves the swarmer will eat; what the swarmer leaves the licker will eat; what the licker leaves the consumer will eat.

Somebody has described the locust as "the incarnation of hunger." They have been known to devour, over an area of almost ninety miles, every green leaf, herb, and blade of grass, leaving behind them a desolation that looks as though the whole area had been scorched by fire.

We have numerous descriptions in print of the horror of a locust invasion. W. M. Thompson in *The Land and the Book* says that when the millions upon millions of locust eggs hatch, the very dust seems to waken to life, and the earth itself to tremble with them; and later, when the vast new breed have acquired wings, the very heavens seem tremulous with them.[1]

One observer tells how the young locusts rapidly attain the size of the common grasshopper. They all move forward in the same direction, first crawling then leaping and consuming every green thing in their path. Fields of standing grain, vineyards, orchards, groves of olive and fig trees are swiftly stripped of every green blade and leaf, even the bark of trees being often destroyed. The ground over which they have passed has been visited by sterility and death. The Romans called locusts "the burners of the land."

Still their hordes move on, completely blanketing the ground. Their numbers are so great it often takes three or four days for the mighty host to pass by.

From a distance, a swarm of advancing locusts looks like a cloud of dust or sand hovering a few feet above the ground, as the countless insects leap forward. The only thing that seems to stop them for the moment is a sudden change to colder weather, for that benumbs them. They rest at night, swarming like bees on the bushes and hedges, but the morning sun warms and revives them and on they go.

They have no king nor leader, as Solomon observed, but that does not deter them. Their endless ranks march on, turning aside for nothing. Buildings are no obstacle, for when a wall impedes them they simply climb up one side and down the other. If a house is before them they march in at open doors and windows. Water does not halt their forward march. A puddle or a river, a lake or the open sea is taken in their stride. They never attempt to go around it, but march right on in and are drowned. The bodies of the dead, floating on the surface, make a bridge for the rest to pass over. Often the only hope for an infested area is for a strong wind to arise and blow them out to the open sea to be drowned. Even when the scourge comes to an end, it often happens that the decomposition of their bodies produces pestilence and death.

Once the locust has developed its wings, a strong breeze will often favor its progress. A sudden darkening of the sun in a summer sky, together with the noise a swarm of locusts makes when moving through the air, heralds their coming. Like billowing clouds they pass overhead, while everyone below hopes and prays that they will keep on going—usually a vain hope, indeed.

Thompson, in describing one locust swarm he observed, says,

> Their number was astounding; the whole face of the mountain was black with them. On they came like a living deluge. We dug trenches, and kindled fires, and beat and burned to death heaps upon heaps; but the effort was useless. Wave after wave rolled up the mountainside and poured over rocks, walls, ditches, hedges—those behind covering up and bridging over the masses already killed. It was perfectly appalling to watch this animated river as it flowed up the road, and ascended the hill above my house. For four days they continued to pass on toward the east . . . millions upon millions. In their march devoured every green thing, and with wonderful expedition. The noise they made in marching and foraging was like that of a heavy shower on a distant forest. Nothing is more striking than the pertinacity with which they all pursue the same line of march, like a disciplined army.[2]

Such is the background of Joel 1:1–14. The land had been invaded by locusts.

The prophet calls the invaders "a nation" and calls on the people to lament as a young bride who has just lost her bridegroom in death—surely, the bitterest of all weeping. People and priests alike are to weep. They are to call for a fast and bring the assembly of the people together and cry unto the Lord.

All this, however, is preliminary and preparatory. Beyond the Day of the Locust, Joel saw another day:

II. The Day of the Lord (1:15–3:21)

He recognized that, dreadful as was the plague of locusts, it was nothing compared with what lay ahead. In chapter 2 his vision focused on the future, but on the nearby future—the day of the Assyrian. In chapter 3 he focuses on the future, but the far distant future—the day of the Antichrist. But he sees it all as "the day of the Lord" for the one was a type of the other.

A. The Day of the Assyrian (1:15–2:32)

It must be noted at the outset that the Assyrian is not directly mentioned. But there can be little doubt that Joel, writing perhaps a century or more before the events, could clearly see two things as inevitable: (1) Athaliah's seizure of the throne and her blatant introduction of Baal-worship into Judah was bound to have ominous consequences. Baal-worship was the deadliest of all threats to Judah—far more deadly than bubonic plague. For if Judah followed in the steps of Israel and embraced the worship of Baal and Ashtoreth, then judgment would be inevitable. (2) The most likely world power to threaten the states of Palestine was the Assyrian. Even though it was no threat as yet, it would become a threat. God would use Assyria as His scourge to chastise the sinful people of both Israel and Judah. So Joel warns of a coming invasion but he doesn't specify either the *power* that would invade or the *period* when the invasion would take place. He only saw invasion as inevitable.

Joel's description of the invasion derives its vivid force and horror from the recent locust invasion, under the curse of which the land was still suffering. Furthermore, the coming armed invasion itself, dreadful and pitiless as it would be, would be nothing compared with the invasion of Israel that would take place in "the day of the Lord." Joel's vision seems, in fact, to waver back and forth from the one to the other. The one was the shadow, the other the substance. The nearer invasion, terrible as it would be, was merely illustrative of the later invasion.

With that in mind, we can look at the four things he has to say about the nearer invasion. He uses "the day of the Lord" three times in his description of it.

1. A Day of Destruction (1:15–20)

He sees, first of all, *The Farms.* All happiness is removed from the festivals because all harvests are rotting in the furrows and all herds are ravenous in the fields. He paints a picture of devastation, utter and complete.

Then he turns his eyes from the farms and he looks at *The Forest*—and sees the same. Everywhere there are burned woodlands and dry waterways. It is a day of destruction. He cries, "Alas for the day! for the day of the LORD is at hand, and as a destruction from the Almighty shall it come" (v. 15).

War always ravages a land. War is a ready tool in God's hand, used by Him to punish nations that refuse to acknowledge His goodness and His grace. Joel saw just such a war ahead for his people—in the near future, and in the distant future in "the day of the Lord." In spirit he was transported down the ages and viewed it as though it were already at hand.

He tells us more.

2. A Day of Darkness (2:1–10)

Blow ye the trumpet in Zion, and sound an alarm in my holy mountain: let all the inhabitants of the land tremble: for the day of the LORD cometh, for it is nigh at hand; a day of darkness and of gloominess, a day of clouds and of thick darkness. (vv. 1–2)

This whole section vividly portrays the onward march of a ruthless, relentless, and resistless army. Joel tells how the enemy *mobilizes* and how the enemy *marches*. He describes his *destructive tactics* and his *disciplined troops*. He tells of the *fearful policy* the enemy supports and of the *fearful pace* he sets. He tells of the terrible *power* he shows and of the terrible *panic* he spreads.

All this was highly descriptive of the ravages of Assyrian-style war. It was the kind of war we, in the twenty-first century, have come to call "total war." But the prophet was not restricted to the coming Assyrian invasion but was transported at once to the end times. He saw the last-day invasion of Israel as though it were before his eyes, imminent, about to take place. It was to be indeed a day of darkness, a dreadful time of horror and despair, especially for the nation of Israel.

That day was more, though, than a day of destruction and a day of darkness.

3. A Day of Deliverance (2:11–27)

The LORD shall utter his voice before his army: for his camp is very great: for he is strong that executeth his word: for the day of the LORD is great and very terrible; and who can abide it? Therefore also now, saith the LORD, turn ye even to me with all your heart. (vv. 11–12)

We know now from history just how the Lord spared Jerusalem from the Assyrian. True, the Assyrian army overran most of Judah, but it was stopped by divine intervention at the walls of Jerusalem. And only because godly King Hezekiah had led the nation in a return to the Lord.

This, too, was a foreshadowing of the end-time "day of the Lord," and a fore view of the coming last-minute deliverance of the Jews. The call to repent and the call to rejoice that throbs down through this section will have its ultimate fulfillment at the return of Christ.

But that day is yet another thing.

4. A Day of Discovery (2:28–32)

And it shall come to pass afterward, that I will pour out my spirit upon all flesh; and your sons and your daughters shall prophesy, your old men shall dream dreams, your young men shall see visions: and also upon the servants and upon the handmaids in those days will I pour out my spirit. And I will show wonders in the heavens and in the earth, blood, and fire, and pillars of smoke. The sun shall be turned into darkness, and the moon into blood, before the great and the terrible day of the LORD come. (vv. 28–31)

Now the prophet's eye leaped clean over the rest of the Old Testament period, lighted for a moment on the day of Pentecost, then passed right over the church age to the end time. For what happened at Pentecost was only a partial and a preliminary fulfillment of the prophecy of Joel. The prophecy awaits a full and final completion in the end times.

After the rapture of the church, things will revert back again, dispensationally, to Israel and to God's Old Testament way of dealing with mankind. There will be another outpouring of the Spirit and an enormous multitude of people will be saved during the tribulation period. They will not be in the church but they will be in the kingdom. But not even that posttribulation outpouring of the Holy Spirit will be the final fulfillment of this remarkable prophecy. It looks on to those end-time events connected with the millennial reign of Christ. *That* is when all men and all women will know such an outpouring of the Spirit that the world will be "full of the knowledge of the LORD, as the waters cover the sea" (Isa. 11:9).

These chapters, then, focus, for the most part, on the day of the Assyrian, but Joel is not yet finished. His vision sharpens.

B. The Day of the Antichrist (3:1–16)

The coming of the Antichrist will force people to take sides, one way or the other, once and for all.

"Multitudes," Joel cries, "multitudes in the valley of decision: for the day of the LORD is near in the valley of decision" (v. 14). Two things will mark this day: a gathering of the *Hebrew* peoples in joy, and a gathering of the *heathen* peoples in judgment. "For, behold, in those days, and in that time, . . . I shall bring again the captivity of Judah and Jerusalem" (v. 1). The Lord will come and rescue Israel from her foes.

Some of those foes are listed by the prophet. He mentions Tyre and "the coasts of Palestine" (v. 4), in modern terms called the Gaza Strip and Lebanon. He also mentions Egypt and Edom—Edom today being the country of Jordan.

The prophet sees the nations massing against Israel. North, east, south, and west they encircle the land. They are determined to uproot the nation of Israel and rid the world, once and for all, of the hated Hebrew people.

It is all in vain, for the Lord is actually behind their gathering.

I will also gather all nations, and will bring them down into the valley of Jehoshaphat. . . . Let the heathen be wakened, and come up to the valley of Jehoshaphat: for there will I sit to judge all the heathen round about. . . . Multitudes, multitudes in the valley of decision: for the day of the LORD is near. (vv. 2, 12, 14)

It is generally agreed that this refers to the great assize of the nations mentioned by the Lord in Matthew 25. At this judgment He will separate the "sheep" from the "goats," those among the nations who have helped Israel in the time of trouble and those who have been set for her destruction. The Antichrist will think that he has gathered the people to exterminate Israel; he will discover that God has assembled them to execute judgment.

C. The Day of Anticipation (3:17–21)

"So shall ye know that I am the LORD your God dwelling in Zion, my holy mountain: then shall Jerusalem be holy, and there shall no strangers pass through her any more" (v. 17). With all her foes banished from the earth, Israel will head the nations that eventually will fill the millennial earth. People will know, to use Joel's resounding closing word, that "the LORD dwelleth in Zion" (v. 21).

Today we are living on the threshold of that "great and terrible day of the Lord." We are living in the day of man, when man judges and runs the affairs of this planet—and not for better but for worse. But the day of Christ is about to dawn and we shall be summoned to our home on high. Then the Lord will make those final moves on this earth that will bring to an end man's mismanagement of affairs down here. Our heart's cry is, "Even so, come, Lord Jesus" (Rev. 22:20).

CHAPTER 26

JONAH

The Unwilling Prophet

The Lord Jesus believed that Jonah (784–772 B.C.) was a literal person. Jesus believed, too, that Jonah's experience in the belly of the great fish was authentic history, for He referred to the incident as an illustration of His own death, burial, and resurrection (Matt. 12:40). As Jonah was a sign to the Ninevites, so was the Son of Man to His generation (Luke 11:30). The Lord referred to Jonah in the same context as the Queen of Sheba and Solomon, thus placing him on the same level of historical validity.

Jonah lived in the northern kingdom of Israel and prophesied of the prosperity Israel came to enjoy in the days of Jeroboam II (2 Kings 14:25). He must have lived, therefore, about this time or perhaps a little earlier. His name means "dove," and certainly his ministry to Nineveh was Spirit-anointed, resulting in one of the greatest religious revivals in history. His home was at Gath-hepher, not far from Nazareth, the well-known Galilean town where the Lord Jesus in later years spent the greater part of His life. Jonah is the only prophet to whom the Lord directly likened Himself. Following is an outline of Jonah.

   I. What Made Jonah Glad (1:1–16)
      A. His Secret Rejoicing (1:1–2)
      B. His Swift Rebellion (1:3–5)
      C. His Sudden Realization (1:6–8)
      D. His Stubborn Resolve (1:9–16)
  II. What Made Jonah Sad (1:17–2:10)
      A. His Dreadful Prison (1:17)
      B. His Desperate Prayer (2:1–8)

I. What Made Jonah Glad (1:1–16)

We cannot understand the book of Jonah without some understanding of the book's historical background. The vast and growing city of Nineveh cast its long and heavy shadow on Jonah's book—Nineveh, the great and guilty city with extensive suburbs that sprawled along the east bank of the Tigris River. The city itself was resplendent with terraces and storied palaces, with arsenals and barracks, with libraries and temples. It had massive embankments, vast irrigation canals, and mighty gates, especially those that fronted the river. Its walls were great and high, and so thick through that Chariots could drive abreast along the top. The circumference of the city was about sixty miles, a three days' journey. Beyond the walls, the suburbs and other towns sprawled one into another mile after mile. Endless dwellings huddled so closely together on the plain they formed one vast complex of buildings. Jonah could have passed the temples and palaces in an hour, but these endless warrens and mazes where the common people dwelt—through these Jonah would have to tramp day after day if he was to cover the whole city with his message of doom.

In Jonah's day this city already had a long history of aggression and atrocity. As a prophet, given the fearful sins of his people and the growing imperial lusts of Nineveh, Jonah knew full well what Nineveh meant to Israel. It meant destruction, deportation, doom. Nineveh glowered over that ancient world as Moscow glowers over Israel and the Middle East today—and to Nineveh Jonah was sent.

The first part of the story consists of four movements. It did not take Jonah long to make up his mind when once the word of the Lord came unto him.

A. His Secret Rejoicing (1:1–2)

"Yet forty days, and Nineveh shall be overthrown" (3:4). So ran the divine decree. It was the best news Jonah had ever heard! He was a prophet at the court of Jeroboam II, the successful king who ruled over the northern tribes of Israel. His capital city was Samaria. The moral and spiritual condition of his kingdom was dreadful. The prophets Amos and Hosea would soon be pouring out their impassioned denunciations against Israel, and Jonah was enough of a prophet to know that, apart from repentance, Israel was doomed, that repentance was nowhere on the horizon, and that Nineveh would surely be the instrument of doom. Thus the news, "Yet forty days, and Nineveh shall be overthrown" filled his heart with joy.

He read the message of Nineveh's doom like many Christians read Ezekiel 38 and 39 today. They derive comfort from these chapters, which chronicle the coming crash of the Soviet Union, a total and unprecedented crash the like of which the world has never seen and the memory of which will become a proverb and a byword throughout the long ages of the millennium. Christians should read that chapter to weep and pray; instead they read it all too often to rejoice and rub their hands for the comfort it brings. Whereas Jesus wept over a doomed city and nation, Jonah rejoiced. Those who rejoice over the prewritten doom of Russia, her allies, and her armies manifest the spirit of Jonah rather than the spirit of Jesus.

B. His Swift Rebellion (1:3–5)

"Jonah," we read, "rose up to flee" (v. 3). It did not take him long to make up his mind. Forty days to the downfall of Nineveh? Just forty days? Well, it would take the Lord more than forty days to catch up with him! The only thing that could possibly avert the fall of Nineveh was the voice of a prophet in her streets. That voice would never be heard if he could help it. He rose up to flee from the presence of the Lord, planning to go as far as a ship would take him. By the time the Lord caught on and caught up with him it would be too late. The forty days would have run their course.

We can picture Jonah haunting the quayside of Joppa, questioning the ship-masters, looking for a ship going as far as possible from Nineveh. At last he finds a ship going to Tarshish. "How far is Tarshish?" he asks. The shipmaster replies, "Well, mister, Tarshish is as far west as most men go, at the end of the Great Sea. We sail westward day after day, week after week, hugging an endless line of coast, hopping from isle to isle. Ever westward we sail. Then we come to a great narrows where two worlds meet, and we sail out and beyond those rocky gates to where mighty breakers march in from a vast and endless ocean beyond. We turn north and hug the shore for a farther stretch of coast until we come to Tarshish, the great seaport at the end of the earth. Beyond Tarshish the ocean stretches farther than we can see from our masthead and then drops over the edge of the world."

"Tarshish!" we hear Jonah. "That's the place for me! How much does it cost to sail to Tarshish?" We can see him as he makes his way into town to the shipping agents. He pays the fare to Tarshish in the golden coin of the realm, stamped with the image and superscription of Jeroboam II.

But no booking clerk in Joppa could have told Jonah what it was *really* going to cost him to set sail for Tarshish. Jonah would pay a great price, indeed, for trying to flee from the presence of the Lord when he should have been hurrying up the great north road from Samaria to Damascus and Nineveh beyond.

So he paid the fare and he went *down*. Down to Tarshish, down into the ship, down into the bottom of the ship, where the sailors had a berth for landlubbers who hated the sea. There he flung himself down to sleep, rocked at first by the wavelets of the bay but soon heaved up and down by the rougher rollers of the sea. Down and down he went until only the thickness of the rough-hewn planks of the ship's hull and a coating of barnacles stood between him and the horrors of the mighty deep. Down he went into a deep, deep sleep, unaware that just below the keel of that ship there swam a mighty monster of the sea with iron jaws agape.

C. His Sudden Realization (1:6–8)

Jonah slept through the departure from Joppa before a stiff, accommodating breeze. He slept through the first alarms of the oncoming storm as mate and skipper gazed with anxious eye at the thick, black, angry clouds that sprang up out of nowhere to darken the sky. He slept through the desperate attempts of the crew to shorten sail and get the ship before the wind. He slept through the panic that swept the ship from stem to stern so that every last man on board began to pray to his gods. He slept through the panic-stricken attempts to lighten the ship by dumping overboard the valuable cargoes in the hold. He slept through it all.

But he was brusquely awakened. We see a rough, hairy hand tear the blankets from Jonah's bed, and we hear a voice edged with fear pierce through Jonah's heavy sleep: "What meanest thou, O sleeper? arise, call upon thy God" (v. 6). He was hauled from his bed to face the grim fact that it was impossible to run away from God. The stormy wind was, indeed, obeying the voice of the living God, lashing the waves into mountains of doom. As the wind screeched through the rigging, Jonah could very likely hear the angry Voice in the wind: "What meanest thou, O sleeper? What meanest thou?"

The sailors hauled him up from below and looked askance at this man who could sleep through such a storm and who could gaze untroubled at the mighty seas. Little did they know their man. If he died in the deep, then Nineveh died! This was even better than Jonah had planned. He would gladly throw away his life if his death would mean the salvation of Israel. Like an apostle born out of season, he would count himself accursed from Christ for his brethren, his kinsmen according to the flesh. He was willing to give his life for them, willing to go to hell, willing to come under the everlasting curse of God if so be his kinsmen could be saved. Whatever else might be said about Jonah, he cannot be accused of cowardice.

"What is your occupation?" "I am a prophet!" "Where do you come from?" "From the presence of the Lord." "What is your country?" "I am from the Promised Land." "Of what people are you?" "The people of God!" (see vv. 8–10). The sailors tried to pump him and the answers they got confused them more and more. Then he told them something that tormented them even more. "I am an Hebrew: and I fear the Lord, the God of heaven, which hath made the sea and the dry land" (v. 9). The men were exceedingly afraid.

The worst kind of company one can keep is the company of a backslidden believer who is knowingly, deliberately, willfully out of step with the mind and will of God. Such was Jonah, and he was a peril to all who had to do with him.

So we have Jonah's secret rejoicing and Jonah's swift rebellion and Jonah's sudden realization. It dawned on him finally that he could not escape God and that his rebellion endangered the very pagans on the deck of whose ship he stood.

D. His Stubborn Resolve (1:9–16)

The hardest man to reach is not a benighted pagan. These wretched men, in all their heathen blindness, turned with eager hearts to Jonah's God before that day was through. The hardest man to reach is not a blind idolater. The hardest man to reach is the backslider—the man who knows the truth of God and who deliberately runs away from it because it doesn't fit in with his own desires and plans.

"Take me up," said Jonah, "and cast me forth into the sea" (v. 12). Did he say, "Wear ship and set a course for Joppa"? Did he say, "Land me on the coast of Canaan as far north as you can and set me on the way to Nineveh"? Not he! "Cast me into the sea!" he said. He was as stubborn as ever, as hard to reach, as unwilling and as adamant as ever not to do what God wanted him to do.

They tried hard to bring the ship to land. They had more conscience than Jonah—much more—but in the end, with a fervent prayer to Jonah's God, they picked him up by arms and legs and heaved him into the sea.

So, at the beginning, *Jonah was very glad*. When we come to chapter 2, however, we see a very different Jonah. The man who was very glad in chapter 1 now sings a different tune.

II. What Made Jonah Sad (1:17–2:10)

A. His Dreadful Prison (1:17)

He calls it "the belly of hell" for that is what it was to him. His dreadful prison was the belly of a great whale.

Uninformed people have said that a whale could not swallow a man; that, although it is the largest animal that has ever lived, its throat is so small that it will choke on a herring. That is true of some species of whale. But the sperm whale can certainly swallow a man. When mortally wounded, sperm whales have been known to disgorge chunks of cuttlefish six feet long and four feet wide. On one occasion, the eighteen-foot skeleton of a shark was found in the stomach of one sperm whale.

In February 1891, a whaling ship, *Star of the East*, sighted a large sperm whale off the Falkland Islands. The whale was harpooned and in its death throes swallowed one of the harpooners—a man named James Bartley. It was not until a day and a half later that his shipmates, who thought he had been drowned, found him living and unconscious in the belly of the whale. He lived to tell the tale. His whole appearance, however, had been changed. His neck, face, and hands, which had been exposed to the action of the gastric juices of the whale, were bleached to a shocking whiteness, from which they never recovered their natural hue. In his testimony, which was written up in the press of the time, he described his sensations as he slid down into the innermost parts of the whale. He said he could easily breathe inside the whale but the heat was terrible.[1]

Such was Jonah's dreadful prison. It is no wonder he called it "the belly of hell." Down he went into the dark, into the heat, into the physical horror and mental terror of the most fearful prison house one could imagine. He had rejoiced at the thought of a million Ninevites going to hell. So God sent him into one of its suburbs for three days and three nights so he could find out what it was like. No wonder almost all of chapter 2 is concerned with Jonah's prayers.

B. His Desperate Prayer (2:1–8)

How we pray when we get into a tight corner! There is nothing like peril for putting an edge on our prayers, for adding a note of urgency and desperation and sincerity to our cries. Like the Lord Jesus, in that dark hour when He entered the dark valley of death for us, Jonah turned instinctively to the Psalms. He quoted eleven times from the Psalms in eight short verses—from Psalms 3, 5, 16, 18, 31 (twice), 42, 69, 88, 116, and 120.

He prayed! He piled up verse after verse of Scripture to add point and pungency to his prayer. He hammered at the door of his prison. He hammered at the heart of God. He acknowledged his sin, acknowledged the justice of God that had locked him up in so dreadful a place, acknowledged that he had no hope but in the salvation of which God had a sole monopoly. "Salvation," he said at the end of his prayer, "is of the LORD" (v. 9)—something he dredged up in his reeling, failing mind from Psalm 3:8. Salvation is of the Lord!

C. His Dying Pledge (2:9–10)

"I will pay my vows," he promised (see v.9). "Lord, if You get me out of here, I will do what you say. I will go to Nineveh, I will preach to the Gentiles. I will keep my vows." Like many another man, Jonah, in his desperation, made promises to God. How many have we made? Have we kept them? "Defer not to pay thy vows," the Lord says (see Eccl. 5:4).

Give Jonah his due, he kept his word. He paid his vow. He went to Nineveh. He went because he was afraid not to, but he went.

Which brings us to the third point. This man who began by being very glad and who goes on by becoming sad, now ends up by being very mad!

III. What Made Jonah Mad (3:1–4:11)

He went to Nineveh. He went not because he wanted to but because he had to, not because he had learned anything about hell, not because he had learned compassion for lost men and women—he went because he was afraid God might have another jailer even worse than the first waiting to arrest him if he did not go.

A. His Successful Mission (3:1–10)

He picked himself up off the sand of the seashore when the whale disgorged him. We can see him wash the slime and stench off his body, look with horror at his hands, fearful even to look at his face. Then off he went to Nineveh.

His message was *brief* and it was *blunt* and it was *blessed*. It was not so much what he said—his actual message is reduced to eight short words: "Yet forty days, and Nineveh shall be overthrown" (v. 4). He *himself* was the real message—"a living epistle, known and read of all men" (see 2 Cor. 3:2). People would have started at that frightful face of his, all ravaged and ruined by the gastric juices of the whale. They saw a man who was a veritable incarnation of both the severity and the salvation of God. It filled them with horror and hope at the same time.

They did something that Jonah did not tell them to do, something he secretly hoped they would not do. They repented! They believed God!

The people of Nineveh were soundly and truly saved—just as saved as any person today who puts his faith and trust in Christ. We read that "the people of Nineveh believed God" (v. 5). That is all that Abraham did. "Abraham *believed God*, and it was counted unto him for righteousness" (Rom. 4:3). That is all *we* do—except, with New Testament light shining on us, we sharpen the focus and trust Christ.

Then, too, we read of the Ninevites that the king issued a decree in which the national repentance was extended not only to the lords and ladies of the land and to the meanest beggar on the city streets—it was extended to the beasts in the field, to the herds and flocks. There is something remarkable about that. Here we see the fierce Ninevites, who made their name a terror to every surrounding nation, concerned over their very cattle—concerned that their animals should be brought into the sphere of the goodness and grace of God. That proves that a work of righteousness had been done in their hearts, for the Bible says "a *righteous* man regardeth the life of his beast" (Prov. 12:10).

When my father was a young man, revival swept through my homeland of Wales, and it revolutionized the lives of thousands of tough miners. Saved by the grace of God, they went singing to the pit head, making the Welsh valleys ring with the songs of Zion. An even stranger thing happened. Down in the mines the pit ponies refused to work because they were not used to kindness! "A righteous man regardeth the life of his beast." The saved Welsh miners spoke softly to their ponies, treated them with kindness instead of kicks, and the astonished beasts were not used to it, and did not know how to respond! The men of Nineveh were motivated by a like compassionate spirit.

B. His Sullen Mood (4:1–9)

Any other man would have rejoiced at the tremendous revival that broke out in Nineveh—one of the greatest revivals, indeed, in all of the recorded history of God's dealings with men—but Jonah was mad. He had marched into Nineveh just one day's journey, had preached for only a single day, and in that one day a million souls were saved—and Jonah was mad. Why? Because it would ruin his standing back home. The Israelites would never understand how he could have preached to Gentiles and particularly to Ninevites.

The Holy Spirit now sets before us the sad story of Jonah's shanty and Jonah's shrub. When he had finished preaching that first day and could see that revival had broken out at Nineveh—such revival as had never fallen on Israel—Jonah retired to the heights over the city. He built a shanty there and sat down angrily to see what would happen next.

The morning broke. Jonah got up and glared down into the city spread out before him. He could hear the music, he could see the dancing, and he was angry. He had prophesied doom, and doom was not coming. Nineveh had repented, and God had withheld His hand. Jonah was angry.

Then a gourd sprang up outside his shanty. It grew swiftly until it overshadowed him, and Jonah was grateful for the shade it provided. Then along came a worm and smote the gourd and it died, and Jonah was enraged about that. He was more concerned about a plant in his back yard, blighted by a bug, than he was with the souls of a million people, including the little ones, who now danced with newfound joy up and down the back alleys of that great city below. How like so many of us today!

C. His Surrendered Mind (4:10–11)

Like the father of the prodigal, God came and sought to reason with Jonah, but he sat there and scowled and hugged his fierce hate to his heart. His name means "dove," but in his attitude toward the lost Gentile world, Jonah was a hawk, not a dove.

God finally broke through, however, into Jonah's soul. His heart was unchanged; he never came to love the Ninevites so far as we know; he did not stay on to teach them the way of God more perfectly. We can see him, instead, as he picks up his stick, takes one last look at the hated city and one last look at his shanty and the withered remains of his shrub—and he heads for home.

But by the time he crosses the Jabbok, having spent the night, as did Jacob, at

Peniel, Jonah was ready to pay his vow to the last farthing. He arrives home and the men of Gath-hepher come out to see him. The news spreads. Soon the whole city is standing around looking with horror and awe at Jonah's terrible face. He now becomes a living epistle to the men of his own land—a land needing repentance as much, if not more than Nineveh.

They say, "What happened, Jonah? Why is your face so marred, more than any man's?" And he says, "The word of the LORD came unto Jonah the son of Amittai, saying, Arise, go to Nineveh, that great city, and cry against it; for their wickedness is come up before me. But [I] rose up to flee unto Tarshish from the presence of the LORD" (1:1–3).

In other words, Jonah sat down and wrote the book that bears his name. He told the whole story. He did not keep back part of the price, he told it all, even his own disgraceful behavior. He wrote it all down. Thus he gave the world a priceless document on the goodness and severity of God: the goodness of God in salvation to those who repent; the severity of God in judgment to those who don't. Jesus believed in this story. We would do well to take it to our own hearts.

CHAPTER 27

ISAIAH

The Evangelical Prophet

Isaiah was called to the prophetic ministry in the year that King Uzziah died. Uzziah was a leper, smitten with "the stroke of God," as it was called in those days, for his presumptuous intrusion into the priest's office. According to Mosaic Law, Uzziah, as a leper, should have cloistered himself outside the city walls, covered his lip when anyone approached, and cried, "Unclean! Unclean!" It is not likely he went to this extreme, although almost certainly he had to observe a measure of strict personal quarantine. The very year that King Uzziah died of his loathsome disease, the young Isaiah saw a throne vacated on earth and a throne forever set in heaven.

Isaiah lived through a stormy era, living to see the sister-kingdom of Israel in the north overthrown by the Assyrians and its capital city sacked after a stubborn three-year siege. The prophets Amos and Hosea had preceded him in the ministry, pouring out their warning to the ten northern tribes. In later years the young prophet Micah joined Isaiah in preaching against the sins and follies of Judah.

He prophesied through the reigns of four of Judah's kings and was martyred in the reign of the fifth. Moreover, he watched four kings ascend to the throne of Israel in the north by the simple expedient of murdering the currently reigning monarch. And he watched them descend just as quickly into the night.

During the days of Isaiah the great Assyrian Empire dominated the stage of history. The Assyrians were the terror of their age. Pitiless, vengeful, delighting in cruelty, bloodthirsty and fierce, their aggressive foreign policy was implemented by a highly efficient military machine. They had one method of dealing with conquered peoples who had refused to submit to their demands: they tortured to death, in particularly horrible ways, the leaders of the opposition and then deported the rest of the population. Thus their terror descended on future victims, undermining the will to resist.

But in Isaiah's day, Assyria's long and dreadful domination of the world scene, though seemingly at its zenith, was already numbered by the prophet as a thing of the past. Their place would be taken by the Babylonians. Hence, years before the Babylonians became a world power, Isaiah foretold their rise and their conquest of Jerusalem. When Hezekiah was miraculously delivered from a fatal sickness, the Babylonians sent an embassy to court the goodwill of Hezekiah. Flattered, he foolishly showed the envoys all his treasures. Isaiah clearly foresaw that Babylon was the nation Judah had to fear, not Assyria. He saw that the cupidity of the Babylonians would be excited by the sight of such treasure, and he did not hesitate to roundly reprimand his king for such an exhibition of pride and folly.

Isaiah lived on into the reign of Manasseh, the son born to Hezekiah during the fifteen-year extension of his life. Manasseh reigned longest of all the kings and was one of the very worst to sit on the throne of David. Tradition has it that he murdered Isaiah by having him "sawn asunder."

Coming now to Isaiah's prophecy, we find that one moment his book is black with the thunder and the darkness of the storm; the next, the rainbow shines through, and the prophet sweeps his readers on to the golden age that still lies ahead for the world. He speaks with equal conviction about the Messiah as a Savior, and the Messiah as a Sovereign. He brings into focus both the cross and the crown in turn. Christ is as much the Lamb of God to Isaiah as He is the Lion of the tribe of Judah.

Isaiah is often quoted in the New Testament. The Lord Jesus quoted frequently from the book of Isaiah. It was from Isaiah 53 that Philip the evangelist was able to lead the Ethiopian chancellor to a saving knowledge of Jesus (Acts 8:26–38). As long as the message of the gospel is preached on earth, as long as there remains a soul to be saved, the great book of Isaiah will be needed. Jew and Gentile alike are caught up in its themes and led with directness and conviction to a consideration of the person and work of God's beloved Son.

When studying the Old Testament prophets, it is of the utmost importance that we put each prophet back into the historical perspective of the times in which he lived. For first and foremost the prophets were preachers to the conscience of their nation in the day and age in which they lived. Much that they say can be understood only in the light of that. So let's put Isaiah where he belongs—back in the days in which he lived.

In the north, the Assyrian king Tiglath-pileser was inaugurating a new era in the history of Assyrian conquest. A born general and an able statesman, he spent the first three years of his reign subduing the Armenians and the Medes in the east. Then he turned his attention to the west.

On the throne of Israel in Samaria was Menahem. As soon as Menahem saw which way the wind was blowing in the north, he tried to purchase immunity from invasion by paying tribute to the Assyrians. He had to raise enormous sums of money in cold cash (2 Kings 15:19) and to do so had to impose onerous taxes on the nation. This policy sparked an outburst of patriotism in Israel, and Pekah, who was the head of Israel's military establishment, led a successful coup against Menahem and seized the kingdom.

As soon as he was firmly enthroned, Pekah approached Rezin, king of Syria, and suggested an alliance against the Assyrians, one they hoped Judah would join. Ahaz, the king of Judah, however, was too petrified at the thought of Assyrian reprisals and he refused to join. Instead of conserving their forces against Assyria, the foolish kings of Syria and Israel attacked Judah because she would not join their alliance. The resulting Syro-Ephraimitic war, as it is called, dominates the early pages of Isaiah.

Ahaz, the young and inexperienced king of Judah, was desperate and, in an act of abysmal folly, he appealed to Tiglath-pileser, the Assyrian, for aid. Moreover, he did this despite the pleadings of the prophet, who urged him to trust God and not to pursue such a suicidal policy of inviting the Assyrians to intervene in the affairs of the Middle East. Naturally the Assyrians were only too ready to oblige Ahaz since his appeal gave them a perfect excuse for marching south. Israel was invaded and Gaza, Galilee, Gilead, and Damascus were all taken. Ashkelon, Ammon, Moab, Edom, and Arabia were made tributaries, and King Ahaz of Judah was forced to send expensive presents to his ominous ally. Many of Isaiah's prophecies were to warn the nations round about what they could expect at the hand of the Assyrians. The cat had been invited into the cage to keep peace among the canaries.

It was not long before Judah began to feel the baneful religious effects of the alliance with Assyria. Ahaz was summoned to Damascus to meet his Assyrian overlord. While there he was shown an altar, which so impressed him that he had his workmen run off its pattern and send it back to Jerusalem with the demand that a copy of it be made and be set up in the temple. The altar of the Lord was pushed aside to make room for this pagan altar. Ahaz became more and more infatuated with foreign ways. He decided to set up pagan-style religion in Jerusalem and even went so far as to make his own son "pass through the fire" to a demon god. Isaiah was about thirty years of age at this time.

When Ahaz died, his son Hezekiah came to the throne. He was destined to become one of the greatest and godliest of Judah's kings, but he inherited a heavy burden of political and religious compromise from his father. During Hezekiah's reign, Tiglath-pileser completed his campaign in the north, carrying two-thirds of the nation of Israel into captivity, putting Samaria and the remaining Israelites under tribute. The Assyrian menace now moved much closer to Hezekiah and Judah.

Courageously, however, Hezekiah set about the work of religious revival by sweeping his little land clean of its idols. Then he arranged for a Passover to be kept—the first for many, many years—and he invited the surviving remnant of Israel to join in the celebration.

But Israel's final end was near. Hoshea, a vacillating puppet king, was now on the shaky throne in Samaria. He foolishly listened to the advice of Egypt and stopped paying his tribute to Assyria. About this time Tiglath-pileser died and was succeeded by his son Shalmaneser, who promptly marched south to punish Israel. Samaria was put under siege.

The siege lasted for three years. Shalmaneser died without taking the city and was succeeded by Sargon II. During the first year of Sargon's reign, Samaria fell and was subjected to the usual horrors of an Assyrian conquest. Some 27,290 of its people were deported, and colonists from other parts of the Assyrian Empire were brought in to take their place. There was now no buffer state between Assyria and Judah. Discouraged, Hezekiah agreed to pay tribute to Assyria to buy off the Assyrian army.

In 714 B.C., Hezekiah fell dangerously ill and was miraculously restored to life in answer to prayer. The Babylonians who, so far, had been able to fight off the Assyrians, sent ambassadors to Hezekiah to congratulate him on his recovery and to arrange terms for a secret alliance.

The alliance came to nothing. In 711 B.C., the Assyrian army again appeared on the horizon. This time Sargon's purpose was to punish the Philistines for seeking a similar alliance with Egypt.

Judah now began to feel the full weight of the Assyrian arm. But then Sargon was assassinated, and in the confusion that followed a general revolt of vassal states broke out. Encouraged, Hezekiah also joined in the revolt and was given the solid backing of the pro-Egypt party in Jerusalem. He stopped paying tribute.

In 705 B.C., Sennacherib, who had seized the Assyrian throne, again marched south to punish the rebels. Tyre was placed under siege. Joppa, Ekron, Ashkelon, Moab, Ammon, and Edom swiftly surrendered. Hezekiah was panic-stricken and sent an enormous gift of conciliation, even robbing the temple to do so. But Sennacherib was not satisfied. He overran a large part of Judah, carrying 200,000 people into captivity, and demanding further large sums of tribute money from Hezekiah. Then, while the bulk of his army stopped to besiege Lachish, he sent a strong detachment under Rabshakeh to besiege Jerusalem. Rabshakeh was unable to do anything against Jerusalem's formidable fortifications, so he returned to Sennacherib, who had conquered Lachish in the meantime and was now attacking Libnah.

A great Assyrian force was now detached from the main army and sent against Jerusalem together with a letter addressed to Hezekiah and demanding his immediate surrender. Isaiah prevailed upon Hezekiah not to submit. Then God stepped in and miraculously smote the Assyrian army. From then on Sennacherib left Jerusalem alone. This great Assyrian invasion of Judah is the great background event in Isaiah's ministry. It provides the framework for many of his prophecies and becomes the inspiration for larger and wider prophecies concerning the end of the age.

With this background, we are now ready to see what Isaiah has to say. He has been called the "evangelical prophet" because so many of his prophecies ring with the gospel message of salvation and because so many of his predictions point clearly and unmistakably to Christ. His very name means "Jehovah saves" or, as we would put it today, "Jesus saves."

The prophecy of Isaiah falls into three main divisions—two prophetical and one historical.

I. Isaiah's Predictive Statements (chaps. 1–35)
   A. His Prophetic Concern (chaps. 1–4)
      1. The Wrong Standards of the Nation (chap. 1)
      2. The Wretched State of the Nation (chaps. 2–4)
   B. His Prophetic Convictions (chap. 5)
      1. Judah's Complete Failure (5:1–7)
      2. Judah's Common Faults (5:8–23)
      3. Judah's Coming Foes (5:24–30)
   C. His Prophetic Call (chap. 6)
   D. His Prophetic Concepts (chaps. 7–12)
      1. Judah's Monarchy (chaps. 7–8)
      2. Israel's Misery (9:1–10:4)
      3. Assyria's Mastery (10:5–34)
      4. God's Messiah (chaps. 11–12)
   E. His Prophetic Compass (chaps. 13–24)
   F. His Prophetic Chorus (chaps. 25–27)
      1. A Song of God's Faithfulness (chap. 25)
      2. A Song of God's Favor (chap. 26)
      3. A Song of God's Forgiveness (chap. 27)
   G. His Prophetic Cries (chaps. 28–35)
II. Isaiah's Practical Statesmanship (chaps. 36–39)
   A. The King of Assyria (chaps. 36–37)
   B. The King of Judah (chap. 38)
   C. The King of Babylon (chap. 39)

III. Isaiah's Prophetic Stature (chaps. 40–66)
  A. Judah's Miseries (chaps. 40–48)
  B. Judah's Messiah (chaps. 49–57)
  C. Judah's Millennium (chaps. 58–66)

I. ISAIAH'S PREDICTIVE STATEMENTS (CHAPS. 1–35)

Most of the prophecies in this long section are arranged in chronological order. All the dates mentioned are in strict historical sequence:

> In the year that king Uzziah died . . . (6:1)
> In the days of Ahaz . . . (7:1)
> In the year that king Ahaz died . . . (14:28)
> In the year that Tartan came unto Ashdod, (when Sargon the king of Assyria sent him,) . . . (20:1)
> In the fourteenth year of king Hezekiah . . . (36:1)

The first four chapters belong to the closing years of Jotham's reign. Jotham was the son of Uzziah the leper. He was a good king who "prepared his ways before the LORD" (2 Chron. 27:6), and his reign was fairly prosperous. Isaiah, however, was not deceived by outward prosperity. Beneath the surface of public conformity to religion smoldered all those horrible vices that later flourished in the days of Ahaz, the wicked son of Jotham. As we check off the list of national inconsistencies, we can think of the condition in the United States and the West today.

In the first place, the religious climate in Isaiah's day was deceptive. People were attending the place of worship but the numbers were deceptive. Isaiah begins at once to strip aside the outward facade to show the rottenness within. "Hear, O heavens, and give ear, O earth: for the LORD hath spoken, I have nourished and brought up children, and they have rebelled against me" (1:2).

He hammers away at the basic truth that a living, meaningful, dynamic faith in God is a nation's only hope for a healthy society and defense from the enemy.

Spiritism had become a national danger. Isaiah warns against "the soothsayers from the east" (see 2:6)—what we would call today "psychics."

Materialism was undermining Judah as well: "Their land also is full of silver and gold," Isaiah says (2:7). When a country becomes prosperous it usually becomes complacent and independent of God.

Then, too, the worship of idols was sapping spiritual vitality. "Their land also is full of idols," the prophet said (2:8).

Trust in the military was another factor contributing to lack of trust in God in Isaiah's day: "Their land is also full of horses, neither is there any end of their chariots," he says (2:7).

Wickedness was unbridled among men in high places. Army officers, cabinet members, judges, lawmakers—all were corrupt (3:1–4). Corruption had become a way of life, calling for the judgment of God.

And all this with a virile, aggressive, and well-armed foe, Assyria, mopping up country after country in readiness for an ultimate attack upon Israel—a nation that once knew God and still had an Isaiah, an Amos, a Hosea, and a Micah in its midst.

Isaiah was convinced that Judah's sins would be punished by armed invasion. Six times in his opening chapters he pours out his woes on the nation.

1. Woe against the *Slum Landlord* (5:8–10). This was the kind of man who, in the city, was building what we would call tenement property and exploiting the poor; the man who, in the country, was overworking the land.

2. Woe against the *Giddy Playboy* (5:11–17). This was the kind of person who, from morning to night, and late into the night, had only one thought—to wring as much pleasure as he could out of every moment.

3. Woe against *Syndicated Crime* (5:18–19). This was the man who made vice a profession and whose whole life was the professional exploitation of sin.

4. Woe against the *Humanist* (5:20). Isaiah castigated "them that call evil good, and good evil; that put darkness for light, and light for darkness." This kind of people tells us that an alcoholic is sick and that a homosexual simply has "an alternate lifestyle." This is the kind of person who excuses criminal behavior, blaming society for the lawless behavior of criminals.

5. Woe against the *Conceited Philosopher* (5:21). This is the person who is wise in his own eyes and prudent in his own sight.

6. Woe against the *Besotted Judge* (5:22–24). This was the man who was not only a habitual drunkard but also an evil judge who justified the wicked for reward.

These sins made judgment inevitable, and Judah would know the power of the Lord's displeasure. The scourge in the hand of God would be war and the rod of His anger would be the Assyrian. God is never short of instruments when the time comes to punish a people for their sins.

Thus the prophet hammered away at the sins and follies of Judah. But ever and again he lifted up his eyes and looked far down the ages unborn. He foresaw, for instance, the coming of Christ. Far beyond the rise and fall of Assyria, beyond the rise and fall of Babylon and Persia, Greece and Rome, he saw God's Son arriving on the scene: "And there shall come forth a rod out of the stem of Jesse. . . . And the spirit of the LORD shall rest upon him" (11:1–2). The full and final answer to the problems that plague mankind is the coming of Christ.

In the same chapter, Isaiah's prophetic vision took wings once more. He saw the Jews scattered abroad throughout the nations of the earth. He saw beyond the Babylonian Empire, beyond the Roman age, beyond the long age of the church—ages dim and dark to him that shed no light into his mind—to the end times. He saw Israel regathered from all nations: "And it shall come to pass in that day, that the Lord shall set his hand again the second time to recover the remnant of his people, which shall be left, from Assyria, and from Egypt, and from Pathros, and from Cush, and from Elam, and from Shinar, and from Hamath, and from the islands of the sea. And he shall set up an ensign for the nations, and shall assemble the outcasts of Israel, and gather together the dispersed of Judah from the four corners of the earth" (11:11–12).

When Isaiah wrote that, the nations of Israel and Judah were still in the land, still intact. Neither the Assyrian deportation of Israel nor the Babylonian captivity of Judah had taken place. Babylon was not even a world power. He saw beyond the Babylonian captivity, beyond the Roman dispersion of the Jews, right on to the end-time regathering of the Hebrew people. He saw what we today can see. He saw the regathering of Israel *from the ends of the earth*. He saw Israel again a nation with its own flag. He saw Israel gathered into the land, not just from Egypt as in the days of Moses, not just from Babylon as in the days of Zerubbabel, but from every nation under heaven. He saw, indeed, the rebirth of the State of Israel, which has become a reality in our own day. What was *prophetic* to Isaiah has become *historical* to us.

Then, again, his vision took wings. There are three comings of the nation of Israel into the promised land. The first time they came into the land, it was from Egypt—and they gave the world the *Bible*. The second time they came into the land it was from Babylon—and they gave the world the *Savior*. The third time is now. This time, after the purging of the nation in the fires of the great tribulation, they will give the world the *millennium*. Isaiah foresaw that in this same remarkable eleventh chapter: "The wolf also shall dwell with the lamb, and the leopard shall lie down with the kid; and the calf and the young lion and the fatling together; and a little child shall lead them . . . and the lion shall eat straw like an ox" (11:6–7).

There is no reason to doubt that this will happen. Both of the other predictions of this chapter have had a literal, actual, historical fulfillment in history. Jesus came yesterday. The Jews are coming home today. Joy cometh in the morning.

II. Isaiah's Practical Statesmanship (chaps. 36–39)

So important an event was the miraculous destruction of the hosts of Sennacherib outside the walls of Jerusalem that the Holy Spirit actually records the incident in full three times. Happy indeed was Hezekiah, king of Judah, to have at his side in those crisis days a preacher-prophet like Isaiah. Happy is that people who have godly rulers in power and men of biblical, spiritual vision to guide their steps in statecraft. If America needs anything today, that is what it needs. It doesn't need better *weapons* or better *colleges* or better *institutions*. It needs better *men*.

Now let us turn our attention to the last magnificent chapters of Isaiah.

III. Isaiah's Prophetic Stature (chaps. 40–66)

In these chapters the prophet passes from the contemporary scene of his day to the future. He is no longer addressing a people facing the imminent Assyrian invasion. He is looking a century into the future for, in the long run, it was Babylon, not Assyria, that posed the greatest threat to Judah. The Babylonian era passes before his prophetic eye when as yet there was no sign that Babylon was to be a threat to the Jews.

And as always, the prophet's vision is filled with the vision of Christ. He sees His two comings—His coming to redeem and His coming to reign. Like all the other prophets of the Old Testament, while he clearly saw both aspects of Christ's coming, he did not see the church age, which lay between. He saw two great mountain ranges of truth, one behind the other, but he could not see the valley in between.

The last twenty-seven chapters of Isaiah are divided into three sections. In the first, the prophet sees Judah's *miseries*. In the next, he sees Judah's *Messiah*. In the third, he sees Judah's *millennium*.

It is of interest that the book of Isaiah has 66 chapters—the same number of chapters as there are books in the Bible. As the Bible is divided into two major sections—an Old and a New Testament—so Isaiah is in two major sections, one dealing with the *Assyrian* era and the other with the *Babylonian* era. As there are 39 books in our Old Testament and 27 books in our New Testament, so there are 39 chapters in the first major section of Isaiah and 27 chapters in the second section. All who read through Isaiah notice the change in language, style, and subject matter when they cross from chapter 39 into chapter 40, just as they notice the vast difference between the Old Testament and the New Testament. Indeed, the difference in Isaiah is so marked that the critics have postulated the false theory that there were actually two Isaiahs—one who wrote the first thirty-nine chapters and another who wrote the last twenty-seven chapters.

It is the purpose of this survey, however, to point out one interesting feature of this last section of Isaiah. In its twenty-seven chapters, there are three main segments, each containing nine chapters:

- Nine chapters deal with Judah's miseries (chaps. 40–48).
- Nine chapters deal with Judah's Messiah (chaps. 49–57).
- Nine chapters deal with Judah's millennium (chaps. 58–66).

For this current survey, we will look at only the center section, the section dealing with Judah's Messiah. These chapters set before us the *Messiah* as God's perfect *Servant* (chaps. 49–54) and as God's perfect *Savior* (chaps. 55–57). It is interesting that the very center chapter of this central section is Isaiah 53. There, at the heart of the "New Testament" section of Isaiah, is the one great chapter that deals with the cross of the Lord Jesus. Indeed, so clear, so unmistakable, so utterly embarrassing to Christ-rejecting Jews is this chapter that they leave it out of their liturgies.

Now look at Isaiah 53. In verses 1–3 we are *approaching Calvary*; in verses 7–12 we are *apprehending Calvary*, taking note of the Lord's *violent death* (vv. 7–8) and the Lord's *victorious death* (vv. 9–12). Isaiah saw it all seven hundred years before it happened.

So we have found the central section of this part of the book of Isaiah and we have found the central chapter. Now let us find the central statement: "All we like sheep have gone astray; we have turned every one to his own way; and the Lord hath laid on him the iniquity of us all. He was oppressed, and he was afflicted, yet he opened not his mouth: he is brought as a lamb to the slaughter, and as a sheep before her shearers is dumb, so he openeth not his mouth" (53:6–7). And there it is. Isaiah, the evangelical prophet; Isaiah, the great gospel preacher of the Old Testament; Isaiah, whose very name means "Salvation of Jehovah" brings us step by step to Calvary and leaves us standing as guilty sinners before the One who loved us enough to die for us. It was this very sentence that the Ethiopian eunuch was reading in his chariot when Philip led him to Christ. For that is what this great book of Isaiah is all about. It is about *Christ*, God's answer to man's desperate need.

Years ago the great evangelist, D. L. Moody, was boarding a train. He had been conducting evangelistic meetings. Many had been saved. There was one man, however, who had kept on putting it off. He knew he was a sinner, knew he was lost, knew he needed to be saved. He had intended to go forward and get the matter settled, but he had put it off and put it off. Now the meetings were over, and D. L. Moody, the man who had been used of God to hammer away at his conscience, was leaving town. The man rushed off to the station, hoping to have a word with the preacher before he left, but he arrived there just as the train was about to leave the station. He spotted D. L. Moody waving good-bye to a group of friends. He rushed down the platform. "Mr. Moody! Mr. Moody!" he cried. "What must I do to be saved?" The train was beginning to move and the desperate man ran alongside the coach. D. L. Moody looked at him. What could he say to point a man to Christ in just five seconds as the train was gathering speed? "Isaiah 53:6," he called. "Go in at the first 'all' and go out at the last one."

The man went home, found his Bible, and turned to Isaiah 53:6. He went in at the first *all*: "All we like sheep have gone astray." "Yes," he said, "that's me, alright. I have gone astray." He went out at the last *all*. "All we like sheep have gone astray, we have turned every one to his own way; and the *Lord hath laid on him the iniquity of us all*." "Thank God," he said. "I am a sinner, but Jesus died for me."

And there we shall leave this great book.

CHAPTER 28

AMOS

The Country Cousin

The firmament of the Hebrew great is ablaze with stars. There are supernovas like David and Daniel, Moses and Elijah, Abraham and Isaiah. There are giants like Samson and Samuel and Caleb and Joshua. There are whole constellations of stars like David's mighty men and Gideon's noble three hundred and the sons of Jacob.

Not to be forgotten are "the Twelve." The Latin church fathers had a poor eye for brilliance, for they counted the brief pages of the writings of these prophets and dubbed them "the *Minor* Prophets!" The Hebrews knew better—a man is not measured by the length of his manuscript. The Hebrews called these prophets the Twelve.

The Twelve carry us across the whole prophetic age, that period when prophecy was written down to become part of the living, eternal Word of God. Elisha and Elijah were not writing prophets, so—although they rank among the greatest prophets of the age—they were not numbered among the Twelve. Elijah took his stand *against* the throne and wrought his miracles in the teeth of Ahab, Israel's sorriest king. Elisha took his stand *for* the throne, preaching repentance, revival, and restoration. All the prophets wore the mantles of these two great men of God.

From Elisha, only forty years elapsed until the time of Amos, among the first of the Twelve. Bur during those four decades the whole scene changed, making urgent, even imperative, the coming of a new breed of prophet—men who would write.

For upon the international scene there emerged *Assyria*, a new and terrible world power, rapacious, cruel, strong, as different from the Egyptians as day is from night. From remotest antiquity, Egypt had dominated world affairs. But, for the most part, Egyptians were a peace-loving people and—except for the coming of new and vigorous dynasties eager for fame and fortune—left others alone. But not Assyria. This new world power, soon to threaten the world, was driven by an appetite for conquest. It was ruthless, fierce, and driven by a lust for blood and conquest.

The emergence of Assyria changed everything. Its national policy was to uproot conquered peoples, tear them forcibly from their homes, transport them across the width of the empire, and scatter and rule them abroad. It was imperative, therefore, that God's messages be written down against the coming of an age like that. So Isaiah came and Jeremiah came and Ezekiel came and Daniel came. And around each of these men, like planets around a sun, clustered one, two, or three of the Twelve.

We can understand the age full well. Just as the discovery of atomic energy and the sudden emergence of Russia as a major world power has slammed the door upon the past irrevocably and confronted the world with enormous, deadly, unthinkable problems and perils—so did the sudden rise of Assyria to world power. The Assyrians were, in fact, the Russians of their day. The Assyrians were warlike, they intrigued far and wide, they crushed their neighbors, used terror as a policy of state, and scoffed at the decadent world power that stood in their path. They trampled on the weak, they changed the map of the world. Propaganda was a favorite weapon. They ridiculed the religion of Israel, they had an awesome military machine, they ground conquered peoples to powder, using every form of terror and intimidation to sap all will to resist. There they were—the great northern power of their day, soon to dictate the policies of the world.

So God raised up the writing prophets. God's answer to the sword was the pen. Long centuries after Assyria had passed away and its place erased from the map—so completely indeed that Alexander the Great could march his armies over the site of Nineveh not knowing that the ruins of a mighty empire lay beneath his feet—long centuries later, the words of these Hebrew prophets still stand.

But all this was in the future when the first star of the Twelve began to gleam in the darkening Hebrew sky. In fact, the Hebrews did not even know it was getting dark. The Hebrew people in those days were divided into two kingdoms—*Israel*, with its capital in *Samaria*, composed of ten of the tribes; *Judah*, owing its allegiance to *Jerusalem* and the throne of David, composed of two of the tribes and gathered remnants of the best of the other ten.

The kings of Israel and Judah, about this time, had been strong, capable, and vigorous. By the time of Amos, a whole generation had grown up in an Israel that had never known defeat—the lesser kingdoms round about, especially Syria, had been put in their place. Along the same length of years, Judah, too, had grown strong. As Israel pushed north toward Damascus, so Judah had pushed south. All this meant such security across the borders as the twin kingdoms had not known since the golden age of David and Solomon, centuries before.

Moreover, a cultural revolution had taken place among the Hebrews. Until now they had been a nation of fighting farmers, but with this new feeling of security and mutual national power, the twin nations had become urbanized, sophisticated, worldly wise, cultured, and proud. Only once before had the Hebrew people taken such a giant step, and that was when they had left nomadic life in the wilderness for agricultural life in Canaan. That step had been fraught with peril, for it had brought the Hebrews into contact with the temptations of idolatry, and with the filthy fertility cults of Canaan. God's answer had been *the temple*. Now they had taken another giant step—from the agricultural form of life to the urban. This step was equally filled with peril for it brought the Hebrews into confrontation with the world superpowers and created in the nation a wealthy, aristocratic ruling class who cared little for the real woes of the people. God's answer this time was *the Twelve*.

At this point it will be useful to tabulate the possible order in which the writing prophets appeared. The chart below shows the nations to which they chiefly poured out their warnings and delivered their appeals.

Joel	To Judah
Jonah	To Nineveh
Amos	To Israel
Isaiah	To Israel and Judah
Micah	To Judah
Hosea	To Israel
Nahum	To Nineveh
Zephaniah	To Judah
Habakkuk	To Judah
Jeremiah	To Judah
Obadiah	To Edom
Ezekiel	To Judah and the Exiles
Daniel	To the Exiles
Haggai	To the Remnant
Zechariah	To the Remnant
Malachi	To the Remnant

This current survey of the early minor prophets speaks repeatedly of Jeroboam II. It was he who brought the northern kingdom of Israel to the peak of its prosperity. He sat upon his throne in Samaria and looked out across the ten tribes of Israel and the surrounding nations with feelings of complacency and pride. He was monarch of all he surveyed. Scattered throughout his realm were numerous idolatrous shrines where Jehovah was supposedly worshipped, but done so in ways that were anathema to Him. At Dan, at Gilgal, at Tabor, at Carmel, at Penuel, the people thronged to religious festivals that had no scriptural warrant. At Bethel—where once heaven had opened and the father of the nation had communed with the living God, where Jacob had received his life-transforming vision—now stood a mighty temple, sacred to the worship of a calf—a temple lavishly endowed and supported by the throne.

In the cities, people were preoccupied with getting rich, and the grandees of the court were building great mansions for themselves from the money extorted from the poor. Deep poverty coexisted with fabulous wealth. Mammon was supreme. The coming of an earthquake could not shake the grasping rich from their greed: "The bricks are down," they cried, "we will build with granite; the sycamores are down; we will build with cedars" (see Isaiah 9:10). The whole scene was one of strength founded on wealth, and of serenity founded on an immoral religion.

It was in such a day and to such an age that Amos came. He was a rustic from way down south, from that wild stretch of country known as the wilderness of Judea. His hometown was Tekoa, some six miles from Bethlehem. He was a herdsman—or, as we would say today, a cowboy. He was also a gatherer of sycamore fruit—or, as we would say today, a farmer—and not too prosperous a one at that.

With the burden of the Lord upon him, this country boy wended his way north—past Jerusalem, on out of Judah, across the frontier into the sister kingdom of Israel, and on north to Bethel. And there he saw sights that brought his blood to the boil.

He saw vast numbers of people worshipping, in the name of Jehovah, a god shaped like an ox. He saw not only the masses but also the governors and the priests worshipping a golden calf. This was a cattle-rearing people—so they worshipped a cow! Foul nature cults flourished, the vigorous undergrowth of a half-true, half-pagan faith. Things done in the name of religion were a shame even to mention. Amos viewed all this with growing indignation and scorn.

Then, too, he saw opulence and luxury everywhere, riding hand in hand with social injustice and with the oppression of the poor. He saw the vilest immoralities, drunkenness, idolatry. His puritan morals were outraged, and his strict belief in the true and living God was offended to the core. His sense of right and wrong was stirred. Like the apostle Paul gazing upon the religious folly of the cultured Athenians, Amos felt his spirit stirred in him—only Amos was not an educated, polished Paul, able to quote from the classics and able to denounce idolatry with barbs drawn from the popular poets of the day. Amos was a cattle herder. If we could imagine an Ozark country boy clomping into the fashionable clubs of New York's elite, we could picture the impression made by Amos.

Yet he was not without an eloquence of his own. He knew how to barb his points and how to drive them home with the force of a telling illustration. He drew his imagery from the country life of his own familiar hills. The wild beasts, the starry sky, the growling elements—these were the threads from which he wove his fabric of truth. Plowing, herding, winnowing corn—his tapestry came to life with the sights and sounds of the farm.

There was a bluntness about his speech that must have caused a shudder to run up and down the spines of the sophisticated college-trained professional priests and prophets of the Bethel temple. One can almost see eyebrows go up and scorn and disdain appear upon the astonished and offended faces of the society butterflies as Amos addressed the upper-class women of Samaria as "cows" (see 4:1).

He began his prophecies by hurling anathemas at the surrounding heathen nations. No doubt his stock went up. He even denounced his own country of Judah. This, too, would bring an approving smile: "You know, that cowboy fellow—what's his name?—you should have heard what he said about Judah last night. I'll bet when the *Jerusalem Post* gets hold of his statement he'll find himself in hot water at home. He predicted the coming of a conflagration in Jerusalem! They'll roast him for that. You should go and hear him. But be sure to sit in the back. The fellow smells of the barn."

But then Amos turned his broadsides on Israel—and that was an entirely different matter: "That Amos fellow. They should clap him in jail. Last night he denounced the temple here in Bethel. I understand the Primate has reported him to Jeroboam. The fellow's nothing but a troublemaker. They should kick him out of the country. If he doesn't like it up here he should go back to Judah or we should feed him to the hogs."

Let us now turn to the outline of Amos.

I. Introduction (1:1–2)
II. The Vigilance of the Prophet (1:3–2:16)
   A. Lands Near to God's People (1:3–2:3)
      1. Those Always Considered as Gentile Foreigners by Israel (1:3–10)
         a. Damascus (1:3–5)
         b. Gaza (1:6–8)
         c. Tyre (1:9–10)

I. Introduction (1:1–2)

In his opening statement, Amos denied that he had any particular antecedents or training that fitted him for the prophetic office. He was simply God's instrument. By way of background he identified himself as a "herdman" (v. 1); the reference seems to be to his shepherding a special breed of stunted sheep with fine wool and also the fact that he did, indeed, herd cattle (7:14). His hometown of Tekoa was five miles south of Bethlehem and ten miles from Jerusalem.

II. The Vigilance of the Prophet (1:3–2:16)

A. Lands Near to God's People (1:3–2:3)

Passions always ran high in Israel when thoughts were directed across the frontiers to the hostile lands around. Then as now, the nation of Israel kept up an incessant border warfare with the hostile Gentile nations by which she was surrounded.

Today, the hostile are, if not Egypt, then Syria, or Jordan, or Iraq. Way back then it was just the same. If Israel wasn't fighting for her life against Syria, then she was warring with Ammon or Moab or Tyre. Amos skillfully gained the ear of Israel by hurling his bombshells at Syria, at the Philistines, at Tyre, at Ammon (Jordan), at Edom, at Moab—even at Judah. The news media was for him one hundred percent. Overnight he became the equivalent of front-page news, and people all over the country were eager to see which of the detested neighboring states would be bombarded next.

1. Those Always Considered as Gentile Foreigners by Israel (1:3–10)

a. Damascus (1:3–5)

"For three transgressions, and for four I will not turn away the punishment of Damascus" (see v. 3). The hostility we see between Israel and Syria today is the same hostility that has existed between these two nations from remotest times. Some forty or fifty years before Amos prophesied, the Syrians had invaded Israel and had massacred the population—just as they would do today if they could. Drawing on his country background, Amos said "[They] threshed Gilead with threshing instruments of iron" (v. 3). These threshing instruments were curved slabs, studded with sharp basalt teeth, which were drawn over the heaped corn by horses and used not only to thresh the wheat but to chop the straw into little pieces. The Syrians had treated Israel like that. Wanton war, soldiers slain without mercy, pregnant women treated with horrifying cruelty, little children dashed in pieces. God had not forgotten. Time had passed but judgment would come. "For three transgressions, and for four." This is not a mathematical formula but a poetic statement of justice—the measure was full, and more than full. Syria had sinned once too often.

b. Gaza (1:6–8)

Again it is the same formula, but this time it is Gaza and the whole country of the Philistines that are handed over to doom. The Philistines were not denounced for the accepted custom of selling into slavery captives taken in war (the "Geneva Convention" of those days permitted that) but for something worse. They had raided Israel and swept up whole populations so as to catch slaves to sell abroad for commercial gain. Four of the five great Philistine cities were denounced by Amos—Gath being already destroyed. God had seen these sins and remembered.

c. Tyre (1:9–10)

Once more the ominous phrase rang out: "For three transgressions, and for four" (see v. 9). The cup of iniquity was full, and more than full. For over two hundred years Tyre and Israel had been at peace one with the other. Tyre was the ancient capital of the vigorous Phoenician nation, the imperialist kings of which had founded Carthage, the very rival of Rome itself. Between Israel and Tyre there were treaty obligations dating back to the days of Solomon. But Tyre, in its lust for commercial gain, had betrayed Israel and had handed over to Edom all the Jews who had come into their hands. Men may tear up treaties at their whim but in so doing they offend the living God, who is a God of absolute integrity. When Britain, for instance, tore up her solemn promises to the Jewish people, the *Balfour Declaration*, in order to keep her hands on Arab oil, giving up the Mandate over Palestine and treacherously turning over all the strong points in Palestine to the Arabs, she tore up her right to her empire and has been little more than an island nation ever since. God takes note of the way the nations treat the Jews.

2. Those Always Considered as Genetic Family by Israel (1:11–2:3)

a. Edom (1:11–12)

Again the death knell tolled: "For three transgressions, and for four" (see v. 11). Edom was to be treated like a brother by Israel, for according to the dictates of the Mosaic Law, Jacob and Esau were twins: "Thou shalt not abhor an Edomite," God declared (Deut. 23:7). Not a foot of Edomite territory was to be taken from them by the Hebrews, nor were the Jews to forbid an Edomite access to the congregation of the Lord.

But the Edomites ever hated the Hebrews. Just as today, the other nations around Israel rarely attack each other, but they are united in attacking Israel, bound together by a common hatred of the Jew. Just so, Edom's resentment against Israel was a deliberately fostered and fomented hatred. All this God saw and remembered and amply rewarded in the day when He settled His accounts. The Arabs today, like Edom of old, are, by their inveterate hatred of Israel, paving the highway along which God's vengeance will come.

b. Ammon (1:13–15)

Again the idiomatic phrase rang out: "For three transgressions, and for four." Ammon had added the last straw of iniquity that broke the back of the forbearance of God. Its appalling cruelty to the pregnant women of Gilead betrayed a national character deserving the sharpest judgment of God. Ammon's was a deliberate war of extermination for the sole end of seizing land owned by the Jews. The Ammonites had a cruel religion, one that gloried in placing little children on the red-hot lap of Moloch to be dropped living into the raging furnace in the idol's belly. Savage belief produces savage behavior. God will avenge both.

c. Moab (2:1–3)

"For three transgressions, and for four" (see v. 1). It had become a hypnotic refrain. The hearers knew what was coming—more judgment, judgment richly deserved as any Israelite could see. What could be more fitting than that judgment should be poured out upon Syria and Philistia, upon Tyre and Edom, upon Ammon and now Moab! Give it to them, Amos! Rub it in with salt! But, for some reason, Moab was denounced, not for its persistent hostility to Israel, but for its treatment of a king of Edom. God has no favorites. Evil wrought by Moab on Edom was as culpable as evil wrought by Moab against Israel. At some time Moab had found itself at war against Israel and Edom (see 2 Kings 3:26). The Moabite king, unable to secure the king of Edom alive, had wreaked his vengeance upon the dead king's bones. It was hatred carried beyond the grave, hatred so insensate and insatiable that, unable to touch the living, it contemptuously desecrated the dead. Hatred that death cannot extinguish is the beginning of eternal hate in hell. And all because the king of Edom, probably against his will, was in alliance with Israel in, so to speak, an enforced service for God.

Such hatred, after all, was but another expression of unquenchable Moabite hostility toward Israel—the same kind of hatred the Arabs have today. Such hatred must bring a nation into collision with the judgment of God.

B. Lands Native to God's People (2:4–16)

1. The Doom of Royal Judah (2:4–5)

"For three transgressions, and for four" (see v. 4). The shots were now to come close to home, but still there were plenty in Israel who would rub their hands with glee to hear a Judean prophet denouncing Judah and Jerusalem. The great apostle Paul, in hammering home to the human conscience the criminality of human sins, says concerning the Gentile and the Jew, "There is no difference: For all have sinned, and come short of the glory of God" (Rom. 3:22–23). The arrows of conviction now began to strike within the inner circles of the target. So Judah was condemned.

The Gentile nations were condemned, but not for having cast aside the law of God; Judah was. Judah had sinned against greater light: "Their lies deceived them," said Amos (v. 4). It is always thus that part of God's moral judgment of the universe is a man's becoming deceived by the lies he has invented himself.

Moreover this lying rejection of God was of long standing. Amos spoke of the lies "after the which their fathers have walked" (v. 4). Evil acquires a sort of authority with the passing of time. The popular error of one generation becomes the idiom of the next generation; the children canonize the errors of their fathers; the second generation of error demands implicit submission to that error as truth.

God hates deception and visits it with judgment. There is moral blindness first, followed by fiery vengeance. Judah was warned that fire would devour the land. It took some two centuries before that fire fell—but fall it did as Jerusalem and the temple went up in flames before the hordes of Babylon; and Babylon, at this time, was not even remotely a world power. The mills of God grind slowly but they grind exceeding small. Well may we as individuals and as a nation heed the lessons so plainly spelled out here.

2. The Doom of Rebellious Israel (2:6–16)

So then the *neighbors of Israel* were denounced by the prophet. And then, turning swiftly, he began to hurl his broadsides into the *nation of Israel*. "For three transgressions of *Israel*, and for four, I will not turn away the punishment thereof" (v. 6). The hammer blows at Israel's conscience fell quick and hard. Israel was guilty of heartless exploitation of the poor. It was not enough to garnishee a poor man's wages or to throw him into a debtor's prison—they sold him into slavery. Nor was it done for some vast debt owed—they did it when the poor man owed only a trivial sum. They sold a man for a pair of shoes.

Israel was guilty of deliberate perversion of justice. The victims were the meek, the inoffensive, the simple. What chance did such people have of obtaining justice in the courts against rich and powerful business magnates? None whatsoever!

Israel was guilty of the vilest immorality—moreover the father was an evil example to the son. Men, sated with ordinary sin, sought to gratify their lust in the very utmost of sin. Israel was guilty of such profanity and callousness as brought the very name of God into disrepute. The rich not only exploited the poor, and deprived them of their barest necessities, but they then employed their ill-gotten gains in revelry and debauchery in the idol's temple.

Israel was guilty, too, of deliberately undermining the testimony of the godly. Not all in Israel were debauched, for God always has His little flock. Nazarites, people set apart for God, dwelt in the land, and they were evidently numerous because they are spoken of by the prophet as a known class, like the prophets. Deliberate attempts were being made to seduce these believers from their allegiance to God.

So the hammer blows fell upon Israel. God would visit the nation with judgment! And with these stinging remarks the prophet Amos, the country boy from the south, stepped into his stride. Nothing has escaped his eye. The vigilance of the prophet has taken in everything from the sins of the neighbors of Israel to the sins of the nation of Israel. Now Israel must hear his voice louder than ever.

III. The Voice of the Prophet (3:1–6:14)

In this current survey we can only summarize Amos's message and put our hand here and there upon the pulse of the book. In the next four chapters Amos preached three sermons. The first had to do with Israel's terrible guilt, evident on every hand. The second dealt with Israel's repeated sins and failures in the past. The third anticipated inevitable judgment to come. The present! The past! The prospect! Everywhere sin and failure and doom.

Let us take an example or two to illustrate the themes of Amos. He says, "Thus saith the Lord, As the shepherd taketh out of the mouth of the lion two legs or a bit of an ear, so shall the children of Israel be left over—they who sit in Samaria in the corner of a couch" (see 3:12). In an eastern house the corner of a couch was the seat of honor. To Amos, the desert shepherd—used to lying out at night beneath the open sky with the hard ground for a bed—the ivory couches upon which the rich reclined at their meals must have seemed the very symbols of extravagance. But judgment was coming—judgment swift and sure. What was on the way was not the ordinary ebb and flow of war between Israel and her neighboring states. What was coming was a fearful foe who would ravage, destroy, and devour. Those pampered bodies that lolled so lazily upon their couches would be left like the crumbs of a lion's meal—a couple of shinbones here, the bit of an ear over there. That was one of the vivid sketches painted with swift bold strokes by Amos on the dark canvas that held the prospect of the future.

The prophet pours scorn on their religion (4:4–5). He calls their false worship nothing but sin. He caricatures their zeal: sacrifices every morning instead of every year; tithes every three days instead of every three years. And public announcement of their donations to the cause! All was vanity and foolishness. Their religion had not a single shred of divine truth in it anywhere. Famine! Drought! Locusts! Blight! Pestilence! Overthrow! That is what they would reap from God in payment for their false and filthy religion.

The prophet put his finger upon terrible days to come, days when plague would rampage through the land. He pictured a household of ten people, all dead, and the funeral left to a distant relative; the plague had made off with the rest. An uncle or a cousin comes along with the body-burner. So dreadful is the plague that normal rites for the dead are abandoned—the best that can be done is to dump the corpse into a burial pit to be burned with lime or to add it to a public funeral pyre. They pause outside the house and call in a loud voice: "Is there anyone there?" From somewhere deep within the house they hear a muffled cry from the single survivor of a family of ten. "Are there any more with you?" Back comes the dread answer: "None!" And then the urgent, superstitious, fearful plea: "Hush! Hold your tongue! For we may not make mention of the name of the Lord" (see 6:9–10).

For over it all, darker, more sinister even than the plague, the terror beyond all terrors—the name of the Lord. All life was believed to be overhung with accumulations of divine anger like cliffs of snow on a mountainside. It is as though the whole world were some shadowed hollow in the Alps, where any noise might bring down the masses of snow in a roaring avalanche, so the fearful traveler creeps gingerly along in silence. So men, filled with superstition, cautioned against using the name of the Lord. "Hush!" they said, "lest even to utter the name of the Lord should unloose some further avalanche of His wrath."

So the voice of the prophet was heard and his voice drove like a plowshare through their consciences, turning over and over the barren soil of their souls.

IV. THE VISIONS OF THE PROPHET (7:1–9:10)

At this point in the prophecy, direct utterance gave way to a more dramatic form—vision. The prophet could see the future as clearly as though it had already come. He was given a vision of locusts, of fire, of a plumb line, of overripe fruit, and of the false altar. And as he saw, he spoke.

A. Judgment Restrained (7:1–6)

1. The Devouring Locust (7:1–3)

He saw the Lord forming the locust, fashioning it so that, at the appointed time, He might send it forth to ravage and destroy. The grass has already been mown down—now comes the locust to devour. The locust was a symbol for a ravaging army. The nation, just recovering from a disaster in which it has been mown down, was to be overrun by a numerous enemy.

2. The Devouring Flame (7:4–6)

Hard on the heels of the locust was to come the fire. The two visions pictured the same general disaster. The fire was to be terrible, even licking up the great deep—a solemn description of the sea used only on rare and significant occasions. The fire would devour a portion of the sea. Like the vision of the locust, the vision of the fire foretold the coming of the Assyrian army into Israel. As the avenging armies of that great and terrible northern power descended at last like locusts on the northern and eastern portions of the land under Tiglath-pileser, the godly remnant would remember the words of Amos who foretold only a partial, initial destruction by the foe.

After both these visions—the vision of the locust and the fire—the prophet burst into intercessory prayer. True, he had been moved and stirred beyond measure by the sins of Israel—but that such a scourge should come! The prophet pleaded with God for mercy and, in answer to his prayer, the great aggressor was restrained—at first. How strange it must have seemed to observers when the conquering and ravaging hordes, having utterly destroyed Damascus and killed Rezin, its king, and after having carried off all the Syrians and laid waste a portion of Israel—how strange that Tiglath-pileser should withdraw! No doubt there were human policies of state which dictated such an unexpected move. But in the background is the prayer of Amos, offered nearly half a century before. How few would remember that. But God remembered. As the revolution of the earth upon its own axis does not hinder its greater movements around the sun, so human policies revolve around themselves only to move, after all, around the greater and more enduring will of God.

B. Judgment Required (7:7–17)

1. The Plumb Line (7:7–9)
The prophet saw the Lord standing by a wall, a wall made straight and true with a plumb line. The Lord has the plumb line in His hand. He calls Amos by his name and tells him to stop praying. Two judgments have been mitigated, not because of the repentance of the people but because of the entreaty of the prophet. But no more! He is to be entreated no more. The wall was the symbol of the strength of Israel—the symbol of whatever held it together and held out the foe. God stood over the nation. He had made it upright, He had given it its laws, and now He stood over it determined to destroy it. The same fixed laws of righteousness and straightness would ensure the downfall of the nation as once ensured its building up. The plumb line marked all its inequalities—how greatly it was bowed out of line.

The prophet was told, too, that the pagan shrines would be destroyed and that the house of Jeroboam II would perish absolutely by the sword—and so it did within a generation.

2. The Priest (7:10–17)
The primate of the false religious system, Amaziah by name, now ran off to the king with a distorted account of the prophecy. Since the king merely shrugged his shoulders, the furious priest turned on the prophet and told him to get out of the

country. He simply brought down the thunderbolt upon his own head, for Amos foretold the priest's own end and that of his wife and his sons.

C. Judgment Restored (8:1–9:10)

The prophet next saw a basket of summer fruit. That is, he saw the last harvest of the year. When the summer fruit was gathered, the circle of farming for the year came to an end. No more could be done for the crop, the end had come and, good or bad, it must be harvested. The whole circle of God's mercies, prophecies, testings, chastenings, warnings had run out. The sun can only injure ripened fruit. The nation of Israel was ripe, and overripe for judgment, and a terrible judgment it was to be. The prophet could see it as clearly as though it were already taking place. He heard the music ascending from the false temple, then heard it suddenly end in a shriek. He saw corpses everywhere and sensed the terrible hush of silence that would fall over the land. He saw the land heaving like the troubled sea, like the flooding waters of the Nile. He saw midday darkness—perhaps describing an eclipse of the sun but certainly describing sudden, catastrophic plunging of the nation into night. He saw a famine of God's Word and men running here, there, and everywhere for a word from God—except south to Jerusalem, where it was still to be found.

Amos next saw the Lord standing over the false altar in Bethel, sending forth His emissaries of doom. The false temple was destroyed. He saw the people flee— but no matter where they fled, ever they were pursued by the sword. Would they wish to find refuge in hell, would they wish to hide behind the stars, would they wish to hide in the thousands of serpentine caves that honeycomb Mt. Carmel, would they seek refuge across the sea—all would be in vain. The sword pursued. Would they find safety in captivity? No! Even there the sword would pursue them. And so it has. From generation to generation, bitter anti-Semitism has dogged the steps of the Jew in country after country of the world.[1]

V. THE VINDICATION OF THE PROPHET (9:11–15)

And then, at last, in a closing word, the prophet caught a glimpse of a better tomorrow, after the storm clouds and judgments have rolled away. He saw God raising up again the kingdom of David after it had fallen down. He saw the coming golden age with its prodigal harvests and its regathered captives and its restored and blessed people of God.

And thus the prophecy ended. Amos was the prophet of moral order in the universe. Break God's moral laws, and disaster follows in the natural realm as night follows day. Righteousness is the hinge upon which the whole world hangs. Loosen it and all history and nature will conspire to punish the sinful nation. Drought, pestilence, earthquake, and war are the answers of an outraged universe to human and national sin. Truly Amos has a message for the nations today.

CHAPTER 29

HOSEA

The Prophet of the Broken Heart and Broken Home

To understand the book of Hosea we need to put ourselves in the day and age in which he lived. The prophet Amos had completed his ministry. Soon Isaiah would raise his voice, and the prophet Micah also would begin to preach. Micah, however, and to some extent Isaiah, would concentrate their prophecies on the southern kingdom of Judah. It was up to Hosea to pick up the mantle of Amos and concentrate on the wretchedly apostate northern kingdom of Israel.

Amos and Hosea are a study in contrasts. Amos thundered out the righteousness of God; Hosea wept out the mercy of God. Amos took the heathen nations into his prophecy; Hosea limited his utterances to Israel, with an occasional reference to Judah. The style of Amos is clear and lucid, his illustrations being drawn from the countryside; Hosea's style dispenses short, sharp sentences, his broken home giving him ample illustration to convey the truths that were heavy on his heart. Hosea is the prophet of outraged love—that love which never lets us go; the love that many waters cannot quench; the love that suffers long and is kind. Amos is the prophet of *law*, but Hosea had no such unhampered vision of great laws. He was the prophet of *love*. He tells us that in its deepest aspect, sin breaks not merely God's law, it breaks His heart.

Hosea prophesied through the reigns of Uzziah, Jotham, Ahaz, and Hezekiah of Judah and through the reign of Jeroboam II of Israel. He long outlived the one northern king he mentions. It will be seen, then, that although his prophecy is quite brief—just fourteen fairly short chapters—the prophet himself ministered for a quite a long time, well over fifty years (some think as long as seventy years).

He was the Jeremiah of the northern kingdom. His sob-choked prophecies were dreadfully fulfilled in his own lifetime. He lived to see the terrible crash of the nation he loved, as the fearful Assyrian war machine moved in to crush Samaria and uproot and haul away the ten tribes into that captivity from which the majority never returned.

Year after year Hosea preached and prophesied. His preaching was a mixture of story, reflection, sarcasm, upbraiding, recollection, denunciation, promise, and appeal. But it was all to no avail. The land was filled with lawlessness.

Jeroboam II, the king Hosea mentions in his date mark, was a capable king. He recovered for Israel more territory than any northern king had ruled over since the division of the kingdom upon the death of Solomon. He even annexed Damascus, which had been lost to the Hebrew people since Solomon's day. But along with all this seeming success, the forces of decay were at work, eating heart and soul out of the nation.

Jeroboam II was the last king to reign with a semblance of legality. After him almost every king who ascended to the throne in Samaria did so by murdering his predecessor. Zechariah reigned only six months when he was murdered by Shallum. Shallum reigned for only one month and was murdered by Menahem. Menahem did manage to survive, but no sooner did his son Pekahiah ascend the throne than he was murdered by Pekah who, in turn, was murdered by Hoshea.

Loyalty to the throne soon died in the face of such unblushing crime in high places. The land was filled with murder and bloodshed, adultery and sexual perversion; drunkenness was widespread, accompanied by utter indifference to God. Debauchery, lawlessness, and violence ran rampant everywhere. Adultery was consecrated as a religious rite. There was no settled foreign policy. Those in power vacillated between alliance with Egypt and appeasement of Assyria. Israel had entered into what Sidlow Baxter[1] calls "the last lap" of iniquity.

The real cause of the chaos was Israel's abandonment of the gold standard of faith in the true and living God. It had started back in the beginning, when the ten tribes had first incorporated as a separate kingdom. To prevent his people from making their annual pilgrimages to Jerusalem to keep the feasts of the Lord, Jeroboam had instituted new altars, consecrated new priests, inaugurated a new religious calendar, and set up golden calves at Bethel and at Dan. At first these idols were supposed to represent Jehovah but, like all idol worship, the images soon became direct objects of worship themselves. Then the gods of other nations were incorporated into Israel's religious pantheon, and the vile immoralities and crude idolatries of the Phoenicians became a regular part of popular worship. All this so deadened the conscience and blunted spiritual sense that before long Israel was practicing the atrocities of child sacrifice and reveling in the unblushing licentiousness of Canaanite religion.

Hosea's prophecy divides into two unequal parts. The first three chapters set before us a page of domestic history—*the tragedy in Hosea's home life*. The rest of the book is an exposition of this. The domestic tragedy in which Hosea was involved is the basis for a series of messages dealing with *the tragedy in Hosea's homeland*.

This current survey gives just the worst of those tragedies.

       c. Sure Disillusionment (13:4)
       d. Stubborn Defiance (13:5–6)
       e. Swift Destruction (13:7–8)
       f. Smitten Defenses (13:9–11)
       g. Sordid Depravities (13:12–13)
       h. Salvation Delayed (13:14)
       i. Successes Despoiled (13:15)
       j. Shocking Doom (13:16)
    4. Israel's Peace (chap. 14)

I. THE TRAGEDY IN HOSEA'S HOME LIFE (CHAPS. 1–3)

The first three chapters deal with signs, with sins, and with salvation.

A. The Signs (chap. 1)

1. The Challenge to the Prophet (1:1–2)

The first chapter of the prophecy focuses on Hosea's children. The prophet was ordered by God to get married, and he married a woman he sincerely loved. She turned out to be a woman with wanderlust, however, who soon became unfaithful to her husband. At first the prophet only suspected that she was not being true to him, but by the time he came to write up his prophecy he knew her for what she was—a common harlot.

The relationship of marriage is often used in the Bible to illustrate spiritual relationship. In the New Testament the church is the bride of Christ; the false church, on the other hand, is a scarlet woman, the great harlot that sits upon the waters (the nations). In the Old Testament, Israel was the wife of Jehovah, a nation brought into a relationship with Him that was unique among all the nations of mankind. God likened this relationship to that which exists within the marriage bond. As adultery is a sin against the marriage union, so unfaithfulness to God is spiritual adultery. When that unfaithfulness becomes a flagrant way of life, it is likened to harlotry.

2. The Children of the Prophet (1:3–11)

At first Hosea seems to have given his wife the benefit of the doubts that were beginning to grow in his mind. There were three children born to his wife, Gomer, at this time. The first he acknowledged as his.

The first child was *Jezreel*. The name means "May God scatter; may God sow." The name of this son spoke of the nation of Israel.

a. The Nation Defeated (Jezreel)

Jezreel was a significant place in the history of the northern kings. The name takes us back to the days of Ahab and Jezebel and to the cold-blooded plot to murder Naboth the Jezreelite because he refused to sell his family inheritance to the king. For this crowning sin, judgment was pronounced on Ahab and his house. His dynasty came to an abrupt end when Jehu was raised up as God's instrument of wrath. He, in turn, founded a dynasty, which in the end was similarly terminated under the judgment of God. By calling his son Jezreel, Hosea struck the note that was to characterize his whole prophecy—the end of the Jehu dynasty and the destruction of the northern kingdom with its military power in the valley of Jezreel. Both these events took place, though with a span of forty years between them.

The beginning of the end for Israel was heralded by Shalmaneser's victory at Betharbel, a city in Galilee. The cruelty and barbarity of the Assyrian there was a warning to Israel that Hosea's prophecies had come to the birth. The valley of Jezreel is the great plain of Esdrealon in central Palestine, where the battle of Armageddon will one day be fought.

The name of this first son, then, was ominous. It announced the defeat of the nation. Although the prophet owned the son as his own, he already suspected, perhaps, that Gomer was not being faithful to him.

b. The Nation Deported (Lo-Ruhamah)

The second child was Lo-Ruhamah. The name of this child means "unloved," or "she who never knew a father's love," by which name Hosea disowned the little one as being any kin of his. The poor little girl was the daughter of some nameless man with whom Gomer had committed adultery. Feinberg tells us that there is a great depth of feeling in the original Hebrew word. The name of this little girl speaks of the nation deported, for with the birth of this child the prophet announced the coming withdrawal of mercy from the house of Israel by the God the nation had betrayed.

c. The Nation Discovered (Lo-Ammi)

Some time later, probably about two or three years later, a third child was born, a second son. The prophet called this son Lo-Ammi. The name means "not my people" or "no kin of mine." He disowns any relationship to this child at all. He knew now that his wife was just a common tramp. The name of this boy speaks of the nation discovered—discovered for what it was as seen in the lives of its people. Yet, at the same time, a note of hope for the future, the distant future, when time and trouble would have done its work.

These were the signs, wrung out of Hosea's soul by the terrible thing that had happened to him. The wife he loved not only did not love him, but she showed her contempt for him by courting other men. The nation of Israel, so greatly loved of God, repaid Him with indifference and contempt. It openly courted the pagan nations round about by embracing their vile religions and by cleaving to them in devotion—the kind of devotion Israel denied to the living God.

B. The Sins (chap. 2)

The second chapter concentrates on the wife. We can imagine the emotions that tore the heart of Hosea. Oh, what a sense of shame, of desolation, must have been his as he looked around his desecrated home! He had forgiven his wife once, yea, twice. He loved her still. He had pleaded with her, warned her, but all to no avail.

1. The Personal Note (2:1–4)

We have the wooings of grace (vv. 1–2) and the warnings of grace (vv. 3–4). Hosea could do no more. In defense of his own good name he disowned the woman, divorced her, and refused to extend mercy to the children she had begotten in her sin.

In all these domestic tragedies, Hosea came to know something of the heartache of God. He, who knew all things from the beginning, had allowed His servant to marry such a woman. The public shame that had come upon Hosea, and the deep, deep sorrow that was his, enabled him to enter into the public shame of Israel's conduct and the unfathomable sorrow in the heart of God.

2. The Prophetic Note (2:5–23)

Hosea had been forced, at last, to disown his wife, so God would disown Israel. Israel, now an unblushing harlot, had declared her intention of pursuing her "lovers," that is, the idols of her pagan worship. She was obdurate, unyielding, determined. God would let her go, let her have her fill of her folly, until at long last, when betrayed and stripped, crushed and beaten, she would think back to her first husband.

C. The Savior (chap. 3)

The third chapter concentrates on the husband. This chapter is very brief (only eighty-one words in the original) but it is one of the great prophecies of the Bible.

Time has passed. The Lord speaks to the prophet and tells him to love again that woman who has so grievously sinned against him. The command was a fresh revelation of God's boundless love for Israel. No wonder Hosea has been called the first prophet of grace. Isaiah might be a greater statesman, a more powerful writer, and a deeper theologian, but he did not have Hosea's tenderness.

Hosea did as he was told and sought out his former wife. She had sunk so low that she had sold herself into slavery. Hosea bought her. She was now so wretched and abject and so undesirable in the eyes of the sinful men she had once so eagerly sought that she was to be sold in the slave market at a bargain price. The normal price of a slave was fixed at thirty pieces of silver (Exod. 21:32); Hosea bought Gomer for fifteen. She was on sale for half price—for fifteen pieces of silver plus one and one half homers of barley. The barley speaks of her utter worthlessness—barley was food for animals.

The prophet took the unhappy woman home. He told her that never again must she play the harlot, and that before he could again become a husband to her, she would have to go through a lengthy period of trial and preparation.

Then came one of the greatest prophecies of the Old Testament regarding the nation of Israel: "For the children of Israel shall abide many days without a king, and without a prince, and without a sacrifice, and without an image, and without an ephod [i.e., without a priest], and without teraphim [i.e., idols of any kind]" (v. 4). No more sovereign! No more sacrifices! No more sanctuary! No more superstition! This is *exactly* how Israel has been ever since the crucifixion of Christ and the subsequent destruction of the temple by the Romans. For nearly two thousand years they have been without a king, without a priest, without animal sacrifices, and without any desire for idolatry.

In a coming day, the nation will be restored to the Lord and will take her place again, thoroughly cleansed, as the wife of Jehovah—the nation He loves above all others. God loves all men, but in terms of nations, Israel holds His heart.

Thus the tragedy in *Hosea's home life* became the text from which he could adequately preach about the tragedy in *Hosea's homeland*. Through the rest of the book, however, he never again mentioned his home, his wife, or the children she bore. When God forgives, He forgets.

In the first major section of the book, Israel is to be seen in the nation's relationship to Jehovah. Gomer represents the nation, Israel; the children are the people of the nation; Hosea's sorrow, patience, judgment, compassion, and final act of redemption illustrate God's attitude toward Israel. Chapter 2 applies the parable of chapters 1 and 3. Hosea came to understand the true meaning of Israel's sin—it was spiritual adultery and even harlotry.

II. THE TRAGEDY IN HOSEA'S HOMELAND (CHAPS. 4–14)

It has been claimed that this section of Hosea does not lend itself to analysis. Here we have the hot outpourings of a broken heart, here the fountains of the great deep are broken up, here a storm of tears and woe bursts upon us, being driven by a score of conflicting winds. Here we have the eruption of a white-hot volcano, the pent-up passions simply flow forth, pouring out here, there, and everywhere. That may be so, but at the same time, there *is* an order here. The remaining chapters *do* lend themselves to analysis, as we have shown. *Ordeal* may be the theme, but *order* is there as well.

A. The Polluted People (chaps. 4–7)

The Lord had a *controversy* with Israel, He made a *commentary* about Israel, and He issued a *caution* about Israel (chaps. 4–5).

God had a lawsuit to bring against the nation because of its moral and its ministerial sins. "Hear the word of the LORD" (4:1). That is how He begins. Swearing, lying, killing, stealing, immorality—these were the broad categories of national sin, but worst of all was idolatry, that fountainhead of all wickedness. "Ephraim is joined to idols: let him alone" (4:17) was God's aside to neighboring Judah.

Yet there was *compassion* for Israel, too (chap. 6), but a compassion that was swept away by *contempt* (chap. 7). Ephraim (the general name for Israel) was "a cake not turned" (v. 8). In eastern lands bread was baked on a hot stone. The flour was kneaded, made into a circular, thin disc and put on the hot stone. The important thing was to turn it at just the right moment. If it was left too long, the one side burned to a cinder and the other side was still raw dough. Such was Ephraim. God intended Israel to be a nation in which He could find satisfaction, but it had turned out about as useless for His purpose as a cake not turned.

Israel was "a silly dove" (v. 11)—a dove that listened to every beck and call and that flitted to and fro without purpose or aim. Thus Hosea scornfully depicted Israel's foreign policy of flitting back and forth between Egypt and Assyria in hopes of playing one against the other.

Israel was a polluted people, a people given over to sin, sin in which the nation's leaders were as much involved as the people themselves.

B. The Punished People (chaps. 8–10)

Retribution was to be swift and sure. In this section of his prophecy, Hosea underlines *the trampled covenant* (chap. 8), *the tragic consequences* (chap. 9), and *the terrible conditions* (chap. 10). It is in this section that he employs his famous proverb: "For they have sown the wind, and they shall reap the whirlwind" (8:7), a reference both to their rulers and their religion. They had set up kings without God's authority; now they were getting the kind of rulers they deserved—murderers, useless, foolish men bent on policies that could land the nation only in ruin. They had indulged themselves in idolatry, and now they must reap what they had sown—the Assyrian was coming to deport them to lands where all that was known was idolatry. They had turned their backs upon God; now God turned His back upon them. "Ephraim shall bring forth his children to the murderer" (9:13) was Hosea's lament. So much misery was building up for their children that the prophet, in his distress, prayed that they might not have any children (9:14).

C. The Pardoned People (chaps. 11–14)

In spite of their *persistence* (chap. 11), their *past* (chap. 12), and their *punishment* (chap. 13), they would be *pardoned* (chap. 14). God takes no delight in punishing people even though He must punish them in His holiness. "How shall I give thee up, Ephraim?" He cried (11:8). In the last chapter, at the very end, love wins.

We look back, then, over this outpouring of grief on the part of Hosea at the *tragedy in his homeland*. We mark the succession of impassioned phrases that pour from his pen—"Make her as a wilderness." "I will hedge up thy way with thorns." "My people are destroyed for lack of knowledge." "Ephraim is joined to idols: let him alone." "Will I be unto Ephraim as a moth." "They make the king glad with their wickedness." "They are all adulterers, as an oven heated by the baker." "Ephraim is a cake not turned." "Ephraim also is like a silly dove." "The calf of Samaria shall be broken in pieces." "They have sown the wind, and they shall reap the whirlwind." "Their glory shall fly away like a bird." "Israel is an empty vine." "Ye have plowed wickedness, ye have reaped iniquity." "He is a merchant, the balances of deceit are in his hand." "They shall be as the morning cloud, and as the early dew that passeth away, as the chaff that is driven with the whirlwind." "I will meet them as a bear that is bereaved of her whelps."[2]

Hosea was, indeed, a preacher who poured out his heart. He knew only too well the doom that awaited Israel. The Assyrian was already sharpening his sword. All the world of that day knew what it meant for a people to be handed over to the cruelties of the Assyrian.

But all of this preaching grew out of the personal tragedy in Hosea's life, which gave him the basis on which to build.

CHAPTER 30

MICAH

A Tale of Two Cities

Isaiah and Micah stood shoulder to shoulder in the prophetic ministry. Isaiah was the older of the two. Isaiah was from the court; Micah was from the country. Isaiah prophesied to the nation from the standpoint of one who had the ear of the king. Micah prophesied from the standpoint of one who rose up from the ranks of the rural yeomen of the nation.

We know nothing about Micah except the place of his birth and the approximate dates of his prophecy. He preached during the days of Jotham, Ahaz, and Hezekiah, kings of Judah. He prophesied, therefore, during the dark days that saw Assyria swoop down like a wolf on the fold and uproot the northern tribes and haul them off into captivity.

He was primarily a prophet to Judah and Jerusalem, though Samaria and the tottering northern kingdom comes well within his view. He mentions no kings of the northern kingdom. Only prophets who prophesied in the northern kingdom make mention of Israel's kings.

He came from Moresheth, a little city located on the hills and glens that ran from Judah eastward to the Philistine plain. His homeland was fair and fertile, with red, alluvial soil and ever-flowing streams. It was a land of cornfields and cattle, with bees humming through the grass and flowers, and with larks rising skyward on the wing. It was not a place for large towns. It was a place for rearing men of sturdy stock, men in love with the soil, men living sufficiently close to hostile neighbors as to be watchful and ready, and sufficiently removed from the capital as not to be under great subservience to its ways and whims.

Only bare traces of the reigns of the earlier kings of Judah are mentioned by Micah. His prophecies seem to lie squarely within the reign of godly King Hezekiah—Hezekiah, who fought so hard and stubborn and losing a battle to instill righteousness back into the minds and hearts of his largely apostate people.

The valley mouth near which Moresheth stood was the gateway to Egypt. Roads converged there from the various points of the compass. It was a place where travelers passed and a place where battles were fought. It was there that Asia defeated the Egyptians. It was there that Vespasian and Saladin, in their different days, drove in their stakes in preparation for the attack upon Jerusalem. Most of the early pilgrims heading from Jerusalem to Sinai passed by here. It was much the same in Micah's day.

From his home he must have seen the embassies hurrying down to Egypt from Hezekiah's court. From there he must have seen the ambassadors hurrying back with the empty, useless news that Egypt would back up Judah in war with the Assyrian kings.

They were days of great excitement. The mighty Assyrian army had rolled down from the north under Shalmanaser, and Samaria was besieged. Shalmanaser died and Sargon took his place, and after long and stubborn siege, Samaria fell. Then came Sennacherib and the invasion of Judah. It was this region of Micah's homeland that the mighty Assyrian king attacked. His plan was to capture these outposts of Judah while sending an army, at the same time, to invade Jerusalem. The doom of northern Israel, so long pronounced by Amos and Hosea, came and went during the time Micah preached.

It was but a day's journey from Moresheth to Jerusalem, a scant twenty miles. The prophet looked at the capital, he looked at the countryside, he saw the sins of his people calling down the inevitable judgment of God. He saw a godly king fighting a losing battle against entrenched injustice, wickedness, and sin in high places. He saw that Judah, just as much as Israel, must come under the scourge of God. Yet, beyond it all, beyond the rise and fall of kingdoms, dynasties, and empires, in the far, far future, was hope. God was still on the throne. Ruin there must be, but beyond that, redemption and a new reign with the long delayed, oft-promised coming of the *King*.

I. The Prophecy of Retribution (1:1–3:12)
   A. The Calamity (1:1–16)
      1. The Coming Forth of Jehovah (1:1–4)
      2. The Coming Focus of Judgment (1:5–16)
         a. The Salient Points of Focus (1:5–9)
            (1) The Sin of Samaria Was Spiritual (1:5–8)

I. THE PROPHECY OF RETRIBUTION (1:1–3:12)

A. The Calamity (1:1–16)

The *salient point of interest* on the first page and paragraph of the prophecy was Samaria, the capital of the northern tribes of Israel. Samaria's sins were beyond recall. Her doom was long since sealed.

The prophet began by inviting the whole world to witness the coming of the Lord to execute His judgment upon his abandoned people. The prophetic focus, after all, was on a very little land, scarcely the size of Wales. Yet twice within the compass of his prophecy, Micah called upon the world, including the hills and mountains, to pay attention to the judgment of God.

This was no mere oratorical flourish. This was in keeping with the purpose for Israel's national existence. Israel was unique. It was a nation specially created to be brought into unique covenant relationship with God. With no other nation has God ever entered into such an agreement. Israel was raised up to be a testimony to all other nations of the goodness, the grace, the government of God.

Since she had so dramatically, abjectly, wretchedly failed, then the nations must come and watch her punishment. Since Israel, in *advancement*, had failed to be a testimony, then Israel in *adversity* must be a testimony. One way or another the nations must know that God is, and that He is holy and righteous, just and true, as well as compassionate, gracious, and kind. The salient point of interest, then, was Samaria. But there was more.

There was also *a subsequent point of interest*. The calamity was by no means to be confined to Israel and Samaria. It was to embrace Judah and Jerusalem. So the prophet turned his attention to his native land, to Judah, to its capital and, particularly, to a cluster of townships and villages he had known since his boyhood days. One of the towns, indeed, was his own hometown.

His eye ran from one town to another. As each came before his vision, a vision quickened by the Spirit of God to see these towns in the light of prophecy, he did something very interesting indeed. He took the name of each town and made a pun out of it. Town after town—each one pungent with prophecy.

Gath and Acco, Aphrah, Saphir, Zaanan, Bethezel, Maroth, Jerusalem, Lachish, Moresheth, Achzib, and Mareshah. Just dull names to us. But Hebrew names! Names alive with meaning! Names that lent themselves to pun and prophecy. "Tell it not in Tell-town! Weep not in Weep-town! Roll in the dust at Dust-town! No neighborliness at Neighbor-town!" Like the rolling of the thunder across the Judean hills, the names were ominous with doom. The prophet began with the far west and moved steadily inland toward the capital city. The storm of judgment rolled relentlessly on and on.

A dozen names, a dozen prophecies. *Baseness* beyond telling and tears (Gath and Acco), *brokenness* (Aphrah), *blight* (Saphir), *bondage* with no freedom left and no friends left (Zaanan and Bethezel), *bitterness* (Maroth), *battle* with all peace gone and all power gone and all prosperity gone (Jerusalem, Lachish, and Moresheth), *betrayal* (Achzib), *bankruptcy* (Mareshah).

A dozen towns' names, a dozen tragedies. The names spoke of all that went with war and defeat and the sack of cities, of all that spoke of human misery, of a nation reaping the due reward of its deeds, and at the hand of an invading power raised up by God to thrash a people He had blessed beyond measure and who had scornfully turned their backs upon Him. It certainly was an original way to prophesy!

The prophet had set forth the calamity and now turns his attention to *why*.

B. The Cause (2:1–3:12)

Judah's sins were deeply engrained. People, princes, and prophets alike were indicted. Micah scourged the landowners and the judges for their corruption.

During the days of King Uzziah (upon whose death the prophet Isaiah began to preach) Judah experienced a tremendous increase of wealth. Prosperous times are often more perilous times than are poor times. The sudden increase of wealth and the concentration of that wealth in the hands of a few created an atmosphere of luxury and laxness that had not been known in the land since the days of Solomon. The new commercial power brokers threatened to upset the simple national economy, which had always depended, under law, on each man having his own piece of freehold land. Under the Mosaic Law, a man could not sell his ancestral property. He might lease it for a period of years, but every fifty years all property reverted to its original freeholder or his heirs. In this way economic power could not be concentrated in the hands of a few.

The rise of a new class of independently rich merchant princes resulted in the oppression of the poor and the forcible seizure of land from the peasants by the new barons of finance. Micah denounced this.

The oppression was made more bitter by the deliberate connivance of the judges who accepted bribes from the powerful and wealthy financiers in order to circumvent the law on their behalf. Anyone who has tried to take a giant corporation to court knows what these unorganized Hebrew peasants were up against. "Woe to them that devise iniquity," cried Micah, "and work evil upon their beds! when the morning is light, they practice it, because it is in the power of their hand [to do so]. And they covet fields, and take them by violence; and houses, and take them away" (2:1–2). There was no conscience. Even widows and orphans were being exploited.

The wealthy overlords of finance and commerce simply told the prophet to shut up (2:6). They were aided in their contempt by a band of false prophets, men who would say anything so long as they were properly rewarded for it.

In such a case when people, princes, and prophets are in alliance to keep the unjust establishment in power, there could be but one remedy. Since wealth and financial power were at the root of the problem, then the power base for the corruption would be removed. And God would remove it by allowing the Assyrians and later the Babylonians to come and spoil the land. So then Micah's prophecy was first and foremost a prophecy of retribution.

II. The Promise of Restoration (4:1–5:15)

This restoration is depicted, then delayed, then described. The prophet's vision soared down the ages.

A. The Restoration Depicted (4:1–8)

"And they shall beat their swords into plowshares, and their spears into pruning-hooks: nation shall not lift up a sword against nation, neither shall they learn war any more" (4:3). It is the millennial dream, a vision of a coming day when Jesus will reign "where'er the sun doth his successive journeys run."[1] It is the vision of a day when armies will be disbanded, when tanks will be turned into tractors, when the war academies will be turned into seminaries, when peace and prosperity will come to all mankind because the Prince of Peace Himself has come.

The first three verses here in Micah 4 are practically identical with Isaiah 2:2–4. It does not really matter who uttered the prophecy first—Micah or his fellow prophet Isaiah. The same inspiring Holy Spirit evidently wanted the glorious news to be repeated. "They shall sit every man under his vine and under his fig tree; and none shall make them afraid" (4:4). Peace and justice at last!

B. The Restoration Delayed (4:9–5:6)

The prophet begins a long section in which he peered into the future. He focused on two coming world empires. Assyria no longer interested him. It was true that the Assyrians were to be the immediate scourge of God for the Hebrew people, and a terrible scourge indeed, but Assyria's day would soon be done. Beyond that, for Judah, were two other oppressors. For sin is so stubborn a thing in the life of a person and a people that once it takes a firm hold it is almost impossible to uproot.

1. The Times of Israel's Misery (4:9–13)

a. The Babylonian Empire (4:9–10)

"Go even to Babylon," he cries (v. 10). The stroke he envisioned in a pregnant sentence or two did not fall until a century after it was uttered. There it lay, written on the prophetic page, slumbering in the womb of time, gradually growing and developing to the terrible moment of birth. It was a sentence of corroboration to what Isaiah, too, was preaching—Judah's true oppressor was to be Babylon. People wrote the pair of them off as crazy.

Then Micah's vision leaped ahead by giant strides until it came to rest in the last days.

b. The Beast's Empire (4:11–13)

He saw the last days come sharply into focus, saw the *threat of the nations* as they mobilized in anti-Semitic hate against a future Israel: "Now also many nations are gathered against thee, that say, Let her be defiled, and let our eye look upon Zion" (v. 11). That will be their threat—bring about the downfall of Israel and the defilement of her holy places. We can hear the rumblings of this today in the growing world dislike of Israel and the problem Israel poses to politicians, situated as it is in the oil-rich Middle East. Even nations that have traditionally been Israel's friends might one day well consider her expendable for the sake of Arab oil or for influence in the vital lands where Islam holds sway. Russia and the West both know the strategic importance of these lands. The day will come when the West will consider Israel to be just as expendable as she is to the Soviet Union today.

But if we have here the threat of the nations, we also have the *thrashing of the nations* (4:12–13). God will not let them get away with it. "Arise and thresh, O daughter of Zion," cries the prophet (v. 13). The nations will be united against Israel, and the Beast's empire will spearhead the final attack on Israel. What they will not realize is that, behind their own evil schemes, God is simply orchestrating everything. It is He who is really bringing the nations together against Israel so that He, as Israel's Redeemer, might give those nations the greatest thrashing in all of history.

2. The Times of Israel's Messiah (5:1–6)

Like those of so many of the Old Testament prophets, Micah's vision jumps back and forth between the first and second comings of Christ. We must always remember that the prophets had no view of the church age, which has been inserted by God between these two comings. Accordingly, they often telescoped the two comings of Christ. This caused great confusion to Jewish readers of the Old Testament because they did not understand what is so obvious to us, that Christ would come twice—once to *redeem* and once to *reign*. These Old Testament prophets wrote and then read remarkable statements that pointed to a *sovereign* Messiah. They wrote and then read equally remarkable statements that spoke of a *suffering* Messiah. Isaiah, for instance, wrote Isaiah 9:6 concerning a Christ and a *crown*; he also wrote Isaiah 53 concerning a Christ and a *cross*. Peter tells us that the prophets themselves were greatly perplexed by these divine revelations, these Spirit-inspired utterances.

Were there to be *two* Messiahs? How could such conflicting utterances be re-solved? Obviously an omniscient God could not contradict Himself! The New Testament makes it all clear—there were not to be two *Christs* but there were to be two *comings*. The failure to realize this fact sometimes makes many Old Testament prophesies seem confusing. We need to remember that the prophets often jumped back and forth. They could see the prophetic peaks in the distance but they could not see the two-thousand-year-long valley in between.

Thus the prophet Micah here, in the compass of a half-dozen verses, spoke of an *invasion* and of an *incarnation*; of an *interval* and of an *investiture*. The most famous statement he made, of course, is in 5:2: "But thou, Bethlehem Ephratah, though thou be little among the thousands of Judah, yet out of thee shall he come forth unto me that is to be ruler in Israel; whose goings forth have been from of old, from everlasting."

His companion prophet Isaiah said that the Christ would be born of a virgin; Micah declared He would be born in Bethlehem. He said, further, that the One who would come to Bethlehem would be from the everlasting ages. In other words, His birth would not be a beginning at all. Moreover, this coming One would be the ruler of Israel. Now we know that Christ came to Bethlehem; but He has not yet been the ruler of Israel. There is no country nor people in the world more op-posed to Jesus than the Jewish people. But one day this people will accept Him. His first coming was literally fulfilled—He came to *redeem*; His second coming will be just as literal—He is coming to *reign*. The literal fulfillment of the one part of the prophecy is the guarantee of the literal fulfillment of the other part.

C. The Restoration Described (5:7–15)

In the remainder of the chapter, Micah speaks of a *remnant* and about a *recovery* and about a *revival*. It anticipated the day when the Jewish people will be dispersed among the nations, not in judgment as now, but in millennial blessing and as a benediction to all mankind.

III. THE PLEA FOR REPENTANCE (6:1–7:20)

The prophet came back abruptly to the present—to the day and age in which he lived, to the pressing perils from Assyria that threatened his people, to the sins and apostasies that made judgment inevitable. He spoke to these issues, and his message is as relevant to us as it was to the Hebrew people of old. He spoke of the nation's *sins* and of the nation's *sorrows* and of the nation's *Savior*. He revealed what sin is really like as a despoiler of mankind.

As he reached forward into the future, so now he reached back into the past. He reminded Israel of the exodus from Egypt and of the facts of their national birth. He mentioned Balak and Balaam who sought to curse Israel, and wrote a magnificent passage on Balak's folly in thinking he could bribe God by making ever-increasing bids for His favor. "Will the LORD be pleased with thousands of rams, or with ten thousands of rivers of oil? shall I give my firstborn for my transgression, the fruit of my body for the sin of my soul?" (6:7). Nonsense! Do justly! Love mercy! Walk humbly with thy God! Micah picked up the story and hammered its lesson home to a land given over to injustice, hardness of heart, and arrogant pride.

He finished his prophecy, however, on a high note by again painting the picture of a future day when Israel will acknowledge her Savior. Revival and restoration lie ahead. Israel's future is bright! Israel's foes are beaten!

Then the prophet seems to have flung down his pen. But he picked it up again before the ink was dry and wrote, "Who is a God like unto thee, that pardoneth iniquity . . . thou wilt cast all their sins into the depths of the sea" (7:18–19). Maybe he was going to sign his name to the prophecy. His name, *Micah*, means "Who is like Jehovah?" Who, indeed!

> Great God of wonders! All Thy ways
> Display Thine attributes divine;
> But the bright glories of Thy grace
> Above Thine other wonders shine.
> Who is a pardoning God like Thee?
> Or who has grace so rich, so free!
>
> —Samuel Davies

But instead he eulogized God Himself.

This prophet out of the past, speaking to a people long since passed away, has a message for us today in all our own personal sin and need. What we need is the very Savior about whom Micah spoke—He who came to Bethlehem that He might go to Calvary that we might come to Him and go to heaven. Who, indeed, is like unto Jesus!

CHAPTER 31

NAHUM

The Prophet of Nineveh's Doom

There was not a cloud in the Assyrian sky when Nahum wrote (648–620 B.C.). Mighty Nineveh, capital of Assyria and mistress of the world, was at the peak of its prosperity and power.

The city of Nineveh seemed impregnable. It stood on the left bank of the Tigris, its walls towering one hundred feet toward the sky and further strengthened by more than twelve hundred mighty towers. Three chariots could drive abreast along the top of its walls, which enclosed 1,800 acres. The city could maintain its own food supply in case of a siege, and the sides not protected by the Tigris were surrounded by a moat. Nothing seemed more unlikely than the fate Nahum announced against Nineveh.

In the days of Jonah, Assyria was the rising world power, destined, as Jonah must have foreseen, to destroy Israel. The notorious brutality of the Assyrians made the surrounding nations to shudder. John Urquhart wrote,

> No considerations of pity were permitted to stand in the way of Assyrian policy. It could not afford to garrison its conquests, and it practiced a plan which largely dispensed with the necessity. . . . There was unsparing slaughter to begin with. The kings seem to gloat in their inscriptions over the spectacle presented by the field of battle. This carnage was followed up by fiendish inflictions upon individual cities. The leading men, as at Lachish when Sennacherib had conquered that city, were led forth by the executioners, and subjected to various punishments, all of them filled to the brim with horror. Some of the victims were held down while one of the band of torturers, who are portrayed on the monuments gloating fiendishly over their fearful work, inserts his hand into the victim's mouth, grips his tongue

and wrenches it out by the roots. In another spot . . . the man is stretched out, unable to move a muscle. The executioner then applies himself to his task; and beginning at the accustomed spot, the sharp knife makes its incision, the skin is raised inch by inch till the man is flayed alive. These skins are then stretched out upon the city walls, or otherwise disposed of so as to terrify the people. . . . For others, sharp poles are prepared. The sufferer, taken like the rest from the leading men of the city, is laid down; the sharpened end of the pole is driven in through the lower part of the chest; the pole is then raised, bearing the writhing victim aloft; it is planted in the hole left for it, and the man is left to die.

Nahum, prophesying some 130 years after Jonah, delivered a message of unmitigated doom for the city that, once spared, had returned to its diabolical ways. The message was addressed to Judah but was intended for the ears of Nineveh.

Nahum must have been the most popular prophet who ever lived! He prophesied the impending downfall of Nineveh, cruel capital of the fierce Assyrian people, and the complete and permanent overthrow of Assyria. Two of the Hebrew prophets had a message for Nineveh and Nineveh alone—Jonah and Nahum. When Jonah preached, the result was *repentance*. Revival swept the city, and Nineveh was spared. It was an instance of the goodness of God. When Nahum preached the result was *ruin*. Nineveh was swept off the map. It was reduced to such a state of rubble that for centuries its very site was lost to mankind. In the nearly century and a half between Jonah and Nahum, however, the city rose to new heights of wickedness. When Nahum preached the impending doom of Nineveh he must have been cheered in capital after capital of the ancient world.

His name means "consolation." The peoples of that part of the world must have often consoled themselves with the thought that, sooner or later, all empires grow old, wax feeble, and fall. Though, as the ages came and went, it must have seemed that Nineveh would never grow old. Now their hopes were to become a reality. Nineveh was to fall. When Nahum preached he struck a note in every heart. Nineveh was doomed! Thank God for that! At last, at long, long last!

We know nothing at all about the prophet himself. We are told that he was "the Elkoshite." And even about this there is disagreement. Some had located a city by the name of Elkosh about twenty-four miles north of Nineveh, but it hardly seems likely that Nahum came from there. Others have seen a connection with Nahum in the Galilean town of Capernaum—which literally means "town of Nahum." Nahum's references to Carmel, Lebanon, and Bashan have led some to think he was a Galilean.

He preached to Judah, however, and probably lived in Judah. Perhaps he was born in Galilee and later migrated to Judah. Many of the more spiritually minded Galileans did so when the Assyrian conqueror Esarhaddon repopulated the vacated farms and villages of Israel with a mongrel population imported from other parts of his kingdom.

Controversy has raged, too, about the date of Nahum's prophecy, some placing it at an earlier and others at a later date. The one date Nahum gives us is the fall of the Egyptian city of Thebes. The reference seems to be to the devastating overthrow of that great Egyptian city by Ashurbanipal, which took place in 665 or 664 B.C.

Nineveh itself fell in the year 612. So Nahum's prophecy must be somewhere in between those two dates. Possibly Nahum was a young contemporary of the aging Isaiah. He might have prophesied during the reign of Manasseh, the most wicked king ever to disgrace the throne of David in Jerusalem.

Sir George Adam Smith[1] has pointed out that there are no references to Israel or Judah once Nahum gets down to the business of unburdening himself of his prophecy of Assyria's doom. It was not in Judah's name that he exulted over the downfall of the great world power of Assyria; he exulted in the name of all mankind. He gave vent to no national passion, but to the outraged conscience of all mankind.

It might be helpful at this point to briefly survey the history of Assyria. Assyrian power first began to make itself felt in the Middle East when Tiglath-pileser came to the throne, about the time of the death of Jeroboam II of Israel. This Assyrian warlord had himself crowned as king of Babylon and then began his westward conquests. That which Jonah had foreseen, when he fled to Tarshish rather than preach to Nineveh, was about to come to pass. Nineveh's repentance was short lived. The Assyrian sword was now being sharpened for Israel, which had known no repentance at all.

Shalmanaser V brought Assyrian armies into Israel and began the siege of Samaria, the capital of the northern kingdom. The siege lasted for three long, weary, desperate years and was not ended until Sargon II took and sacked the city with all the attendant horrors that accompanied an Assyrian victory—especially one purchased at so high a price. The ten tribes, what remained of them, were physically uprooted and deported far and wide across the length and breadth of the Assyrian Empire.

Then came the terrible Sennacherib, whose name was a household word of terror in every nation round about. He carried victorious Assyrian arms down into Judah, besieged Jerusalem, and would have taken it had not God intervened and smitten his army before its very gates. His crimes against humanity reached fearful proportions and were brought to the violent and appropriate end they deserved by his murder at the hands of his own son.

His son, Esar-haddon, carried the tide of Assyrian conquest into Egypt. It must have seemed to the terrified nations of the area that the Assyrian nightmare would never end.

The last important king of Assyria was Ashurbanipal, who finished his father's goal of subduing Egypt. The fall of No-Ammon, the famous city of Thebes in Upper Egypt, is the one great date mark in the book of Nahum. If Nahum wrote his prophecy right after the downfall of one of the oldest and most magnificent cities of antiquity—a city whose temples and monuments are still viewed with awe even today—then at that time there was scarcely a cloud in the Assyrian sky. For although soon after, the Assyrian supremacy began to ebb from Egypt, never to return, Ashurbanipal was by no means through thrashing other nations round about. Elam, Babylon, and Syria were all given large doses of the very nasty Assyrian medicine.

Nothing, then, seemed more unlikely than the fall of Nineveh. Yet Nahum foretold something unprecedented for this haughty capital of empire—utter extinction. Other empires would fall but their capital cities would survive—but not Assyrian Nineveh.

Now all this was not just dull history to the Hebrews. It was exciting prophecy. It is history, perhaps to us—but vivid, passionate, inspired, accurate prophecy as it was pronounced and penned by the prophet.

Moreover, it embodies a great principle. Nahum had hardly dipped his pen in the ink before he was writing down these words: "The LORD is slow to anger." The history of Assyria and Nineveh surely affords us with proof of that—of His great patience and longsuffering with an utterly vile and ruthless people. "The LORD is slow to anger, and great in power" (1:3a). His delays were not caused by impotence. It was simply that "His love is as great as His power, and knows neither measure nor end."[2] "The LORD is slow to anger, and great in power, and will not at all acquit the wicked" (1:3). He may hold back His hand for what seems to us an interminable length of time. But when He does act, it will be in full.

I. Nineveh's Doom Declared (chap. 1)
  A. The Lord's Patience (1:1–3a)
  B. The Lord's Power (1:3b–5)
  C. The Lord's Presence (1:6–8)
  D. The Lord's Purpose (1:9–14)
  E. The Lord's Protection (1:15)
II. Nineveh's Doom Described (chap. 2)
  A. The Siege of Nineveh (2:1–8)
  B. The Sack of Nineveh (2:9–13)
III. Nineveh's Doom Deserved (chap. 3)
  A. The City's Fierceness (3:1–3)
  B. The City's Filthiness (3:4–7)
  C. The City's Folly (3:8–10)

D. The City's Fear (3:11–13)
E. The City's Fall (3:14–19)

Nahum foretold for Nineveh utter desolation, and this was something new because normally empires fell, but cities survived. Babylon, for example, the seat of the Babylonian Empire, passed in turn to the Persians and the Greeks, but not so Nineveh. God reserved for it "an utter end" (1:8). The city of Nineveh passed so completely into oblivion that for centuries the place where it had once stood was not known.

I. Nineveh's Doom Declared (chap. 1)

Let us remember as we look at this book, which is wholly absorbed with the overthrow of a nation that has been extinct now for some 2,500 years, that this prophecy embodies living principles. The world has to cope with nations today that are just as fierce, just as unscrupulous, just as terrible as Nineveh ever was—nations armed to the teeth and spoiling for conquest. We have only to think of the rise and fall of Nazi Germany and of the still great threat of Russian imperialism to see that this book of Nahum is by no means out of date. It embodies profound principles—God waits in patience and then suddenly intervenes in wrath with godless nations, especially nations that tamper with His people Israel. What we have in Nahum is an illustration, enacted on the international stage, of God's methods with those high and mighty nations that defy His laws.

A. The Lord's Patience (1:1–3a)

Despite the fearful and prolonged centuries-long provocation of Assyrian aggression and atrocity, the Lord stayed His hand. What He felt all this long time is stated in the second verse of the prophecy: "God is jealous, and the Lord revengeth; . . . and is furious; the Lord will take vengeance . . . he reserveth his wrath for his enemies." The Old Testament idea behind God's jealousy is not that of petty human vindictiveness—it is the thought of God's burning zeal and passion for justice and right, and His feeling toward injustice and wrong.

The great mystery of the age was how God could stay His hand so long, just as it is today when we think of the atrocities being committed by the Communists in their God-hate and lust for world power. But God never acts in haste, and He never smites without warning.

Nineveh had repented once at the preaching of Jonah. Doubtless reports of Nahum's preaching were heard at the Assyrian capital. Ashurbanipal simply sneered. Memories of Sennacherib's encounter with the living God of Israel at the gates of Jerusalem were long since obliterated in other Assyrian conquests.

But people mistake God's patience for impotence.

B. The Lord's Power (1:3b–5)

"The Lord hath his way in the whirlwind and in the storm, and the clouds are the dust of his feet. . . . The mountains quake at him, and the hills melt" (vv. 3b, 5). God is an omnipotent God; thunderbolts are His weapons. He can kindle the volcano, uproot the mountain range, command all the fierce forces of the storm. He can dry up mighty rivers or turn fertile lands into searing wastes. Just because He does not visibly use His weapons is no proof that He does not have them to command.

It is like the silly atheist who pulled out his watch before an audience and said, "I give the Almighty five minutes to strike me dead!" And because nothing happened, he declared, "There! That proves there is no God!" As if he could order God around.

C. The Lord's Presence (1:6–8)

God is invisible, and often He works in secret. He is there just the same, even if men in their folly and pride ignore His presence. "Who can stand before his indignation? . . . with an overrunning flood he will make an utter end" (vv. 6–8).

God had made His presence felt once already to the Assyrian army—He had visited those invincible regiments before the gates of Jerusalem and had left the land littered with their dead. Now He was about to visit Nineveh itself. The prophet gave his first hint at the way Nineveh's mighty battlements would be breached—by an overrunning flood. The prophet's vision was as clear and sharp as though he were actually standing as an eyewitness to what actually happened some fifty years later.

D. The Lord's Purpose (1:9–14)

Abruptly the prophet turned to address the Assyrians themselves: "What do ye imagine against the Lord?" (v. 9). He likened the proud Assyrian army to knotted, entangled thorns—an impenetrable and formidable and hurtful force. Like a hedge of thorns they presented a seemingly impenetrable front. But "they shall be devoured as stubble fully dry," says the prophet (v. 10). There is one answer to a hedge of thorns—fire! To sweep the Assyrian army into oblivion was nothing at all to God—it was as easy to Him as a man setting fire to a tinder-dry bramble.

"He will make an utter end" (v. 9). The prophet said it again. This was God's purpose. His purposes in grace and mercy and forgiveness and forbearance were now to be replaced by His purposes in judgment and wrath. Nineveh was to be made an age-long example to all such nations that rise up to plague and torment the peoples of the earth. God has His ways of sweeping them onto the garbage heaps of time.

"The Lord hath given a commandment concerning thee, that no more of thy name be sown: out of the house of thy gods will I cut off the graven image. . . . I will make thy grave; for thou art vile" (v. 14). The Assyrian people would come to an end, their gods become extinct.

We can go to the British Museum today and see the colossal winged bulls sculptured in stone, which once stood in front of the royal palace and which were supposed to ward off evil. We feel dwarfed by the immense size and power of the carvings. But there they stand, objects of curiosity to us today, gracing the halls of a museum of a people who were still wild barbarians in Assyria's day. Nothing is left of the Assyrian people save a memory preserved in books and museums. Even its vast city of Nineveh remains largely unexcavated because it is crowned by villages and Moslem cemeteries.

E. The Lord's Protection (1:15)

The prophet turned to Judah: "Behold upon the mountains the feet of him that bringeth good tidings, that publisheth peace! O Judah, keep thy solemn feasts, perform thy vows: for the wicked shall no more pass through thee; he is utterly cut off." The news would soon be heralded around the world! Fear of Assyria had kept people away from the feasts during the days of Hezekiah. But never again would Assyria menace Judah.

If Nahum preached during the godless reign of King Manasseh, the injunction would be particularly appropriate. Manasseh did his level best to undo all the religious reforms of his godly father Hezekiah. He sought to saturate Judah with the obscenities of paganism. He did not go unpunished. He was taken to Babylon as a prisoner of the Assyrians in the days of Esar-Haddon and came back to Jerusalem cured of his pagan desires. In the days of his son Josiah, a further revival broke out in Judah and it was in those days that Nahum's prophecy was fulfilled. Tidings came that Nineveh was no more.

II. Nineveh's Doom Described (chap. 2)

The prophet now begins a thorough description of the doom that was already rushing down upon the great city and empire, which had for so long scourged the nations. His description is in two parts.

A. The Siege of Nineveh (2:1–8)

"He that dasheth in pieces is come up before thy face" (v. 1). The Hebrew word for "dasheth" means literally "the breaker" or "the battle-ax" or "the hammer." The prophet painted a vivid picture of what was to follow. In due time the armies of the Medes and the Babylonians carried out the divine decree.

For a long time Assyria was on the defensive. First her empire was taken away and she was reduced to the limits of her native land—a fertile, fruitful triangle covered with town after town, fortress after fortress, with the roads drawing in upon Nineveh itself. Nahum describes the fighting along those great roads. He saw the shields of the advancing hosts dyed red with the blood, no doubt, of the defeated Assyrian armies and the sack of cities. He saw the dreadful war chariots armed with scythes extending from the wheels to mow down men like standing corn. He saw those chariots racing for the capital, cutting to ribbons all who stood in their way. He saw the Assyrian army fall back upon its final stronghold, Nineveh itself.

Nineveh—on the left bank of the Tigris with its towering walls and its hundreds of towers, each two hundred feet high, protected, too, by the Tigris and by deep moats—seemed impregnable. The Assyrians, behind their triple line of defense, felt themselves invincible. They had plenty of water, cultivated land lay enclosed behind their fortifications; they could defy God Himself.

But the prophet had only just begun. Those mighty walls would soon come tumbling down. Nahum saw exactly how: "The gates of the rivers shall be opened, and the palace shall be dissolved" (v. 6). This was just what happened. The siege of Nineveh lasted for three years. Then came heavy rains as God brought one of His weapons to bear upon Nineveh.

The city lay on the east bank of the Tigris, the river Khasr ran through the city, and a manmade canal connected the Khasr and the Tigris. The flood would have caused these waters to rise. Presumably the "gates of the rivers" were the heavily fortified and guarded gates at the points where the rivers and canal came in contact with the walls. Any break in these gates would give a determined foe immediate access to the city. These gates were opened—either by the enemy, by traitors within the city, or by the flood waters. Possibly part of the walls, undermined by the flood waters, gave way, too.

"And Huzzab shall be led away captive," Nahum prophesied (2:7). Some scholars think that *Huzzab* refers to the capture of the queen mother. Others think the word is a verb meaning "it is decreed." If the latter is true, Nahum's prophecy meant that Nineveh itself, stripped of all its fabulous wealth, would be helpless in the hands of an eager and vengeful foe.

B. The Sack of Nineveh (2:9–13)

This passage is a prophetic description of the sack of Nineveh. "Take ye the spoil," said Nahum (2:9). The spoils of countless cities overthrown by the Assyrians in centuries of war had flowed into Nineveh. Now the invaders took all the treasures and apparently carted much of the spoils off to Babylon.

Nahum described Nineveh as "empty, and void, and waste" (2:10). The city was so completely ruined by the invaders that Xenophon scarcely recognized the site. Alexander the Great marched his men past the location, not knowing that the capital of a world empire was buried beneath his feet. Gibbon confirmed that even the ruins of Nineveh disappeared. It was not until Layard and Botta identified the site in 1842 that the city was rediscovered by the modern world.

"Where is the dwelling of the lions?" asked the prophet (2:11). The lion, the lioness, the young lion, the lion's whelp—Nahum mentioned them all. As a roaring and ravening lion, Assyria had terrified and devoured the world. No one could tame the wild beast. Nineveh's kings had boasted, "Where are the gods of Hamath, and of Arpad? where are the gods of Sepharvaim, Hena, and Ivah?" (2 Kings 18:34). But now the prophet demanded in effect, "Where is Nineveh?" His contemporaries must have looked at Nahum in astonishment, for when he prophesied, there was not a cloud in the Assyrian sky. In Nahum 2:13 we read the Lord's words to Nineveh: "Behold, I am against thee."

III. Nineveh's Doom Deserved (chap. 3)

A. The City's Fierceness (3:1–3)

In his last chapter Nahum recapitulated his dirge of doom for Nineveh. "Woe to the bloody city! it is all full of lies and robbery; the prey departeth not" (3:1). Again, much that is said of Nineveh could be said of Moscow and the Kremlin. Who can count the millions of people who have been killed to spread communism around the world? What nation has been more guilty of treachery in its treaty obligations than Russia? Assyrian promises were also notoriously untrustworthy, and vengeance was on the way.

Transported into the future, Nahum could hear "the noise of a whip, and the noise of the rattling of the wheels, and of the prancing horses, and of the jumping chariots" (3:2). He could see the carnage and horror of battle as the cavalry hunted down the foe. Mounds of the dead littered the landscape, and the living tripped on the rotting corpses. Nineveh had become an abode of the dead.

B. The City's Filthiness (3:4–7)

Nahum described Nineveh as a harlot, for the city was full of whoredom and witchcraft. Idolatry was one of Nineveh's cardinal sins. The Assyrians waged religious wars: all their wars were fought in the name of one or another of their false gods. Wherever their victorious armies went, their gods went, too. Conquered nations were compelled to pay their gods honor, and gross immorality always accompanies idolatry.

In 3:5 the living God again declared His opposition to this vile people. He warned that He would expose Nineveh's shame to the world and heap filth on the city's nakedness. The nations witnessing Nineveh's defilement would distance themselves from the disgraced city. Reaping the harvest of what it had sown, Nineveh would have no friends—none to pity, none to help, none to lament. One great universal cheer would go up at the news of its downfall.

Usually, when connected with Israel, whoredom is a symbol for idolatry. In connection with Assyria it was more than that. It was idolatry, of course—but it was Assyria's traffic with the occult, with witchcraft, with evil spirits that the prophet underlined. No nation can stand that opens the floodgates to intercourse with the powers of the pit. Occultism opens the door for every form of immorality.

C. The City's Folly (3:8–10)

"Art thou better than populous No [No-Ammon, the city of Thebes]. . . . Ethiopia and Egypt were her strength. . . . Put and Lubim were thy helpers. . . . Yet was she carried away" (vv. 8, 9, 10). The Assyrians had sacked that great city. And Thebes was indeed a mighty city, located on both banks of the Nile. The famous temples of Karnak and Luxor were there, and Homer described it as having one hundred gates. Its ruins cover an area of twenty-seven miles. Thebes was much better off than Nineveh. It had strong allies, whereas Nineveh had alienated every nation with which it had ever had anything to do. Thebes could call on all Egypt to its defense. It could look abroad and summon aid from Ethiopia, Samaria, and Libya.

Yet Assyria had captured Thebes. Nahum described the atrocities the Assyrians had committed in the fallen city. What folly for Nineveh to think that she could escape now that the hour of her doom had come. Nineveh had no allies. There was not a nation in the world that would not rejoice at her fall.

Nineveh had demolished great cities. Let her read her own fate in that. What folly to think that she was impregnable when she herself had overthrown other impregnable cities!

D. The City's Fear (3:11–13)

The nation that had kept the ancient world in a state of abject terror for centuries would now know to the full the paralyzing bite of fear: "Thou also shalt be drunken: thou shalt be hid, thou also shalt seek strength because of the enemy. . . . Behold thy people . . . are women" (vv. 11–13). The mighty men of Nineveh who had marched far and wide, spreading desolation and destruction, would be like frightened women when the final defenses crumbled and the foe came surging in like the sea through broken dikes. All its strongholds would fall like ripe figs before the shaking of the tree.

E. The City's Fall (3:14–19)

With elaborate irony Nahum told the Assyrians to provision their capital for the siege—to make bricks and mortar with which to strengthen the invincible walls soon to totter and fall. He told them to make sure that Nineveh had a plentiful water supply. Yet for all that the avenging fire would sweep through the city. Before the avengers were done the place would look like a field after the locusts have finished with it.

Nahum closed his prophecy of doom with the final pronouncement that the Assyrians would be scattered upon the mountains like sheep without a shepherd and with none to care what became of them. "There is no healing of thy bruise," he said, "thy wound is grievous: all that hear the [rumor] of thee shall clap the hands over thee: for upon whom hath not thy wickedness passed continually?" (v. 19).

Place yourself for a moment among the peoples of the ancient world, so long intimidated, crushed, and demoralized by the most brutal empire that was ever allowed to roll its force across the world. Stand with those people as the runners come panting in with the glorious news: "Assyria is no more! Nineveh has vanished from the earth!" Would you not clap your hands? Would you not pause for a moment to give thanks to Almighty God?

Just so did the people of the world rejoice at the collapse of the Soviet Union, and in a day soon to dawn will yet rejoice at the disintegration of the Russian war machine, the downfall of the Kremlin, and the annulment of any remaining schemes and plans for empire. Just so, too, will the remnant of mankind rejoice at the downfall of the empire of the Beast.

Nahum tells us that when God makes an end, He makes an utter end. There is not much *gospel* in Nahum. But, thank God, there is a great deal of *government*—and it is as much a truth of Scripture that God *rules* as it is that He *redeems*.

CHAPTER 32

JEREMIAH

The Weeping Prophet

As Isaiah lived through the turbulent Assyrian period, so Jeremiah (627–575 B.C.) lived through the equally heartbreaking Babylonian period. In Isaiah's day, Israel was carried into captivity, and in Jeremiah's day a like fate overtook Judah. Jeremiah stood in the same relationship to godly King Josiah of Judah as Isaiah had to godly King Hezekiah. As Amos, Hosea, and Micah had clustered around Isaiah, so Zephaniah, Habakkuk, and possibly Obadiah clustered around Jeremiah.

Jeremiah saw five kings on the throne of David in Jerusalem: Josiah, Jehoahaz, Jehoakim, Jehoiachin, and Zedekiah. He lived about a century after Isaiah. Isaiah had lived to see Judah delivered from the Assyrians, but Jeremiah wept out his prophecies on deaf ears and lived to see his beloved people given over to famine and the sword. His loftiest counsels were ignored, his writings torn to shreds by a tyrant king, his name blackened, his life hunted, and his worst predictions horribly fulfilled before his tear-filled eyes. He was indeed a weeping prophet, "a man of sorrows, and acquainted with grief" (Isa. 53:3).

He recorded the bitterest feelings of his broken heart in the book of Lamentations. He was forbidden by God to marry. And, even when his preaching produced results, as in the days of King Josiah, he could clearly see that the reforms were superficial and could not last. The disastrous reign of Manasseh had been too long, and his apostasies had taken too great a hold. Idolatry and corruption had seeped too deeply into the lives of the people. The sepulcher of Judah might be whitened by a godly and well-meaning king, but inwardly it was filled with corruption and dead men's bones.

JEREMIAH'S STYLE

Jeremiah has been criticized because so many of his utterances are in no kind of order. E. W. Bullinger, in his *Companion Bible*, said it well concerning this that "it is the historical portions, which concern Jehoiakim and Zedekiah, that are chiefly so affected. And who was Jehoiakim that his history should be of any importance? Was it not he who 'cut up the word of Jehovah' with a penknife, and cast it into the fire? Why should not his history be 'cut up'? Zedekiah rejected the same word of Jehovah. Why should his history be respected? Secular authors take the liberty of arranging their own literary matter as they choose; why should this liberty be denied to the sacred writers?"

HISTORICAL BACKGROUND

Jeremiah was born during the days of Manasseh, the wicked son of Hezekiah. He was called to prophesy at the tender age of fourteen, and his feelings of helplessness and incompetence are recorded in the opening chapter.

He was told that God would be with him and that his words would be inspired. He would have a twofold ministry—first, to root out and overthrow, and second, to plant and build. He was told he could expect violent opposition from the princes, the priests, and the people, but that he had no cause for alarm.

He began to prophesy in the thirteenth year of Josiah and continued until the capture of Jerusalem in the fifth month of the eleventh year of the reign of Zedekiah—about forty-one years all told.

The men of Anathoth, his paternal home, were the first to oppose him and threatened to kill him if he did not stop prophesying. He was looked upon as a traitor, aiding and abetting Judah's foes.

The short-lived reforms of Josiah came to an abrupt end with his death, and his son Jehoahaz reigned only three months, when he was deposed by the Egyptian Pharaoh Necho. His father, Josiah, had lost his life in a vain attempt to stem an Egyptian army marching across Judah on the way to Carchemish.

At Carchemish, Pharaoh suffered a resounding defeat at the hands of the Babylonians. That defeat assured the inevitable ascendancy of Babylon over the nations and guaranteed the ultimate total humiliation of Egypt at the hands of the Babylonians. On his way back to Egypt, the humiliated Pharaoh vented his spite on the nation of Judah.

From this point on, Judah was just a pawn in the power play between Egypt and Babylon. Pharaoh Necho put the brother of Jehoahaz on the throne in Jerusalem, carrying the rightful king to Egypt as a hostage. Jehoiakim reigned for eleven years and, coming out boldly for idolatry, was a bitter foe of Jeremiah. But by now the Babylonians felt themselves strong enough to curb the ambitions of Egypt, and in 605 B.C. the first Babylonian invasion of Judah took place.

In the fourteenth year of Jehoiakim's reign, Jeremiah began dictating his prophecies, which he had been uttering for twenty years, to the scribe Baruch. Jeremiah told Baruch to take the book to the sanctuary and read it to the people coming to the temple. The roll finally reached the king, who listened to a few pages and then cut it up with a penknife and threw it in the fire.

By divine direction, Jeremiah immediately prepared a second roll like the first, but with additions. Pashur the priest had Jeremiah put in the stocks, but he was released the next day (20:2–3). Still Jeremiah went unheeded.

Jehoiakim was deposed, and threatened with deportation to Babylon, and Jehoiachin, his son, was placed on the throne of David as a puppet of Babylon. A second and more severe invasion of Judah took place in March, 597 B.C., to end this evil king's short reign. Every able-bodied man, including Jehoiachin, was carried into captivity.

The last king of Judah was then set on the throne by Nebuchadnezzar, who, generously enough, chose Zedekiah, a prince of the royal Davidic line and another son of Josiah. Zedekiah was a weakling, who, although inclined to be friendly to Jeremiah, was little better than a tool in the hands of the princes.

During the siege of Jerusalem, Jeremiah was violently opposed as a traitor. The siege was temporarily raised because of a Babylonian expedition against Egypt, and Zedekiah, despite a solemn warning from Jerusalem, broke his oath to the Babylonian monarch and rebelled. Assured of success by false prophets, he listened to accusations of treachery against Jeremiah and allowed him to be persecuted. When Jeremiah prepared to leave Jerusalem he was seized as a deserter and thrown into prison (37:1–15). After many days, Zedekiah released him and committed him to the court of the guard, but the princes had him cast into a miry pit to die (38:1–6). An Ethiopian eunuch took pity on him and obtained the king's permission to put him back in the court of the guard. He was still there when Jerusalem was taken (vv. 7–13).

Soon the Babylonians were back. This time, after a bitter siege, Jerusalem fell and was sacked and the temple destroyed. The book of Lamentations speaks of the horrors of this time. Zedekiah fled, only to be captured and treated after the barbarous fashion of the times. His sons were slain before his eyes, his eyes were put out, and he was marched away in chains to exile in Babylon.

The Chaldeans looked upon Jeremiah as a friend who had suffered in their cause and Nebuchadnezzar gave express orders he was to be treated with kindness. He was accordingly taken to Ramah and set free with permission to go to Babylon or return to Jerusalem as he wished. Jeremiah chose to go to Jerusalem. Nebuchadnezzar gave him a present and sent him to Jerusalem under the protection of Gedaliah, the new governor.

Some time later, the people of Jerusalem revolted again and murdered Gedaliah. The authors of this crime fled. Jeremiah strongly urged the remaining Jews in

Jerusalem to remain there and not to flee to Egypt. It was in vain. They not only went themselves but they forced Jeremiah to go with them. In Egypt he continued to weep out his warnings but, as ever, he went unheeded. Ancient tradition has it that Jeremiah was finally stoned to death in Egypt.

Jeremiah's message was one of doom. He delivered it faithfully despite persecution. His warnings were ignored and ridiculed, and his best counsels treated with contempt. He was a lonely man, maligned, misunderstood, maltreated, and without the solace of family. He loved Jerusalem with a patriotic fervor, yet was accused of being a traitor because he told the truth to his people.

I. Jeremiah's Call Received (1:1–15:9)
  A. The Prophet's Mandate (chap. 1)
  B. The Prophet's Message (2:1–15:9)
    1. During Days of Incomplete Revival (chaps. 2–12)
      a. Prior to the Finding of the Law (chaps. 2–6)
        (1) Theme 1: The Tainted People (2:1–3:11)
        (2) Theme 2: The Two Places (3:12–6:30)
          (a) The Survivors of the North (3:12–4:2)
          (b) The Scorners in the South (4:3–6:30)
      b. Pertinent to the Finding of the Law (chaps. 7–9)
        (1) Theme 1: The Temple Precincts (7:1–8:3)
          (a) Judgment Against the Temple in Jerusalem (7:1–19)
          (b) Judgment Against the Tribe of Judah (7:20–8:3)
        (2) Theme 2: The Transgressing People (8:4–9:26)
          (a) Jehovah's Sorrow (8:4–19)
          (b) Jeremiah's Sorrow (8:20–9:9)
          (c) Judah's Sorrow (9:10–26)
      c. Pursuant to the Finding of the Law (chaps. 10–12)
        (1) Theme 1: The Broken Commandment (chap. 10)
        (2) Theme 2: The Broken Covenant (chaps. 11–12)
          (a) Words Concerning Judah (11:1–17)
          (b) Words Concerning Jeremiah (11:18–12:6)
          (c) Words Concerning Judgment (12:7–17)
    2. During Days of Increasing Rejection (13:1–15:9)
      a. Novel Warnings (chap. 13)
      b. No Water (chap. 14)
      c. New Woes (15:1–9)
II. Jeremiah's Call Repeated (15:10–45:5)
  A. The Focus on Jeremiah (15:10–16:9)
  B. The Focus on Judah (16:10–45:5)

1. Judah's Sins (16:10–17:27)
2. Judah's Signs (chaps. 18–20)
   a. The Sign of the Potter (chap. 18)
   b. The Sign of the Pitcher (chaps. 19–20)
3. Judah's Sovereigns (chaps. 21–22)
4. Judah's Savior (23:1–8)
5. Judah's Seers (23:9–40)
6. Judah's Servitude (chaps. 24–25)
7. Judah's Scorn (chap. 26)
8. Judah's Salvation (chaps. 27–33)
   a. The Present Hope (chaps. 27–29)
   b. The Promised Hope (chaps. 30–33)
9. Judah's Situation (chaps. 34–38)
   a. Jeremiah's Final Messages Delivered (chaps. 34–35)
   b. Jeremiah's Final Messages Disregarded (chaps. 36–38)
      (1) The Impiety of Jehoiakim (chap. 36)
      (2) The Imprisonment of Jeremiah (chaps. 37–38)
10. Judah's Surrender (chaps. 39–45)
    a. The Fate of the Jews (39:1–10)
    b. The Fate of Jeremiah (39:11–45:5)
       (1) His Captivity Ended (39:11–40:6)
       (2) His Concern Endured (40:7–45:5)
          (a) For His Countrymen (40:7–44:30)
             i. The Remnant in the Land (40:7–43:7)
             ii. The Refugees in Egypt (43:8–44:30)
          (b) For His Colleague (chap. 45)
III. Jeremiah's Call Redirected (chaps. 46–51)
   A. Egypt (chap. 46)
   B. Philistia (chap. 47)
   C. Moab (chap. 48)
   D. Ammon (49:1–6)
   E. Edom (49:7–22)
   F. Damascus (49:23–27)
   G. Arabia (49:28–33)
   H. Elam (49:34–39)
   I. Babylon (chaps. 50–51)
IV. Jeremiah's Call Reviewed (chap. 52)
   A. The Fate of Jerusalem (52:1–23)
   B. The Fate of The Jews (52:24–30)
   C. The Fate of Jehoiachin (52:31–34)

I. Jeremiah's Call Received (1:1–15:9)

Jeremiah began to prophesy forty years before the destruction of Jerusalem. This period corresponds to the apostolic testimony that preceded the fall of Jerusalem after the crucifixion of Christ. Some think it indicates that a similar period of forty years will precede the future destruction of Jerusalem by the Antichrist (Zech. 14).

A. The Prophet's Mandate (chap. 1)

Jeremiah was converted in his boyhood during a period of revival, and he immediately began to witness for the Lord. His call to the ministry took place during the reign of King Josiah, some sixty-six years after the death of Isaiah. It is inferred that he was probably about twenty-one at the time, a mere child according to the notions of his day.

He shrank from the work thrust upon him by God, but God would not take no for an answer. He gave the young man two signs to strengthen him for the task. There was the sign of the *almond tree* and the sign of the *boiling pot*. The almond tree is the first tree to awaken after the winter's sleep, and this sign symbolized the nearness of the events that were to come. The boiling pot symbolized the eruption of the Babylonians into Palestine.

In warning Jeremiah what he would be up against, God said, "I will utter my judgments against them. . . . For, behold, I have made thee this day a defensed city, and an iron pillar, and brazen walls *against* the whole land, *against* the kings of Judah, *against* the princes thereof, *against* the priests thereof, and *against* the people of the land. And they shall fight *against* thee; but they shall not prevail *against* thee; for I am with thee, saith the Lord, to deliver thee" (1:16–19). The constant repetition of the word *against* is intended to underline that when man's ways and thoughts are opposite to those of God, it is impossible for the prophet who is God's spokesman to be other than against that man or that people. Jeremiah's path was to be no bed of roses. It was to be battle and blood, opposition, resentment, persecution, and difficulty all the way. I don't wonder that he shrank from his mandate.

B. The Prophet's Message (2:1–15:9)

1. During Days of Incomplete Revival (chaps. 2–12)

The most important event of this period was the finding of the law of God in the ruins of the temple in the days of godly King Josiah. Josiah desperately tried to stem the rising tides of apostasy all about him, but with little success. All he succeeded in doing, despite his noble efforts and genuine longing for a spiritual awakening, was to whitewash the tomb of the nation, which was inwardly filled with dead men's bones. Chapters 2–6 give us a summary of Jeremiah's preaching during this period when Josiah's vigorous attacks on idolatry reached their height. Josiah's determined efforts carried him even to the abandoned cities of the deported northern tribes of Israel—to the wastes of Manasseh, Ephraim, Naphtali, and Simeon (2 Chron. 34:1–7). Jeremiah could see, though, that nothing lasting was being accomplished. The king's heart was right with God, and his intentions were good, but the princes, the priests, and the people were not heart and soul in the thing at all.

> For my people[, cried the prophet in the name of his God,] have committed two evils; they have forsaken me the fountain of living waters, and hewed them out cisterns, broken cisterns, that can hold no water. (2:13)

> Judah hath not turned unto me with her whole heart, but feignedly, saith the LORD. (3:10)

> O Jerusalem, wash thine heart from wickedness, that thou mayest be saved. (4:14)

> A wonderful and horrible thing is committed in the land; the prophets prophesy falsely . . . and my people love to have it so. (5:30, 31)

> They have healed also the hurt of the daughter of my people slightly, saying, Peace, peace; when there is no peace. (6:14)

Because the revival was incomplete, there could be nothing but judgment ahead. Josiah was, in fact, the last good king Judah ever knew until Jesus came.

After doing his best to spread revival abroad, King Josiah set himself to restore the temple, which had fallen into a terrible state of neglect and decay. A copy of the law of God was found, the reading of which greatly troubled the king (2 Chron. 34:18–32). So far had the nation drifted from God that, at this time, not even the king had a copy of the Scriptures in his home. The nation had utterly forgotten that God had ever spoken.

The finding of the law resulted in even greater efforts on the part of Josiah to awaken the nation to spiritual things. The temple! The law! These two things occupied the mind of the king. They occupied the mind of Jeremiah, too. In chapters 7–9 we find notes of Jeremiah's preaching in connection with this most dramatic discovery—the forgotten law in the forsaken temple.

In chapter 7 Jeremiah speaks about the temple. There he stands outside its principal entrance, a youthful figure proclaiming the Word of the Lord at the risk of his life. It is easy to picture the scene. The temple, long neglected, now repaired; its doors and courts open and crowded with people—people going through all the motions of worship without any sense of repentance at all. And there stands Jeremiah accusing them of worshipping the temple instead of worshipping the Lord. "Trust ye not in lying words," he cried. "The temple of the LORD, the temple of the LORD . . ." (7:4). Stealing, murdering, committing adultery, swearing falsely, burning incense to Baal, walking after other gods, they yet came and stood before the Lord in His house. Little wonder the prophet cried, "We are delivered to do all these abominations?" (7:9–10). The deluded people believed that the presence of the temple in their city secured their national independence and guaranteed it from all attack. Therefore they could sin as they pleased and pay mere lip service to God. They had turned the house of God into a den of thieves.

The people were so incensed by the preaching of Jeremiah that they demanded his death. He was a lonely man indeed. So terrible was the condition of the people that God told Jeremiah he was not even to pray for them (v. 16).

So little was Judah's regard for the temple, and as for the law—they had abandoned it completely. "The LORD saith, Because they have forsaken my law which I set before them, and have not obeyed my voice, neither walked therein; . . . Therefore thus saith the LORD of hosts, the God of Israel; Behold, I will feed them, even this people, with wormwood, and give them water of gall to drink. I will scatter them also among the heathen . . . and I will send a sword after them . . ." (9:13–16).

Following the finding of the law, more drastic reforms than ever were carried out, climaxing in the commemoration of what was called the Great Passover (2 Chron. 35:1–19). In Jeremiah 10–12 we have the notes of the prophet's preaching during this period. These works were all so pitiful. The king's efforts were fruitless. The people were wedded to their idols. Jeremiah preached with passion and with power against idolatry, in order to support the king, but it was all in vain. Nothing but judgment lay ahead. "And the LORD said unto me, A conspiracy is found among the men of Judah, and among the inhabitants of Jerusalem. They are turned back to the iniquities of their forefathers. . . . Therefore thus saith the LORD, Behold, I will bring evil upon them, which they shall not be able to escape" (11:9–11).

2. During Days of Increasing Rejection (13:1–15:9)

It was increasingly evident that Josiah's reforms had failed to touch the heart of the people. Jeremiah resorted to symbolism. God visited the nation with a drought. New woes were announced.

II. Jeremiah's Call Repeated (15:10–45:5)

The prophecies that followed continued on down to the fall of Jerusalem. The prophecies were embodied in signs, in sermons, and in sufferings. We shall just take some representative samples.

There was, for example, the sign of the *Unmarried Prophet* (16:1–2). "The word of the LORD came also unto me, saying, Thou shalt not take thee a wife, neither shalt thou have sons or daughters in this place." Closely coupled with this sign was that of the *Unmourning Prophet* (16:5). "For thus saith the LORD, Enter not into the house of mourning, neither go to lament nor bemoan." The prophet was to abstain from mirth and from mourning. He was to maintain a thorough separation from the ordinary and legitimate functions of social life. He was about to witness the desolation of the people, and he must be desolate himself as a sign to the people.

There was the sign of the *Potter's House* (18:1–6). The prophet stood and watched the turning of the wheel and the plastic yielding of the clay. He saw a thought in the mind of the potter being made manifest in clay. He saw the constant pressure kept upon the clay by the potter's hand. Then suddenly the whole thing was marred. It no longer expressed the potter's thought. But the potter did not abandon the clay—"He made it again another vessel" (v. 4) until the remolded clay fulfilled what the potter had in mind. It was a sign of the goodness, of the government, and of the greatness of God. It was a sign that the marred vessel of the nation would one day be shaped anew to fulfill the sovereign will of God. These were some of the signs. There were others, too, but these will serve to show the vivid way in which truth was taught to a people bent away from God.

The sufferings of Jeremiah were severe. In his book of Lamentations he cried, "Behold, and see if there be any sorrow like unto my sorrow" (1:12). His sufferings were mental as well as physical—agony of soul as well as agony of body. He was an Old Testament "man of sorrows and acquainted with grief."

On one occasion, Pashur, the chief officer of the temple, scourged Jeremiah and then condemned him to twenty-four hours in the stocks. The stocks were made of a beam of timber with five holes in it through which the head, the hands, and the feet were thrust, bending the body into an unnatural position and causing terrible cramps and suffering. On being finally released from the stocks, far from being intimidated, Jeremiah, under inspiration of the Holy Spirit, not only repeated his prophecy against Jerusalem but singled out his tormentor for special attention (20:1–6).

For his prophecies, Jeremiah was accused of being a traitor to his country. The princes clamored for his death, and the king allowed him to be cast into the most loathsome dungeon in Jerusalem, and he sank down deep in the mire (38:6). There his enemies left him to die, and no doubt he would have perished from hunger and from thirst in the stink and slime of this horrible pit. But Ebedmelech, an Ethiopian courtier, persuaded King Zedekiah to have mercy on the man.

Jeremiah was a great preacher. It is impossible to do justice to his preaching by sampling some of his sermons, but that is all we can do in this brief survey. He saw far ahead of his day. Take, for example, his famous sermon on the seventy year captivity (25:1–35): "And this whole land shall be a desolation, and an astonishment; and these nations shall serve the king of Babylon seventy years. And it shall come to pass, when seventy years are accomplished, that I will punish the king of Babylon" (vv. 11–12). It was this prophecy that stirred Daniel to prayer when the seventy years were almost done.

His equally famous sermon on the time of Jacob's trouble was also far seeing: "Thus saith the LORD; We have heard a voice of trembling, of fear, and not of peace. . . . Alas! for that day is great, so that none is like it: it is even the time of Jacob's trouble; but he shall be saved out of it" (Jer. 30:5, 7). That terrible day is yet future. We often call it "The Great Tribulation." The sorrows of Judah in the days of Jeremiah were as nothing compared with the terrible days yet ahead for the State of Israel and the Jew in general.

Nor could we talk about the sermons of Jeremiah without mentioning his great sermon on the millennium: "Behold, the days come, saith the LORD, that I will perform that good thing which I have promised unto the house of Israel and to the house of Judah. . . . For thus saith the LORD; David shall never want a man to sit upon the throne of the house of Israel" (Jer. 33:14, 17).

So by signs, by sermons, and by sufferings, Jeremiah prophesied to the nation of Israel during days of increasing rejection.

III. JEREMIAH'S CALL REDIRECTED (CHAPS. 46–51)

The prophet's voice was now lifted up against the various Gentile nations involved in the turmoil of the times. One by one the Egyptians, the Moabites, the Ammonites, the Edomites, the city of Damascus, Elam, and Babylon came into view.

The two most important nations in these prophecies were Egypt and Babylon. The policy of Judah's leaders was to lean on Egypt instead of heeding Jeremiah. But Egypt was a broken reed. Not only did the Babylonians roundly defeat Pharaoh at Carchemish, but Egypt itself was to be sold to the Babylonians. Egypt, however, had defeated and slain godly King Josiah at Megiddo, and afterward taken his son, Jehoahaz, as a vassal to Egypt and set up Jehoiakim in his place (2 Kings 23:29–35). After that, the kings of Judah were dazzled by what they imagined to be Egyptian military prowess. They scorned Jeremiah's warnings that Egypt could not save Jerusalem from the Babylonians.

The immediate future lay with Babylon. All the surrounding nations would fall before her. But eventually even Babylon would fall. Throughout all Jeremiah's prophecies, Babylon was seen as the instrument of God's judgment. But finally, because of her own sin and corruption, judgment must inevitably fall on Babylon, too.

In chapters 50–51 Jeremiah describes in detail the ultimate doom of Babylon:

"Thus saith the LORD of hosts; The broad walls of Babylon shall be utterly broken, and her high gates shall be burned with fire; and the people shall labor in vain, and the folk in the fire, and they shall be weary" (51:58). "So Jeremiah wrote in a book all the evil that should come upon Babylon, even all these words that are written against Babylon. And Jeremiah said to Seraiah, When thou comest to Babylon, and shalt see, and shalt read all these words; Then shalt thou say, O LORD, thou hast spoken against this place, to cut it off, that none shall remain in it, neither man nor beast, but that it shall be desolate for ever. And it shall be, when thou hast made an end of reading this book, that thou shalt bind a stone to it, and cast it into the midst of Euphrates: And thou shalt say, Thus shall Babylon sink, and shall not rise from the evil that I will bring upon her: and they shall be weary" (vv. 60–64).

IV. JEREMIAH'S CALL REVIEWED (CHAP. 52)

Some think that the last chapter of the book was written by another's hand. It records the sad details of the fall of Jerusalem before the Babylonians. Famine! Fire! Flight! Fetters! Frightfulness! All the terrible things that had broken Jeremiah's heart came to pass. The ache and breaking of his heart over the terrible doom of Jerusalem, the city he so greatly longed to save, is recorded in the book of his Lamentations. He stands there weeping out his heart like One, in later years, far greater than he, who wept over this selfsame city.

> O Jerusalem, Jerusalem, thou that killest the prophets, and stonest them which are sent unto thee, how often would I have gathered thy children together, even as a hen gathereth her chickens under her wings, and ye would not! Behold, your house is left unto you desolate. (Matt. 23:37–38)

The man of sorrows of the Old Testament was, after all, only a faint foreshadowing of the Man of Sorrows of the New Testament.

CHAPTER 33

LAMENTATIONS

The Story of a Prodigal City

Jeremiah's lamentations, written in the form of an acrostic dirge, consist of five poems. The first, second, and fourth are of twenty-two verses each, corresponding to the letters of the Hebrew alphabet. The third poem is built on the same principle except that each letter of the alphabet is repeated three times. The acrostic is dropped for the fifth poem, which is a prayer. It has twenty-two verses but the emotion of the prophet outstrips his acrostic style. The dirge has to do with the fall of Jerusalem and the terrible sufferings connected with its overthrow. "O Jerusalem, Jerusalem," wept Jeremiah, as did the Lord Jesus Himself in later years. No wonder some thought Jesus was Jeremiah returned from the dead (Matt. 16:14; 23:37–38).

The book of Lamentations occupied a significant place in the Hebrew Bible. The Jews divided their Bible into three parts: (1) *The Law* (the five books of Moses); (2) *The Prophets* (divided into two—*the former prophets* [Joshua, Judges, Samuel, and Kings] and *the latter prophets* [Isaiah, Jeremiah, Ezekiel, and the minor prophets]; and (3) *The Writings*—Psalms, Proverbs, Job, *Song of Solomon*, *Ruth*, Lamentations, Ecclesiastes, Esther, *Daniel*, *Ezra/Nehemiah*, *Chronicles*.

The books italicized above formed a separate category within and central to the writings. These five books were called the *Megiloth*. Central to the Megiloth (and also to the Writings) was Lamentations, which was separated from the book of Jeremiah, put in a different part of the Hebrew Bible, and made central to it.

We can visualize the five books of the Megiloth thus:

A **Canticles**: The Song of Solomon. *Goodness* illustrated. Solomon and the woman who defied him.

   B **Ruth**: *Grace* illustrated. Virtue rewarded. The heathen woman who married a Hebrew man.

    C **Lamentations**: *Grief* illustrated.

  A **Ecclesiastes**: The Sermon of Solomon. *Glory* illustrated. Solomon and the world that defiled him.

   B **Esther**: *Government* illustrated. Valor rewarded. The Hebrew woman who married a heathen man.

It is significant, too, that the Jews read all these five books at various times in their annual religious celebrations, as follows:

  A **Song of Solomon**. Read at the *Feast* of Passover—which celebrates a deliverance, the deliverance from Pharaoh, the great persecutor and exterminator.

   B **Ruth**. Read at the *Feast* of Pentecost—which celebrates God's goodness in the land.

    C **Lamentations**. Read at the *Feast* of the ninth of Ab (which commemorates the destruction of Jerusalem).

   B **Ecclesiastes**. Read at the *Feast* of Tabernacles—which celebrates God's goodness in the wilderness.

  A **Esther**. Read at the *Feast* of Purim—which celebrates a deliverance, the deliverance from Haman, the great persecutor and exterminator.

It will be seen that both these structures place Lamentations at the center. Central to all God's dealings with men is a great sorrow, a sorrow that finds its fullest expression at Calvary. It is no accident, surely, that the great cry of the book is this: "Is it nothing to you, all ye that pass by? Behold, and see if there be any sorrow like unto my sorrow, which is done unto me, wherewith the LORD hath afflicted me in the day of his fierce anger" (1:12). That statement could be the very expression of the Savior Himself as He hung upon the cross of Calvary.

Central, too, to the various celebrations, as brought to mind in the annual reading of these five books, is a *fast*. As the Jews remembered God's dealings with them, central to all was not a feast, but a fast—a fast that found expression in the book of Lamentations.

The fast of the ninth day of Ab, the fifth month (our August) developed into a significant day of remembrance among the Jews. On that day they commemorated the five great calamities of the Jewish people:

1. the return of the twelve spies and the subsequent wilderness wanderings;
2. the destruction of Solomon's temple by the Babylonians;

3. the destruction of Herod's temple by the Romans in A.D. 70;

4. the taking of Bether by Hadrian's troops when 580,000 Jews perished;

5. the plowing of Zion as foretold in Jeremiah 26:18 and Micah 3:12.

The best way to grasp the theme and thrust of Lamentations is to get its outline before us.

I. Desolation (chap. 1)
   A. The Far Country (1:1–5)
   B. The Forsaken Covenant (1:6–10)
   C. The Final Curse (1:11–15)
   D. The Forlorn Cry (1:16–22)
      1. No Comfort for Jeremiah (1:16)
      2. No Comfort for Jerusalem (1:17–22)
         a. A City Defiled (1:17–18)
         b. A City Deceived (1:19–22)
II. Destruction (chap. 2)
   A. The Lord's Wrath (2:1–7)
      1. His Protection (2:1–5)
      2. His Presence (2:6–7)
   B. The Lord's Will (2:8–16)
      The Destruction of Jerusalem's:
      1. Walls (2:8–9a)
      2. Wisdom (2:9b–12)
      3. Witness (2:13–16)
   C. The Lord's Word (2:17–22)
      1. Truly Fulfilled (2:17)
      2. Terribly Fulfilled (2:18–19)
      3. Totally Fulfilled (2:20–22)
III. Desperation (chap. 3)
   Jeremiah's:
   A. Present Sadness (3:1–21)
      He was:
      1. Visibly Aged (3:1–4)
      2. Vindictively Arrested (3:5–7)
      3. Vitally Alienated (3:8–9)
      4. Viciously Attacked (3:10–13)
      5. Verbally Affronted (3:14)
      6. Verily Abused (3:15–17)
      7. Victoriously Abased (3:18–21)

    B. Pathetic Sermon (3:22–39)

    C. Proposed Supplication (3:40–51)

    D. Past Suffering (3:52–57)

    E. Persisting Sorrow (3:58–66)

IV. Destitution (chap. 4)

    A. Described (4:1–10)

       1. No Homes Left (4:1)

       2. No Honor Left (4:2)

       3. No Heart Left (4:3–6)

       4. No Holiness Left (4:7–8)

       5. No Humanity Left (4:9–10)

    B. Deserved (4:11–20)

       1. By Israel's Monarchs (4:11–12)

       2. By Israel's Ministers (4:13–20)

    C. Derided (4:21–22)

       1. Edom's Petty Triumphs (4:21a)

       2. Edom's Prophesied Troubles (4:21b–22)

V. Degradation (chap. 5)

    A. The Existing Gloom (5:1–18)

       1. The Conquerors (5:1–2)

       2. The Captives (5:3–8)

          a. Bereavement (5:3)

          b. Bankruptcy (5:4–6)

          c. Bondage (5:7–8)

       3. The Calamities (5:9–15)

          a. The Siege (5:9–10)

            (1) Fear Without (5:9)

            (2) Fear Within (5:10)

          b. The Surrender (5:11–15)

            (1) Rape (5:11)

            (2) Ridicule (5:12)

            (3) Repression (5:13–15)

       4. The Cause (5:16–18)

    B. The Extinguished Gleam (5:19–22)

       1. Hope Revived (5:19–21)

          a. The Reality (5:19)

          b. The Request (5:20–21)

       2. Hope Removed (5:22)

The background of Lamentations is a ruined city. The stench of death assailed the nostrils. Rubble and ruin were heaped everywhere. The smoke of burning buildings hung yet in the air. The cries of widows and orphans, the desolate sobs of the bereaved rose like a dirge on every hand. The walls and gates of the once proud Jerusalem lay in heaps. The magnificent temple of Solomon was no more. Its treasures had been plundered and carried off to Babylon to enrich the shrines of Bel and Marduk. God's altars had been thrown down and the holy places desecrated and burned with fire. The royal family, descended—father and son—from David, had been marched away to oblivion, and the throne of David was no more. The majority of survivors of the siege were in chains and on their way to exile, and a Babylonian governor and Babylonian troops held what was left of Jerusalem.

Jeremiah had seen it coming. He had warned and pleaded with the apostate people he had loved with a great and tender care. His dire predictions had all been fulfilled. The rulers of Jerusalem had called him a traitor for preaching unconditional surrender to Babylon. He had been persecuted and abused, his written prophecies cut to ribbons and flung in the fire. But they had all come true.

And in Lamentations, Jeremiah wept out his heart over the desolate city. "No comforter! No comforter!" he cried again and again (see 1:2, 9, 16, 17, 21).

Jerusalem! O Jerusalem! The city where God had put His name, the city where once He had dwelt between the cherubim upon the mercy seat in the glory cloud, upon the ark, behind the veil, in the Holiest of all! The city that was intended to be that city set upon a hill, a city that could not be hid, set on high as a beacon to the nations to draw them to the living God in their midst. Now a ruin!

And the human tragedy! Can we not see the weeping prophet as he picks his way through the ruins of the city? He sees a starving little girl with unwashed face and uncombed hair, in rags, suffering from malnutrition, sobbing her little heart out in utter lostness, loneliness, fear, and desolation by her mother's putrefying corpse. The sight of it breaks afresh the prophet's heart and starts once more the tears from the dried up fountain of his heart. He sees a woman, weeping in shame and despair, her mantle rent, her virginity gone, ravished by the heartless storm troops of the Babylonian king. It breaks his heart afresh.

And above and beyond the lamentations of Jeremiah is the great sorrow in the heart of God.

In the Jewish Bible the name of the book is derived from its first word—Alas! The word is one of grief and power. In the interesting history of the inspiration, preservation, revision, and protection of the sacred Hebrew text, the *Sopherim* were the authorized revisers and the *Masserites* the custodians of the revised text. The older MSS of the Hebrew Bible, beside the text, arranged in columns, contain comments in smaller writing in the margins and here and there between the columns. These comments consist of facts and phenomena—the number of times the several letters occur, the number of words, the middle word, the middle verse, things of like matters—all intended to protect the text from alteration and copyist's mistakes.

The Masorah reminds us that this exclamation "Alas" was used by three prophets: Moses in connection with Israel's multiplication (Deut. 1:12); Isaiah in connection with Israel's corruption (Isa. 1:21); and Jeremiah in connection with Israel's desolation (Lam. 1:1).

Alas! At the heart of the sacred Jewish writings was that one woeful word, *Alas!* At the heart of all God's dealings with the human race is that sob-choked, tearful, agonized word of woe. The cross rears its dreadful head above the ages, casts its shadow across the centuries, holds enthralled the two eternities. "Alas!" Yet now, because of that cross, because the Man of Sorrows has suffered, bled and died, yea, and risen again and ascended on high, a new note has been sounded, a new and major key been introduced, a new and higher octave found. The last word in the Bible is not "alas," but "amen" (Rev. 22:21)—and that is just another name for Jesus, the glorious Son of the living God and Savior of the lost sons of men (Rev. 3:14).

The last two verses of Lamentations should be observed. "Turn thou us unto Thee, O LORD, and we shall be turned; renew our days as of old" (v. 21). There we have supplication. "But thou hast utterly rejected us; thou art very wroth against us" (v. 22). There we have silence. In the public reading of the Hebrew Scriptures, the Jews always repeat verse 21 after verse 22 to soften the blow, to minister some comfort. They do the same with Ecclesiastes, Isaiah, and Malachi. God does not do that. He deliberately ends the book the way He does to underline the reason for the sob—their sin.

CHAPTER 34

ZEPHANIAH

The Royal Prophet

His great, great grandfather was godly King Hezekiah. He was a prince among the prophets—a true prince of the house of David, wearing David's prophetic mantle even though he did not wear David's royal robe. His name is Zephaniah, a name that means "He whom Jehovah hides" or, as some suggest, "Jehovah is hidden." His pedigree is given more fully than any other of the prophets.

Given, too, is the time of Zephaniah's prophecy—during the days of Josiah, the last of the godly kings of Judah. In other words, Zephaniah was a contemporary of the prophet Jeremiah.

The nation of Judah had come through a disastrous period. The death of good King Hezekiah had brought Manasseh to the throne. Manasseh was the son born to Hezekiah during the fifteen-year extension of his life. Manasseh reigned longer and more wickedly than any of the kings who sat on David's throne. Amon, who followed Manasseh, was a wicked king as well, and between the two of them, they carried the nation of Judah beyond the line of God's patience. Vile and vicious sins were publicly paraded, sodomy was an accepted lifestyle, idolatrous worship was accepted as a matter of course, false cults flourished, people were infatuated with astrology, and corruption saturated the courts.

Then came godly Josiah. His one great wish was to lead the nation back to God in revival. But revival cannot be legislated. Though the king was heart and soul in the effort to restore the pure, pristine faith embodied in the law of Moses and the earlier prophets, it was all in vain. The best that was effected was reform, not revival. Even such reforms as the king was able to enact did not penetrate below the surface of Judah's national life. The princes were skeptical, and the people were wedded to their wicked ways. Zephaniah, who doubtless helped spark the reforms of Josiah, completely ignores them in his book.

The prophet could see that with Josiah's reforms it was a question of too little, too late. For too long, wickedness had been enthroned; the forces of ungodliness had entrenched themselves too deeply, so Zephaniah ignored Josiah's reforms. The party of reform in the country was headed by the king. The party had a program. The program was based solidly on the Scriptures. But Zephaniah was a prophet, and the mantle of Isaiah and Amos and Joel and Hosea had fallen on him. Surely he would give his endorsement of this new move to clean up the national life of the nation and to put the Bible back into the schools and courts? But no! He ignored it and did so with true prophetic insight. The reforms would not be sufficient to change anything for long.

Indeed, Josiah was cut off in his prime by a disastrous Egyptian invasion of Judah. Thereafter a succession of weak puppet kings occupied the throne—kings who brought down on their heads the increasing denunciation and ire of the prophet Jeremiah. The reforms of Josiah were stillborn, and Zephaniah had the insight to see it.

So then, he arose to preach in Judah at a critical time. Nahum was dead and gone, and Nineveh's fall was imminent. The ten tribes were already in captivity, their fate was a warning to Judah, a warning cynically ignored. The sins of Manasseh had pushed Judah over the line to certain judgment. Zephaniah's mission, therefore, was not to the whole people, whose sentence was already fixed, but to the remnant, who would flee from the wrath to come.

Zephaniah saw beyond the frontiers of Judah and beyond the limits of his own time. His prophecy is essentially a prophecy of the *Day of the Lord*. This coming "day of the Lord" was the burden of Joel, Amos, Hosea, Micah, and Isaiah as well as that of Zephaniah. These prophecies concerning the day of the Lord had a partial, illustrative fulfillment in the Assyrian and Babylonian invasions, but these visitations did not exhaust the prophecies. They all pointed on to a time yet to come—a time not far distant any more but at the very threshold of the door of our day.

Here is the outline of Zephaniah's prophecy:

I. The Determination of the Lord (1:1–6)
   A. The Prophet's Pedigree (1:1)
   B. The Prophet's Perspective (1:2–6)
     1. The Decision of the Lord (1:2–4a)
     2. The Discrimination of the Lord (1:4b–6)
       a. Judah's Idolatrous Priests (1:4b)
       b. Judah's Idolatrous Practices (1:5–6)
II. The Day of the Lord (1:7–3:8)

I. The Determination of the Lord (1:1–6)

A. The Prophet's Pedigree (1:1)

Zephaniah allied himself with the throne, a throne that was occupied so valiantly by Zephaniah's distant cousin Josiah. The blood of great David runs in the prophet's veins, and the Spirit that moved David to the very pinnacle of prophecy in so many of his psalms moved Zephaniah as well.

B. The Prophet's Perspective (1:2–6)

What a dreadful perspective it was! It was the perspective of one who saw that the wrath of God could not be much longer averted from a nation that had been given every possible spiritual privilege, every possible advantage, every possible blessing, every possible warning and example—yet still persisted in its sins.

1. The Decision of the Lord (1:2–4a)

The prophet saw the devouring flame and the divine focus. It was Judah's turn now to experience those outpourings of divine judgment that the sister nation of Israel had so dreadfully and thoroughly experienced. "I will consume . . . I will consume . . . I will cut off . . . Man and beast, fish and fowl, idols and wicked men" (see vv. 2–3). George Adam Smith says that "no hotter book lies in all the Old Testament."[1] Everywhere Zephaniah turned his prophetic eye he saw fire and smoke, darkness and drifting chaff, ruins, nettles, salt pits, empty decaying houses and palaces, and owls and ravens looking from the windows of desolate ruins. That was his perspective. All he had to say was ruled by the irrevocable decision of God to thoroughly thrash Judah for its sins.

2. The Discrimination of the Lord (1:4b–6)

And Zephaniah saw right through to the real source of the problem—the idolatrous priests who infested the land. He used an interesting word to describe the priests. The King James Version has the word "Chemarims." It comes from a root that means "black-robed" or "cassocked." The prophet saw them going about their business of encouraging the people in their worship of graven images. He saw the idolatry, the astrology, the insincerity, the cruelty, the apostasy, the infidelity of the people, wedded as they were to their false religious practices. He saw the people given over to the lewd and licentious rites of Baal. He could look out over the flat roofs of the city in the twilight and see the men and women bowing to the stars. He heard people, in crass insincerity, swearing by the name of the Lord. Worse than all that, he saw little children being offered up on the red-hot lap of Moloch. He saw that, despite all Josiah's valiant efforts, the people had "turned back" from the Lord, and that they "have not sought the LORD" (v. 6).

It is no wonder he was so convinced of the determination of the Lord to visit this people with judgment. That is his first great theme.

II. THE DAY OF THE LORD (1:7–3:8)

As always, with these Old Testament prophets, Zephaniah merged the near and the far, the impending, immediate, partial, illustrative fulfillment with the ultimate, distant, complete fulfillment. And, like all the prophets, he did not distinguish between the two comings of Christ.

A. The People Mentioned (1:7–13)

1. The Summons (1:7)

"Hold thy peace at the presence of the Lord GOD: for the day of the LORD is at hand: for the LORD hath prepared a sacrifice, he hath bid his guests." The consecrated guests were the Chaldeans—the Babylonians. The picture anticipates the one we have in the Apocalypse, in which God summons the vultures to come and feast upon the slain.

2. The Sacrifice (1:8–13)

God was about to immolate the wicked in a holocaust of judgment, a judgment long delayed, amply depicted, and thoroughly deserved. The power-brokers, the sin-seekers, the money-mad, the leisure-lovers, each came up before the prophet's gaze and each was scathingly bundled up for the flames. His eye swept over the city, beginning with the fish gate in the northern part of the city, where the produce of the Sea of Galilee and the Jordan was brought in (what we would now call the Damascus Gate). This was the side of the city from which the Babylonian threat would first come. Then his eye took in the heights, the second quarter of the city, the hill Acra where Huldah the prophetess lived (2 Kings 22:14). Then he saw disaster embrace Zion, Moriah, and Ophel as the enemy penetrated deeper and deeper into the city. Finally he saw disaster come to the hollow mortar, perhaps the Tyropoeon Valley where the Phoenician merchants and money-lenders carried on their business.

The Lord would grind the wicked as corn is crushed by the pestle in the mortar. It is a sweeping view of the whole city. Neither Jeremiah nor Isaiah tell us more about Jerusalem.

B. The Period Mentioned (1:14–18)

1. The Nearness of Judgment (1:14)

"The great day of the LORD is near, it is near, and hasteth greatly, even the voice of the day of the LORD: the mighty man shall cry there bitterly" (v. 14). Zephaniah saw the swift onrush of events as the Babylonians gathered their strength and surged across the world to build their empire in the Middle East. With the death of Josiah the pace on the international scene began to increase. Once Nineveh was swept aside, Egypt and Babylon began a struggle for the mastery of the world, and Judah was crushed between the upper and nether millstones of events beyond her control.

Zephaniah's prophecy, however, leaped far beyond the immediate, impending fall of Jerusalem before the Babylonians. With scarcely a pause for breath he speaks of events far in the future.

2. The Nature of Judgment (1:15–18)

His vision carried him over the long centuries of time to the judgments of the end-times to describe what he calls "a day of wrath" (v. 15). We learn from the Apocalypse that the day of wrath dawns after God's preliminary judgments under the seals and trumpets. These convulsions hand the world over to man and then over to Satan. It is not until *then*, when men have finally hardened their hearts against God and set themselves in an attitude of defiant unrepentance, that the vials of God's wrath are outpoured. Zephaniah saw that period as the time when God will fulfill prophecy, finally punish and fully purge. "For," he says, "he shall make even a speedy riddance of all them that dwell in the land" (v. 18).

Having looked at the people and the period, the prophet looks at places.

C. The Places Mentioned (2:1–3:8)

1. The Country of Judah (2:1–3)

Zephaniah called upon the people to repent: "Seek ye the LORD, all ye meek of the earth, . . . seek righteousness, seek meekness: it may be ye shall be hid in the day of the LORD's anger" (v. 3). We know from Old Testament history that there was a believing remnant in the land. There were men like Ezekiel and Daniel, men like Meshach, Shadrach, and Abednego. Even though they were carried away into Babylon as captives as part of God's clean sweep of the wicked land of Judah, there they prospered, and there they maintained a tremendous testimony for God. Daniel, at least, lived to see the captivity come to an end and a new world power repatriate those of the Jewish people who wished to return and rebuild the land.

2. The Conquerors of Judah (2:4–15)

The prophet looked *westward* to the land of the Philistines, the ancient, heredi-tary and persistent foes of Israel; he looked *eastward* to Moab and Ammon, likewise entrenched enemies of Judah for centuries; he looked *southward* to Ethiopia, the land south of Egypt—a country that figures again and again in end-time prophe-cies, especially as being confederate with Russia in her coming invasion of the Promised Land; he looked *northward* to Nineveh, which had not yet fallen but whose doom was gathering rapidly and was about to fall in unmitigated fury and thoroughness.

The collapse of Nineveh was the close of an epoch. As George Adam Smith says, "We can hardly overestimate what it meant. Not a man was then alive who had ever known anything else than the greatness and glory of Assyria. It was two hundred and thirty years since Israel first felt the weight of her arms. It was more than a hundred since her hosts had swept through Palestine, and for at least fifty her supremacy had been accepted by Judah. Now the colossus began to totter. As she had menaced, so she was menaced. The ruins with which for nigh three centuries she had strewn Western Asia—to these were to be reduced her own impregnable and ancient glory. It was the end of an epoch."[2]

Again Zephaniah turned his vision from the country of Judah and from the conquerors of Judah to Jerusalem.

3. The Capital of Judah (3:1–8)

He denounced Jerusalem, the city that, above all other cities ever built upon this planet, had been favored and chosen and blessed and privileged of God.

"Woe to her that is filthy and polluted, to the oppressing city!" (v. 1). He spared the king but he lashed out at the ruling classes. They were roaring lions, and the judges were nothing but wolves. He castigated the priests who perverted the law, and the prophets, who were nothing but boasters. He denounced the people who had no shame. Jerusalem had refused all the Lord's warnings and wooings; now must come her wars and her woes.

Zephaniah pointed out that Jerusalem had no regard for God's presence, no response for God's patience, no repentance to God's persistence, and no realization of God's purposes. Therefore God would assemble all nations and make a full and final end. The nations would fulfill His purpose in punishing Jerusalem, and then He would punish them for their own sins.

Thus Zephaniah finished his burden regarding the day of the Lord—a day both near and far—and turned to his final theme. For now his prophetic vision soared across the centuries beyond the storm clouds gathering in his day, beyond all that, to the consummation of the age.

III. THE DELIVERANCE OF THE LORD (3:9–20)

Zephaniah still had "that day" in view, but now he saw its consummation in the future blessing of his people. He had picked up the dominant thread of Joel and woven it into the tapestry of his own utterances—at least nineteen times he mentions "the day."[3] Now he shows how it is all going to end.

A. Israel's Regathering (3:9–10)

He saw the exiled Hebrew people coming from "beyond the rivers of Ethiopia"—that is, the White Nile and the Blue Nile. The Jews of our day have already trekked back from there to the reborn State of Israel. The Abyssinian Jews who came back were flown to Israel and literally believed that they were being borne on eagles' wings to the Promised Land. When they saw snow for the first time, they called it "manna," not knowing what it was.

Zephaniah saw something else in connection with this. He saw the Gentile nations having their language purified. "For then will I turn to the people[s] [not just the people, as in the King James version] a pure language . . ." (v. 9). The phrase "a pure language" can be rendered "a lip purified." That is, a clean lip in contrast with the leper's cry as echoed by Isaiah: "I am a man of unclean lips" (Isa. 6:5). That is one of the evidences of a genuine conversion—a person's vocabulary is cleaned up. God intends to convert the remnant of the Gentiles as well as a remnant of the Jews.

Israel's final regathering will be a time of blessing for the Gentiles, who will be cleansed and able to praise and worship God aright.

B. Israel's Repentance (3:11–13)

1. A New Humility (3:11–12)

Every shameful deed will have been cleansed. The age-long attitude of unbelief will be over. National, hypocritical pride will be gone. "Thou shalt no more be haughty because of my holy mountain" (v. 11). The Beast's defilement of the temple and the horrors of the great tribulation will bring the Jewish people to the end of themselves, and they will be ready at last to embrace the Christ.

2. A New Holiness (3:13)

"The remnant of Israel shall not do iniquity, nor speak lies; neither shall a deceitful tongue be found in their mouth: for they shall feed and lie down, and none shall make them afraid." Jesus said, "Out of the abundance of the heart the mouth speaketh" (Matt. 12:34). A filthy heart runs over in filthy words; a false heart betrays itself in false words; a foolish heart expresses itself in foolish words. Similarly, a redeemed heart displays itself in redeemed speech.

C. Israel's Rejoicing (3:14–15)

Our attention is drawn to joy.

1. A Merry People (3:14)

"Sing, O daughter of Zion; shout, O Israel; be glad and rejoice with all the heart, O daughter of Jerusalem." The prophet piles up phrase after phrase to emphasize the time of rejoicing that lies ahead for Israel. Down through the long centuries their history has been one of blood, sweat, and tears. They have been hounded and hunted from country after country in century after century. They have known no rest, no safety. At times they have prospered in the land of their exile but sooner or later anti-Semitism always reared up its head and the tale of their woes has begun again. But Zephaniah saw a day when all that will be over. He saw Israel as a merry people, rejoicing, singing, and shouting with joy.

Our attention is drawn, too, to Jesus.

2. A Messianic Presence (3:15)

"The king of Israel, even the LORD, is in the midst of thee." Jesus has come back! He sits enthroned in their midst. What nation will dare now to lift hand or heel against Israel? Israel's new happiness will stem from Israel's new holiness. God has joined the two together whether for the nation or for the individual.

The prophet has almost finished. He has spoken of Israel's regathering and of Israel's repentance and of Israel's rejoicing. He concludes on a high note.

D. Israel's Redeemer (3:16–20)

1. The Climax of the Lord's Blessings (3:16–17)

"The LORD thy God in the midst of thee is mighty" (v. 17). What more could be said than that! The prophet saw God Himself dwelling in the midst of a nation that was resting as on the Sabbath and rejoicing and singing! Such a thing has never been said of any other nation under heaven.

2. The Context of the Lord's Blessings (3:18–20)

Zephaniah goes over the ground again. He talks once more of the Lord gathering Israel, guarding Israel, guiding Israel, glorifying Israel, and governing Israel: "I will make you a name and a praise among all people of the earth, when I turn back your captivity before your eyes, saith the LORD" (v. 20). That has not happened yet. The nations of the earth still hate Israel—are still hostile to Israel. But as God's Word is sure, the day *will* come when every tribe and tongue, every land and people will have nothing but words of praise for Israel.

Before leaving this prophet and his message, we need to recall his main burden. He was preaching to a nation that had sinned away the day of grace, that had abused its privileges, that had so angered God by its lusts and lies that judgment simply had to come.

Zephaniah, therefore, has a word for us. We who live in the United States of America live in a land singularly blessed of God, a land of prodigal wealth from sea to shining sea. It is a land that has been generous beyond anything known in all history—generous to friend and foe alike. It is a land that has known freedom to an extraordinary degree, a land that was built by men who feared God and who stamped their faith on the coin of the realm and wrote it into the articles of its national faith.

But it has become a land that has denied the principles of its existence. It has become, to an alarming extent, a land where juvenile delinquency flourishes, where marriage is no longer sacred, where pornography is big business, where crime is syndicated, where God is ruled out of all institutions of learning, where false prophets flourish, where the vilest sins are legislated into respectability. Zephaniah had a word for the people of his land and a word for the people of ours as well. God is the same yesterday and today and forever.

CHAPTER 35

HABAKKUK

The Prophet with a Problem

Habakkuk has been called "the doubting Thomas of the Old Testament." He seems more concerned with solving a problem than with delivering a message. We can learn a valuable lesson from Habakkuk, for this man, when faced with a seemingly unsolvable problem, took it to God instead of abandoning his faith as some would do.

He was a contemporary of Jeremiah and clearly saw the handwriting on the wall for Judah. The rising power of the Babylonians filled his vision, and herein lay his problem. That the Judeans were wicked was an obvious fact, but still they were the people of God. Habakkuk could see that God must punish sin, and that Judah could not possibly escape His chastening. But when he looked at the Babylonians, the people whom God would use to chastise Judah, he could see that they were worse than the Jews. How could God punish a nation by a less righteous nation? Habakkuk's problem is perennial and is as pertinent today as it was in his day. How Habakkuk took his doubts and difficulties to God and how he found his answer is the theme of the book.

Other prophets addressed themselves to Israel or Judah or Edom or Nineveh or Babylon; Habakkuk addressed himself to God.

We know nothing at all about the man, but he has a significant name. "Habakkuk" means "to embrace." The great ministry of this prophet was to take the people of Judah into his arms—his sinning, erring people, about to know all the horrors of invasion, battle, siege, defeat, and exile—to take them into his arms and comfort them as one comforts a weeping child. He wrestled with questions as old as man—why is God silent? Why do the wicked triumph? Why does God stand back and allow the earth to be plowed and plowed again by the wicked? How can He remain aloof so long? The mills of God grind slowly, but they grind things very small. It was with the seeming slowness of God's governmental methods that Habakkuk was concerned.

Nobody has the last word as to when this prophecy was given. Controversy revolves around the fifth verse of the first chapter: "Behold ye among the heathen, and regard, and wonder marvelously: for I will work a work in your days, which ye will not believe, though it be told you." The great question is—what *was* that work? It certainly had to be one of startling significance and unusual magnitude. It was, as we shall see.

I. The Prophet Is Troubled (1:1–17)
  A. The Crimes of Judah (1:1–4)
    1. A Personal Sorrow (1:1–2a)
    2. A Perilous Situation (1:2b–3)
    3. A Permissive Society (1:4)
  B. The Coming of Judgment (1:5–17)
    1. The Invincibility of the Chaldeans (1:5–11)
      a. Their Conquest of Mighty Nineveh (1:5)
      b. Their Conquest of Many Nations (1:6–11)
    2. The Iniquity of the Chaldeans (1:12–17)
      a. God's Revelation (1:12)
      b. God's Reasons (1:13)
      c. God's Righteousness (1:14–17)
II. The Prophet Is Taught (2:1–20)
  God's righteousness seen:
  A. On the Individual Level (2:1–4)
  B. On the International Level (2:5–20)
    1. The Wars of the Chaldeans (2:5)
    2. The Woes of the Chaldeans (2:6–20)
      a. Their Crimes (2:6–8)
      b. Their Covetousness (2:9–11)
      c. Their Cruelties (2:12–14)
      d. Their Carousings (2:15–18)
      e. Their Cults (2:19–20)
III. The Prophet Is Triumphant (3:1–19)
  A. Faith Surrenders (3:1–2)
  B. Faith Sees (3:3–15)
    1. The Lord's Presence (3:3–5)
    2. The Lord's Power (3:6–9)
    3. The Lord's Path (3:10–15)

C. Faith Soars (3:16–19)
    1. The Prophet Trembling (3:16)
    2. The Prophet Trusting (3:17–19)

Habakkuk's world was in upheaval. Momentous things were happening abroad, and within his own nation things were ripening fast for judgment. The prophet had his hand upon the pulse of his people and knew his nation's sins could not go unpunished.

I. The Prophet Is Troubled (1:1–17)

He looks first at the situation at home.

A. The Crimes of Judah (1:1–4)

It is possible that Habakkuk began to preach and wrestle with his great problem in the days of King Josiah—perhaps shortly after the great prophet Jeremiah began to preach. Josiah was the last king with any semblance of divine authority to sit on the throne of Judah, and the last king to even try to bring revival to Judah. After his tragic and sudden death, first the Egyptians and then the Babylonians interfered increasingly in Judah's affairs, and her kings became mere puppets of foreign powers.

Josiah's reforms did no more than scratch the surface of Judah's moral and spiritual needs. The long and disastrous reign of Manasseh had taken the rot too deeply into the fiber of the nation. Habakkuk looked around him with dismay. If things were this bad, even with a godly king on the throne, what hope was there for Judah?

"O Lord, how long shall I cry, and thou wilt not hear! Even cry out unto thee of violence, and thou wilt not save!" (1:2). Thus Habakkuk began. He saw a land where society had become so permissive that, as he puts it, "the law is slacked" (1:4). That is, the law was powerless to restrain the rising tides of wickedness. The Lord, however, is all powerful.

B. The Coming of Judgment (1:5–17)

1. The Invincibility of the Chaldeans (1:5–11)

a. Their Conquest of Mighty Nineveh (1:5)

Behold ye among the heathen, and regard, and wonder marvelously: for I will work a work in your days, which ye will not believe, though it be told you.

God challenged the prophet's skepticism. He said, in effect, "I am about to act on the stage of history in a way that will draw the attention of everybody. I am not going to tell you what it is, however, because even if I did you would not believe it." This seems to be a veiled reference to the impending downfall of the Assyrian Empire. For hundreds of long, terrible years, that monstrous world power had tyrannized mankind, and it seemed as hale and strong as ever. Yet within a few short years it would be swept aside and so completely buried in the rubble of the ages that its very place would be forgotten. The collapse of the Assyrian Empire was to be an event of unprecedented magnitude in that ancient world—just as the catastrophic, overwhelming collapse of Russia will be in a not too far distant day in our world.

b. Their Conquest of Many Nations (1:6–11)

For, lo, I raise up the Chaldeans, that bitter and hasty nation, which shall march through the breadth of the land, to possess the dwellingplaces that are not theirs. They are terrible and dreadful. (vv. 6–7)

And there follows a description of their character, their cruelty, and their conquests. And, sure enough, in 612 B.C., not many years after Habakkuk began to prophesy, Nineveh came crashing down, Babylon and the Medes accomplishing this great service to the rest of mankind. The whole world breathed a sigh of relief, but it was to be a sigh that was short-lived. For a new oppressor had arisen among men. Instead of Nineveh, it was Babylon—and Habakkuk knew his Bible well enough to know that it was Babylon that Judah had to fear.

2. The Iniquity of the Chaldeans (1:12–17)

Many years before, the prophet Isaiah had warned godly King Hezekiah about the Babylonians; now Habakkuk was picking up the theme. Judah's sins would be punished by the Babylonians, Judah's sons would be carried captive into Babylon.

The prophet was aghast! So that was the way God kept order among the nations! He used one nation to thrash another, and now it was to be Judah's turn. Judah, for her unceasing sins and apostasies, was to be handed over to the Babylonians for judgment. "Art thou not from everlasting, O LORD," he cried, "my God, mine Holy One? . . . O mighty God, thou hast established them for correction. Thou art of purer eyes than to behold evil, . . . wherefore lookest thou upon them that deal treacherously . . . ?" (vv. 12–13).

Then Habakkuk described the way in which the Babylonians, in common with all world conquerors, dealt with the nations round about. Tyranny is the same no matter who is in power. Nineveh was bad, and Babylon was no better. Like all other mighty world powers, Babylon treated the nations as though they were so many fish in the sea to be swept up into her net and callously dumped on shore while she went fishing for more. Habakkuk came very close to the complaint of Job, almost charging God with being the cause of all the carnage and cruelty inflicted on the nations by unchecked tyrants.

The prophet was troubled. True, Judah deserved punishment for her sins, but how could God use Babylon, which was much more wicked and ruthless than Judah, to punish Judah's sins? The thought came as a painful shock to the prophet. It not only outraged his innate sense of right and wrong, but it seemed morally wrong. It shook his belief in the righteousness of God and in the fairness of His judgment.

So chapter 1 leaves the prophet more puzzled than ever. He decided that something must be done. He did not, however, throw away his faith like so many have done when faced with the same imponderable issues of God's moral judgment of the world.

II. The Prophet Is Taught (2:1–20)

Instead of running away from the problem or saying foolish things about God, the prophet put himself in a position where God could speak to him about the problem: "I will stand upon my watch, and set me upon the tower, and will watch to see what he will say unto me, and what I shall answer when I am reproved" (v. 1).

In this chapter, faith finds a solution. It is not so much an intellectual solution as an intuitive solution; it is a solution that lies in the reality of faith. The prophet was shown that God is righteous and that this righteousness has to be seen both individually and internationally.

First, this righteousness has to be applied.

A. On the Individual Level (2:1–4)

The prophet was taught something of the *truth* of God and something of the *timings* of God and something of the *trustworthiness* of God.

One of the great lessons he had to learn was that "the vision is yet for an appointed time, but at the end it shall speak, and not lie: though it tarry, wait for it; because it will surely come, it will not tarry" (v. 3). We are in such a hurry. We are creatures bounded by time. Our little lives ebb so swiftly away, and before we know it our allotted span is over. We are like people traversing a deep valley between two high hills. We have never been anywhere else, never seen anything else, being narrow, limited, circumscribed by the very nature of our confinement, even in our most expansive thoughts. What we need is a different perspective. We need to climb one of those hills or, better still, borrow an eagle's wings, climb the heights of the heavens, and look down. Things would take on a better perspective. The hills that hedge us in are the extremities of time, as we know it, bounded by the date of our birth and the date of our death. We need to see things from the standpoint of eternity rather than the standpoint of time, to soar beyond the narrow, restricting confines of our circumscribed mortality and see things from the perspective of God's throne. We would then see the nations as a drop in the bucket. Assyria! Babylon! Greece! Rome! What are these! Their comings and goings are mere markings on the sands of time. God is working to a much bigger plan than ours and, in the end, everything will work out right. God *is* in control, He is still sovereign, He has not abdicated His throne. We must be patient. The timings of God are controlled by a much bigger clock than Big Ben.

Such was the first great lesson God taught the prophet. He had the wrong perspective—even his watchtower was not nearly high enough. He must learn a lesson about the *timings* of God.

More! He must learn a lesson about the *trustworthiness* of God. The Lord had already weighed the soul of the oppressor and found it sadly wanting. "Behold, his soul which is lifted up is not upright in him: *but the just shall live by his faith*" (v. 4). Let the believing man remember that. "The just shall live by *faith*." In one sweeping statement, God set before the prophet the way of death and the way of life.

"The just shall live by faith!" Faith is the key to seeing the big picture. Faith looks up into the face of a wise and loving and powerful God and says, "I believe; help thou mine unbelief" (Mark 9:24)! On the individual level *that's it!* Faith is the key to seeing God's perspective.

The text became famous even in Bible times. It is quoted three times in the New Testament. It became the watchword of the Reformation. It was the text that changed Martin Luther, shook the corrupt church of his day to its foundations, and gave birth to movements of revival and reform that changed the map of Europe and the world.

Let us recall what happened. Martin Luther crossed the Alps and came to Rome looking for peace for his soul. He had far exceeded his brethren in watching and fasting, in mortification of the flesh, in prayers and penance, but it had brought him no relief. He had carried his extremes to the very doors of death, but all in vain. He hoped to find in Rome the peace he had sought so long. Penniless and barefoot, he begged his way toward the city of his dreams. If only he could see Rome!

Then came the shock. He arrived in Italy and saw monasteries of marble, and monks faring sumptuously every day. He pressed on—Rome would be different, Rome was the holy city, Rome was sanctified by the tombs of the apostles, by the monuments of the saints, and by the blood of the martyrs.

He hastened to the holy places, listened to the legends, earnestly believed all he was told. He would not allow even the arrogance and profanity of the priests to disturb him at first. He saw the triumphal pomp of the pope, saw cardinals carried like lords of the land upon the shoulders of men, riding fiery steeds and driving in carriages studded with gems, sheltered from the sun by canopies of peacock feathers. The revolt began in his soul.

Still, stifling his inner doubts, he hurried from shrine to shrine until at last he arrived at the Scala Sancta. He decided to earn the indulgence promised for those who ascended Pilate's Stairway on their knees, making the proper pause and saying the proper prayers at each stage. We can see him crawl painfully to the first step, and we can hear his prayer: "My Jesus! Through the sorrow you suffered in being separated from your dear Mother and your beloved disciples, have mercy on me. Holy Mother pierce me through, in the heart each wound renew of my Savior crucified." It brought no relief. Like Naaman's first dip in Jordan, his disease of soul remained as vile, as leprous as ever.

He struggled on. Another step, another, another. "My Jesus! My Jesus! Holy Mother! Holy Mother!" Step after step. Prayer after prayer.

Then, like a flash of lightning, the light burst through, and like the voice of thunder the Spirit of God spoke directly to his darkened soul. "*The just shall live by faith!*" Faith, Martin, faith! Not works, *faith!*

Halfway up the staircase he stopped, rose to his feet, dusted off his robe, turned around, and marched resolutely down the worn steps, out of the place altogether, and into the full experience of life as it is in Christ.

Until that moment, Martin Luther's thought of God had been a pagan thought. When the pagan thinks of God he thinks of God as cruel. From head to foot the pagan bears the marks of self-inflicted wounds, his back a tangle of scars, his flesh rent and torn, his tongue pierced by pitiless hooks. What does it mean? It means he worships a fiend. His god lives to see him in pain. His ceaseless round of pain represents his futile attempts to appease his idol's lust for blood.

Martin Luther made the same mistake. His life had been one long drawn-out agony. His body was wasted to a skeleton. More than once his brother monks had to pick him up exhausted from the floor. "The just," we can imagine him saying to himself, "the just shall live by *pain* and *punishment*, by *fasting* and by *fear*." "*The just shall live by faith!*" thundered the voice of God in his soul.

In describing this experience at a later date, Martin Luther said of this text,

> It was like entering into Paradise. Before those words broke upon my soul I hated God and was angry with Him because, not content with frightening us sinners by the laws and by the miseries of life, He still further increased our torture by the gospel. But then, by the Spirit of God I understood these words *the just shall live by faith*—then I felt born again like a new man; I entered through these open doors into the very Paradise of God.[1]

So it was with Habakkuk. He was taught that, on the individual level, he must learn something about the truth of God and the timings of God and the trust of God. But more.

The righteousness of God has to be applied much more broadly.

B. On the International Level (2:5–20)

The prophet's attention was now turned to the Babylonians, who would soon be pouring across the frontiers of his native land to execute the purposes of God.

He discovered that God knew all about them! He was given a series of five woes to pronounce against them. Their crimes, covetousness, cruelty, carousing, and their cults are all denounced. God was not blind to their character—they were but a ready instrument to His hand. When He had used them as a stick to chastise Israel, then He would break them out of hand. Nations march their armies across the world and sow bloodshed, tears, and wretchedness wherever they go, but God takes full account.

The chapter ends on a significant note. "*But* the LORD is in his holy temple: let all the earth keep silence before him" (v. 20). The prophet was told that all was well. God was still there. The Babylonians might indeed destroy the magnificent temple of Solomon still standing in Jerusalem, so recently cleansed by Josiah, but so often polluted by Judah's other kings, but there was a temple no weapon of theirs could ever touch.

III. THE PROPHET IS TRIUMPHANT (3:1–19)

The last chapter is a psalm. Sobs gave way to a song! It is a real psalm. Three times the prophet uses the word "Selah!" (vv. 3, 9, 13), which may be roughly rendered "There! What do you think of that!" He sends it to "the chief singer" (v. 19), and he uses a word often found in the psalms—*neginoth* (smitings). The psalm, in other words, has to do with God's smitings of His foes, and relates to an appearance of God upon the earth.

In response to the challenge, "The just shall live by faith," in this closing chapter faith *surrenders*, then faith *sees*, then faith *soars*.

A. Faith Surrenders (3:1–2)

"O LORD, I have heard . . . revive thy work in the midst of the years . . . in wrath remember mercy" (3:2). With true spiritual insight, Habakkuk bowed to the obvious fact that an unrepentant people must be punished—especially a people such as Judah, which had been blessed with so many spiritual privileges, so many opportunities, such great accountability. Where Judah stood in Habakkuk's day, Britain and the United States stand today.

With spiritual insight, Habakkuk saw that judgment must come, and he bowed to the inevitable. The Babylonians would be God's rod. But Habakkuk also saw that one thing that could avert judgment—not legislation, but revival. He prayed that perhaps the Lord in His mercy would send revival, real revival.

B. Faith Sees (3:3–15)

The prophet caught a glimpse of God coming down to earth to take personal charge of the affairs of men. This vision blended pages of the past into portents of the future. He saw the coming of One whose glory covers the heavens, brighter than the noonday sun, as bright as all light. He saw Him coming down and taking His stand in territory that belonged to Edom. He saw pestilence running ahead of Him, reducing the nations to nothing. He saw Him shaking Ethiopia and striding across the Red Sea to desolate Arabia. He saw all nature tremble; he saw all nations tremble. He saw right down the ages to the end of "the times of the Gentiles" (Luke 21:24).

C. Faith Soars (3:16–19)

Habakkuk bowed to the revelation of God to his soul. Judgment was irreversible, he could see that, but joy was irrepressible: "Yet I will rejoice," he says. "I will joy in the God of my salvation. The LORD God is my strength, and he will make my feet like hinds' feet" (vv. 18–19). The problem is *solved*—to *faith's* satisfaction, anyway!

There has probably never been a darker hour in this world's history than the one in which we live. When our hearts begin to fail us with fear, looking on those things that are coming upon the earth, it is time to turn back to this little-known book of Habakkuk and read his message again. He tells us that "God is still on the throne" and that all appearances notwithstanding, His wise and loving purposes cannot be thwarted—that

> Deep in unfathomable mines
> Of never-failing skill,
> He treasures up His bright designs
> And works His sovereign will.
> —William Cowper,
> "God Moves in a Mysterious Way"

CHAPTER 36

OBADIAH

The Prophet of Edom's Doom

A certain man had two sons. They were twins, born the same day, within the same hour. Unlike many twins, these boys were as different as night is from day. Their differences were so obvious it was remarked from the moment of their birth. They were different in appearance, different in their appetites, different in their appeal. The one was hairy, the other was smooth; the one was hungry for spiritual things, the other craved sensual things; the one appealed to the mother, the other to the father. The one boy was by instinct a *killer*. He liked to tramp the wild woods in search of prey. Nothing pleased him more than to bring down a deer with a well-aimed arrow, to skin it and to bring back the red meat to camp. The other boy was by instinct a *keeper*. He liked to roam the green pastures, sit down beside still waters, and gather around him a flock. Nothing pleased him more than to mind and multiply sheep, to care for the lambs, and to bring back the strays to the fold.

There was something about the older boy that fascinated the father. The father was a mild man easily ruled, but given to appetite. He always felt drawn toward the wilder of the two boys. Doubtless the older boy's daring met a need in his soul. In any case, he encouraged the instincts of the killer. He liked to eat of his son's venison.

There was something about the younger boy that fascinated the mother. She was a somewhat willful woman herself, not easily ruled, a woman given to precipitous action. She always felt drawn to the younger, the wiser of the two boys. Perhaps there was something in his disposition that matched the mother instinct in her soul. She encouraged the instincts of the keeper. She was clever with a leg of lamb, clever, too, with the sleek hair of the goat. The younger boy was always mother's boy.

The one boy grew up to be a lover of this world. He cared nothing for the world to come, nothing for God, nothing for the verbal traditions of truth that were the great heritage of the family into which he was born. The other boy grew up to be a lover of the world to come. He cared a great deal about God, about the family faith, about the covenant, about the things that spoke of Christ, about those pleasures that are at God's right hand for evermore.

Thus the one boy grew up wild, a killer, a despiser of spiritual things. The other boy grew up wise, a keeper, a desirer of spiritual things.

They quarreled, these two boys, as we might expect—quarreled bitterly, and to such an extent that bad blood stood between them. So much so that the younger boy was sent away from home and only came back, many years later, a sadder and a wiser man, a man broken by God and born from above. The older boy strayed away and stayed away, growing wilder and bolder and more a partaker of the spirit of the age.

Both boys married. The younger boy chose his bride from among those who had some knowledge of the truth, a knowledge derived from the godly testimony of his grandfather in days gone by. The older boy had a taste for the carnal, the exotic, the sensual. He chose for himself a dark daughter of a local pagan Canaanite and also a daughter of banished Ishmael.

From the families of these two boys, related by blood, riven apart by all else, there developed in the process of time two nations. The one nation was wild, godless, secure in its inaccessible hills and in the power of its might. The other nation was chosen of God, secure in His love, shepherded by the Most High, despite its self-will and sin.

And as we might expect, there was little love lost between the two peoples as there had been little love lost between the two persons from whom they sprang. The name of the older son was *Esau*, the name of the younger was *Jacob*. The nation that sprang from Esau was *Edom*, the nation that sprang from Jacob was *Israel*. God, in summing up the ebb and flow of their national characters, declared, "I loved Jacob, and I hated Esau" (Mal. 1:2–3).

Esau, before ever he and his brother were born, sought to murder Jacob, and Edom, long after Esau's death, took pleasure in the misfortunes of Israel. Esau and Jacob! Israel and Edom! Locked together in history; locked together in prophecy. The prophet Obadiah tells us how. For his prophecy is a tale of two cities—two cities the origins of which are lost in the mists of a distant past. His prophecy is the tale of Petra, the famous capital of Edom, and of Jerusalem, the famous capital of Judah.

Nobody knows for sure just when this man Obadiah preached. He has been placed all the way from among the very earliest of the prophets to among the very latest. Some six hundred years divide the era championed by the one view from the era championed by the other. So there is wide disagreement as to the date of Obadiah. There are a number of people in the Old Testament with the name of Obadiah but none of them can be positively identified as the prophet of that name.

The dating of Obadiah hinges on the interpretation of verses 11–14. Some relate the reference to events in the days of Jehoram (2 Chron. 21:16–17); others relate the reference to events in the days of Ahaz (2 Chron. 28:16–17). Still others link the passage with Jeremiah 49:14–16 and make these two prophets contemporaries. It is not necessary to assume that either prophet quoted the other, although there is a close similarity between these two passages. Jude and 2 Peter give us just such an example of God inspiring two men with a like message. It is true that the prophecy in Obadiah 11–14 contains many verbal parallels to the one found in Jeremiah 49:14–16. But who quoted whom? Did Jeremiah quote from Obadiah or did Obadiah quote from Jeremiah? Or did each prophesy quite independently of the other?

Little in the book enables us to give a conclusive verdict. No mention is made in the book either of the Assyrians or the Babylonians; the book raises no doctrinal issue, and we know nothing of the prophet beyond the bare mention of his name, a common enough name in Israel. Obadiah simply means "Servant of Jehovah." We know that he prophesied to the southern kingdom of Judah, and could have prophesied either before the Babylonian invasion, during it, or even after it was over. He is filled with indignation against Edom—with ample cause, as we shall see.

The prophecy of Obadiah is a classic warning against anti-Semitism. The nation that curses and persecutes the Jew will inevitably reap what it sows. The nation that harbors and protects the Jew will surely enjoy the blessing of God (Genesis 12:2–3).

I. The Doom of Edom Predicted (vv. 1–16)
   A. The Doom Declared (vv. 1–2)
      1. The Ambassador's Mission (v. 1)
      2. The Ambassador's Message (v. 2)
   B. The Doom Described (vv. 3–9)
      1. Edom's Territory Subdued (vv. 3–4)
      2. Edom's Treasures Stolen (vv. 5–6)
      3. Edom's Treaties Subverted (v. 7)
      4. Edom's Troops Slaughtered (vv. 8–9)
   C. The Doom Deserved (vv. 10–14)
      Edom had:

When the children of Israel were on their way to Canaan after their exodus from Egypt, the Edomites refused them passage through their territory. In later years the Edomites were often at war with the Hebrews and were thrashed again and again by kings of Judah, but they were never completely subdued. When at last Nebuchadnezzar sacked Jerusalem, the joy of the Edomites knew no bounds, and they did all they could to befriend and assist the Babylonians. As the wall of Jerusalem was assaulted, the Edomites screamed with delight. "Down with it, down with it, even to the ground," they cried (see Psalm 137:7). Their exultation was brief, however, for within four years Edom itself was invaded by Nebuchadnezzar and completely overthrown. This was clearly foreseen by Obadiah (assuming he was a contemporary of Jeremiah) and stated in a most emphatic way. Long centuries afterward we find Edomite hostility to the things and people of God still in evidence, for Herod the Great, who massacred the babes of Bethlehem in his efforts to slay the infant Christ, was an Idumean and a descendant of the Edomites.

I. The Doom of Edom Predicted (vv. 1–16)

"The vision of Obadiah. Thus saith the Lord God concerning Edom; We have heard a rumor from the Lord, and an ambassador is sent among the heathen, Arise ye, and let us rise up against her in battle" (v. 1).

A. The Doom Declared (vv. 1–2)

Already the summons had gone forth from on high. Battle and belittlement await Edom for its sins. The Lord has sent His ambassador among the nations to stir them up to war against Edom. War is the rod of God's anger, the whip of His chastisement. He used it against His own people Israel; He will certainly use it against those who ill-treated Israel. He always has and He always will. It is written right into the original draft of His covenant with Abraham (Gen. 12:1–3). No nation has ever prospered that made it a policy of state to persecute the Jew.

B. The Doom Described (vv. 3–9)

The prophet expands the theme, going into detail and giving four special particulars of the doom and downfall of Edom.

1. Edom's Territory Subdued (vv. 3–4)

The pride of thine heart hath deceived thee, thou that dwellest in the clefts of the rock . . . that saith in his heart, Who shall bring me down . . . ? Though thou exalt thyself as the eagle, and though thou set thy nest among the stars, thence will I bring thee down, saith the LORD.

The Edomites dwelt in Mount Seir, a mountainous region reaching from south of the Dead Sea to the Gulf of Akabah (territory now included in the kingdom of Jordan). Bozra was its ancient capital. In Obadiah's day the capital was Sela (Petra), the rock city, which, although desolate now, still remains one of the wonders of the world. The Edomites had good grounds, humanly speaking, for thinking their city impregnable, but they failed to reckon on God.

The dwellings and temples of Petra were hewn out of the rock. The purple mountains into which the wild sons of Esau clambered run out from Syria upon the desert for some one hundred miles and embrace some of the finest scenery in the world. From Mount Hor, which is their summit, the traveler can look down upon a maze of mountains, chasms, rocky shelves, and strips of valley.

On the east side, the range is but the crested edge of a high, cold plateau covered for the most part with stones, but with stretches of corn fields and forests. On the west, however, the walls of rock spring steep and bare, black and red from the yellow of the desert. The interior is reached by defiles so narrow that two horsemen can barely ride abreast, and from which the sun is shut out by overhanging rocks. Eagles and hawks scream in the sky above the traveler. The people of Edom perched on high shelves or hid away in caves at the end of deep gorges.

Mount Esau, however, was no mere citadel, stocked and provisioned against siege. It was a well-watered country, full of food and men, yet lifted up so high and locked so fast by precipice and treacherous mountain that it called for the minimum of defense.

The main gorge by which Petra was approached, called today "the valley of Moses," looks down on a rivulet, which threads its entire length. Its rocky steeps are awesome and impressive. Its valley, with its branching side valleys, is about 4,500 feet long and it is flanked on all sides by precipitous sandstone cliffs. An invading army would have to creep down that narrow, precipitous canyon, twisting and turning through the mountains, before the prize could even be seen. With incredible industry, the inhabitants of Petra had carved their actual fortress from the beetling crags, tunneling into the flinty rock, and beautifying its face with the sculptured lines of temples and palace tombs.

"Who shall bring me down?" boasted the Edomite. "I will bring thee down, saith the LORD" (v. 4). What difference did rocks and precipices make to the One who reared up the Rocky Mountains and plowed out the Grand Canyon? Edom's territory was to be subdued. Armies specially commissioned for the task were already being summoned from afar. The prophet Obadiah had heard the tidings, and with evident relish he passed the tidings on.

2. Edom's Treasures Stolen (vv. 5–6)

> If thieves came to thee, if robbers by night, . . . would they not have stolen till they had enough? If the grapegatherers came to thee, would they not leave some grapes? How are the things of Esau searched out! how are his hidden things sought up!

For Edom was not only protected, it was prosperous. The wealth of Edom derived from its standing astride several of the main caravan trade routes of the ancient world. The masters of Edom held a sword over the harbors of the Gulf of Akaba, into which the gold ships of Ophir came, and they levied their tribute on that trade. They cut the roads and intercepted the caravans that ran from Damascus to Gaza. Merchants from Arabia and the East, from Egypt and from Greece were forced to pay tribute to Edom or else have their goods stolen. The Edomites filled their caves with plunder. Solomon, Jehoshaphat, Amaziah, Uzziah, and other Judean kings had all sought to command the Eastern trade through Elath and Ezion-geber, but to do so they had to subdue Edom.

But Obadiah saw the coming of a conqueror who would leave Edom with *nothing*—nothing at all. An ordinary thief would take just the portable valuables. An ordinary harvester would at least leave the gleanings on the vines. But Edom was to be plundered until there was nothing left, nothing at all. Edom's territories would be subdued. Edom's treasures would be stolen.

3. Edom's Treaties Subverted (v. 7)

> All the men of thy confederacy have brought thee even to the border: the men that were at peace with thee have deceived thee, and prevailed against thee; they that eat thy bread have laid a wound under thee.

Their allies, their confederates were to play a major part in Edom's downfall. Her treaties would be found to be worthless—worse than worthless. The very countries she thought she could count on would make their peace with the invader at her expense.

4. Edom's Troops Slaughtered (vv. 8–9)
Sages and soldiers alike would perish:

> Shall I not in that day, saith the LORD, even destroy the wise men out of Edom, . . . and thy mighty men . . . shall be dismayed . . . that every one of the mount of Esau may be cut off by slaughter.

The wise men of Esau were famous. It is the race that gave to history its Herods—clever, scheming, ruthless statesmen. "That fox!" is how Jesus characterized the Herod of His day, and thus He stamped the race. The cunning craftiness of the Edomites would not save them in the hour of divine visitation. Their domains would become a slaughterhouse.

And sure enough, along came the Babylonians, and the rocky bulwarks of Edom yielded to the superior military craft of Nebuchadnezzar, the man to whom God symbolically gave the whole world. Then, during the days of the Maccabees, John Hyrcanus laid them low. And when the Romans came, they lost their national character altogether.

Thus the doom of Edom is declared and described.

C. The Doom Deserved (vv. 10–14)
Edom had done three unforgivable things. The prophet notes them.

1. Edom Had Encouraged Judah's Foes (vv. 10–11)
They participated in the *spread of violence* and they participated in the *spoils of victory* (vv. 10–11): "For thy violence against thy brother Jacob shame shall cover thee, and thou shalt be cut off for ever. In the day that thou stoodest on the other side, in the day that the strangers carried away captive his forces, and foreigners entered into his gates, and cast lots upon Jerusalem, even thou wast as one of them." The Edomites had encouraged the Babylonians in their sack and plunder of Jerusalem. They had looked on gloatingly, and had become active participants. Consider the situation. It was the darkest hour of Israel's history. City and temple had been overthrown. Up over the desolate land came wave after wave of Babylonian troops. And with them came the Edomites, eager to gloat over Jerusalem's downfall. Edom had not merely encouraged, though, Judah's foes.

2. Edom Had Enjoyed Judah's Fall (vv. 12–13)
They found both pleasure and profit in it. "But *thou shouldest not* have looked

on the day of thy brother in the day that he became a stranger; *neither shouldest thou* have rejoiced over the children of Judah in the day of their destruction; *neither shouldest thou* have spoken proudly in the day of distress; *Thou shouldest not* have entered into the gate of my people in the day of their calamity; yea, *thou shouldest not* have looked on their affliction in the day of their calamity, nor have laid hands on their substance in the day of their calamity." *Thou shouldest not have . . .* It rings out again and again. It was one thing for God to be punishing His people. It was something else again for Edom, near of kin to the Hebrew people, to stand back and enjoy the dreadful spectacle.

3. Edom Had Enslaved Judah's Fugitives (v. 14)

This was the crowning act of wickedness—to stand at the fork of the road, on the mountain pass, at "the crossway," and catch the fleeing women and children and the panting, frightened, fleeing, beaten men—to catch them and hand them over to the Babylonians for death or deportation. That was Edom's final wickedness, Edom's unforgivable sin: "*Neither shouldest thou* have stood on the crossway, to cut off those that did escape; *neither shouldest thou* have delivered up those of His that did remain in the day of distress."

Edom had indulged in treachery against Judah; treachery was what Edom would reap. Edom had not hesitated to seize a share of the spoil of Jerusalem; Edom too would be spoiled. Edom had lifted the sword in violence against Judah; violence would recoil upon Edom. Edom had urged on the utter destruction of Jerusalem; utter destruction would be Edom's lot. Edom had ravished the remnant of Judah, handing over even the refugees to the invader; the remnant of Judah would one day possess the land of Edom. It was judgment deserved, fully deserved. Coming judgment on Edom was as inevitable as the rising of tomorrow's sun.

D. The Doom Dated (vv. 15–16)

Here we have one of those instances in prophecy where the prediction leaps over the ages of time to point to a fuller and more final fulfillment in the last days. Many Old Testament prophecies are like that—they have both a near and a far fulfillment. They have an initial, partial fulfillment and then a second and more complete fulfillment. This is especially true of prophecies that look on to the end of the age.

"For the day of the Lord is near upon all the heathen: as thou hast done, it shall be done unto thee: thy reward shall return upon thine own head. For as ye have drunk upon my holy mountain, so shall all the heathen drink continually." There was an initial, partial fulfillment in the case of the Edomite nation; there is a postponed fulfillment that has reference to the nations in the end time.

Thus the prophecy is dated as having its ultimate focus of fulfillment in the "day of the Lord," the coming day when all nations will come up against Jerusalem, a reborn Edom with them. For these ancient hostilities are to come back into the focus of world affairs again as the end-time approaches. The rebirth of the State of Israel today heralds the approaching fulfillment of these end-time prophecies. The ancient land of Edom is now part of the territory of the Arab country of Jordan. Jordan joins with the other Arab states of the Middle East in bitter hostility toward the nation of Israel. The revived kingdom of Edom, perhaps known under its new name, will play its part in the battle of Armageddon, on the side of the Beast and the other Gentile nations, in seeking to exterminate the Jewish people once and for all, fully and forever.

God will see to it, however, that justice is done. The Arab lands of the Middle East, so vehement, so bitter, so unrelenting in their hatred of Israel, will surely reap what they are sowing: "As thou hast done, it shall be done unto thee" (v. 15). That is the principle of poetic justice in God's dealings with men. The penalty corresponds to the crime as one line of poem corresponds to another.

The prophecy of Obadiah ends with a fresh focus on Israel.

II. THE DELIVERANCE OF ZION PREDICTED (vv. 17–21)

Three things are noted by the prophet.

A. The Character of It (v. 17)

"But upon mount Zion shall be deliverance, and there shall be holiness; and the house of Jacob shall possess their possessions." Rescue! Regeneration! Recovery! Israel is to be at last a holy nation and will enter into the full territorial grant deeded by God to Abraham, to Isaac, and to Jacob—a grant that takes in not only the little land we know today as Israel but a very large slice of the Middle East as well. The promised boundaries run from the Nile to the Euphrates. The Jews have never possessed more than ten percent of their promised land.

B. The Completeness of It (vv. 18–20)

"There shall not be any remaining of the house of Esau; for the LORD hath spoken it. . . . And the captivity of this host of the children of Israel [i.e., the whole twelve tribes] shall possess that of the Canaanites." The prophet lists some of the place names to make sure it is understood that possession is to be literal and not just symbolic.

C. The Consummation of It (v. 21)

"And saviors [deliverers] shall come up on mount Zion to judge the mount of Esau; and the kingdom shall be the LORD's." How did this judgment fall? Jeremiah distinctly prophesied that Edom would be subjected to Nebuchadnezzar: "Thus saith the LORD to me; Make thee bonds and yokes, and put them upon thy neck, and send them to the king of Edom, . . . by the hand of the messengers which come to Jerusalem unto Zedekiah king of Judah; and command them to say unto their masters, . . . And now have I given all these lands into the hand of Nebuchadnezzar the king of Babylon, my servant" (Jer. 27:2–4, 6).

Malachi, after the captivity, when upbraiding Israel for its lack of thankfulness to God, bears witness to the desolation of Edom: "I loved Jacob, and I hated Esau, and laid his mountains and his heritage waste for the dragons of the wilderness" (Mal. 1:2–3).

The occasion of this desolation was doubtless the march of Nebuchadnezzar against Egypt when, as Josephus tells us, he subdued Moab and Ammon. Edom lay on his way from Moab to Egypt. It is probable he found occasion against this petty state whose submission was needed to give him free passage between the Dead Sea and the Gulf of Akaba—that very access that Edom had denied to Israel when she came out of Egypt. Edom fell into the hands of Nebuchadnezzar and met with the usual lot of conquered peoples—plunder, death, captivity.

The closing verses of Obadiah leap the centuries to "the day of the LORD" (v. 15). The *day of the Lord* was already a well-known prophetic phrase. It is the day when God's judgment will fall upon all nations, the day in which God will judge all the heathen, especially for their outrages against the Jewish people.

Obadiah closes by depicting that day when Israel will be restored and when "the kingdom shall be the LORD's" (v. 21).

The key thought in the book of Obadiah is this: "As thou hast done, it shall be done unto thee." Thus the prophet announces one great rule of God's retribution, one law of His righteous judgment.

CHAPTER 37

EZEKIEL

The Exile Prophet

Like Jeremiah, Ezekiel was a priest as well as a prophet. He was one of ten thousand captives taken to Babylon by Nebuchadnezzar at the time Zedekiah, Judah's last king, began his miserable reign (2 Kings 24:11–20). Thus Ezekiel spent eleven years in Babylon before the final fall of Jerusalem. His exile home was Tel-abib (3:15) on the river Chebar, which flows into the Euphrates north of the city of Babylon. The colony of deported Jews at Tel-abib consisted probably of better class Jews.

Ezekiel gives dates for his visions thirteen times, and he reckons from the tragic year of his life when he was deported to Babylonia.[1] He began prophesying in the fifth year of his arrival in Babylon, six years before Jerusalem fell. That is why in the first twenty-four chapters there is so much about the coming judgment on Jerusalem.

Ezekiel's ministry to the exiles was a difficult one. Ominous blows had already fallen on Jerusalem. Two deportations had robbed the land of the flower of her nobility. Yet (as we saw in Jeremiah) instead of being humbled by these things, the Jews in Jerusalem sank ever lower in immorality, idolatry, and intrigue.

After the deportation of the ten thousand, to which group Ezekiel belonged, God gave the prophet Jeremiah the sign-message of good and evil figs (Jer. 24). The good figs were those who had been carried from Jerusalem; the bad figs were those who remained. Yet so insensitive had the people become to spiritual truth that the Jerusalem Jews regarded themselves as the good figs and their deported kin as the bad figs being punished for their sins. Those left behind in Jerusalem thought themselves heaven's favorites to whom the land was given for possession.

The Jerusalem Jews had no doubt that the Babylonian armies would return no more. It was in vain that Jeremiah told them that the city's fate was sealed.

The same mood prevailed among the exiles in Babylon. The majority clung to their idolatries and clung to the delusion that their captivity would soon be ended and that Jehovah could never allow Jerusalem, His chosen city, to be ruined. To these deluded exiles Jeremiah wrote a letter urging them to settle down in Babylonia and seek the good of that land (Jer. 29).

Clearly, there was a need for a prophet not just to the wicked remnant in Jerusalem but to the exiles as well. Ezekiel was God's man for this latter task. His first work was to attack the false hopes entertained by the exiles. He also had to set before them the stern logic of their history. His task was difficult and one that required much moral courage. Probably his task was eventually made easier by the fall of Jerusalem. His messages were not all of doom for, like Jeremiah, he had great visions of the after-days.

Ezekiel's messages were threefold in form: visions, sign-sermons, and direct prediction. In the first twenty-four chapters, the prophet's main burden is the impending doom of Jerusalem. In these chapters are ten sign-action sermons. Three times in these chapters we are told that Ezekiel was to be in a certain sense *dumb* until the fall of Jerusalem.

> I will make thy tongue cleave to the roof of thy mouth, and thou shalt be dumb. (3:26)

> In that day [when Jerusalem falls] shall thy mouth be opened . . . and thou shalt speak, and be no more dumb. (24:27; this word was given him four-and-a-half years after he became dumb)

> One that had escaped out of Jerusalem came unto me, saying: The city is smitten . . . and my mouth was opened, and I was no more dumb. (33:21–22)

The point is this: to a people whose ears were largely closed, God was largely mute. So deaf had they become to God's word that even the warning of judgment must be conveyed to them in the form of sign-actions, with the purpose of at least arousing their curiosity. That these sign-actions did cause them to ask questions we know from 12:9 and 24:19.

Ezekiel's last sign-sermon to his own people before his total dumbness for about a year and a half was the culminating tragic sign of his own wife's death (24:15–17). On the very day Jerusalem was invaded by the armies of Nebuchadnezzar, God revealed the fact of it to Ezekiel in far-off Babylonia. In the same chapter, also, his wife ("the desire of his eyes") dies. Ezekiel was instructed not to mourn his wife nor express his heartbreak in any way. He was to have his personal sorrow swallowed up in the bigger bereavement, namely, the ruin of Jerusalem and his nation.

The key thought in Ezekiel is summed up in a statement that occurs seventy times in the book: "They shall know that I am Jehovah."[2] The expression occurs thirty-four times in connection with God's punishment of Jerusalem, eighteen times in connection with God's judgment of the Gentile nations, and eighteen times in connection with the coming restoration of Israel. This is the heart of the book. The elect people of Israel, and all nations, must learn the truth that Jehovah is the one true God. They will learn it in a threefold way—by the *punishment* of Israel, by the *judgments* on the Gentile nations as predicted, and by the *restoration* of Israel in the last days.

The book begins with *heavenly glory* in the vision of the Cherubim. It ends with *earthly glory* in the vision of the new temple. In between is the story of the departing *glory* of the Shechinah cloud. The idea of glory runs through the whole prophecy.

According to Dr. Scofield, the major divisions in the book are indicated by the expression, *The hand of the Lord was upon me*, and the secondary divisions by the expression *And the word of the Lord came unto me*.

The book of Ezekiel is in three well-defined divisions. The prophet first addresses his own exiled people before the final siege of Jerusalem. At the time of the fall of Jerusalem he turns his attention to the Gentile nations and addresses seven of these. Then again he turns his attention to his own people and, with Judah fallen and her people in exile, comforts the captives with glowing accounts of the glory yet future.

I. The Fall of Judah (chaps. 1–24)
   Prophecies before the siege of Jerusalem
   A. Judgment Decided (chaps. 1–3)
   B. Judgment Demonstrated (chaps. 4–5)
      1. The Sign of the Tile (4:1–3)
      2. The Sign of the Prophet's Food (4:9–17)
      3. The Sign of the Prophet's Hair (chap. 5)
   C. Judgment Declared (chaps. 6–7)
   D. Judgment Demanded (chaps. 8–11)
   E. Judgment Decreed (chaps. 12–19)
   F. Judgment Deserved (chaps. 20–24)
II. The Foes of Judah (chaps. 25–32)
   Prophecies during the siege of Jerusalem
   A. Ammon (25:1–7)
   B. Moab (25:8–11)

C. Edom (25:12–14)
D. Philistia (25:15–17)
E. Tyre (26:1–28:19)
F. Sidon (28:20–26)
G. Egypt (chaps. 29–32)
III. The Future of Judah (chaps. 33–48)
Prophecies after the siege of Jerusalem
A. The Nation's Troubles Removed (chaps. 33–36)
B. The Nation's Tribes Regathered (chaps. 37–39)
C. The Nation's Temple Rebuilt (chaps. 40–47)
D. The Nation's Title Restored (chap. 48)

Ezekiel's prophetic utterances were in the forms of visions, signs, and direct prophecy. He also made use of parables, poems, and proverbs to convey the message of God.

I. THE FALL OF JUDAH (CHAPS. 1–24)

Prophecies before the fall of Jerusalem begin with Ezekiel among the exiles on the banks of the Chebar River, a tributary of the Euphrates, which joins that mighty river about forty-five miles north of Babylon.

A. Judgment Decided (chaps. 1–3)

First there was the *vision*. A strange and mysterious vision it was, too. It was a vision of the Cherubim, unearthly creatures connected with the throne of God, particularly as that throne is seen in its relationship to earth. First, the prophet saw a whirlwind and a great cloud and a twisting flame of fire all aglow with a lurid amber light descending from the north. The picture is that of a terrific, whirling thundercloud enwrapped in flaming fire. The symbols are those of judgment. The judgment was coming from the north, that is, from Babylon, via the north.

In the midst of the fire Ezekiel saw four living creatures emerge. They were the Cherubim (Ezekiel calls them so in chapter 10). They had four faces; like a man, symbolizing intelligence; like an ox, depicting strength in service; like a lion, suggesting majesty; like an eagle, typifying soaring splendor. They had four wings and four hands each, symbolic of capacity for service. They went wherever the Spirit was to go, indicating undeviating execution of the divine will. They looked like burning coals of fire, like the flashing of lightning, suggesting utter holiness and swiftness in action. Strength, service, intelligence, splendor, great capacity for service, total dedication to God's will, absolute holiness, unmatched speed. Such were the Cherubim!

Beside the Cherubim was another wonder, equally mystical and strange. Wheels! Wheels within wheels! The size and circle of the wheels was vast. They reached down to earth and touched the very heaven. Ezekiel says that their rims were so high, they were dreadful (v. 18). Each wheel was two wheels in one, one wheel bisecting the other as the rings on a child's gyroscope. The four living creatures (with their four faces) faced all four points of the compass simultaneously. The bisected wheels were such that they could move in all four directions without having to change direction. The wheels connected the Cherubim with earth, they whirled like lightning, and their awesome rims were full of eyes, looking simultaneously in all directions. They saw everything. Nothing could be hidden from them.

Finally, these terrible wheels were filled with the life of the living creatures, expressing by their movement the will of the living creatures themselves. Then, as the climax, he saw the *throne* and the *man*.

What does all this mean? Judgment was about to overtake the earth. But that judgment was but the expression of the government of God. Behind events on earth is the vast and only dimly apprehended machinery of the government of God. These fearful wheels are the wheels of divine government, and that government touches both earth and heaven. It is living, dynamic, awesome, omniscient, swift, terrible, and unimpeachable. The wheels connect events on earth with the Cherubim in heaven. The Cherubim, in turn, connect them with God. Ezekiel no sooner saw the vision than he fell on his face.

Next there was the voice. The first command was that Ezekiel get up. The prostrate soul, prepared by the fearful vision, was to adopt a new attitude. In order to deliver His message to mankind, God needs more than a man prostrate in worship. He needs a man erect in the attitude of alertness and attention, ready to do what God commands. "Son of man, stand upon thy feet, and I will speak unto thee" (2:1). Immediately the Spirit entered into the prophet. This was divine enabling for the great task of service.

It is of interest to note that Ezekiel is called "son of man" some ninety-two times in the book.[3] He was a mere human being; a natural descendant of Adam. In contrast with this, the Lord Jesus is called *the* Son of Man at least eighty-four times in the New Testament.[4] Jesus is the Second Man, the last Adam—the One who came to claim the dominion that Adam so recklessly threw away. Jesus is the true Son of Man.

Listening to the voice, Ezekiel learned that he was to prophesy the downfall of Jerusalem and he was told that his words would go unheeded. Yet he was to be a watchman to the house of Israel; he was to faithfully discharge his duties of warning the people so as to clear his own soul of guilt for their blood. Judgment was decided. Ezekiel was to sound the alarm but by both silence (he was to be dumb) and by speech.

At the beginning of his ministry his dumbness was declared. It was to be partial (3:26–27) and then removed (24:27—four and a half years later). He was told that upon the fall of Jerusalem his mouth would be opened (33:21–22) and he would be dumb no more.

What does all this mean? To a people who stopped their ears, God closed His mouth. The unbelief of the Jews was obdurate. As we have seen, those left behind in Jerusalem after the first deportation congratulated themselves as heaven's favorites, and in this they were encouraged by false prophets (Jer. 27:9). Those carried to Babylon remained infatuated with their idolatries and evil lifestyle, and they fondly imagined that their exile would be brief. To such people God would speak directly no more. Indeed, so infantile had they become regarding spiritual things, God had to resort to the sign language of the dumb to at least awaken some curiosity. Also this arresting form of communication was intended to impress the children who were the hope of the future.

B. Judgment Demonstrated (chaps. 4–5)
In these two chapters, Ezekiel was to act out by signs that Jerusalem was doomed.

1. The Sign of the Tile (4:1–3)
The prophet had to take a tile. The tile was two feet long and one foot wide. The Babylonians engraved figures and letters on such tiles, and many have been dug up in the ruins of ancient Babylon. On this tile Ezekiel was to draw the picture of Jerusalem, and around the city to depict the details of a siege. Then, between himself and the picture of the city, he was to place a flat piece of iron. The sign was to depict the siege of Jerusalem—the last terrible siege by Nebuchadnezzar. His listeners were to learn that it was far better to be a captive by the river Chebar than to be in Jerusalem in the days that lay ahead.

2. The Sign of the Prophet's Food (4:9–17)
The next sign was of the food Ezekiel was to eat during this period. It was the simplest, coarsest, and scantiest kind, and it was to be cooked with filth. For a Hebrew, and above all, for a priest, to have to do such a thing was to become ceremonially unclean. The sign was to indicate the straits to which the siege would reduce Jerusalem—the famine and destitution that would accompany it.

3. The Sign of the Prophet's Hair (chap. 5)
He was to take shavings from his head and face, and to divide the hair into three parts—a third was burned, a third smitten with the sword, and a third scattered to the wind. This sign was carefully explained to Ezekiel. The hair symbolized

Jerusalem. The treatment of it showed the method of God's judgment against Jerusalem. A third part of its peoples would die by pestilence and famine in the city; a third would die in battle; a third would be scattered to the winds.

C. Judgment Declared (chaps. 6–7)

In the next two chapters are two sermons by Ezekiel denouncing the nation for its sins—one attacking Jerusalem and the other attacking the land. "Son of man, set thy face toward the mountains of Israel, and prophesy against them. . . . Behold, I, even I, will bring a sword upon you" (6:2–3). "Son of man, thus saith the Lord GOD unto the land of Israel; An end, the end is come upon the four corners of the land" (7:2). This prophecy preceded by only a short time the final siege of Jerusalem. This siege ended in the burning of the city, the destruction of the temple, and the exiling of what remained of the people. The prophet announced the dissolution of the kingdom of Judah. Time had run out. There was to be no more waiting. Ezekiel was telling the exiles in Babylon what Jeremiah was telling the Jews in Jerusalem. The end had come. History is filled with illustrations of like sad endings to cities, kingdoms, and empires. Nor will any country be exempt from God's governmental dealings with those who reject and spurn His Word.

D. Judgment Demanded (chaps. 8–11)

In these chapters, Ezekiel was carried away in spirit to Jerusalem to see for himself, in ecstatic vision, exactly what was going on there that made judgment so irrevocable. He saw the awful idolatries being practiced in Jerusalem. In the inner court of the temple, the Jews had set up what God calls an "image of jealousy" (8:3). The prophet was instructed to dig a hole in the wall. He did so and saw, in his vision, all kinds of secret abominations before which the Jews were burning incense. So far had the Jews departed from any knowledge of God that they imagined God could not see what they were doing.

Yet again the prophet was bidden to look and he saw the women of Jerusalem weeping for Tammuz—an idol. Tammuz was supposed to be the son of the Queen of Heaven, who was supposed to have lost her son and later on to have found him again. The loss was celebrated by the pagans by a festival of weeping, the recovery by a festival of rejoicing. Then, as now in Romish and other religious circles, the favorite divinity of women was the virgin and her child. These Jewish women were not weeping in the temple for their sins, nor were they weeping to Jehovah; they were weeping for Tammuz.

But there was more yet. Worse still! He saw the high priest and the chiefs of the twenty-four courses of Aaron standing in the Holy Place with their backs to the Holy of Holies, worshipping the sun.

Now begins a solemn movement—chapter 9. The Shechinah glory rose from its resting place in the Holy of Holies and stood at the threshold of the temple (9:3). Ezekiel saw, in his vision, a man with a bottle of ink. This man was sent through Jerusalem to mark all those who mourned the abominations taking place in the city. Six men followed him, slaying without pity every man, woman, and child without the mark. This vision of judgment appalled Ezekiel so that he fell on his face in intercession. He was told, however, that the sin of the nation was so great that judgment was demanded and irrevocable.

Slowly, reluctantly, step by step, the Shechinah began to depart from Jerusalem. First it left the Most Holy Place (8:4) to take up its stand at the threshold of the temple (9:3); then it rose above the threshold (10:4); then it retired to the Eastern Gate (11:23). Finally, it moved to the mountain on the east side of the city (11:23). Thus did God reluctantly leave His city and His temple, not to return until a future day. The vision over, Ezekiel told the captives in Babylon what was taking place in Jerusalem.

E. Judgment Decreed (chaps. 12–19)

There followed more signs and sermons. The people had to learn that the decree of judgment had gone forth and must inevitably run its terrible course.

First there was the sign of the removal (12:1–16). The prophet had to make up a bundle as for a journey and act as though he were an exile going into captivity. The bundle was to be made up during the daytime, after which he was to dig a passage through the wall that surrounded his house. At nighttime he was to disguise his face and creep through the hole with his bundle and pretend to go into exile. The sign was necessary because of the unbelief of the captives. False prophets were promising speedy restoration for them and victory for King Zedekiah in Jerusalem. The prophet play-acted the flight of Zedekiah exactly as it happened five years later.

Coupled with this was another sign—the prophet was commanded to eat his food with outward signs of fear. It was to endorse the truth that terror was coming to Jerusalem.

So, then, with signs, with blunt messages, with graphic figures of speech and with laments, Ezekiel continued to foretell the imminent woes to come upon Jerusalem.

One of the most graphic statements he made is in chapter 14. The prophet was told by God that so great was the wickedness of the Jews that even though *Noah, Daniel,* and *Job* were in Jerusalem they would deliver nobody but themselves (14:14, 20). Daniel was a fellow captive in Babylon with Ezekiel. His position at the court, his piety, his personal testimony were already proverbial. God has a special word of commendation for each of these men. *Noah* was "perfect in his generations" (Gen. 6:9), and he was used of God to deliver his family from wrath. *Daniel* is called "greatly beloved" (Dan. 9:23). *Job* justified God's estimate of him: "there is none like him in [all] the earth" (Job 1:8).

F. Judgment Deserved (chaps. 20–24)

In this section is a series of prophecies showing that God was absolutely righteous in His purpose of judging Jerusalem. These five chapters contain Ezekiel's final messages before the fall of Jerusalem.

False prophets among the captives were at this time foretelling the speedy restoration of the exiles to Palestine. Some of the elders of the people came to Ezekiel and desired him to give the same voice of comfort. He refused. Instead he gave five proofs from history of Israel's incurable devotion to any other god than Jehovah:

1. In Egypt (20:5–9)
2. The fathers in the wilderness (vv. 10–17)
3. The children in the wilderness (vv. 18–26)
4. The people in the land (vv. 27–29)
5. Now the people in exile (vv. 30–38)

It is no wonder that judgment was deserved. These five proofs were followed by four more in Israel's later history:

1. After the return from the captivity
2. Under the ministry of John the Baptist
3. During the ministry of the Lord Himself
4. During the period covered by the book of Acts

During these nine periods of appeal with alternating mercy and judgment, the nation persisted in its rejection of God. It is no wonder that the Jew has been scattered for two thousand years.

One of the closing five messages concerned Samaria and Jerusalem under the figure of two shameless women, each utterly lewd, filthy, and vile, but with Jerusalem far exceeding the spiritual infidelity and harlotry of Samaria (chap. 23).

The last message is in chapter 24. In this chapter, the date of which burned its way into Ezekiel's mind and heart, the armies of Nebuchadnezzar encompassed Jerusalem. It was the beginning of the end. That very day, at eventide, Ezekiel's wife, "the joy of his heart," died, and God revealed to Ezekiel, in Babylon, the fact that Jerusalem was now under siege. He was forbidden by God to show any emotion over the death of his wife. His own sorrow was to be eclipsed by a greater sorrow—the ruin of Jerusalem and Judea.

II. THE FOES OF JUDAH (CHAPS. 25–32)

Ezekiel prophesied during the siege of Jerusalem, addressing other nations that needed attention. A glance at the map will show that the prophet dealt first with the nations on the east (Ammon, Moab, and Edom), then with those on the west (Philistia, Tyre, and Sidon), and finally with the nation to the south (Egypt).

The first four cities are Ammon, Moab, Edom, and Philistia. Ammon had mocked the people of God in the day of their desolation. Moab had rejoiced in the degradation of Judah. Edom had been brutal in her treatment of Judah. Philistia had taken vengeance with undying enmity.

The next two are the twin cities of Tyre and Sidon. Tyre, one of the most important cities of antiquity, is the subject of a long prophecy. It was wealthy and powerful, a Phoenician city whose colony, Carthage, on the north coast of Africa, almost conquered Rome in later years. One of the most remarkable prophecies in the Bible is found in this section—a prophecy concerning the King of Tyre, the imagery of which makes it quite evident that the personal history of the Devil himself is being described. The prophet foretold for this proud, prosperous, and powerful city-state of Tyre utter and complete extinction. The prophecy was literally fulfilled, in part by Nebuchadnezzar and then later in full and literal detail by Alexander the Great.

Sidon was a twin city on the Phoenician coast. Whereas complete overthrow and eventual extinction was foretold for Tyre, Ezekiel predicted for Sidon suffering but not extinction. The city, founded by a son of Canaan (Gen. 10:15), was famous for its idolatry. Jezebel was a Sidonian, and she it was who introduced the lustful rites of Sidonian religion into Israel.

Finally, Ezekiel turned his attention to Egypt. He delivered a series of six prophecies against this nation, one of the most remarkable nations of antiquity. Pharaoh was denounced for his pride in imagining that the river Nile, the lifeline of Egypt, the longest river on earth, was his own creation. He was told that Egypt would be given to Nebuchadnezzar as payment for the overthrow of Tyre. The series of prophecies climaxed in a funeral dirge for Pharaoh (chap. 32). The word of the Lord came to the prophet, who spoke of the descent of Pharaoh into hades, accompanied by his slaughtered hosts. As he passed into the underworld, he found himself in the company of the slain multitudes of Asshur and Elam, of Meshech and Tubal, of Edom and Sidon. Ezekiel said, "Pharaoh shall see them, and shall be comforted" (v. 31). It is an appalling concept. The only comfort that can come to him is the sense of the justice of God—all who have been guilty of abomination are treated alike.

Throughout all these prophecies to Judah's foes is one refrain. It is repeated to every one of them—sometimes more than once: "Ye shall know that I am the Lord." Here is the one purpose of God in His dealings with these nations. Those who fail to find Him when He reveals Himself in mercy will find Him when He reveals Himself in judgment. But in the end they will all know Him.

III. THE FUTURE OF JUDAH (CHAPS. 33–48)

The first prophecy in the series after the siege of Jerusalem was given to Ezekiel on the evening before the arrival of a messenger from Jerusalem announcing the fall of the city (33:21). This news liberated Ezekiel from the silence that had been enjoined on him (24:15–27), and he was now permitted to resume his spoken ministry to the exiles.

A. The Nation's Troubles Removed (chaps. 33–36)

His preparation for the coming of the messenger is to hear again the voice of the Lord, which reminded him that he is a watchman to the house of Israel (33:7). It is the same message he had received at the beginning of his ministry (3:17). Ezekiel is to tell the people that God has no pleasure in the death of the wicked. His desire is that the wicked man should turn from his wicked way and live (33:11).

Next came a message denouncing the false shepherds, and promising that one day God would send David, the great shepherd-king, back to Israel: "And I will set up one shepherd over them, and he shall feed them, even my servant David; he shall feed them, and he shall be their shepherd. And I the LORD will be their God, and my servant David a prince among them; I the LORD hath spoken it" (34:23–24).

The land, too, would ultimately be restored to its original bounty: "O mountains of Israel, ye shall shoot forth your branches, and yield your fruit to my people of Israel; for they are at hand to come. For, behold, I am for you, and I will turn unto you, and ye shall be tilled and sown: And I will multiply men upon you . . . and the cities shall be inhabited, and the wastes shall be builded: And I will multiply upon you man and beast . . . and I will . . . do better unto you than at your beginnings: and ye shall know that I am the LORD" (36:8–11). It is a great prophecy looking forward to the day when the land of Israel will be like the garden of Eden (v. 35). The Jews today are well on the way to making these prophecies leap to life.

B. The Nation's Tribes Regathered (chaps. 37–39)

Unquestionably, for us today, these chapters are the most interesting and fascinating in the whole book. They deal with the valley of dry bones, with two sticks, and with the invasion of the land by Gog and Magog. First, the nation of Israel will have its *national sovereignty* restored. It will be recognized again as a living nation. Its scattered people will be regathered to the land, and the old division of the nation into two will be a thing of the past. It will be a single, united nation. We are seeing this part of the prophecy fulfilled today.

Next, the nation will have its *national security* restored. Then, when the time is ripe, a great northern power, allied with certain European, Middle East, and African nations, will swoop down to wipe out Israel. The rise of Russia and her satellites, together with her growing influence in the Middle East, shows that the fulfilling of these predictions is to take place soon. The northern invader will come to a terrible end on the mountains of Israel.[5]

C. The Nation's Temple Rebuilt (chaps. 40–47)

These chapters in the prophecy foretell the building of the millennial temple. The visions were given to Ezekiel fourteen years after the sack of Jerusalem. His description of the new temple begins with the outer courts and the inner courts; then he describes the temple itself. He describes it first from the outside, detailing the actual temple with its Holy Place and the Holy of Holies. Then the side chambers and the separate buildings are described. Finally, he gives the dimensions and a description of the ornamental woodwork.

D. The Nation's Title Restored (chap. 48)

The temple has been rebuilt. The Shechinah glory has returned (43:2–6). Rivers of blessing flow from the temple. The tribes are regathered and set in the land in order around the sanctuary. The New Jerusalem is there with its twelve gates. The nation at last fulfills the role that God had planned for it from the very beginning. Its title is restored.

The last words of Ezekiel ring on and will continue to ring until Jesus comes again to make his visions a reality. Looking at the city and at the temple and at the nation he cries, "The name of the city from that day shall be, The Lord is there." And who can imagine what it will be for this poor old world when all nations look toward Jerusalem and see *the Lord is there!*

CHAPTER 38

DANIEL

The Prophet Greatly Beloved

Daniel was both a saint and a seer, and his book is both practical and prophetical. The courage, conviction, and commitment of Daniel and his friends, as recorded in the first half of the book, teach valuable lessons. Those who would "know their God . . . and do exploits" (11:32) in days of testing and trial should spend much time in the good company of these choice young men.

Since much of Daniel's prophecy has now been fulfilled in history, and that in minute detail, the book is especially valuable. It not only confounds the critics but it confirms the faith of the believer. It is little wonder, therefore, that the book of Daniel has been a storm center of criticism. The battle has been waged around four chief issues: the miracles, the predictions, the language, and the history. Today, archaeology and the philological studies by men like Dr. Robert Dick Wilson have done much to refute the claims of the critics. Professor Wilson's claim is "that the time at which any document of length, and often even of small compass, was written can generally be determined by the character of its vocabulary, and especially by the foreign words which are embedded in it."[1]

The book of Daniel contains three Greek words, and the critics claim that this proves the book could not have been written as early as 533 B.C. as is maintained. They would place it at least during the reign of Antiochus Epiphanes, when the majority of its most remarkable predictions had already been fulfilled. The three Greek words, however, refer to musical instruments. There is no reason why a world monarch like Nebuchadnezzar could not have imported Greek instruments into Babylonia. Actually Daniel's use of foreign words is an incidental proof of his presence at a royal court that was constantly being visited by emissaries from other lands. Moreover, if the book had been written in the Greek period of Antiochus, the author would not have simply inserted three Greek words (and these restricted to musical instruments) but his book would have incorporated many Greek words, expressions, and ideas.

Daniel was an actual historical person famed even in Ezekiel's day for his piety. Ezekiel mentioned Daniel by name three times and regarded him as such an outstanding person as to link his name with those of Noah and Job. The Lord Jesus mentioned Daniel by name, looked upon him as a historical person, and regarded his prophecies as inspired. He identified Himself with the Son of Man of Daniel's vision (cf. Dan. 7:13 with Matt. 16:13; 26:64), and in Matthew 24:15 (Mark 13:14), He referred to Daniel 8:13; 9:27; 11:31; 12:11. In Matthew 24:30; 26:64; Mark 14:62; Luke 22:69, the Lord referred to Daniel 7:13, and in Matthew 24:15–17, He referred to Daniel 12:1. For the believer, this settles the issue of Daniel's historical existence.

Daniel was deported from Judah in 605 B.C., began his ministry three years later, and lived in Babylon through the entire period of the seventy-year captivity. He was probably of royal descent, and was good-looking, intelligent, courageous, and devout. He was a contemporary of Jeremiah, Habakkuk, Ezekiel, and possibly Obadiah.

Daniel lived in Babylon during the reigns of the following Babylonian and Medo-Persian kings: Nabopolassar, Nebuchadnezzar, Evil-Merodach, Neriglassar, Labash Marduk, Nabonidus, and Belshazzar (all Babylonians), Darius the Mede, and Cyrus the Persian.

Daniel lived to a ripe old age. The following chart shows his age when he wrote the various chapters of his book:

CHAPTER	DANIEL'S AGE
1	19
2	22
3	?
4	?
5	87
6	88
7	84
8	87
9	88
10	92
11	92
12	92

The book of Daniel is in two parts—one part largely historical and the other largely prophetical. It was written chiefly in two languages—Aramaic and Hebrew.

 I. Daniel and His Personal Friends (chaps. 1–6)
    Key Thought: Personal Victory
    A. Times of Testing (chaps. 1–3)
       1. The Challenge of a Believer's Walk (chap. 1)
       The Matter of the King's Meat
       2. The Challenge of a Believer's Witness (chap. 2)
       The Dilemma of the King's Dream
       3. The Challenge of a Believer's Worship (chap. 3)
       The Implications of the King's Image
    B. Times of Triumph (chaps. 4–6)
       1. The Triumph of Truth (chaps. 4–5)
          a. Before Babylon's First World Emperor—Boasting Rebuked: The Conversion of Nebuchadnezzar (chap. 4)
          b. Before Babylon's Final World Emperor—Blasphemy Rebuked: The Condemnation of Belshazzar (chap. 5)
       2. The Triumph of Trust (chap. 6)
       The Den of Lions
 II. Daniel and His People's Future (chaps. 7–12)
    Key Thought: Prophetic Vision
    A. The Character of the Future (chaps. 7–8)
       1. The Nature of the Facts (chap. 7)
       Four Beasts: Babylon, Persia, Greece, Rome
       2. The Narrowing of the Focus (chap. 8)
       Two Beasts: Persia and Greece
    B. The Control of the Future (chaps. 9–10)
       1. Daniel's Vision (chap. 9)
          a. He Believes an Old Prophecy: The Prophecy of the Seventy Years (9:1–23)
          b. He Receives a New Prophecy: The Prophecy of the Seventy "Weeks" (9:24–27)
       2. Daniel's Visitor (chap. 10)
          a. The Herald Angel
          b. The Hindering Angels
          c. The Helping Angel
    C. The Course of the Future (chap. 11)
       1. The Coming of the Typical Antichrist (11:1–35)
       2. The Coming of the True Antichrist (11:36–45)

D. The Climax of the Future (chap. 12)
  1. The Turmoil Is Seen (12:1–4)
  2. The Tribulation Is Sure (12:5–7)
  3. The Truth Is Sealed (12:8–10)
  4. The Times Are Set (12:11–13)

Daniel carefully dates his various prophecies and writings. It is helpful to see their relationship to the kings of Babylon and Persia under whom he lived and attained such prominence.

THE DATING OF DANIEL'S PROPHECIES			
Historical		**Prophetical**	
Chapters	*Kings*	*Chapters*	*Kings*
1–4	Nebuchadnezzar	7–8	Belshazzar
5	Belshazzar	9	Darius
6	Darius	10–12	Cyrus

I. Daniel and His Personal Friends (chaps. 1–6)

A. Times of Testing (chaps. 1–3)

Daniel and his friends were deported to Babylon at the time of Nebuchadnezzar's first invasion of Judah in 605 B.C. In that year Pharaoh-Necho of Egypt marched east against Babylon. He was overwhelmingly defeated at Carchemish on the west bank of the Euphrates as had been foretold by Jeremiah (46:1–26). The defeat of the Egyptians made Nebuchadnezzar master of the world. He pursued Necho to Egypt and, having completely conquered that land, invaded Judah and besieged Jerusalem in the third year of Jehoiakim. Jehoiakim was defeated and put in fetters. Later he was released and restored, as a puppet of Babylon, to the throne. Nebuchadnezzar returned to Babylon carrying with him treasure from the plundered temple and the cream of Judean nobility, including young Daniel. In Babylon, Daniel and his friends ran into some severe tests.

1. The Challenge of a Believer's Walk (chap. 1)

God always proves His man before He promotes His man. The four Hebrew captives, Daniel, Hananiah, Mishael, and Azariah, were of royal blood—all descended from godly King Hezekiah. Nebuchadnezzar's first act was to change their names. They were given names that glorified the false gods of Babylon, in a deliberate attempt to wean them away from their ancestral faith and get them to adopt the religion and habits of the heathen nation where they were to spend their future.

Next they were called upon to eat meat from the king's table, and here was the test. The dishes would be savory and appetizing—tempting indeed to the carnal man, but it was ceremonially unclean (Lev. 11:1–47).

At the outset of a spiritual venture, God brings into the life of the believer a crisis, a cross, and a crown. The crisis involves the mortgaging of some strict demand of the faith. The cross involves the mortifying of some strong desire of the flesh. The crown involves the maturing of some sovereign design of the Father. Daniel, tested along all three lines, triumphed gloriously.

2. The Challenge of a Believer's Witness (chap. 2)

Nebuchadnezzar had a dream. The next morning he asserted that he had forgotten it and put to the test the claim of the Babylonian soothsayers that they were able to divine the future. He summoned his magicians, astrologers, sorcerers, and Chaldeans and ordered them to tell him his dream.[2] His rage knew no bounds when they told him he was demanding the impossible. He decided they were charlatans and ordered their extermination. Daniel and his friends, being numbered among the wise men of Babylon, were in instant peril.

Now comes the challenge to their witness. Being put to the test, Daniel spoke out boldly: "Give me time and I will show the king the interpretation" (see v. 16). During the night, God gave Daniel the same vision He had given to Nebuchadnezzar. Daniel was able to recount the dream to the king and to give him its interpretation. The king had seen an image with a head of gold, breast and arms of silver, belly and thighs of brass, legs of iron, feet of a mixture of iron and clay, and having ten toes. The feet of the image were smitten by a "stone cut without hands" (see v. 34), which resulted in the dissolution of the whole and its replacement by the stone, which then became a great mountain filling the whole earth. The following chart shows the deterioration in the image as the vision progresses from beginning to end.

			Specific Gravity[3]
Head	Gold	Intellect	19.3
Breast and Arms	Silver	Emotions	10.51
Belly and Thighs	Brass	Digestion	8.5
Legs	Iron		7.6
Feet	Iron/Clay	Walk in dust	1.9

Also, there is another deterioration. The image begins first with the head, the seat of the intellect; then with the breast, the seat of the vital organs; then with the belly, the seat of the digestion; finally with the feet, which walk in the dust.

Not only was there deterioration as the vision unfolded—the image was top heavy from the start.

The interpretation of the dream concerned the course of Gentile world empire beginning with Babylon. Nebuchadnezzar was "the head of gold" (v. 38) an absolute monarch to whom God gave the right to rule the earth. With him the "times of the Gentiles" began. None of the kings who followed him on the throne of Babylon amounted to much. One was assassinated, one was killed in battle, and one was an imbecile.

The two arms of the image showed that the kingdom that would follow the Babylonian era would be a dual kingdom (the Medo-Persian Empire), the left arm of the image signifying the weaker kingdom of Media. Cyrus, the first of the Persian emperors, was forenamed in Isaiah 44:28; 45:1–4, about 175 years before Cyrus's birth. After conquering Babylon in 538 B.C., he assigned the governorship of Babylon to his uncle Darius, king of Media, and went off to finish his campaigns. During the Persian era the Babylonian captivity was ended.

In Nebuchadnezzar's dream the belly and thighs were of brass (copper), which signified the Greek Empire, although this is passed over very quickly. In later revelations, God had much to say about the Grecian era. Brass is inferior to silver; the brilliant campaigns of Alexander the Great did not profit him much. He died a young man, and his empire was carved up among four of his generals.

The legs of iron symbolized the Roman Empire, though this empire is not specifically named in Daniel. The image had two legs, symbolizing the division of the Roman Empire into two empires ruled respectively from Rome and Constantinople. The last ten-kingdom stage of Roman world empire, partly weak, partly strong, is seen in the iron and clay of the ten toes. The Roman Empire is described in more detail later in this current chapter.

The end of it all was sudden and calamitous. The "stone" is a figure of the Lord Jesus, and the mountain filling the earth a picture of Christ's coming millennial reign over all the earth—an empire to be suddenly and forcefully imposed by heaven on mankind. All the other kingdoms were literal—Christ's will be, too.

3. The Challenge of a Believer's Worship (chap. 3)

Everything Nebuchadnezzar did was big. The image he erected was no exception—away out on the Plain of Dura and towering ninety feet toward the sky. In places it was nine feet wide. Made of gold, in the brilliant eastern sunshine it must have dazzled every eye.

Presumably, Nebuchadnezzar was inspired to make this image by his dream.

World Empires	THE RISE AND FALL OF GENTILE WORLD EMPIRES		
	Nebuchadnezzar's Dream	Daniel's Dreams	
	Daniel 2:31–45	Daniel 7:1–28	Daniel 8:1–27
Babylonian	Head of gold	Lion	
Medo-Persian	Breast and arms of silver	Bear	Ram
Grecian	Belly and thighs of brass	Leopard	He-goat
Roman	Legs of iron	The beast with ten horns	
Antichrist's	Ten toes of iron and clay		
Christ's	The stone cut out without hands		

He saw Gentile world empire and particularly his part in it as something to be put on a pedestal and worshipped. Not content with being the head of gold, he determined his image would be of gold from top to bottom. The biblical description of the dimensions of the image are significant—sixty cubits by six cubits.

It is stamped, then, with the number 6—the number of man. The first king of Babylon's image foreshadowed the image that will be erected in a coming day by the Antichrist, the last king of the "times of the Gentiles." We are moving rapidly today toward the final deification of man.

Nebuchadnezzar demanded that everyone worship his image, and thus tried to enforce a universal "state religion." When his image was completed, leading men from all parts of his empire were summoned to Babylon and amassed on the Plain of Dura to render public homage to the colossal idol. Among them were Shadrach, Meshach, and Abednego.

The day for the dedication of the image arrived. The king's instructions were clear. A vast band had been prepared to sound the signal for all to prostrate themselves, and a terrible furnace was prepared for anyone daring not to worship the image. As all others fell flat on the ground, three figures could be seen standing straight and tall—Shadrach, Meshach, and Abednego. They were victorious in this challenge to their worship.

Nebuchadnezzar was angry but he gave them a second chance. What a noble answer he received to his sneering, "Who is that God that shall deliver you out of my hands?" The three young Hebrews replied, "If it be so, our God whom we serve is able to deliver us from the burning fiery furnace, and he *will* deliver us out of thine hand, O King. But *if not*, be it known unto thee, O King, that we will *not* serve thy gods, nor worship the golden image which thou hast set up" (3:16–18). And God did deliver them in a way that made a deep impression on the king.

B. Times of Triumph (chaps. 4–6)

1. The Triumph of Truth (chaps. 4–5)

a. Before Babylon's First World Emperor—Boasting Rebuked: The Conversion of Nebuchadnezzar (chap. 4)

Chapter 4 is a Babylonian state document that recounts the conversion of Nebuchadnezzar. In chapter 2, after the interpretation of his dream, Nebuchadnezzar made this statement: "Of a truth it is, that your God is a God of gods, and a Lord of kings, and a revealer of secrets, seeing thou couldest reveal this secret" (v. 47).

In chapter 3, after the deliverance of Shadrach, Meshach, and Abednego from the fiery furnace and the vision of the Son of God in the flames, he said this: "Blessed be the God of Shadrach, Meshach, and Abed-nego, who hath sent his angel, and delivered his servants that trusted in him, and have changed the king's word, and yielded their bodies, that they might not serve nor worship any god, except their own God. Therefore I make a decree, That every people, nation, and language, which speak any thing amiss against the God of Shadrach, Meshach, and Abed-nego, shall be cut in pieces, and their houses shall be made a dunghill: because there is no other God that can deliver after this sort" (vv. 28–29).

In this chapter, God so dealt with Nebuchadnezzar that he was brought into a living relationship with Him. The opening salutation to the whole world sounds almost like a Pauline epistle! "Nebuchadnezzar the king, unto all people, nations, and languages, that dwell in all the earth; Peace be multiplied to you" (v. 1).

First Nebuchadnezzar had a dream, which his wise men could not interpret. Then came Daniel, who had the sad and dangerous task of telling the king that he was going to become temporarily insane because of his pride. "Break off thy sins by righteousness, and thine iniquities by showing mercy to the poor," he said (v. 27). Bold words indeed to speak to such a one as Nebuchadnezzar.

Time passed. Then one day the king walked in the palace of the kingdom of Babylon. His heart was lifted up with pride. He said, "Is not this great Babylon that I have built?"[4] Instantly God smote him.

The type of insanity that overcame the king is called lycanthropy, in which the sufferer imagines he is some sort of a beast. The king imagined he was an ox and even took on some of the characteristics of this beast for seven years, after which his sanity and kingdom were finally restored according to the prophecy. When he was recovered, Nebuchadnezzar became a true convert to Jehovah and issued his testimony in this state document, which ends with these remarkable words:

> And at the end of the days I Nebuchadnezzar lifted up mine eyes unto heaven, and mine understanding returned unto me, and I blessed the most High, and I praised and honored him that liveth for ever, whose dominion is an everlasting dominion, and his kingdom is from generation to generation: and all the inhabitants of the earth are reputed as nothing: . . . and none can stay his hand, or say unto him, What doest thou? . . . Now I Nebuchadnezzar praise and extol and honor the King of heaven, all whose works are truth, and his ways judgment: and those that walk in pride he is able to abase. (4:34–37)

b. Before Babylon's Final World Emperor—Blasphemy Rebuked: The Condemnation of Belshazzar (chap. 5)

Daniel was able to witness to Nebuchadnezzar, Belshazzar, and Darius. The humbling of Nebuchadnezzar, foretold by Daniel, led to the conversion of this king, who immediately issued a most remarkable document in which he bore witness to his faith in the living God. Unlike Nebuchadnezzar, Belshazzar refused to be humbled when he came to power. Though terribly frightened when his blasphemous feast was interrupted by God, whose hand wrote its message of doom on the palace wall, this dissolute king refused to repent.

Belshazzar's feast was given in a spirit of contempt and defiance. At the time, the city of Babylon was in a state of siege. The armies of the Medes and Persians were encamped outside its walls, but Belshazzar felt secure. He considered his city to be impregnable. His feast was at its height when the king commanded they bring the golden vessels from the treasury that Nebuchadnezzar had looted from the temple of the Lord in Jerusalem. He wanted to toast the idols of Babylon in these sacred and consecrated cups as an expression of contempt for the God of the Jewish people.

"In the same hour came forth fingers of a man's hand, and wrote over against the candlestick upon the plaster of the wall of the king's palace: and the king saw the part of the hand that wrote" (5:5). Such a message conveyed by such a means at such an hour struck Belshazzar with terror. He summoned his soothsayers with promises of vast reward if they would interpret the mysterious message to him.

Eventually Daniel was summoned (now 87 years of age) and, scorning the king's gifts, fearless of his wrath, and contemptuous of his promises, he turned his eye on the wall and then on the king. Instead of expounding the handwritten message of God, he first preached Belshazzar a sermon and told him that he was "without excuse" (Rom. 1:20) because of the example of Nebuchadnezzar. Then he read out to the king the message of doom.

It was fitting that Belshazzar's doom be read out to him by a Jew, for it was the Jew's God he had set at naught with his sacrilege. If Belshazzar continued on the throne, there was little chance of the return of the Jews and the sacred vessels to Jerusalem, according to prophecy, in two years' time. "MENE, MENE, TEKEL, UPHARSIN [PERES]," ran the cryptic message. "God hath numbered thy kingdom, and finished it. . . . Thou art weighed in the balances, and art found wanting. . . . Thy kingdom is divided, and given to the Medes and Persians" (vv. 25–28).

"That night was Belshazzar the king of the Chaldeans slain" (v. 30). The Persians, realizing the futility of trying to take Babylon by siege, had resorted to strategy. They diverted the waters of the Euphrates and marched into the city on the riverbed. Cyrus the Persian took the kingdom and committed its governorship to his uncle Darius, king of Media. Thus, world empire passed out of Hametic and Semitic hands into the hands of a Japhetic race, where it has been ever since and where it will remain until it falls into the hands of the Antichrist, the last of the Caesars and the last Gentile king to oppress Jerusalem.

2. The Triumph of Trust (chap. 6)

This chapter introduces us to the second world empire of Nebuchadnezzar's dream—the Medo-Persian Empire, which lasted for nearly seventy years. Darius appointed Daniel to a high post in the kingdom despite his now being eighty-eight years of age. His appointment stirred the envy of the other ministers of state, and they plotted his downfall. They based their plan to trap Daniel on his being devoted to his God and on the king's not being an absolute monarch. He was subject to the unanimous will of his counselors, and once a decree was signed, he could not revoke it.

They proposed that for a period of thirty days no one be permitted to ask any petition of any god or man save the king, on penalty of death in the den of lions. The plot succeeded because Daniel scorned to pray to his God in secret. So the trap was sprung, not to the dismay of Daniel but of Darius. He labored to the setting sun to save his beloved counselor and then spent a sleepless night thinking of Daniel in the lion's den. In the morning he found that Daniel's God was "mighty to save" (see Zeph. 3:17). The wicked counselors and their families were cast instead to the lions, and Darius issued a decree:

Unto all people, nations, and languages, that dwell in all the earth; Peace be multiplied unto you. I make a decree, That in every dominion of my kingdom men tremble and fear before the God of Daniel: for he is the living God, and steadfast for ever, and his kingdom that which shall not be destroyed, and his dominion shall be even unto the end. He delivereth and rescueth, and he worketh signs and wonders in heaven and in earth, who hath delivered Daniel from the power of the lions. (6:25–27)

These decrees of Nebuchadnezzar and Darius show how, during Israel's dispersal during the first captivity, light came upon the Gentiles.

Daniel continued and "prospered in the reign of Darius, and in the reign of Cyrus the Persian" (6:28). Thus he became chief adviser to the first two monarchs (Darius the *Mede* and Cyrus the *Persian*) of the dual second world empire. There can be little doubt that behind the books of Ezra and Nehemiah, with their story of the returned remnant, is the influence in the Persian Empire of Daniel. Perhaps Daniel was the one who showed to Cyrus his name written aforetime in Isaiah 44:28–45:4.

II. DANIEL AND HIS PEOPLE'S FUTURE (CHAPS. 7–12)

A. The Character of the Future (chaps. 7–8)

These two chapters detail visions given to Daniel during the reign of Belshazzar. For about twenty-three years since the death of Nebuchadnezzar, Daniel had been in retirement. It is easy to suppose that much of his time had been spent in studying the Scriptures and in earnest seeking of the face of God to learn what the future held for Israel. In chapter 7 we have the *nature of the facts* concerning the future and then in chapter 8 we have a *narrowing of the focus*, as the Spirit of God gives more detail concerning one part of the vision in chapter 7.

1. The Nature of the Facts (chap. 7)

The vision of this chapter is of world empire. It is depicted under the imagery of four wild beasts, and it covers much the same ground as Nebuchadnezzar's dream of the image in chapter 2. Nebuchadnezzar saw world empire from the standpoint of a Gentile conqueror, as something to be admired, put on a pedestal, and glorified. God sees Gentile misrule of the earth as bestial. As a "prophetic philosophy of history"[5] the book of Daniel brings into sharp focus the contrast between the godless empires of earth and the coming kingdom of God. Nowhere is this contrast more evident than in the vision of the four beasts of Daniel 7.

The first beast represented Babylon. It was like a lion with eagle's wings, suggesting Babylon's supremacy over the nations. The wings were plucked, symbolizing the fact that Nebuchadnezzar lost his lust for conquest. Then it was lifted up and walked on two feet as a man and was given a man's heart. This suggests the conversion of Nebuchadnezzar.

The second beast represented Medo-Persia. It was like a bear raised up on one side. Medo-Persia was ponderous in its movements, and its victories were gained laboriously and at great expense in human life. The bear had three ribs in its mouth, suggesting the kingdoms of Lydia, Babylon, and Egypt, which formed a futile triple alliance to block the Medo-Persian power. It was raised up on one side reminding us that in the Medo-Persian alliance, Persia was the dominant power.

The third beast was like a leopard with four heads and four wings, and it represented Greece. The leopard is the symbol of grace and power, and the wings suggest the speed with which Alexander the Great brought the world to his feet. The four heads symbolize the four kingdoms into which Alexander's kingdom was afterward divided—Thrace, Macedonia, Syria, and Egypt. Daniel did not fully understand this vision and had to wait for a couple of years until the vision of the next chapter made it clear.

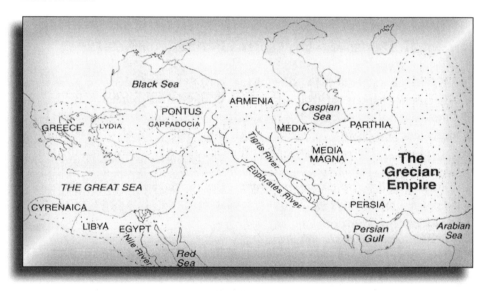

The fourth beast was like no other beast ever seen on earth. It represented Rome. It was hideous to behold. It had iron teeth and ten horns, symbolizing the tenacity of Roman conquest and the end-time division of the empire into ten parts. Daniel saw a little horn spring up among the ten, then saw that this strange horn had the eyes of a man and a mouth speaking great things.

Before Daniel could solve the mystery of this little horn, he received another vision—the vision of the Ancient of Days. As Daniel looked, the thrones were all

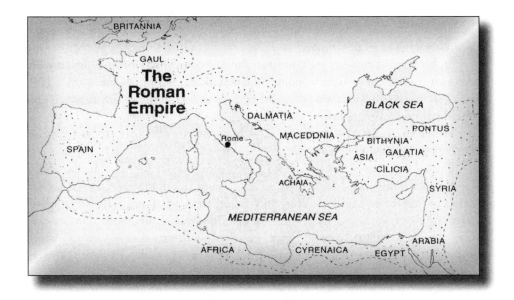

cast down, and the throne of God appeared with the Ancient of Days sitting upon it. The fourth beast was slain and his body destroyed. All empire was handed over to the Son of Man.

Daniel was then told what these visions signified but he was particularly anxious to know the significance of the fourth beast. At this point we need to recognize that, when revealing prophetic truth, the Holy Spirit sometimes ignores certain periods of time and leaps over the centuries without comment. Daniel's vision of the fourth beast represents the Roman Empire as it was in history and the Roman Empire as it will be in a coming day when it will be reconstituted as the last world empire at the end of the age.

Daniel was told that when the final stage of world empire arrived, a person (symbolized by the little horn and known as the *Antichrist*) would come. He would blaspheme God and seek to "wear out the saints of the most High." His day of supreme power would last "a time and times and the dividing of time," in other words, three and a half years (v. 25).

2. *The Narrowing of the Focus (chap. 8)*

In this chapter Daniel receives further light on the coming empires of Persia (the last of the eastern Asiatic empires) and Greece (the first of the western European empires). In chapter 7 these empires were depicted as a bear and a leopard. In chapter 8 they are seen as a ram and a he-goat.

This vision was given in the third year of Belshazzar—two years after the vision of chapter 7. It is no wonder that Daniel, with these visions in mind, cared so little about Belshazzar's promises of promotion. Prophecy should woo us also away from the entanglements of this world.

In this vision Daniel saw a ram from the east come into violent collision with a he-goat from the west. The he-goat had a remarkable horn between its eyes. This horn was snapped off and was replaced by four others in the midst of which another little horn appeared.

The chief characteristics of the visions in chapters 7 and 8 are tabulated in the chart on the next page.

The ram in the vision of Daniel 8 had two horns, one higher than the other. Again we recognize the Medo-Persian Empire and the dominance of Persia over Media in this alliance. The heraldic emblem of Persia was a ram. The ram pushed westward, northward, and southward—westward toward Lydia, northward toward Babylon, and southward toward Egypt. Positive identification was given to Daniel in the interpretation (v. 20): "The ram which thou sawest having two horns are the kings of Media and Persia."

Suddenly a he-goat appeared from the west, moving with incredible speed. The "notable horn" (v. 5) between its eyes depicted Alexander the Great. Alexander became king of Greece at the age of twenty. Two years later, in 334 B.C., he defeated the Persians, and the next year swept eastward and decisively defeated the Persians again at Issus (333 B.C.). More than half a million men were under Persian arms in that battle. Still later he defeated an enormous Persian army in the Battle of Arbela (331 B.C.) and made himself master of the world. He died in 323 B.C. at the age of thirty-three.

The vision continued. When the "notable horn" was strong, it was broken, and four other great horns came up in its place, pointing toward the four winds of heaven. Upon the death of Alexander, his empire was carved up between his four generals—Cassander, Lysimarchus, Seleucus, and Ptolemy.

It will be remembered that in Daniel's vision of the four beasts (chap. 7), a little horn grew up on the fourth, which represented the Roman Empire. That little horn stood for the *Antichrist*. Now Daniel sees a little horn grow upon the he-goat representing Greece. The two little horns are not the same. One stands for the Antichrist (the Roman beast); this one in Daniel 8 stands for *Antiochus Epiphanes*, a later heir to part of Alexander's empire and the most outstanding type of Antichrist in history. More is said about this evil king in Daniel 11.

Some of the things told us of Antiochus Epiphanes look ahead to the true Antichrist of which he was a mere type. Antiochus Epiphanes, a younger son of Antiochus III (the Great), was the eighth king of Syria. There was a trace of madness in his veins. He liked to be called Epiphanes ("the Illustrious") but he was nicknamed "Epimanes" (the madman) behind his back. He tried to introduce the worship of the Olympian Zeus throughout his dominions, as well as introduce

THE VISIONS OF DANIEL 7 AND 8		
Chapter 7	**Chapter 8**	**Interpretation**
Medo-Persia		
Bear	Ram	Medo-Persia
Two sides	Two horns	A dual empire
Raised on one side	One horn higher than the other	Persia the predominant one of the two powers
	The higher horn raised up after the other	Persia raised up after Media
Three ribs between teeth	Pushed west, north, and south	Conquests
Greece		
Leopard	He-goat	Greece
	Came from the west	Its conquests eastward
Dominion given to it	Over the face of the earth	Extent of conquest
Four wings of a bird	Touched not the ground	Rapid conquest
	A notable horn	Alexander the Great
	Four notable horns	Alexander's generals
	The "little horn"	Antiochus Epiphanes

this pagan worship into Judea. He desecrated the temple in Jerusalem and fiercely persecuted those who stood in his way.

The angel who interpreted the vision told Daniel that the part of the interpretation fulfilled by Antiochus Epiphanes would have a later fulfillment at the end of the age. Thus Antiochus, wicked as he was, was but a shadow of a far more sinister and evil king yet to come. When the true Antichrist appears he will eclipse all the efforts of Antiochus to impose an idolatrous worship on Israel. He will "cause craft to prosper" and will "stand up against the Prince of princes; but," says the interpreter, "he shall be broken without hand" (v. 25).

This vision left Daniel weak, exhausted, and sick. He confessed there was much about the vision that he failed to understand.

B. The Control of the Future (chaps. 9–10)

In these two chapters Daniel has a divine *vision* and a divine *visitor*.

1. Daniel's Vision (chap. 9)

This is one of the most remarkable visions in the Old Testament, for it pinpoints the date of the crucifixion of the Lord. The chapter is in two parts.

a. He Believes an Old Prophecy: The Prophecy of the Seventy Years (9:1–23)

"In the first year of Darius . . . I Daniel understood by books the number of the years, whereof the word of the LORD came to Jeremiah the prophet, that he would accomplish seventy years in the desolations of Jerusalem" (vv. 1–2).

Some seventy years or so before this time, Jeremiah had declared, "And this whole land shall be a desolation, and an astonishment; and these nations shall serve the king of Babylon seventy years" (Jer. 25:11).

The false prophets had contradicted this prophesy and encouraged the people to believe that the captivity would be of short duration. To counteract this false prophesy, Jeremiah wrote to the captives, "Thus saith the LORD of hosts, the God of Israel . . . Build ye houses, and dwell in them; and plant gardens, and eat the fruit of them; Take ye wives, and beget sons and daughters; . . . that ye may be increased there, and not diminished. And seek the peace of the city whither I have caused you to be carried away captives, and pray unto the LORD for it: for in the peace thereof shall ye have peace. . . . For thus saith the LORD, That after *seventy years* be accomplished at Babylon I will visit you, and perform my good word toward you, in causing you to return to this place [Jerusalem]" (Jer. 29:4–10).

Daniel had been in exile in Babylon for sixty-eight years, so he knew that the time was almost ripe for this prophecy to be fulfilled. Accordingly, he gave himself over to prayer and intercession. His prayer was answered, and the angel Gabriel was sent to give him further enlightenment on the future.

b. He Receives a New Prophecy: The Prophecy of the Seventy "Weeks" (9:24–27)

An important key to understanding this prophecy is to recognize that it covers only the time the Jews are in their own land.

The word *weeks* means "sevens," and in this case it means sevens of years—490 years. The weeks are divided as follows:

$$7 + 62 + 1 \text{ of } weeks = 70 \text{ weeks}$$
$$49 + 434 + 7 \text{ of years} = 490 \text{ years}$$

The important question is, *When did the prophecy begin to take effect?* Four starting points have been suggested. First, that the decree mentioned in this prophecy was that of Cyrus in 538 B.C. (Ezra 1:1–4), which allowed the Jews to return to the land and rebuild the temple.

The second suggestion is that it refers to the decree of Darius Hystaspes, 519 B.C. (Ezra 5:1–17). This decree was to reaffirm the Jews' right to build their temple when this right was challenged.

The third suggestion is that it refers to the decree of Artaxerxes, 458 B.C. (Ezra 7:11–22). But this was simply a letter giving Ezra permission to go to Jerusalem and take some priests and Levites with him to take part in the sacrificial system at treasury expense.

The best suggestion is that it refers to the decree of Artaxerxes, 445 B.C. (Neh. 2:1–8) given in the twentieth year of his reign. It was a decree permitting Nehemiah to return to Jerusalem and build it. This was not a religious but a political mission and ran into serious opposition as predicted in Daniel 9:25 as "troublous times." Commentators are generally agreed that this is the decree meant in the prophecy.

Daniel was given to understand that the first 69 weeks would be in two parts (7 + 62 or 49 years + 434 years). There is no agreement as to why the first 69 weeks are in two parts, although all are agreed that there is no break between the 7 weeks and the 62 weeks. Some suggest that the first 49 years take us down to the end of the Old Testament canon. After 69 weeks the Messiah was to be cut off.

The period begins in 445 B.C. (69 x 7 = 483 years), which brings us to A.D. 39. The biblical year, however, is only 360 days, so we must deduct the difference (5 x 483 = 2415 days or 6.6 years) and we come to A.D. 32. Sir Robert Anderson calculates that the period ends with the *Lord's triumphal entry as Messiah into Jerusalem.*[6] Then He was "cut off." The seventieth week was dealt with separately by Daniel's angelic visitor and suggests that after Messiah's rejection there will be a gap in God's dealings with His people. The gap has extended down the entire church age, and the seventieth week is yet future. It will coincide with the appearance of the Antichrist and the last half of that "week" will be the great tribulation.

2. Daniel's Visitor (chap. 10)

The last three chapters of Daniel record revelations that Daniel received in the third year of Cyrus. He was about ninety-two years of age and no longer in public office (Dan. 1:21 tells us he continued in office until "the first year of Cyrus").

Daniel tells us he was mourning at the time. Perhaps he was troubled because so few Jews showed any interest in taking advantage of Cyrus's proclamation. The great majority of priests and the chief of the people preferred their ease in Babylon to the rigors of pioneering in Palestine.

At this time he received a visitor from glory. We cannot detail all the chapter except to say that one of Daniel's visitors at this time was the Lord. He also received a visit from Gabriel at the same time, or so it would seem from the context. One of the great values of this chapter is the light it casts on the "principalities and powers" who rule behind the scenes in the affairs of men, and the special relationship Israel has in connection with Michael.

C. The Course of the Future (chap. 11)

We often speak of the "silent years" between Malachi and Matthew. What happened during these years was written out in detail beforehand by Daniel in this chapter, which has to be one of the most amazing in the entire Bible. We shall give a few illustrations of the unerring accuracy of the prophecy.

The chapter is in two parts: the first 35 verses deal with events that lead up to the coming of *Antiochus*; the last 10 verses deal with the coming of the *Antichrist*.

1. The Coming of the Typical Antichrist (11:1–35)

> Behold, there shall stand up yet three kings in Persia; and the fourth shall be far richer than they all: and by his strength through his riches he shall stir up all against the realm of Grecia. (v. 2)

The three Persian kings, Cyrus, Cambyses, and Darius Hystaspes, were followed by the mighty Xerxes—the most powerful of them all. His invasion of Greece and his defeat at Salami is foretold:

> And a mighty king shall stand up, that shall rule with great dominion, and do according to his will. And when he shall stand up, his kingdom shall be broken, and shall be divided toward the four winds of heaven; and not to his posterity. (vv. 3–4)

Alexander's conquests are thus foreseen, also the division of his empire into four upon his death at the height of his success. His kingdom went to his generals:

And the king of the south shall be strong, and one of his princes . . . shall be strong
above him. (v. 5)

One division of Alexander's kingdom was Egypt. This portion went to
Ptolemy I. "One of his princes" is Seleucus Nicator, originally one of Ptolemy's
officers. He became king of Syria and the most powerful of Alexander's
successors.

And [after certain years] they shall join themselves together; for the king's daughter
of the south shall come to the king of the north to make an agreement: but she
shall not retain the power of the arm. (v. 6)

Bernice, the daughter of Ptolemy II of Egypt, was given in marriage to
Antiochus II of Syria. She was murdered.

But out of a branch of her roots shall one stand up in his estate, which shall come
with an army, and shall enter into the fortress of the king of the north, and shall
deal against them, and shall prevail. (v. 7)

Ptolemy III, brother of Bernice, retaliated and avenged his sister's murder by
invading and defeating Syria.

But his sons shall be stirred up, and shall assemble a multitude of great forces: and
one shall certainly come, and overflow, and pass through: then shall he return, and
be stirred up, even to his fortress. (v. 10)

The sons mentioned were Seleucus III and Antiochus III (afterward known as
Antiochus the Great). The story of the reign of Antiochus is one of war. At first he
was entirely successful in his campaigns against Egypt.

And the king of the south shall be moved with choler, and shall come forth and
fight with him, even with the king of the north: and he shall set forth a great multitude; but the multitude shall be given into his hand. (v. 12)

Ptolemy IV of Egypt defeated Antiochus III, who suffered great loss in the
battle of Raphia near the border of Egypt in 217 B.C.

For the king of the north shall return, and shall set forth a multitude greater than
the former, and shall certainly come after certain years with a great army and with
much riches. (v. 13)

Fourteen years later, Antiochus III returned with a great army against Egypt.

> And in those times there shall many stand up against the king of the south: also the robbers of thy people shall exalt themselves to establish the vision; but they shall fall. (v. 14)

Antiochus was supported by apostate Jews or riotous men who defied law and justice.

> So the king of the north shall come, and cast up a mount, and take the most fenced cities: and the arms of the south shall not withstand. (v. 15)

Antiochus III defeated Egypt.

> But he that cometh against him shall do according to his own will, and none shall stand before him: and he shall stand in the glorious land, which by his hand shall be consumed. (v. 16)

Antiochus conquered Palestine and desolated it.

> He shall also set his face to enter with the strength of his whole kingdom, and upright ones with him; thus shall he do: and he shall give him the daughter of women, corrupting her: but she shall not stand on his side, neither be for him. (v. 17)

Antiochus gave his own daughter, Cleopatra, then only eleven years old, in a treacherous marriage to Ptolemy V of Egypt, then a mere boy of twelve. He hoped his daughter would help him complete his control of Egypt. She sided with her husband, however, and defeated his plans.

> After this shall he turn his face unto the isles, and shall take many: but a prince for his own behalf shall cause the reproach offered by him to cease. (v. 18)

Antiochus next invaded Asia Minor and Greece. This drew the Romans against him, and he was defeated at the battle of Magnesia, 190 B.C. Upon returning to Syria, he was slain.

> Then shall stand up in his estate a raiser of taxes in the glory of the kingdom. (v. 20)

Antiochus was succeeded by his son Seleucus, who was forced to pay heavy tribute to the Romans. The raiser of taxes was Heliodorus, sent by Seleucus throughout the land of Judea to extract the needed funds and plunder the temple.

And in his estate shall stand up a vile person. (v. 21)

Antiochus Epiphanes was not the rightful heir to the Syrian throne, but a treacherous usurper. His career is graphically described in verses 21–35. He is one of the greatest types of Antichrist in the Scriptures. His hatred of the Jews, his setting up in the temple of an "abomination of desolation," and his diabolical persecution of the Jews all foreshadow the coming Beast. His excesses gave rise to the Maccabeans.

2. The Coming of the True Antichrist (11:36–45)

At this point the prophecy leaps the ages to pinpoint the end times and to describe events yet future, which lie in the days of Antichrist, the last Gentile ruler of the world.

The sudden appearance of *the king* in verse 36 is one of the marks that signifies the break in the prophecy. This king, of course, is the willful king met in previous visions of the book—the Man of Sin himself. Daniel tells us of this king's blasphemous assumption of the insignia of deity—that he will exalt himself and magnify himself above the gods and speak "marvelous things" (v. 36) against the God of gods. He will be a worshipper of the "God of forces," in other words, whichever god can secure for him the kingdoms of the world—that god being the Devil (v. 38).

Daniel next describes the troubles that will overtake the Antichrist toward the end of his reign. His kingdom will fall apart and "he shall come to his end, and none shall help him" (v. 45). He will be smitten by God Himself.

D. The Climax of the Future (chap. 12)

This chapter speaks of the time of the Antichrist, but goes back to just before the tribulation period. Michael is again introduced for he is the "prince which standeth for the children of thy people." Here, the promise is given of deliverance from the hands of the Antichrist—"and at that time thy people shall be delivered"—the tribulation being described as "a time of trouble, such as never was since there was a nation" (v. 1).

Daniel is assured that "our times are in [God's] hands" (see Ps. 31:15). Three periods are designated in this closing chapter, and while uncertainty prevails as to their full significance, we can be sure of one thing. He who weighs the dust in the balance, who numbers the hairs of our head, who counts the stars, and who numbers our days has not lost control of the world's affairs—no, not for a single day. The days are counted and controlled. Each day that passes brings us closer to that grand and glorious consummation when the kingdoms of this earth shall become the kingdom of God and His Christ.

CHAPTER 39

HAGGAI

First Things First

The prophets Haggai, Zechariah, and Malachi are known as "postexilic" prophets because they prophesied to the returned remnant after the Babylonian exile was over. Haggai and Zechariah were contemporaries, and Malachi prophesied about a century later.

The name of Haggai means "Festal One," and he is the only person in the Bible with this name. It has been thought that he was born on one of the annual feast days of Israel—or perhaps he was such a wanted child that his birth was a festive occasion to his parents.

He was given four prophecies to utter, all of them dated, and all dated according to the reign of the Persian King Darius Hystapses. Several of the prophets date their prophecies according to the years of Gentile kings. It was a tacit acknowledgment that "the times of the Gentiles" were in force, that Israel had forfeited its right for the present time to rule the nations, and that world supremacy had been divinely placed into Gentile hands for the time being. The "times of the Gentiles" will end as Jesus said, but when Haggai wrote they were in force. They are still in force, and they will continue to be in force until Jesus comes back to reign.

The four prophecies of Haggai were all delivered in the space of four months in the year 520 B.C. The prophet delivered his first message in the second year of this Persian king—he gives the month and the day. About seven weeks later, the prophet delivered a second message, and nine weeks after that he delivered a third and a fourth message, both on the same day. The message of this prophet can be summed up in four simple statements.

I. The Call to Build (1:1–15)
    A. The Background (1:1–2)
    B. The Burden (1:3–11)
        1. Its Context (1:3–4)
        2. Its Content (1:5–11)
    C. The Blessing (1:12–15)
        1. The Response (1:12)
        2. The Reassurance (1:13)
        3. The Revival (1:14–15)
II. The Call to Behold (2:1–9)
    A. The Present (2:1–3)
        1. A Special People (2:1)
        2. A Struggling People (2:2)
        3. A Sorrowing People (2:3)
    B. The Past (2:4–5)
        1. An Application of Covenant Position (2:4)
        2. An Appeal to Covenant Principle (2:5)
    C. The Prospect (2:6–9)
        The Messiah and
        1. His Power (2:6–7a)
            a. Shaking All Nature (2:6)
            b. Shaking All Nations (2:7a)
        2. His Presence (2:7b, c)
        3. His Possessions (2:8)
        4. His Peace (2:9)
III. The Call to Behave (2:10–19)
    A. The Blessing Wanted (2:10–14)
        1. The Principle of the Law (2:10–13)
        2. The People of the Lord (2:14)
    B. The Blessing Withheld (2:15–17)
        1. The Neglected House (2:15)
        2. The Niggardly Harvests (2:16–17a)
        3. The Negligent Heart (2:17b)
    C. The Blessing Waiting (2:18–19)
        1. The Ground of the Blessing (2:18)
        2. The Greatness of the Blessing (2:19)
IV. The Call to Believe (2:20–23)

A. God Will Manifest His Power (2:20–22)
1. The Shaking of the Elements (2:20–21)
2. The Shattering of the Enemy (2:22)
B. God Will Magnify His Prince (2:23)

Haggai appeared at a critical time in the history of his people. A remnant of the Jews was back in the Promised Land but their incomplete temple was not only a bad testimony to the surrounding nations but a source of spiritual peril to themselves. With the throne of David gone, it was imperative that the nation realize its true center in the temple. Indeed, within the compass of his brief book, Haggai mentions three temples: Solomon's (2:3a), Zerubbabel's (2:3b–5), and the Messiah's (2:6–9).

I. THE CALL TO BUILD (1:1–15)

A. The Background (1:1–2)

"In the second year of Darius the king, in the sixth month, in the first day of the month, came the word of the LORD by Haggai the prophet unto Zerubbabel the son of Shealtiel, governor of Judah, and to Joshua the son of Josedech, the high priest, saying, Thus speaketh the LORD of hosts, saying, This people say, The time is not come, the time that the LORD's house should be built." That was the background.

We need now to fill in this sketch with a little more detail. On October 29, 539 B.C., the Persian conqueror Cyrus had entered Babylon, bringing to an end the Babylonian Empire. In 538 Zerubbabel and Joshua had led the first contingent of Jews back to the Promised Land. They were accompanied by some priests and by the heads of the tribes of Judah and Benjamin.

In April or May 536 B.C., the foundations of the new temple were laid in Jerusalem, the work being aided by a grant from Cyrus. The Samaritans asked if they could help. When the Jews scornfully turned down their offer, the Samaritans did all they could to harass and hinder. One of the things they did was hire lawyers to misrepresent and slander the Jews at the Persian court. As a result the work came to a halt.

There can be no doubt that the returned remnant had become greatly discouraged. The prophets, especially, had painted glowing pictures of the Promised Land. But it was a far cry from the refinements of the Babylonian culture—to which they had grown accustomed—and a rude awakening to the rigors of pioneer life. There was nothing romantic about having to hoe the flinty soil, quarry stones, and stay up nights on watch against bitter and persistent foes. For some years, before the voice of Haggai was raised in the land, things had been allowed to drift. Poor harvests, declining income, and repeated discouragements had taken their toll.

No further work was done on the temple during the reigns of Cyrus and his successors Cambesis and Smerdis. For sixteen years nothing was done. The Jews, however, were by no means lax about taking care of their own interests. While the foundation of the temple became overgrown with weeds, the Jews were busy building their own houses. They excused themselves, saying, "It is not yet time to build the Lord's house" (see v. 2).

To understand the background of Haggai, we must delve into previous prophetic utterances. We generally speak of the "Seventy-Year Captivity," but actually there were at least two periods of seventy years that ran concurrently.

There was *the servitude* mentioned in Jeremiah 29:10. This period began with Jehoiakim's original submission to Nebuchadnezzar and it ended with the decree of Cyrus. Then there was *the desolations*. This period began with the date that Nebuchadnezzar surrounded Jerusalem with his armies for the last time during the days of Zedekiah (2 Kings 25:1–2; Ezek. 24:1–2). This particular date was of such importance that it is the only date in the historical books of the Kings that gives day, month, and year. The "desolations" ended on the twenty-fourth day of the ninth month of the second year of Darius—the very day on which Haggai uttered his third great prophecy: "From this day," he says at least three times, "will I bless you" (v. 19, also vv. 15, 18). The same day he received another and a final message.

One of the reasons for Jewish apathy toward completing the temple was a wrong attitude toward prophecy. The people seem to have mistakenly inferred (despite God's sign to them in the decree of Cyrus) that even the temple could not be rebuilt until the period of the "desolations" on the city had run its course. They were presuming on prophecy and saying, "The time is not come, the time that the Lord's house should be built." Thus prophecy had become a mere excuse for the neglect of duty. Haggai recalled them sharply: Is it *time* (you who say the time is not come to build God's house) is it *time* to build your own? Where is your prophecy for that? Haggai's rebuke is relevant today. In Haggai's day prophecy had become narcotic instead of a tonic. Present effort, they felt, was useless, the prophetic hour had not struck. We need to beware lest we allow prophetic teaching to be a narcotic—a substitute for vigorous evangelism and missionary activity. The truth of the Lord's coming should spur us on, not slow us down. It should be a stimulant to holy living and to dedicated Christian service.

So the voice of God, through the voice of a prophet, Haggai, rang through the silence to rudely awaken the Jews from their laziness and spiritual indifference. The date was August 29 in the year 520 B.C.—the first day of the sixth month of the second year of Darius I Hystapses, according to the reckoning of the times. It was this king who had reaffirmed the Jews' right to rebuild the temple and who had authorized his governor to help them receive financial aid from tribute money in the province.

The first day of the month was the day of the new moon, when the people were accustomed to gather for worship. Zerubbabel, the civic leader of the nation, was there, and Joshua, the religious leader of the nation, was there. Zerubbabel (his name means "born in Babylon") was the grandson of Jehoiachin and had been appointed by Cyrus to be governor of the new colony in Judah. Joshua was the son of Jehozadek, who had been high priest in Jerusalem at the time of the Babylonian invasion.

B. The Burden (1:3–11)

Haggai ignored the external difficulties since they were of no account. They were nothing at all to God! What could a handful of Samaritans do? What could a Persian despot do? What was in question was the work of God, the building of God's house. The work had ceased solely because it was no longer the chief interest of those engaged in it. Opposition never really hinders the work of God. Only lethargy and disinterest on the part of the Lord's people can do that.

With magnificent sarcasm the prophet says in effect, "It is not the time that the Lord's house should be built? Well, how come it's time for you to dwell in paneled, tapestried homes?" God wanted His people to face the fact that they were barefaced hypocrites.

Great lukewarmness had characterized the return to the Promised Land. For the most part the exiled Jewish people seem to have been taken up with material prosperity. During their exile, they had flourished in a remarkable way. Haman, for instance, had calculated on being able to pay out of his spoils ten thousand talents of silver into the king's treasuries (Esth. 3:9)—about one and one-half billion dollars, two-thirds of the annual revenues of the Persian Empire. Those who returned with Zerubbabel consisted of only about 42,360 free men, and of the twenty-four orders of priests only four orders returned—3, 5, 9, 16 (Ezra 2:36–39), and of the Levites only 74 individuals (Ezra 2:40).

Notice what the people were saying in Haggai's day. They were not saying that the Lord's house should *not* be built. They were saying that it was not a convenient time to get on with that work. They had room and time enough for everything else, but no time for building God's house. They had the Laodicean spirit—a selfish spirit—one all too evident among the Lord's people today. So many have time enough for two jobs, time enough for the demands of school activities, time enough for newspapers and TV shows, time enough for college, for business, and for vacations. But no time for the Lord's work, for Sunday school, for the ministry meeting, for the prayer meeting, for missionary work. No time for the Lord's house.

As a result, the Lord simply brought blight upon their activities and made them profitless. "Consider," said the prophet (v. 5). It is a favorite word with him. It is a call to self-examination. He demanded they take a hard look at the nature of their excuses for not building the Lord's house and see what was happening as a result.

"Ye have sown much, and bring in little; ye eat, but ye have not enough . . . he that earneth wages earneth wages to put it into a bag with holes" (v. 6). That sounds familiar! "Oh," we say, "inflation is running so high. We go to the grocery store and spend thirty dollars and hardly get enough to fill one small bag!" It is a vicious circle. We blame inflation; we say, "We have to have two jobs . . . we have so many payments to make . . . there's the house mortgage and the car payment and Jimmie's schooling, and clothes are so expensive, I simply cannot afford to give God either my time or my tithe." What about putting God first? What about putting the Lord's house first? What about trusting God to take care of those other things? Jesus said, "Seek ye *first* the kingdom of God, and his righteousness; and all these things shall be added unto you" (Matt. 6:33).

There is such a thing as putting the Lord's interests first. Then we will find that, in some mysterious way, our paycheck goes further, our savings don't vanish into thin air, and the cost of living takes care of itself. We are no longer earning wages to put into a bag with holes. "Thus saith the Lord, Consider your ways."

But there was more: "Go up to the mountain, and bring wood, and build the house; and I will take pleasure in it, and I will be glorified, saith the Lord" (v. 8). We need to notice this—God's house cannot be built without material. God's house cannot be built without time and effort and labor and sacrifice. It is not an easy task to go to the mountains, to fell mighty cedars and saw them up into boards. It takes time and money and effort. The very things we say we do not have.

What makes us think that we can do God's work, build God's house with odds and ends of our time? What makes us think that enterprises of evangelism, mighty movements in missions, growing Sunday schools, and flourishing local churches can be built with tips instead of tithes? What makes us think that we can minister the Word of God acceptably with a few borrowed points of an outline and a shallow, cursory commentary based on a few minutes of hasty browsing in the footnotes of the Scofield Bible? It simply cannot be done. God never blesses laziness.

I have a brother who is in demand the world over as a specialist on diseases of the liver. Does he command the respect of his medical colleagues by devoting a few odds and ends of his time to his lectures? Has he become a world authority on hepatitis by reading a few medical journals? He spent ten years of diligent study just to become a pathologist, and has spent decades since in in-depth study of his medical specialty. What makes us think we can be less proficient in building the Lord's house? No wonder we have barely laid the foundation! No wonder even that has been so neglected it is overgrown with weeds! If some of the Lord's people ran their businesses and financial affairs the way they attend to the work of the Lord's house, they would be bankrupt in a month.

"Ye looked for much, and, lo, it came to little; and when ye brought it home, I did blow upon it. Why? saith the Lord of hosts. Because of mine house that is waste, and ye run every man unto his own house" (v. 9). That was Haggai's burden. "Therefore," he says, "the heaven over you is stayed from dew, and the earth is stayed from her fruit" (v. 10). Why is it that even the little that we do attempt for God produces so little fruit? Why is there so little of the dew of heaven upon it? We do not have to look far for the reason. If we loved the Lord more and ourselves less, and if we loved the Lord's house more and our own houses less, why, then He would send the dew and the fruit.

C. The Blessing (1:12–15)

"Then Zerubbabel . . . and Joshua . . . with all the remnant of the people, obeyed the voice of the LORD their God. . . . Then spake Haggai the LORD's messenger . . . saying, I am with you, saith the LORD. . . . And the LORD stirred up the spirit of Zerubbabel . . . and the spirit of Joshua . . . and the spirit of all the remnant of the people; and they came and did work in the house of the LORD." The Lord recorded the exact date—it was just a little over three weeks after Haggai began to preach. Moreover, it was a movement of the Spirit. Theirs was not just a carnal, worldly effort but a spiritual response, and one that made everyone aware of the Lord's presence.

II. THE CALL TO BEHOLD (2:1–9)

Again Haggai dates his prophecy. It was the twenty-first day of the seventh month. We know from Leviticus 23:39–44 that this was the seventh day of the joyous Feast of Tabernacles, the final feast of ingathering or harvest festival.

There were many among the people who were comparing the former glory of Solomon's magnificent temple—which was swept away in flames at the time of the Babylonian invasion—to the inferior structure that was now being built. While the younger generation shouted with joy over what was being achieved, the older people, who had seen the first temple in all its splendor, wept. This was less than two months after things started moving again.

This represents a very subtle attack of the enemy because it seems to make much of the glorious past of God's people. The enemy's goal, however, was to minimize and depreciate the wonderful revival that was going on by pouring cold water and criticism over everything. As though God could ever do an inferior work!

"Who is left among you that saw this house in her first glory?" demanded the prophet. "And how do ye see it now? Is it not in your eyes in comparison of it as nothing?" (v. 3).

The answer to this wretched spirit of criticism and comparison was to direct attention away from the *work* to the *Lord*: "The glory of this latter house shall be greater than of the former, saith the LORD of hosts" (v. 9). Whereas Solomon's temple was graced by the presence of the *Shechinah*, the glory cloud within the

Holy of Holies—this temple, the very temple the revived remnant were building, would be graced by the presence of the *Savior*.

Thus the prophet directed the attention of the remnant to the coming of Christ, urging them on to the work with the tremendous truth that the Messiah Himself would crown their efforts by personally coming and blessing it with His own divine presence. What more could one want than that? To have had a share in building something that the Lord Himself will own and use.

Surely that is the best way to deal with discouragement. We must get our eyes off the work and onto the Lord! After all, our feeble efforts do look so meager, even when we put hearts and souls into them, when the Lord is with us in the work, and when His Spirit is guiding and directing it. It is so easy to compare what we are doing with what others have done for God.

Take the case of William Carey, who has been called the father of modern missions. Carey was a cobbler. He had long been burdened about the plight of the pagan world. He made a leather map of the world and hung it up in his workshop so that it might be a constant reminder to him of "the untold millions still untold." But that was not what sent him out to India to become one of the greatest missionaries of all time. Nor was it his work that spurred him on, even when, illiterate cobbler that he was, he mastered language after language and became one of the great pioneers of the gospel. A vision of the continents does not provide sufficient motivation for braving the perils of the pioneer.

What was it, then, that spurred Carey to go, and what was it that kept him from quitting once he had gone? It was not the vision of the *lost* at all. It was the vision of the *Lord!* According to F. W. Boreham,[1] William Carey was spurred on by a text—"Thou shalt see the King in His beauty!" (see Isa. 33:17). That's it! That is what keeps us going. That is what Haggai set before the people who, after six or seven weeks of effort, began to listen to the criticisms of those who could only minimize the work and compare it unfavorably with the achievements of the past.

III. THE CALL TO BEHAVE (2:10–19)

Another nine weeks passed, and the prophet received another message from God. This time it had to do with behavior. "If one bear holy flesh in the skirt of his garment, and with his skirt do touch bread . . . shall it be holy?" The priests, of course, answered "No" (v. 12). "If one that is unclean by a dead body touch any of these, shall it be unclean?" the prophet asked (v. 13). This time the answer is "Yes" (see v. 13).

It was a message on holiness and uncleanness. Holy things do not have the power to make unholy things holy, but unclean things have the power to make clean things unclean. In other words, impurity, vileness, and carnality is catching; holiness is not. It is a warning against touching the unclean. It is easier to tear things down than build them up.

But Haggai's point was even graver. He was making the point that those who build up their own houses and neglect God's house—those who look after their own interests and who neglect God's interest—these people are really unclean. It is a sobering word.

IV. THE CALL TO BELIEVE (2:20–23)

This message came to the prophet on the same day as the previous one. Evidently a fresh start was made at once on the house of God, and at once came God's two-fold word of encouragement. The first was a promise that God would manifest *His power*: "I will shake the heavens and the earth . . . and I will overturn . . . and overturn" (see v. 22). Let us get our eyes fixed on Christ and our shoulder to the wheel and God will sweep aside all the power of the enemy, all the opposition of nations and kingdoms. When God throws His power behind a work, however feeble it might appear on the surface, then something is bound to happen.

The second word of encouragement was a promise that God would magnify *His prince*: "In that day, saith the LORD of hosts, I will take thee, O Zerubbabel . . . and will make thee as a signet: for I have chosen thee, saith the LORD of hosts." Zerubbabel was set up as a type of Christ. It is God's purpose to use Christ as a signet ring or a seal and put the impress of Christ on the whole created scene. We are all too well aware that the nations do not bear the impress of Christ today. Our task is to get on with building God's house and leave the outcome to Him.

CHAPTER 40

ZECHARIAH

Looking Ahead

Some twenty-nine people in the Old Testament bear the name of Zechariah. The name means simply, "The Lord remembers." The prophet Zechariah was born an exile in Babylon but he was born into a priestly family. So, like Jeremiah and Ezekiel, Zechariah was both a prophet and a priest. His father seems to have died in Babylon, which perhaps explains why Zechariah the prophet is known as the son of Iddo—Iddo being the name of his grandfather.

He was one of the little band of repatriated Jews. Some fifty thousand in all responded to the decree of Cyrus, which gave the exiled Jews the right to return and rebuild their ancestral home in the Promised Land. Zechariah was a young man when he first began to preach (2:4). He began his ministry two months after Haggai began to raise his voice, protest against the carelessness of the Jews in their leaving the unfinished temple to lie neglected and forlorn while being busy building their own houses and careers. So Zechariah began his ministry in the second year of the reign of the Persian king Darius Hystaspes (521–520 B.C.).

Like his companion prophet Haggai, Zechariah encouraged the Jews to finish the temple. Deeply concerned over the spiritual life of the Hebrew pioneers in Palestine, Zechariah's visions were of far greater scope than those of his fellow preacher. He soared on eagle's wings far beyond his own day and age, seeing the coming of the Greeks, the coming of the Romans, the crucifixion of Christ, the scattering again of the Hebrew people, the events of the last days, the rise to power of the Beast, the ultimate horrors awaiting Jerusalem, and the final return of Christ to impose upon this planet a righteous reign for God.

Almost everyone agrees that some of Zechariah's visions and prophecies are complex and difficult to understand. His overall plan, however, is simple, even though the details are difficult. He received three series of revelations—concerning *Israel's future* (chaps. 1–6), concerning *Israel's fasts*, (chaps. 7–8) and concerning *Israel's folly* (chaps. 9–14). The first series of revelations were apocalyptic in character, couched in highly symbolic language, and imparted to him in a series of night visions. The second series of revelations revolved around a question put to him by a delegation of Jews regarding certain fasts the Jews had imposed upon themselves at the time of their exile, fasts that had become irksome religious duties they wished they could now shed. The third series of revelations centered on Israel's sin in rejecting the Messiah and the age-end sufferings that would finally bring to an end the nation's persistent refusal to acknowledge Christ.

The difference in style between chapters 9 through 14 and the earlier part of his book is usually explained on the ground that these later chapters were probably written when the prophet was a much older man. Also, the circumstances under which he wrote would probably be much different.

Woven into Zechariah's prophecy are ten distinct visions and symbols. Circled numerals (❶ – ❿) indicate where they occur in the outline. See page 445 for a complete list.

   I. Revelations Concerning Israel's Future (1:1–6:15)
      A. The Voice of the Prophet (1:1–6)
         1. The Man (1:1)
         2. The Message (1:2–6)
      B. The Visions of the Prophet (1:7–6:15)
         1. God Sees (1:7–21)
            a. The Four Horses (1:7–17) ❶
              (1) The Imperialist Powers (1:7–11)
              (2) The Impassioned Plea (1:12–17)
            b. The Four Horns (1:18–21)
              (1) Gentile Power Displayed (1:18–19) ❷
              (2) Gentile Power Destroyed (1:20–21) ❸
         2. God Speaks (2:1–4:14)
            a. The Matter of Israel's Restoration (2:1–13) ❹
              (1) Perspectives (2:1–5)
              (2) Priorities (2:6–7)
              (3) Punishment (2:8–9)
              (4) Privilege (2:10–13)
            b. The Matter of Israel's Righteousness (3:1–10)
              (1) The Consecrated Priest (3:1–7) ❺
                (a) The Adversary (3:1)

(b) The Advocate (3:2–7)
(2) The Coming Prince (3:8–10) ❻
(a) The Coming Servant (3:8)
(b) The Cornerstone (3:9–10)
c. The Matter of Israel's Revival (4:1–14)
(1) The Testimony Restored to Israel (4:1-7) ❼
(2) The Temple Rebuilt by Israel (4:8–10)
(3) The Tribulation Reviewed for Israel (4:11–14)
3. God Stirs (5:1–6:15)
a. Implicitly to Convict (5:1–4) ❽
(1) The Mystery of the Flying Roll (5:1–2)
(2) The Ministry of the Flying Roll (5:3–4)
b. Impartially to Condemn (5:5–11) ❾
(1) The Container (5:5–6)
(2) The Cover (5:7a)
(3) The Contents (5:7b–8)
(4) The Carriers (5:9)
(5) The Comment (5:10–11)
c. Imperially to Conquer (6:1–15)
(1) The Timely Coming of the Chariots (6:1–8) ❿
(2) The Typical Crowning of the Christ (6:9–15)
II. Revelations Concerning Israel's Fasts (7:1–8:23)
A. The Question Asked (7:1–3)
B. The Question Argued (7:4–14)
1. Their Hearts Exposed (7:4–7)
2. Their History Explained (7:8–14)
C. The Question Answered (8:1–23)
1. Israel and Her Needs (8:1–19)
2. Israel and Her Neighbors (8:20–23)
a. The World Pilgrimage to Jerusalem (8:20–22)
b. The World Prestige of Jews (8:23)
III. Revelations Concerning Israel's Folly (9:1–14:21)
A. The Coming of the King (9:1–17)
1. The Grecian Age (9:1–8)
2. The Gospel Age (9:9)
3. The Golden Age (9:10)
4. The Godless Age (9:11–17)
a. The Blood (9:11–12)
b. The Battle (9:13–16)
c. The Blessing (9:17)

B. The Call of the King (10:1–12)
    1. Israel: A Concerned People (10:1–2)
    2. Israel: A Conquering People (10:3–8)
    3. Israel: A Converted People (10:9–12)
C. The Crucifixion of the King (11:1–17)
    1. The Coming Invasion (11:1–3)
    2. The Crowning Insult (11:4–14)
    3. The Cursed Idolater (11:15–17)
D. The Curse of the King (12:1–14)
    1. A Time of War (12:1–9)
    2. A Time of Woe (12:10–14)
E. The Compassion of the King (13:1–9)
    1. Causes Removed (13:1–5)
        a. Personal Defilement (13:1)
        b. Prophetic Deception (13:2–5)
    2. Calvary Remembered (13:6–7)
    3. Crisis Rementioned (13:8–9)
        a. Those Slain in the End Times (13:8)
        b. Those Saved in the End Times (13:9)
F. The Coronation of the King (14:1–21)
    1. Jerusalem Ravished (14:1–3)
    2. Jerusalem Remade (14:4–8)
    3. Jerusalem Rescued (14:9–15)
    4. Jerusalem Restored (14:16–21)

Let us now fill in some of the features of this book. We shall have to be content, though, with the broad features. The above outline, while by no means complete, is sufficiently detailed to enable the reader to pursue a more in-depth study of this remarkable book.

I. REVELATIONS CONCERNING ISRAEL'S FUTURE (1:1–6:15)

A. The Voice of the Prophet (1:1–6)

The prophecies in this section of the book all center around ten visions given to Zechariah in one night of extraordinary ecstatic revelations.

In a brief survey we cannot even recount in detail, much less expound in detail, these ten visions. Let us first list them, however, and then give the gist of their meaning—no simple task, indeed, since scholarly men have differed about these visions for centuries. Still, we can at least sketch out the overall significance of the visions.

B. The Visions of the Prophet (1:7–6:15)
The ten visions are as follows:

1. The Four Horses (1:7–17)
2. The Four Horns (1:18–19)
3. The Four Carpenters (1:20–21)
4. The Man with the Measuring Line (2:1–13)
5. Joshua the High Priest (3:1–7)
6. The Righteous Branch (3:8–10)
7. The Lampstands and Olive Trees (4:1–7)
8. The Flying Roll (5:1–4)
9. The Ephah (5:5–11)
10. The Four Chariots (6:1–8)

1. God Sees (1:7–21)

a. The Four Horses (1:7–17)
The prophet dreamed of four horses. The first horse was red in color and was ridden by a man identified as "the angel of the LORD" (v. 12). Other horses followed behind. They rode abroad throughout the earth.

In this first vision Zechariah saw Judah, dispersed and scattered, and Jerusalem trodden down of the Gentiles, while the nations remained at rest, quite unconcerned about the plight of the Jewish people.

b. The Four Horns (1:18–21)
Then the prophet saw four horns. That was all—just four horns, enough to stir the slumbering prophet to ask the interpreting angel exactly what four horns could possibly signify.

(1) Gentile Power Displayed (1:18–19)
The vision of the four horns takes in the four world powers that, over the centuries, participated in the scattering of Israel. A horn in Scripture is usually a symbol of power, and it derives its significance from the horns of bulls and wild beasts.

(2) Gentile Power Destroyed (1:20–21)
Next the prophet had a vision of four carpenters, or craftsmen, who were told to destroy the four horns. Again the prophet was moved to ask what was signified by this.

The Gentile world powers that scattered Israel remain unconcerned about the fate of the Jewish people. The vision of the craftsmen summoned to destroy the horns was a reminder that God has His own instruments at hand and is quite able to bring Gentile world power to naught.

2. God Speaks (2:1–4:14)

a. The Matter of Israel's Restoration (2:1–13)

The visions continued. The prophet saw a man with a measuring line, starting out to measure Jerusalem. Before he could get started on his task, however, a messenger angel was sent to him with the information that while the Jerusalem of that day might be small enough to be thus measured, he was to keep one thing in mind—Jerusalem would spread out far, far beyond its parochial bounds. This measuring of the city looks ahead to a coming day when God will fully restore both the nation of Israel and the city of Jerusalem and will give both an enlargement of power and significance never yet realized in the long and checkered history of the Jewish people. "He that toucheth you toucheth the apple of his eye," the Lord assured Jerusalem (v. 8). Woe betide those nations that launch their offensive against the Jewish people!

The first four visions were intended to bring comfort to that struggling remnant of pioneers who were seeking to rebuild the Promised Land. They were engaged in a great work, one that had a scope and significance far beyond their own troublesome times.

But the spiritual condition of the nation needed to be addressed. Thus, the next visions dealt with the whole question of sin among the people and its representative leaders.

b. The Matter of Israel's Righteousness (3:1–10)

(1) The Consecrated Priest (3:1–7)

Joshua, the high priest, was seen standing before the Lord, arrayed in vile and filthy garments, while Satan stood at his right hand to accuse him before God. A divine Advocate came forward to take up Joshua's case and so successfully that the high priest was clothed in new garments and given a new ministry.

This vision shows how God will yet deal with Israel's national sin. In Joshua, symbolically, the guilt of Israel was removed, Satan's accusations were silenced, and a new ministry entrusted to Israel in which the watchword would be, "holiness unto the Lord" (see 14:20). The vision anticipates a coming glorious day when the nation of Israel will undergo its spiritual rebirth. The very name *Joshua* (*Yeshua*) was significant, being the Old Testament form of the name *Jesus*. *He* is the One who will remove Israel's sins just as He removes ours.

(2) The Coming Prince (3:8–10)

Next came the vision of the Branch. "The Branch" is one of the great Old Testament titles of the Lord Jesus. There are twenty-three words translated "branch" in the Old Testament, but one, occurring twelve times, is used specifically of the Messiah on four great occasions: Jeremiah 23:5–6 (see also 33:15); Zechariah 3:8; 6:12; and Isaiah 4:2. It will be seen from the context of these references that the Messiah is referred to as King, Servant, Man, and Jehovah; and it is from these four viewpoints exactly that the four gospels are written.

c. The Matter of Israel's Revival (4:1–14)

Next the prophet saw two olive trees feeding a golden candelabra with a ceaseless supply of oil. The vision of the candelabra and the olive trees anticipates the day when the nation of Israel will shine forth among men as a mighty witness for God. After the rapture of the church, the lamp of testimony will be restored to the Jewish people and, just prior to the great tribulation, God will raise up two very remarkable witnesses, symbolized as olive trees, to make God's name known on earth (Rev. 11).

3. God Stirs (5:1–6:15)

a. Implicitly to Convict (5:1–4)

Then came the vision of the flying scroll. It was a very large scroll, the same dimensions, indeed, as the Holy Place of the tabernacle, and as it flew over the land, it was pronouncing a curse because of Judah's sins against God and man. Sin will yet be judged among the Hebrew people—especially as signified by the vision of the flying scroll with its curse against all those who violate the laws of God.

b. Impartially to Condemn (5:5–11)

The prophet had a vision next of a woman in an ephah. An ephah was the largest dry measure among the Jews—about the size of a bushel. In that container sat a woman, and she was sealed in by a covering of lead weighing a talent—the largest measure of weight among the Jews. Two women appeared, and they carried off the ephah with its burden to Babylon.

According to this vision, sin will find its focal center once more in the very place where so much of it began—back in Babylon. The book of Revelation envisions, indeed, the rebuilding of Babylon and the violent overthrow of that great sin capital of the Beast's empire. Babylon, in Scripture, is associated with "the mystery of iniquity" (2 Thess. 2:7), and it is identified as the home and heartland of all kinds of human wickedness.

c. Imperially to Conquer (6:1–15)

(1) The Timely Coming of the Chariots (6:1–8)

The prophet had a final vision of four chariots. These came into sight from between two mountains of brass, and the prophet was told they represented the four winds of heaven. The chariots were drawn by four horses—again of differing colors. The various points of the compass were the destinations of these chariots but special mention is made of the *north*. Special judgment was reserved for the north, and God's Spirit is said to be quieted only when that particular judgment is accomplished.

The prophet was not left to speculate on the symbolic meaning of these chariots but was expressly told they were "four spirits of the heavens" (v. 5). They were angelic messengers sent forth to hasten the completion of end-time events. Their mission will be to the four points of the compass but with a special emphasis on the north.

Commentators tend to interpret "the north" as Babylon. It would, perhaps, be more fitting to link the north with the great northern power of the last days, whose vitriolic hatred of God, whose militant atheism, whose fierce hatred of Israel makes her overthrow not only imperative but a tremendous witness to the other nations of the tribulation age (Ezek. 38–39, a prophesy believed to apply to Russia). The overthrow of this northern power quiets God's Spirit in the north country. It will be an overthrow long delayed, richly deserved, and satisfying to the righteous holiness of the Spirit of God.

(2) The Typical Crowning of the Christ (6:9–15)

The visions were concluded by the symbolic crowning of Joshua the high priest. In the Old Testament, priests were not crowned, for the office of priest and the office of king were kept apart by divine decree. This symbolic crowning of Joshua, therefore, anticipates the day when the Lord Jesus as Priest-King ("a priest for ever after the order of Melchizedek" [Ps. 110:4]) will be owned and acknowledged by the restored, redeemed, and repentant nation of Israel. No wonder the cry rings forth, "Behold the man" (v. 12). That was Pilate's cry when he tried to persuade the Jews of his day to lay aside their hatred of Jesus. It must have rung in their ears with startling force! Here was a pagan governor pointing to the Christ of God and using the very words of Zechariah to describe Him—words of which he could have known nothing at all. "*Behold the Man!*" This will be the cry of God's Spirit to Israel when, at last, they look upon Him again and see Him as their true and long-rejected Messiah.

These, then, were Zechariah's revelations concerning Israel's future. The prophet was carried down the centuries to see in broad, sweeping outline the plans and purposes of God in connection with His people as the long ages roll their waters down the streams of time.

II. Revelations Concerning Israel's Fasts (7:1–8:23)

The memorable night of visions was past, and two years came and went. It was now the fourth year of the reign of Darius (518 B.C.). The temple had been rebuilt, and Jerusalem itself was beginning to look more like a city. The old scars of invasion were fast being erased, and new life was pulsing through the land.

Then the prophet received a delegation of Jews from Bethel, a city once filled with idolatry. Many of the city's former inhabitants had been among those who had come back from Babylon, forever cured of that curse (Ezra 2:28; Neh. 11:31).

These delegates had a question for Zechariah and his friend and colleague Haggai. What about the fasts? There was a fast in the tenth month—when King Nebuchadnezzar's armies had surrounded Jerusalem and besieged the city. There was a fast in the fourth month—to recall the time when the Babylonians first burst into the Holy City. There was a fast in the fifth month—when Nebuchadnezzar burned the temple of Solomon. There was a fast in the seventh month—to commemorate the slaying of Gedaliah, the Jewish governor of Judea, and the flight of the Jewish remnant.

All these fasts, connected with the fall of Jerusalem in 586 B.C., had become irksome. Was it necessary for the people to continue keeping them?

That, of course, is the basic problem with any merely *religious* duty. If something does not come from the heart, then it becomes a burden and a chore. It is easy enough to make a pledge in a moment of enthusiasm or despair, but keeping it up in the same spirit is something else. Which, of course, is exactly why the New Testament does not impose any such rites and rituals on believers in the Lord Jesus Christ.

In answer to the question about fasts, the prophet read his people a lecture. In the first place, God had never ordained those irksome fasts; they themselves had forged those chains. It did not matter to God whether they kept them or not. What mattered to God was that they keep the Word He *had* given them. All their national calamities stemmed from their failure to obey the law and the prophets. It was far more important to do what God *did* require than to try to salve the conscience with rules and regulations He did not require.

The prophet's vision was again enlarged. He saw once more the last days and the millennial reign when *feasts* would forever replace fasts and when the Jewish people would become the blessing to mankind that God always intended them to be.

The closing chapters of the prophecy all focus on the future—a future inevitably tied up with what the nation would do to the Messiah when, in the fullness of time, He came.

III. Revelations Concerning Israel's Folly (9:1–14:21)

These prophecies were probably written some considerable time later. Although their general burden has to do with the first and second comings of Christ, there is a nearer as well as a farther focus. So it is thought that chapters 9 and 10 envision the nation under *Greek* domination, chapter 11 sees the nation under *Roman* rule, and chapters 12 through 14 anticipate almost entirely events of *the last days*. Christ, as well as the nation's attitude toward Him, is the focus of all the chapters.

A. The Coming of the King (9:1–17)

The chapter contains many interesting prophecies but, probably, the one that holds the greatest interest for us is the prophecy of Christ's triumphal entry into Jerusalem.

"Behold, thy King cometh unto thee: he is just, and having salvation; lowly, and riding upon an ass, and upon a colt the foal of an ass" (v. 9). And when Jesus did just that, with the streets of Jerusalem ringing and resounding with the Hosannas of the people, the elders were infuriated. They demanded of Jesus that He silence the crowds. He told them that so imperative was the fulfillment of this prophecy that if the people were silent the stones would cry out. The problem, of course, was that Jesus was not the kind of king they wanted. The Jews wanted a militant Messiah, one who would smash the power of Rome and make Jerusalem capital of the world. A lordly Christ would have suited them well; a lowly Christ they despised. A militant Messiah they, too, would have hailed; a meek Messiah they scorned.

B. The Call of the King (10:1–12)

The vision leaped ahead to Christ's second coming and to a time when there will be no more defeat, no more division, no more dispersion. Instead, Israel will be a people regathered, rejoicing, and redeemed. During the millennium, the Jews will be sown back among the nations—only in blessing to mankind instead of under the judgment of God.

C. The Crucifixion of the King (11:1–17)

The prophet's astonishing vision came back to the rejection of Christ. He foretold the treachery of Judas: "So they weighed for my price thirty pieces of silver. And the Lord said unto me, Cast it unto the potter. . . . And I took the thirty pieces of silver, and cast them to the potter in the house of the Lord" (vv. 12–13). This, of course, was literally fulfilled—and fulfilled by the enemies of Christ, who certainly had no interest in helping fulfill prophecy concerning Christ. Yet, in spite of themselves, they gave for Jesus the contemptible price of a damaged and worthless slave. And even used the same money a second time to buy a potter's field.

In this same chapter the prophet spoke of the consequent breakdown of Jewish national life, and with astonishing vision even anticipated the cry of the people: "We have no king but Caesar" (see v. 6, wherein the Lord delivers His people into the hands of their chosen king).

D. The Curse of the King (12:1–14)

Zechariah now began a series of statements that run on to the end of the chapter, each statement headed up by the phrase, "In that day" (v. 3), a day he explains as being "the day of the LORD" (14:1). In other words, his vision focused on end-time events.

In this chapter he predicted for Jerusalem a time of war and a time of woe. He tells how Jerusalem will become what he calls "a burdensome stone" to the Gentiles. Every nation that meddles with Jerusalem will find itself cut and crushed by it. He describes how the nations will come to fight against Jerusalem in the last days and describes, too, how Israel will cry out at last to the Lord: "And they shall look upon me whom they have pierced, and they shall mourn for him as one mourneth for his only son." At long, long last the truth about Jesus will break in upon the terrified Hebrew people.

E. The Compassion of the King (13:1–9)

And a marvelous compassion it is. The prophet says, "And one shall say unto him, What are these wounds in thine hands? Then he shall answer, Those with which I was wounded in the house of my friends. Awake, O sword, against my shepherd, and against the man that is my fellow, saith the LORD of hosts: smite the shepherd, and the sheep shall be scattered" (vv. 6–7). Here is a clear Old Testament statement regarding both the *character* of Christ and the *cross* of Christ. The prophet describes him as "the man" but He is the Man who is "the fellow" of the Lord of hosts. In other words, He is both *God* and *Man* in one person.

Moreover, this unique person was to be put to death by crucifixion. And, as a result, the flock He had come to shepherd would be scattered. These statements have been so literally fulfilled in the first coming of Christ that they are self-evident truths.

But in keeping with His compassion, that very "fountain filled with blood, drawn from Emmanuel's veins,"[1] opened there in Jerusalem, would avail to cleanse away the deepest, darkest stains of human sin.

F. The Coronation of the King (14:1–21)

The focus of the prophet's final vision came back once more to the day of the Lord. Jerusalem is to be surrounded by armies. The Lord will come! His feet will touch upon the Mount of Olives! The mountain will rend asunder, making a deep valley and, for the first time in history, Jerusalem will become a city located on the banks of a river! "And the LORD shall be king over all the earth: in that day," says the prophet (v. 9).

The nations will be required to come up to Jerusalem year by year to worship, and those who resist will be punished. Jerusalem will become indeed a holy city. "In that day shall there be upon the bells of the horses, HOLINESS UNTO THE LORD; . . . Yea, every pot in Jerusalem and in Judah shall be holiness unto the LORD of hosts" (vv. 20–21).

With that, the prophet threw down his pen! What more could be said? Well might those struggling pioneers—in that little repatriated land, surrounded by hostile Gentile seas, striving to drive in their stake for the coming of Christ—take courage! They were building for the future, a future upon which, indeed, dark shadows were destined to fall, but a future upon which, at last, the sun would shine in undimmed splendor and power.

What, then, is the burden of Zechariah? Perhaps his message can best be summed up by the hymn writer:

> God moves in a mysterious way;
> His wonders to perform;
> He plants His footsteps in the sea
> And rides upon the storm.
>
> Deep in unfathomable mines
> Of never failing skill,
> He treasures up His bright designs
> And works His sovereign will.
>
> His purposes will ripen fast
> Unfolding every hour;
> The bud may have a bitter taste,
> But sweet will be the flower.
>
> —William Cowper,
> "God Moves in a Mysterious Way"

CHAPTER 41

MALACHI

The Gathering Gloom

Malachi is the prophet of the gathering gloom. Nothing is known of him at all. His name means "My messenger" and employs the usual word for "angel," so he has been called the unknown prophet with the angel's name. He appears among the writing prophets like an Elijah—without father or mother, without beginning or ending of days! He emerges suddenly from the shadows, lifts up his voice in protest and prophecy, then melts back into the shadows from which he came. In the New Testament he is quoted, but he is quoted anonymously, without the use of his name. It is as though Malachi deliberately hid himself so that all attention might be focused on the truth he uttered. He is the voice of one crying in the wilderness: "Make straight the way of the Lord!" (see John 1:23).

Although Malachi did not date his prophecy, there are clues as to when it was written. We can thus arrive at an approximate time for the writing of this prophecy by a process of elimination. Some half-dozen dates stand as signposts of Hebrew history after the ending of the Babylonian captivity until Malachi closes the Old Testament Scriptures.

In 536 B.C. Cyrus the Persian had reversed the policy of the Assyrian and Babylonian tyrants who had ruled the world before him and allowed captive peoples to return back home. Under Zerubbabel and Joshua some 50,000 Jews responded.

In 534 B.C. the foundations were laid for a new temple in Jerusalem. But then complications arose, and the actual building of the temple ground to a halt.

In 520 B.C. the voices of Haggai and Zechariah were raised, urging the Jews to get on with the job and encouraging and strengthening Joshua and Zerubbabel for the task.

In 516 B.C. the temple was finished. By this time some twenty years had elapsed since the Jews first returned to the Promised Land.

In 457 B.C., some fifty years later, Ezra the scribe arrived in Jerusalem, accompanied by a small contingent of Jewish people willing to endure the hardships of pioneering in the Holy Land.

In 445 B.C. Nehemiah showed up in Jerusalem. A high official at the court of the Persian king Artaxerxes, Nehemiah was commissioned by the king with the task of rebuilding the walls of Jerusalem. The decree of Artaxerxes is one of the most important in the Old Testament era for it dates the beginning of that mystical "seventy weeks," which were to terminate first in the crucifixion, and then in the second coming, of Christ.

In 433 B.C. Nehemiah returned to Babylon to make his report to the king as to what had been accomplished at Jerusalem.

In 420 B.C., or perhaps a little earlier, Nehemiah returned to Jerusalem and attacked religious and moral sins that had surfaced among the people.

The question is, at what point did Malachi prophesy? It is generally thought that he prophesied either during the absence of Nehemiah or at some point during Nehemiah's ministry in Jerusalem. There are problems with this view.

We know that Malachi prophesied some considerable time after the rebuilding of the temple and the restoration of the Levitical religious system. In his day the services of the temple had degenerated into mere ritualistic routine, and the sacrifices and offerings had been perverted and profaned by priests and people alike. There is evidence, too, of a callousness and hostility toward the things of God, which had taken some time to develop.

It is hard to place the prophet in the days of either Ezra or Nehemiah. The prophets Haggai and Zechariah are mentioned by name. Malachi is ignored. Nehemiah's reforms were so thorough and so sweeping that it hardly seems possible they could collapse so completely during the comparatively brief time he was away in Babylon reporting to his king. He seems to have had no difficulty in sweeping aside such abuses as had grown up again during his absence.

Nor was Nehemiah of the temperament that would need the presence of a prophet to support him in his reforms. He was quite able to handle things himself.

He was a tough-minded, forceful individual, not at all averse to taking offenders by the scruff of the neck and tossing them head-over-heels out of the temple, baggage and all.

So then, when did Malachi prophesy? Zerubbabel and Joshua had Haggai and Zechariah. Conditions in Ezra's day, while calling for reform, do not suit the circumstances of Malachi. For instance, royal revenues were still subsidizing the temple services, so that there would be no room for Malachi's denunciation of the stinginess of the people. Nehemiah did not need a prophet. The dozen years of his absence from Jerusalem is hardly long enough for the abuses Malachi attacks to have taken such a firm hold, despite the efforts of the latitudinarian party in the commonwealth to return to those evil practices he had so vigorously corrected.

The probability is that Malachi prophesied some time after the days of Nehemiah, at a time, indeed, when the settled corruption he denounces would have had plenty of time to take root and flourish. But just when *did* he prophesy?

Sir Robert Anderson has the best idea. He takes us back to that remarkable prophecy of the seventy weeks in Daniel 9. Daniel was told that seventy weeks of years would sum up the future history of the Hebrew people. The period started with the decree to rebuild Jerusalem. There is little doubt that this is the decree of Artaxerxes given in 445 B.C. and for discharge when Nehemiah first came to Jerusalem.[1]

The actual seventy-weeks period is divided by the Holy Spirit into three. There was to be a period of seven weeks, plus a period of sixty-two weeks, plus a final period of one week. The first two periods take us down to the cutting off of the Messiah. The final one-week period is still future. But what is the significance of that first period of seven weeks (i.e., 49 years)?

The period begins in the year 445 B.C. We deduct 49 from 445, and that brings us to 396 B.C. The suggestion is that *this* was when Malachi prophesied. It would give sufficient time for the conditions he describes to develop. Joshua and Zerubbabel, Haggai and Zechariah had all long since gone. The decline had set in. The spirit of smugness on the one hand and skepticism on the other—which came to full flower in the days of Christ in the sects of the Pharisees and the Sadducees—had plenty of time to take root.

Then comes the last call! Once more, and for the last time for four hundred years, the voice of prophecy rang out in Israel. The temple sacrifices had been restored indeed, but the formalism, skepticism, and hypocrisy—which were seen in flower by Malachi and came to full fruit in the dead ritualism of the Pharisees and the dread rationalism of the Sadducees in the days of the Lord Jesus—were actively at work. The voice of that unknown prophet with the angel's name shattered the silence. Its thunders echoed and reverberated. Then, silence! God had no more to say. When He spoke again it would be to announce the birth of Christ.

At any rate, Malachi's prophecy was late enough for a sharp religious and moral decline to have set in. Sacrilege and profanity marked the religious attitude. Witchcraft, adultery, perjury, fraud, oppression were the prevailing moral sins. Disregarding family responsibilities highlighted social conditions. Robbing God reflected the materialism of the age.

The attitude of the people was one of self-defense. Seven times Malachi confronted priests and people with the issues of true, heart religion. Seven times they answered back with a callous "Wherein?" "Wherein hast thou loved us?" (1:2); "Wherein have we despised thy name?" (1:6); "Wherein have we polluted thee?" (1:7); "Wherein have we wearied [thee]?" (2:17); "Wherein shall we return?" (3:7); "Wherein have we robbed thee?" (3:8); "[Wherein] have we spoken so much against thee?" (3:13).

The last word of Malachi, the last word of the Old Testament, the last word before the long silence fell was the sad, solemn, sobering word *curse* (4:6). With that fearful word ringing in his ears, the Jew came to the end of his Bible. The New Testament begins where the Old Testament ends. Without the New Testament, the Old Testament tells of a beginning without an ending, makes promises without fulfillments, begins in Genesis with blessings but ends in Malachi with curses. Gratefully we acknowledge that the silence of God has been broken. God has spoken again. He has spoken to us in these last days in His Son.

Now let us get an analysis of Malachi's prophecy before us.

I. The Lord's Complaints (1:1–2:17)
   A. The Nation's Spiritual Sins (1:1–2:9)
      1. Denying God's Love (1:1–5)
         a. The Burden Described (1:1–2a)
         b. The Brothers Differentiated (1:2b–4)
         c. The Blindness Dispelled (1:5)
      2. Despising God's Name (1:6)
      3. Defiling God's Altar (1:7–14)
         a. The Contemptuous Attitude of the Hebrews (1:7–10)
         b. The Contrasting Attitude Among the Heathen (1:11–14)
            (1) God's Name Famed by the Gentiles (1:11–14a)
            (2) God's Name Feared by the Gentiles (1:14b)
      4. Disregarding God's Law (2:1–9)
         a. God's Commandment to the Priests (2:1–4)
         b. God's Covenant with the Priests (2:5–7)
         c. God's Contempt for the Priests (2:8–9)
   B. The Nation's Special Sins (2:10–17)
      1. Their Detestable Worship (2:10–13)

After Malachi's prophecies rang out, the voice of prophecy died away.

The minor prophets cover a period of about four hundred years. With the famous last words of Malachi, silence descends—four hundred years of speaking, four hundred years of silence. Malachi brought the one era to an end and inaugurated the other. For four hundred years God shuts up His Book to His people. During that time the Hebrew people began to take that book and add to it their own notions and traditions and ideas until at last they discarded it altogether in favor of the Talmud.

I. THE LORD'S COMPLAINTS (1:1–2:17)

In spite of all the evident tokens of His goodness to them, this people was still perverse and rebellious. True, idolatry no longer plagued the nation, but other sins had taken its place.

A. The Nation's Spiritual Sins (1:1–2:9)

The nation was guilty of four sins related to spirituality.

1. Denying God's Love (1:1–5)

"I have loved you, saith the LORD. Yet ye say, Wherein hast thou loved us?" (v. 2). In answer, the prophet pointed to the contrast between Israel and Edom, between Jacob and Esau. "Was not Esau Jacob's brother? saith the LORD: yet I loved Jacob, And I hated Esau" (vv. 2–3). The love of God for Jacob was undeserved love; it was sovereign grace o'er sin abounding. The hatred of God for Esau was deserved hatred, the result of centuries-long hostility on the part of the Edomite nation toward God and His people.

When the Babylonians destroyed the nation of Judah, the Edomites had gone hysterical with delight, aiding and abetting the invaders in every possible way. Five years after the destruction of Jerusalem, the Lord paid back Edom in full. The Babylonians invaded their country, too. Never again would Edom regain its former might.

The people of the land—restored after their captivity, reconstituted as a nation, blessed and protected by God—callously shrugged their indifference to God. "Wherein has He loved us?" they said. "Prove it!"

They were not only denying God's love, they were guilty of even worse.

2. Despising God's Name (1:6)

A son honoreth his father and a servant his master: . . . where is mine honor? . . . O priests, that despise my name. And ye say, Wherein have we despised thy name?

In the old Semitic world, honor to a parent was due before love. "Honor thy father and thy mother," ran the commandment (Exod. 20:12). "If I am a Father, where is my honor?" Throughout the Old Testament, God revealed Himself primarily through His names. He was Elohim, He was Jehovah, He was Jehovah Shammah, Jehovah Shalom, Jehovah Tsidkenu, Jehovah Jireh. It was left for the last of the prophets to underline the greatest of all the names of God—*Father!* It is the name Jesus took up and glorified, the highest and greatest revelation of God in the Old Testament. The ungodly priests thought so little of it that they flung it back in Malachi's face—and into God's. "Wherein have we despised thy name?" they sneered.

They were guilty of denying God's love and of despising God's name. They were guilty, moreover, of yet worse.

3. Defiling God's Altar (1:7–14)

"Ye offer polluted bread upon mine altar; and ye say, Wherein have we polluted thee?" (v. 7). They were bringing as offerings at the altar what they would not dare have presented as a gift to their governor. He would have been insulted and infuriated. They did not hesitate, however, to offer such gifts to God—the leftovers, the refuse, the torn, the wounded, the crippled.

"I am a great *King!*" the Lord exclaims. "How dare you treat Me with such contempt?"

Then, too, they were guilty of even more.

4. Disregarding God's Law (2:1–9)

"Ye are departed out of the way; ye have caused many to stumble at the law" (v. 8). This, indeed, became the great national sin of Israel in the centuries that followed. Already the first roots of the Midrash had begun to sprout—those Jewish commentaries upon the law that were to develop and flourish until the Midrash became the Mishna and the Mishna became the Torah. By the time of Christ, the process was so entrenched that the Scribes and Pharisees were constantly rebuked by Him for making the Word of God of no effect by their tradition. They had substituted for the plain Scriptures of truth ever-growing volumes of man-made verbiage.[2]

So the prophet dealt with the nation's spiritual sins; with its sins against God.

B. The Nation's Special Sins (2:10–17)

He underlined three things.

1. Their Detestable Worship (2:10–13)

"Judah hath dealt treacherously, and an abomination is committed in Israel and in Jerusalem; for Judah hath profaned the holiness of the LORD which he loved, and hath married the daughter of a strange god" (v. 11). That is, the people of God were marrying idolatrous women. The Lord threatened to destroy completely the family of the offender in this matter. They might think it a light matter to marry those who did not love the Lord, but God looked upon it as a very serious matter. This, after all, was the sin of Solomon, a sin that led directly to all the ills that befell the nation during the long years of the monarchy, and that led, in turn, to the Assyrian and Babylonian captivities.

Perhaps nowhere in the Old Testament is such a high view of marriage preached as what we have in the preaching of Malachi. Marriage for God's people must be "in the Lord." There can be no unequal yoke with an unbeliever, especially with one who is committed to a false religion.

2. Their Deserted Wives (2:14–16)

Malachi next underlines that it was bad enough that the Lord's people were getting married to pagans. Worse, they were divorcing their wives to do it. The altars of Israel were being drenched with the tears of women who had been deserted and divorced in this way: "The Lord hath been witness between thee and the wife of thy youth," says the prophet (v. 14).

Again, nowhere in the Old Testament is there such a clear, ethical stand against divorce as in this remarkable little prophecy that closes the Old Testament. By their behavior, the Jews were circumventing the whole purpose of God, who was seeking to bring in a godly seed—that is, a generation of people who would own and honor God.

3. Their Distorted Words (2:17)

Next the prophet underlines that "Ye have wearied the Lord with your words. Yet ye say, Wherein have we wearied him?" They were parading the old argument against the providence of God—the seeming prosperity of the wicked, and the suffering of the righteous. Their skepticism was exhausting the patience of God. He was weary with listening to their shallow argument that sin was successful.

If such shallow arguments wearied God in the days of Malachi, how much more must they weary Him today! Take, for instance, the reported words of a man who became a popular host-narrator on television. His program was watched by millions. He helped popularize astronomy as few have done. His books are avidly devoured by his fans, having been translated into dozens of languages, with millions of copies having been sold. His lectures on and off campus attracted overflow crowds. Here is one of Carl Sagan's typical statements: "I am a collection of water, calcium and organic molecules."[3] God must get weary of hearing otherwise intelligent human beings making statements like that. "Ye have wearied me with your words."

Malachi turns from "The Lord's Complaints" to the second great theme of his prophecy.

II. The Lord's Coming (3:1–4:6)

With dramatic suddenness the prophet switched from the present to the future. He spoke of the Lord's coming.

A. To Deal in Judgment with Sinners (3:1–15)

God intends to deal with the ungodly in His own time and way.

1. Their Ungodly Actions (3:1–6)

"Behold, I will send my messenger, and he shall prepare the way before me: and the Lord, whom ye seek, shall suddenly come to his temple. . . . But who may abide the day of his coming? . . . for he is like a refiner's fire" (vv. 1–2). The two comings of Christ are mixed together here as is so often the case with the Old Testament prophets, who never saw the valley of the church age, which lay between the two comings.

The messenger envisioned by Malachi was undoubtedly John the Baptist, the forerunner of the Lord Jesus, who announced to the Jewish nation the coming into their midst of the promised Messiah. But then Malachi vaulted the centuries to the day when the Jewish nation, just prior to the second coming of Christ, will have to face Him as the Refiner. The nation will be put through the fire of the great tribulation, the "time of Jacob's trouble," so that the dross might be consumed away.

2. Their Ungodly Attitude (3:7–12)
"Will a man rob God?" cried Malachi in a passage that has taken its place with the great utterances of the Word of God. "Will a man rob God? Yet ye have robbed me. But ye say, Wherein have we robbed thee? In tithes and offerings. Bring ye all the tithes into the storehouse . . . prove me now herewith, saith the Lord of hosts, if I will not open you the windows of heaven, and pour you out a blessing, that there shall not be room enough to receive it" (vv. 8, 10).

In its primary application, the promise and the challenge have to do with Israel. In robbing God of His portion they had robbed themselves. The failure of their harvests, their famines, their national economic woes were all the result of robbing God. The principle applies to us: if we want God to honor us we must first honor Him, and one of the most tangible ways we can do that is by seeing to it that He receives His portion of our income.

3. Their Ungodly Arguments (3:13–15)
"Ye have said, It is vain to serve God: and what profit is it that we have kept his ordinance . . . ?" (v. 14). They claimed that they had served God, and claimed there was no financial profit in it. They regarded the whole of their religious life in a mercenary spirit, as though reaping material benefits was the sum and substance of religious activity. There are plenty of preachers today, with vast television audiences, who are propagating a similar error. They have schemes whereby God will supposedly financially enrich those who give generously to their programs. All such schemes result, ultimately, in the disappointment and disillusionment of those who invest in them. The be-all and end-all of spiritual life is not money in the bank, two cars in the garage, and a cottage at the lake. All such teaching is contrary to the Sermon on the Mount and to the spiritual character of the New Testament age.

Malachi ends his prophecy by focusing on the Lord's people.

B. To Deal in Justice with Saints (3:16–4:6)
He tells us that the righteous are to be remembered and rewarded and recognized and rescued and revived.

1. They Will Be Remembered (3:16)

"Then they that feared the LORD spake often one to another: and the LORD hearkened, and heard it, and a book of remembrance was written before him for them that feared the LORD, and that thought upon his name." Every thought of God that passes through our minds, He appreciates and cherishes and notes down against the day when all such thoughts will be owned.

2. They Will Be Rewarded (3:17)

"And they shall be mine . . . in that day when I make up my jewels." The word for "jewels" is one that means "special treasure" or "acquired property." Malachi was evidently going back to the first use of the word in Exodus 19:5. Israel had come to Mount Sinai. God had put them under the blood and brought them through the water, and now He was going to gather them around the tabernacle, give them His law, own them as His special treasure. They are His! His jewels! That is their reward, and His.

3. They Will Be Recognized (3:18)

"Then shall ye return and discern." There will be a complete separation between the good and the bad, the true and the false, the saints of God and the children of the lawless one.

4. They Will Be Rescued (4:1–3)

The prophet's vision is focused now on end-time events, when God will deal in judgment with the wicked, will pour out millennial blessings on His own, and make an end of the ungodly. They seem to prosper now, but the last chapter has not been written yet.

5. They Will Be Revived (4:4–6)

Before closing the Old Testament canon, Malachi directed his people back to Moses and the law—and then on to Elijah and the coming of the Lord.

"Behold, I will send you Elijah the prophet before the coming of the great and dreadful day of the LORD" (v. 5). Again his eye runs down the ages to the endtimes. John the Baptist was not Elijah, although he came in the spirit and power of Elijah and, had the Jewish people accepted their Messiah, he would have been all the Elijah they needed. Since they did not accept the One he heralded, the stage will need to be set again—at the end of the age. And this time, it would seem, Elijah will come in person. He seems to be one of the two witnesses spoken of in Revelation 11 who expose the Beast for what he is—the Devil's messiah.

"And he shall turn the heart of the fathers to the children, and the heart of the children to their fathers, lest I come and smite the earth with a curse" (v. 6). It was revival or ruin! That was the option set before the people by their last prophet before the silence descends. Ruin or revival! Much the same option lies before the world today. Except, for the church, another possibility is added. For us it is ruin, revival, or *rapture!*

Thus the Old Testament ends with the word *curse!* The Jews always repeat verse 5 after verse 6. Dr. Feinberg tells us that four portions of the Old Testament were treated in the same way.

Isaiah ends on a note of terrible judgment: "And they shall go forth, and look upon the carcasses of the men that have transgressed against me: for their worm shall not die, neither shall their fire be quenched; and they shall be an abhorring unto all flesh" (66:24).

Lamentations ends with a wail of despair: "But thou hast utterly rejected us; thou art very wroth against us" (5:22).

Ecclesiastes ends on a startling note: "For God shall bring every work into judgment, with every secret thing, whether it be good, or whether it be evil" (12:14).

And, as we have seen, The Book of the Twelve, the Minor Prophets, ends with the word *curse!* Thus, the Old Testament ends with that dreadful word *curse!* echoing down the silent centuries. Until at last Jesus came and began His public ministry with the word *blessed!*

The rabbis sought to evade the full force of those four dreadful book endings by going back a verse and repeating the verse before so that the echoes were muted. God tells us that the true way to evade the full force of those dreadful book endings is to find a new beginning in Christ.

THE JEWISH RELIGIOUS CALENDAR

The Jewish religious calendar on the following pages is a reproduction from John Phillips, "Jewish Calendar," in *Exploring the World of the Jew* (Chicago: Moody Press, 1993), 95–104. Originally adapted from Merrill F. Unger, *Unger's Bible Dictionary* (Chicago: Moody Press, 1957), 163–66.

THE JEWISH RELIGIOUS CALENDAR

| | Name of Month | | | | | |
	Hebrew	English	Festivals	Season	Weather	Crops
I	ABIB (green ears) or NI'SAN. Thirty days; first of sacred, seventh of civil year.	March–April	1 New moon (Num. 10:10; 28:11–15). Fast for Nadab and Abihu (Lev. 10:1–2). 10 Selection of paschal lamb (Exod. 12:3). Fast for Miriam (Num. 20:1) and in memory of the scarcity of water (20:5). 14 Paschal lamb killed in evening (Exod. 12:6). Passover begins (Num. 28:16). Search for leaven. 15 First day of unleavened bread (Num. 28:17). After sunset, sheaf of barley brought to temple. 16 "First fruits," sheaf offered (Lev. 23:10). Beginning of harvest, fifty days to Pentecost (Lev. 23:15). 21 Close of Passover, end of unleavened bread (Lev. 23:6, 15, 21). Holy convocations (23:7). 26 Fast for death of Joshua.	Spring equinox	Wind S; sometimes sirocco. Fall of the "latter" or spring rains fill the Jordan channel, and the river overflows in places in its "lower plain" (Josh. 3:15; cf. Zech. 10:11).	Barley harvest begins in the plain of Jericho, and in the Jordan valley wheat comes into ear; uplands brilliant with short-lived verdure and flowers.
II	ZIF (brightness) or I'JAR. Twenty-nine days; second of sacred,	April–May	1 New moon (Num. 1:18). 6 Fast of three days for excesses during Passover. 10 Fast for death of Eli and capture of ark (1 Sam. 4:11). 15 "Second" or "little" Passover for those unable	Summer	Wind S; showers and thunderstorms rare (1 Sam. 12:17–18). Sky generally cloudless until end of summer.	Principal harvest month in lower districts. Barley harvest general (Ruth 1:22); wheat ripening on the uplands; apricots ripen. In Jordan

	eighth of civil year.		to celebrate in Abib; in memory of entering wilderness (Exod. 16:1). 23 Feast for taking Gaza by S. Maccabaeus; for taking and purification of temple by the Maccabees. 27 Feast for expulsion of Galileans from Jerusalem. 28 Feast for death of Samuel (1 Sam. 25:1).		valley hot winds destroy vegetation.
III	SIʼVAN. Thirty days; third of sacred, ninth of civil year.	May–June	1 New moon. 2 "Feast of Pentecost" or "Feast of Weeks"—because it came seven weeks after Passover (Lev. 23:15–21). 15–16 Celebration of victory over Beth-san (1 Macc. 5:54; 12:40–43). 17 Feast for taking Caesarea by Hasmonaeans. 22 Fast in memory of Jeroboam's forbidding subjects to carry firstfruits to Jerusalem (1 Kings 12:27). 25 Feast in memory of rabbis Simeon Ishmael and Chanina; feast in honor of judgment of Alexander the Great, in favor of Jews against Ishmaelites, who claimed Canaan. 27 Fast; Chanina being burned with books of law.	Wind NW, also E; khamseen, or parching wind from southern deserts. Air still and brilliantly clear.	Wheat harvest begins on uplands; almonds ripen; grapes begin to ripen; honey of the Jordan valley collected May to July.
IV	TAMʼMUZ. Twenty-nine days; fourth of sacred, tenth of civil year.	June–July	1 New moon. 14 Feast for abolition of a book of Sadducees and Bethusians, intended to subvert oral law and traditions. 17 Fast in memory of tables of law broken by Moses (Exod. 32:19) and taking of Jerusalem by Titus.	Hot season	Wind usually NW, also E; khamseen from S. Air still and clear; heat intense; heavy dews.	Wheat harvest on highest districts; various fruits ripe. Springs and vegetation generally dried up. Bedouin leave steppes for mountain pastures. Elsewhere,

THE JEWISH RELIGIOUS CALENDAR

Name of Month		Festivals	Season	Weather	Crops
Hebrew	**English**				
					country parched, dry and hard—"a dreary waste of withered stalks and burned up grass" (stubble).
V	AB (fruitful). Thirty days; fifth of sacred, eleventh of civil year.	July–August	1 New moon; fast for death of Aaron commemorated by children of Jethuel who furnished wood for temple after the captivity. 9 Fast in memory of God's declaration against murmurers entering Canaan (Num. 14:29–31). 18 Fast, because in the time of Ahaz the evening lamp went out. 21 Feast when wood was stored in temple. 24 Feast in memory of law providing for sons and daughters alike inheriting estate of parents.		Wind E. Air still and clear; heat intense; heavy dews.	Principal fruit grapes, figs, walnuts, olives, etc.; vintage begins (Lev. 26:5).
VI	E'LUL (good for nothing). Twenty-nine days; sixth of sacred,	August–September	1 New moon. 7 Feast for dedication of Jerusalem's walls by Nehemiah. 17 Fast, death of spies bringing ill report (Num. 14:30). 21 Feast, wood offering.		Wind NE. Heat still intense (2 Kings 4:18–20); much lightning but rarely rain.	Vintage general; the rest of durra and cotton and pomegranate ripen.

No.	Month	Gregorian	Feasts and Events	Season	Weather	Agriculture
	twelfth of civil year.		22 Feast in memory of wicked Israelites who were punished with death. (Throughout the month the cornet is sounded to warn of approaching new civil year.)			Plowing and sowing begin as soon as ground is softened by the rain; in any weather as the time runs short (Prov. 20:4; Eccl. 11:4); cotton harvest.
VII	ETH'ANIM (permanent) or TIS'RI. Thirty days; seventh of sacred, first of civil year.	September–October	1 New moon; new year; Feast of Trumpets (Lev. 23:24; Num. 29:1–2). 3 Fast for murder of Gedaliah (2 Kings 25:25; Jer. 41:2); high priest set apart for Day of Atonement. 7 Fast on account of worship of golden calf. 10 Day of Atonement, "the fast" (Acts 27:9), i.e., the only one enjoined by the law; the first day of jubilee years. 15–21 Feast of Tabernacles. 22 Holy convocation, palms borne, prayer for rain. 23 Feast for law being finished; dedication of Solomon's temple.	Seed time, or earing	Wind NE. Dews very heavy. Former or early, i.e., autumnal, rains begin (Joel 2:23) to soften the ground (Deut. 11:14); nights frosty (Gen. 31:40).	
VIII	BUL or MAR-CHESH'VAN. Twenty-nine days; eighth of sacred, second of civil year.	October–November	1 New moon. 6–7 Fast because Nebuchadnezzar blinded Zedekiah (2 Kings 25:7; Jer. 52:10). 17 Prayers for rain. 19 Fast for faults committed during Feast of Tabernacles. 23 Memorial of stones of altar profaned by Greeks (1 Macc. 4:44). 26 Feast in memory of recovery after the captivity of places occupied by the Cuthites.		Wind N, NW, NE, S, SW. Rainy month partly fine; rains from S and SW.	Wheat and barley sown; vintage in northern Palestine; rice harvest; fig tree laden with fruit; orange and citron blossom; almost all vegetation has disappeared.

THE JEWISH RELIGIOUS CALENDAR

	Name of Month		Festivals	Season	Weather	Crops
	Hebrew	**English**				
IX	CHIS'LEU. Thirty days; ninth of sacred, third of civil year.	November–December	1 New moon. 2 Fast (three days if no rain falls). 3 Feast in honor of Hasmonaeans throwing out idols placed in temple court by Gentiles. 6 Feast in memory of death of Herod the Great. 14 Fast, absolute if no rain. 21 Feast of Mount Gerizim; plowing and sowing of Mount Gerizim with tares, as Samaritans had intended to do with temple ground. 25 Feast of the dedication of the temple, or of Lights (eight days) in memory of restoration of temple by Judas Maccabaeus.	Winter begins (John 10:22)	Snow on mountains and stormy. Greatest amount of rainfall during year in December, January, and February.	Trees bare, but plains and deserts gradually become green pastures.
X	TE'BETH. Twenty-nine days; tenth of sacred, fourth of civil year.	December–January	1 New moon. 8 Fast because the law was translated into Greek. 9 Fast, no reason assigned. 10 Fast on account of siege of Jerusalem by Nebuchadnezzar (2 Kings 25:1). 28 Feast in memory of exclusion of Sadducees from the Sanhedrin.	Mid-winter	Wind N, NW, NE. Coldest month; rain, hail, and snow (Josh. 10:11) on higher hills, and occasionally at Jerusalem.	Flocks leave highlands for the Jordan valley, and its cultivation begins; oranges ripening, and lower districts green with grain.

XI	SHE'BAT or SE'BAT. Thirty days; eleventh of sacred, fifth of civil year.	January–February	1 New moon. 2 Rejoicing for death of King Alexander Jannaeus, enemy of the Pharisee. 4 or 5 Fast in memory of death of elders, successors to Joshua. 15 Beginning of the year of Trees. 22 Feast in memory of death of Niscalenus, who ordered images placed in temple, and who died before execution of his orders. 23 Fast for war of the ten tribes against Benjamin (Judg. 20); also idol of Micah (18:11, sq.). 29 Memorial of death of Antiochus Epiphanes, enemy of Jews.	Winter	Wind N, NW, NE. Gradually growing warmer. Toward end of month the most pleasant "cool season" begins.	Almond and peach blossom in warmer and sheltered localities; oranges ripe.
XII	A'DAR (fire). Twenty-nine days; twelfth of sacred, sixth of civil year.	February–March	1 New moon. 7 Fast because of Moses' death (Deut. 34:5). 8–9 Trumpet sounded in thanksgiving for rain and prayer for future rain. 12 Feast in memory of Holianus and Pipus, two proselytes, who died rather than break the law. 13 Fast of Esther (Esther 4:16). Feast in memory of Nicanor, enemy of the Jews (1 Macc. 7:44). 14 The first Purim, or lesser Feast of Lots (Esther 9:21). 15 The great Feast of Purim. 17 Deliverance of sages who fled from Alexander Jannaeus. 20 Feast for rain obtained in time of drought, in time of Alexander Jannaeus. 23 Feast for dedication of Zerubbabel's temple. 28 Feast to commemorate the repeal of decree of Grecian kings forbidding Jews to circumcise their children.	Cold and rainy season, or spring	Wind W. Thunder and hail frequent, sometimes snow. The latter rains begin, on which plenty or famine, the crops and pasture depend.	In valley of Jordan cultivation draws to an end, and barley ripens.

NOTES

Chapter 2: Genesis

1. That meant, of course, that there would actually be thirteen tribes, although God invariably counts only twelve in any given list.

2. *Reuben, Simeon, and Levi* give the history of the nation down to the first advent of the Messiah. *Judah* gives a sketch of the Messiah's appearing, rejection, and ultimate reign. *Zebulun and Issachar* set forth the dispersal of Israel and the long subjection of the race to the Gentiles. *Dan* foreshadows the appearing and kingdom of the Antichrist. *Gad, Asher, and Naphtali* depict the moral character of the elect in the last days—victorious, royally nourished, and witnessing. *Joseph and Benjamin* foreshadow the second coming and triumphs of Israel's Messiah.

3. Matthew 27 records a significant event that took place at the time of Christ's death and resurrection: "The graves were opened; and many bodies of the saints which slept arose, and came out of their graves after his resurrection, and went into the holy city, and appeared unto many." Is that why the patriarchs coveted burial in Canaan? Could it be that Jacob had an inkling of that and wanted to be where it would happen? Did he hope to be part of that wondrous and mysterious wave-sheaf to be snatched from the grave at the great Feast of Firstfruits on Christ's resurrection morn? We do not know, but the possibility exists.

Chapter 3: Exodus

1. Compare Galatians 3:17. The 430 years are from the time Jacob came to Egypt to the exodus, and thus this Scripture refers to the covenant promises being renewed to Jacob as in Genesis 35:9ff. (cf. Ps. 105:9f.).

2. Quotation is from the novel *Ulysses* by James Joyce, first published in 1922 in Paris.

Chapter 5: Numbers

1. This saying of Balaam is inferred from events in chapters 22–24 and 2 Peter 2:15.

Chapter 9: Ruth

1. The mother of Boaz was Rahab, the harlot of Jericho.

Chapter 11: 2 Samuel

1. Jenney E. Hussey, "Lead Me to Calvary," 1921.
2. See John Phillips, *Exploring Psalms*, 2 vols. (Grand Rapids: Kregel, 2002).

Chapter 13: 1 and 2 Kings

1. John C. Whitcomb (b. 1924) has been a professor of Old Testament and theology for more than fifty years, and is widely recognized as a leading Bible scholar. He gained much recognition for his work on *The Genesis Flood*, which he coauthored in 1961. This book has been credited as one of the major catalysts for the modern creationism movement.
2. William Shakespeare, *King Henry, Part II*, act 3, scene 1.
3. William Shakespeare, *Julius Caesar*, act 3, scene 2.

Chapter 14: 1 and 2 Chronicles

1. E. W. Bullinger, *The Companion Bible* (Grand Rapids: Kregel, 1999).
2. W. E. H. Lecky (1838–1903), historian and politician. Many of Lecky's quotations can be found on atheist Web sites.

Chapter 16: Nehemiah

1. Guy King is author of *Leader Led: First Timothy* (Neptune City, NJ: Paganiniana, 1982).
2. This quote is well authenticated as spoken by Cromwell in concluding an address prior to his troops' crossing a river and attacking an enemy.

Chapter 18: Hebrew Poetry

1. E. W. Bullinger, *The Companion Bible* (Grand Rapids: Kregel, 1999).
2. Ibid.

Chapter 20: The Psalms

1. Isaac Watts, *Psalms, Hymns, and Spiritual Songs*, 78 (Ps. 19:1–2).
2. Ibid., 214 (Ps. 141:1–2).
3. Ibid., 50 (Ps. 34:1–2).
4. Ibid., 6 (Ps. 3:4–6).

5. Ibid., 210 (Ps. 139:1–2).
6. Ibid., 210 (Ps. 139:6–9).
7. Ibid., 211 (Ps. 139:15–16).
8. Ibid., 45 (Ps. 32:1–5).
9. Ibid., 169–70 (Ps. 113:1–4).

Chapter 21: Proverbs

1. According to Jewish authorities, Solomon was called by six names: Solomon, Jedidiah, Koheleth, Son of Jakeh, Agur, and Lemuel.
2. W. Graham Scroggie, *Know Your Bible: A Brief Introduction to the Scriptures* (London: Pickering & Inglis, 1940), 1:140–41.
3. "Is There Life in a Swingers' Club?" *Time*, January 16, 1978.
4. "The Youth Crime Plague," *Time*, July 11, 1977.
5. Prov. 3:32; 6:16; 11:1, 20; 12:22; 15:8, 9, 26; 16:5; 17:15; 20:10, 23.

Chapter 22: Ecclesiastes

1. Eccl. 1:3, 9, 14; 2:11, 17, 18, 19, 20, 22; 3:16; 4:1, 3, 7, 15; 5:13, 18; 6:1, 12; 8:9, 15, 17; 9:3, 6, 9, 11, 13; 10:5.
2. Augustine, *Confessions and Enchiridion*, chapter 2, trans. Albert C. Outler (Philadelphia: Westminster Press, 1955).
3. Benjamin Disraeli in *Coningsby*, an English political novel published in 1844.

Chapter 23: Song of Solomon

1. For a full treatment of this book, see John Phillips, *Exploring the Love Song of Solomon* (Grand Rapids: Kregel, 2003).
2. George Müller (1805–1898), Christian evangelist and coordinator of orphanages in Bristol, England.
3. This is another of the verses in the book that militate against Solomon being a type of Christ.
4. It is reported that Luther uttered these words at the Diet of Worms in 1521.

Chapter 25: Joel

1. W. M. Thompson, *The Land and the Book* (New York: Harper & Brothers, 1882), 297–98.
2. Ibid., 297.

Chapter 26: Jonah

1. It must be noted that current evidence disputes this account. While some scientists concede the possibility, no definitive evidence has been unearthed that either totally verifies or falsifies the Bartley story.

Chapter 28: Amos
1. John Phillips, *Exploring the World of the Jew* (Chicago: Moody Press, 1981).

Chapter 29: Hosea
1. J. Sidlow Baxter (1903–1999), pastor and theologian who authored as many as thirty books. Source of quote is unknown.
2. Hos. 2:3, 6; 4:6, 17; 5:12; 7:3, 4, 8, 11; 8:6, 7; 9:11; 10:1, 13; 12:7; 13:3, 8.

Chapter 30: Micah
1. Isaac Watts, "Jesus Shall Reign Where'er the Sun," 1719.

Chapter 31: Nahum
1. Sir George Adam Smith (1856–?), British divine, was knighted in 1916, and from 1916 to 1917 was moderator of the general assembly of the United Free Church of Scotland.
2. Thomas Hastings and Williams Patton, *The Christian Psalmist* (D. Fanshaw, 1839).

Chapter 34: Zephaniah
1. George Adam Smith, *The Book of Twelve Prophets*, vol. 2 (New York: Harper Brothers, 1928), 48.
2. Ibid., 66.
3. Zeph. 1:7, 8, 9, 10, 14 (2x), 15 (4x), 16, 18; 2:2 (2x), 3, 4; 3:8, 11, 16.

Chapter 35: Habakkuk
1. Taken from Martin Luther, *Preface to the Complete Edition of Luther's Latin Writings*, 1545.

Chapter 37: Ezekiel
1. Ezek. 1:1; 8:1; 20:1; 24:1; 26:1; 29:1, 17; 30:20; 31:1; 32:1, 17; 33:21; 40:1.
2. Exact wording varies, but the intent is the same in the following verses: (34x punishment of Jerusalem) 5:13; 6:7, 10, 13, 14; 7:4, 9, 27; 11:10, 12; 12:15, 16, 20; 13:9, 14, 21, 23; 14:8; 15:7; 16:62; 17:21, 24; 20:12, 20, 26, 38, 42, 44; 21:5; 22:16, 22; 23:49; 24:24, 27; (18x in connection with judgment of the Gentiles) 25:5, 7, 11, 17; 26:6; 28:22, 23, 24, 26; 29:6, 9, 16, 21; 30:8, 19, 25, 26; 32:15; (18x in connection with restoration of Israel) 33:29; 34:27, 30; 35:9, 12, 14, 15; 36:11, 23, 38; 37:6, 13, 28; 38:23; 39:6, 7, 22, 28.
3. Ezek. 2:1, 3, 6, 8; 3:1, 3, 4, 10, 17, 25; 4:1, 16; 5:1; 6:2; 7:2; 8:5, 6, 8, 12, 15, 17; 11:2, 4, 15; 12:2, 3, 9, 18, 22, 27; 13:2, 17; 14:3, 13; 15:2; 16:2; 17:2; 20:3, 4, 27, 46; 21:6, 9, 12, 14, 19, 28; 22:2, 18, 24; 23:2, 36; 24:2,

16, 25; 25:2; 26:2; 27:2; 28:2, 12, 21; 29:2, 18; 30:2, 21; 31:2; 32:2, 18; 33:2, 7, 10, 12, 24, 30; 34:2; 35:2; 36:1, 17; 37:3, 9, 11, 16; 38:2, 14; 39:1, 17; 40:4; 43:7, 10, 18; 44:5; 47:6.

4. Matt. 8:20; 9:6; 10:23; 11:19; 12:8, 32, 40; 13:37, 41; 16:13, 27, 28; 17:9, 12, 22; 18:11; 19:28; 20:18, 28; 24:27, 30, 37, 39, 44; 25:13, 31; 26:2, 24, 45, 64; Mark 2:10, 28; 8:31, 38; 9:9, 12, 31; 10:33, 45; 13:26, 34; 14:21, 41, 62; Luke 5:24; 6:5; 7:34; 9:22, 26, 44, 56, 58; 11:30; 12:8, 10, 40; 17:22, 24, 26, 30; 18:8, 31; 19:10; 21:27, 36; 22:22, 48, 69; 24:7; John 1:51; 3:13, 14; 5:27; 6:27, 53, 62; 8:28; 12:23, 34; 13:31; Acts 7:56; Heb. 2:6; Rev. 1:13; 14:14.

5. For a full discussion of this remarkable prophecy, see John Phillips, *Exploring the Future* (Grand Rapids: Kregel, 2002).

Chapter 38: Daniel

1. Robert Dick Wilson, "Is the Higher Criticism Scholarly?" (Philadelphia: Sunday School Times Company, 1922).

2. In the Babylonian priesthood there were various classes, including *magicians*: those who practiced magic (i.e., all the superstitious rites and rituals of fortune tellers); *astrologers*: those who claimed power to foretell future events by a study of the stars; *sorcerers*: those who claimed to hold communications with the dead; *chaldeans*: those who belonged to a special caste of astronomers and astrologers.

3. A substance's specific gravity is determined by comparing its weight to a like amount of distilled water that has been heated to 62° Fahrenheit. See "Comparison on Hydrometric and Specific Gravity Indications" at http:// albumen.stanford.edu/library/monographs/sunbeam/chap47.html.

4. The city of Babylon was built in an exact square, 15 miles to a side—60 miles around. It was surrounded by a brick wall 87 feet thick and 350 feet high. The walls were strengthened by 250 towers. Six chariots abreast could drive atop of the walls. Outside the walls was a vast moat. Inside the wall was another almost as big, although not quite so wide. The city was bisected diagonally by the great river Euphrates. Wide avenues ran from side to side of the city. Great bridges spanned the river. Near the center of the city, two palaces stood on either side of the river connected by a subterranean passage underneath the bed of the river. In this enormous passage were banqueting rooms.

Near the palace stood the Tower of Bel—one of the famous temple towers reminiscent of the tower of Babel. This one stood 650 feet high. At the top was a chapel containing idols and instruments of worship valued at two million dollars. Then there were the Hanging Gardens—one of the wonders of the world. These gardens were 400 feet square and raised in terraces, one above the other, to a height of 350 feet. The whole had the appearance from a distance of a forest-covered mountain. The rest of the city was equally magnificent. It contained parks and farms and had a population of over one million.

5. The term *prophetic philosophy of history* likely comes from Oswald Spengler, *The Decline of the West*, vols. 1 and 2 (New York: Knopf, 1926). While it is recognized that Spengler was racist and fascist, he was nonetheless prescient in asserting the West's movement toward soullessness in its devaluing of poets, artists, and philosophers in favor of engineers, soldiers, and politicians.

6. Sir Robert Anderson, chapter 10, "Fulfillment of the Prophecy," *The Coming Prince* (1895; Grand Rapids: Kregel, 1957).

Chapter 39: Haggai

1. Frank William Boreham (1871–1959) pastored in New Zealand, Tasmania, and Australia. He wrote the five-volume Great Text Series, and became one of the century's most prolific and well-known religious writers. The precise source for the story on William Carey is unknown.

Chapter 40: Zechariah

1. William Cowper, "There Is a Fountain Filled with Blood," *Collection of Psalms and Hymns*, 1772.

Chapter 41: Malachi

1. Sir Robert Anderson (1841–1918), in *The Coming Prince* (1895; Grand Rapids: Kregel, 1957), a classic interpretation of the prophecies of Daniel.

2. See John Phillips, *Exploring the World of the Jew* (Chicago: Moody Press, 1981).

3. Carl Sagan, *Cosmos* (New York: Random House, 1980), 127.

ALSO BY JOHN PHILLIPS

John Phillips New Testament Commentary Set

Explore the entire New Testament in greater depth! This nineteen-volume, complete set of New Testament commentaries from the pen of expositor John Phillips is known for its rich exposition, sound doctrine, and practical application.

978-0-8254-3369-6 | 6,030 pages | Hardcover

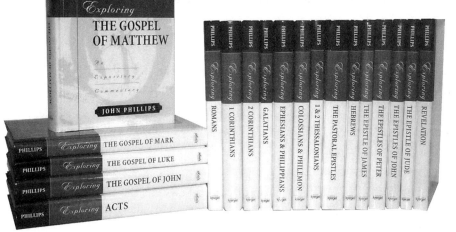

Exploring People of the Bible Set
John Phillips Bible Characters Series

Many pastors, teachers, and students have grown to rely on the John Phillips Commentary series for its sound and practical exposition of Scripture. Written in the same tradition, the Exploring People of the Bible series examines the lives of biblical personalities great and small and shows how their lives are still applicable to today's Christian. This four-volume set includes all of Phillips's Exploring People of the Bible titles.

978-0-8254-3372-6 | 1328 pages | Hardcover

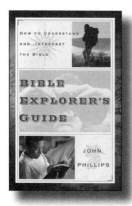

Bible Explorer's Guide
How to Understand and Interpret the Bible

Serious study of the Bible can be a daunting task for any Christian. Dr. Phillips provides the ground rules for handling God's Word—including the "Golden Rule" for studying Scripture; symbols in the Bible's discussion of covenants and dispensations; and interpreting types, parables, and prophecy. He also offers practical "maps" and resources to aid in a discovery study—a survey of Scripture, a harmony of the Gospels, and summaries of Bible history and names.

978-0-8254-3483-9 | 288 pages | Paperback

Exploring the Future
A Comprehensive Guide to Bible Prophecy

Books in the John Phillips Commentary Series are designed to provide pastors, Sunday school teachers, and students of the Scripture with doctrinally sound interpretation that emphasizes the practical application of Bible truth. Working from the familiar King James Version, Dr. Phillips not only provides helpful commentary on the text, but also includes many detailed outlines and numerous illustrations and quotations.

978-0-8254-3380-1 | 400 pages | Hardcover

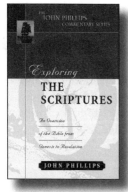

Exploring the Scriptures
An Overview of the Bible from Genesis to Revelation

Exploring the Scriptures gives a panoramic view of God's Word, providing a firm foundation for more detailed study of books, passages, and themes of the Bible. Each book of Scripture is presented through a brief introduction, a concise outline, and a comprehensive summary of the book's content. Included also are special chapters dealing with the major divisions of Scripture and thirty-five maps and charts to help with visualization of important Bible content.

978-0-8254-3487-7 | 256 pages | Hardcover